ALCATRAZ

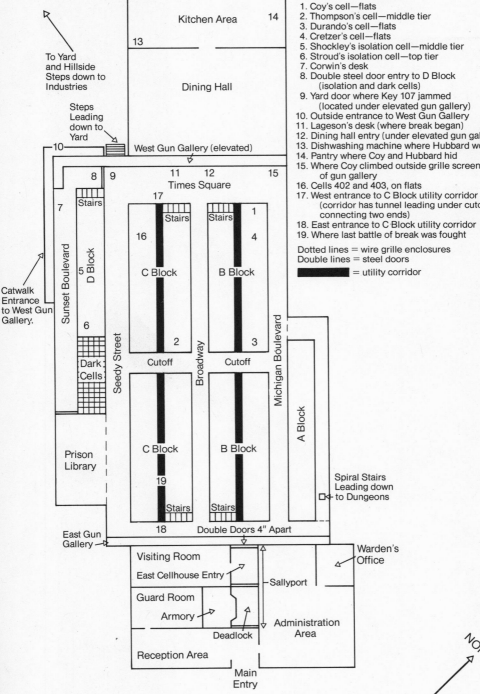

Key to Alcatraz Diagram

1. Coy's cell—flats
2. Thompson's cell—middle tier
3. Durando's cell—flats
4. Cretzer's cell—flats
5. Shockley's isolation cell—middle tier
6. Stroud's isolation cell—top tier
7. Corwin's desk
8. Double steel door entry to D Block
   (isolation and dark cells)
9. Yard door where Key 107 jammed
   (located under elevated gun gallery)
10. Outside entrance to West Gun Gallery
11. Lageson's desk (where break began)
12. Dining hall entry (under elevated gun gallery)
13. Dishwashing machine where Hubbard worked
14. Pantry where Coy and Hubbard hid
15. Where Coy climbed outside grille screen
    of gun gallery
16. Cells 402 and 403, on flats
17. West entrance to C Block utility corridor
    (corridor has tunnel leading under cutoff area,
    connecting two ends)
18. East entrance to C Block utility corridor
19. Where last battle of break was fought

Dotted lines = wire grille enclosures
Double lines = steel doors
███ = utility corridor

Diagram labels:

Kitchen Area — 14
13
To Yard and Hillside Steps down to Industries
Dining Hall
Steps Leading down to Yard
10 — West Gun Gallery (elevated)
8 9 — 11 12 15
Times Square
7
Stairs
17
Stairs Stairs
16 1
Sunset Boulevard
D Block
5
C Block B Block
4
Catwalk Entrance to West Gun Gallery.
6
Dark Cells
2 3
Seedy Street
Cutoff Broadway Cutoff
Michigan Boulevard
A Block
Prison Library
C Block B Block
19
Stairs Stairs
Spiral Stairs Leading down to Dungeons
East Gun Gallery
18 Double Doors 4" Apart
Visiting Room
East Cellhouse Entry
Sallyport
Warden's Office
Guard Room
Armory
Deadlock
Administration Area
Reception Area
Main Entry
NORTH

NOVELS BY CLARK HOWARD

The Killings
Mark the Sparrow
The Hunters

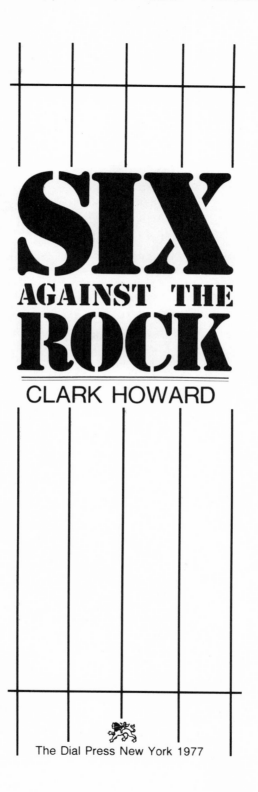

SIX
AGAINST THE
ROCK

CLARK HOWARD

The Dial Press New York 1977

Published by
The Dial Press
1 Dag Hammarskjold Plaza
New York, New York 10017

Manufactured in the United States of America

First printing

Library of Congress Cataloging in Publication Data

Howard, Clark.
Six against the Rock.

1. United States. Penitentiary, Alcatraz Island,
Calif. 2. Escapes. I. Title.
HV9474.A4H68   365'.641   77–5091
ISBN 0–8037–8003–0

To the men,
guards and convicts alike,
who did time on
Alcatraz.

And to the men who died there.

CONTENTS

AUTHOR'S NOTE

On May 2, 1946, one of the most daring and ingenious escapes in the history of American prisons was attempted. On that day, six convicts serving a collective total of 283 years plus three life sentences captured the big cellhouse on the island penitentiary of Alcatraz and staged a prison mutiny that seized the attention of the country. In the middle of San Francisco Bay, while tens of thousands watched from nearby shores, the six convicts waged an incredible battle against almost impossible odds.

The siege of Alcatraz lasted forty-one hours. Ending it required the combined efforts of prison guards not only from Alcatraz but also from San Quentin, Leavenworth, McNeil Island, and Englewood prisons, along with forces of the San Francisco Police Department, the United States Army, Navy, Air Corps, and Coast Guard, and finally, two assault companies of U.S. Marines.

This book is an hour-by-hour narrative of that incident, and of the men on both sides of the battle. The scenes depicted on the following pages have been reconstructed from eyewitness accounts, overheard conversations, personal narratives of men involved, newspaper reports, and records and documents both public and private. Dramatic license has been used in recreating the gamut of emotions that always surface in moments of stress and desperation, but on the whole the battle which newspapers described as "six against the Rock" is described exactly as the many contributors to the book remember it. The people in the book—from the President of the United States to several inmates mentioned only once—are real people. The name and ethnic background of only one person has been changed. That is the person represented by the character of Dan Durando. The reason for the change will be obvious to the reader.

Much of the narrative in the book is being written for publication for the first time. The research and documentation of those scenes that will probably be controversial is contained in the Afterword. Individual versions of specific incidents may differ, but this, we believe, is how it happened.

PART ONE

THURSDAY, MAY 2, 1946

CHAPTER ONE

6:00 A.M.

Cecil Corwin had just finished shaving. He was up early; it was his first day back on the job after a two-week vacation. He had slept well the night before and felt rested, but for some reason he kept yawning. The early hour, he imagined; during his vacation he had fallen into the habit of sleeping a little later than usual.

As he finished in the bathroom and got dressed, Corwin hummed a soft, happy tune. He was a musical man by nature; the tune was one of his own, an original melody he had composed in his head while on vacation. He had not had time yet to sit down at the organ and commit it to paper.

The vacation had been a good one: enjoyable yet restful. Corwin and his wife Catheryn had taken the train down to Fresno to visit his brother and sister-in-law. The four of them had gone by car from there up to Yosemite National Park. It was one of their favorite places; during those last two weeks in April it had blossomed out in its full magnificence. Corwin and his wife had visited there a number of times before, but they never tired of it. To Cecil Corwin, nature, like music, was beautiful.

Straightening his tie in the mirror, he examined his face for a moment. He decided that he looked pretty good for a man of fifty-two. Although he did not know it at the time, he bore quite a resemblance to a British actor some fifteen years younger than he, named Michael Rennie. Corwin himself was a native of Nebraska, the son of a circuit minister.

3

As he was standing at the mirror, the aroma of coffee reached him. Breakfast was almost ready. It was his habit to eat a hearty meal in the mornings: orange juice, scrambled eggs, two or three slices of toast with jam, and plenty of black coffee. A good breakfast, he felt, helped make a good day.

Before he left the bedroom, Corwin picked up a pocket-size book of Shakespeare and slipped it into one of his jacket pockets. He liked to read Shakespeare at work while he ate lunch, and if he had any other idle time.

On his way to the kitchen, Corwin paused to look out the bay window of the living room. He and his wife lived in Apartment 12 at 2955 Van Ness Avenue in San Francisco. From the third-floor window, Corwin had a splendid view of San Francisco Bay and the island a mile out in the water where he worked.

Cecil Corwin was a prison guard.

The island out in the bay was Alcatraz.

•

In Cellblock B on the island prison, Alcatraz inmate number 415 was also starting his day. Bernard Paul Coy, from Kentucky, lean, almost frail-looking, was standing at the single-faucet sink in his five-by-eight cell, washing his face and upper body in cold water— the only kind available to prisoners in their cells. Coy had just had a hot shower the previous night—Wednesday evenings and Saturday mornings were shower and clothing-exchange times—but because he liked to keep as clean as possible, Coy took cold-water sponge baths at least twice a day.

Called Bernie by some, Barney by others, Coy had just passed his forty-sixth birthday ten weeks earlier. He had been on Alcatraz for nearly nine years, since July of 1937. His crime, bank robbery. His sentence, twenty-five years.

When he finished washing, he briskly rubbed himself down with the coarse prison towel and put on an undershirt and denim prison shirt. He combed his thick black hair straight back, rinsed off his comb and put it on the cell's single shelf, and sat down on his bunk to wait for the morning distribution of razor blades so that he could shave. His beard, like his hair, was dark and heavy; he liked to shave closely every morning, even though with cold water it was not a very pleasant task. It always made him feel better, nevertheless, if only because the daily ordeal was over.

Sitting on his already carefully made bunk, Coy took the makings from his shirt pocket and carefully rolled a cigarette. Usually he did not smoke before breakfast, but this particular morning he was a little tight, a little tense inside, and he knew a smoke would help him ease up some. The cigarette he fashioned was neat and well constructed, as it should have been after nearly nine years of practice. Since his arrival at this prison known as the Rock, he had smoked nothing but roll-your-owns. Because Alcatraz was a minimum-privilege penitentiary, tailor-made cigarettes and other niceties were prohibited.

As he smoked, feeling the raw prison tobacco burn his throat and stir up acid in his stomach, Coy looked at one of the canvases stacked on the cell's lidless, seatless toilet. It was a landscape, like nearly everything he painted—this particular one a Kentucky hillside in the fall, the way he remembered it from his boyhood. There wasn't a prettier place in the world, he was convinced, than the Kentucky countryside in the early fall. Unless it was the Kentucky countryside in the late spring. At one time, Coy had worked as a house painter and had traveled all over western Kentucky, painting houses and barns for a contractor. That was before the Depression, when there was work. Back when the young Bernie Coy had believed he could get ahead in life by honest labor, regardless of his background.

Sitting on the bunk, his homemade cigarette half smoked, he shifted his feet slightly and felt his heel hit against the books stacked under the bunk. They were books on psychology and human relations. Bernie Coy had an intense desire to learn what motivated people to do some of the things they did. He was interested in understanding not only people like himself, who committed acts of crime, but also the so-called respectable people of the world. Like prison guards, for instance. There were guards on Alcatraz who went out of their way to torment prisoners; guards who felt that besides maintaining security and discipline, they also had a responsibility to make an individual's incarceration a little bit harder however they could. One guard, a mail clerk, always made it a point to deliver personally any letter in which an inmate's wife wrote that she was divorcing him.

"Well, old Joe D. Grinder has got your wife," he would say as he handed the prisoner his letter, loudly enough for half the men in the cellblock to hear. "Yeah, she's quitting you for old Joe D. Grinder."

"Joe D. Grinder" was any man who took a convict's wife to bed while the con was doing time. It was not a complimentary name.

In contrast to that guard was the Candy Bar Man. This particular guard frequently had a candy bar in his pocket when he came on duty. Sometime during his shift, he would casually toss the candy through the bars onto some con's bunk. As one con would say about him thirty years later, "I felt like he'd given me a little bit of freedom."

Bernie Coy wondered why a guard like the mail clerk felt he had to rub a prisoner's face in his misery that way, while someone like the Candy Bar Man tried to lighten a con's load for a brief moment. After all the years Coy had been reading psychology books, he still did not know.

When he finished the cigarette, Coy reached over, lifted up the canvases, and tossed it in the toilet. Then he sighed anxiously and got up to pace his cell. Today, he thought, rubbing his scratchy stubble of beard. Today, May second. It was finally here. After nearly nine years on the Rock, and more than a year of planning how to get off. May second had come at last.

The day of reckoning between Bernard Paul Coy and Alcatraz.

•

In an apartment in the personnel compound of the island, Joseph Simpson, having finished breakfast, was sitting in his easy chair testing the shutter speed of a 35-mm camera. Over the years, he had taken hundreds of snapshots and color slides of the prison island and its activities. As Simpson sat there, his mixed-breed dog Honey lay at his feet, seeking his attention by pawing at one of his shoelaces, then rolled over to the petting position.

Presently, Marian Simpson entered the room, bringing her husband's uniform coat and tie clip. "Is it broken, Joe?" she asked of the camera.

Simpson shook his head. "No. The shutter is just sticking a little. I'll work it out." He put the camera aside, reached down to temporarily pat away Honey's constant desire for his attention, and rose to put on his coat.

"Honestly, that dog," said Marian. "Sometimes I think she's as crazy about you as I am." Simpson smiled and kissed his wife on the cheek. Then he turned around and Marian held the coat while he slipped his arms into it.

The coat was part of a guard officer's uniform. Joe Simpson was an Alcatraz lieutenant. He was fifty-four years old, tall, nicely built, with an erect military posture and a confident, authoritative bearing.

Both were the result of a military-academy education and service as an army officer during World War I. He wore the uniform coat as naturally as a priest wore his collar. It was almost as if the person of Joe Simpson had been *designed* to wear a uniform of authority.

"I think I'll walk out with you," Marian said. "The flowers look so pretty early in the morning."

Simpson buttoned up his coat and took his wife's arm, and they walked outside together. The personnel compound was on a bluff about halfway between the ocean and the summit. It was on the eastern curve of the island and consisted of the duplex home of the associate warden and the chaplain, six small cottages, and three small apartment buildings. There was also a government-operated general store and post office, and a recreation hall. All over the compound were daisies, geraniums, honeysuckle, wild poppies, and an abundance of ivy and wild ice plant. Among the flowers grew fig trees and eucalyptus. Contrary to what many thought, the Rock was not all rock.

As Joe and Marian Simpson walked arm in arm outside, they met a group of the island's children on their way to catch the prison launch, which would take them to the mainland to school. The children all waved and shouted, "Good morning, Lieutenant Simpson!"

Simpson cheerfully waved back at them. Then he and Marian walked around the side of the building and stood for a few moments admiring the flowers and the panorama of the bay and the city beyond. Finally Simpson gave his wife a hug and said, "Got to go."

He kissed her good-bye and started off. After he had gone a short distance, Marian called and came running after him.

"Your tie clip, Joe," she said, holding out her hand. "I forgot to give it to you."

Simpson laughed, took the clip, and hurried on up the hill.

•

Two of the island children hurrying to catch the launch for elementary school that morning were Robert Stites, fourteen, and his brother Herbert, nine. They were the two younger sons—their brother James was seventeen—of Officer Harold Stites and his wife Bessie. As the boys rushed off to school, their father was still in bed. It was his day off, but Hal Stites was awake: it was impossible to sleep when his boys were up; he might try to go back to sleep as soon as it quieted down.

The Stites family lived in an apartment on the island; Stites, with twenty-one years of prison bureau service, had the seniority to rate an apartment, and it was far less expensive than living over in San Francisco. A five-room apartment in the compound rented for only $40 a month, heat and electricity included. While on duty, Stites could eat his lunch in the officers' dining room for twenty-five cents. The family's dry-cleaning and shoe-repair work—the latter a constant expense with the younger boys—was done in the prison dry-cleaning plant and cobbler shop at a fraction of the mainland cost.

On this day in early May, Hal Stites was one month away from his fiftieth birthday. Still a vigorous man, he was one of the best-liked guards in the island's resident cadre. An easygoing sort, he smiled readily despite slightly bucked teeth. His ears were a little too large for his head, and his hair was thinning noticeably in a half-moon from the top of his skull forward. But he was not a vain man; those things were not important to him. He was happily married, had three fine sons and a married daughter, a good job, and his health. Those were the things that mattered to Hal Stites.

Stites was a good guard; his reputation could be summed up in two words: steady and dependable. Eight years earlier, in May of 1938, he had proved himself in the face of sudden and violent danger. Three bank robbers, Whitey Franklin, Jimmy Lucas, and Sandy Limerick, jumped an unarmed guard, Royal Cline, in the Industries furniture shop and beat him to death with a claw hammer. The convicts then armed themselves with more hammers and some heavy wrenches and made their way to the roof of the building, which was known as the Model Shop. They knew the Model tower had a rifle and a submachine gun in it. On the roof, they split up and charged the tower from three directions at once. As they charged, they began throwing the hammers and wrenches through the windows of the tower.

The tower guard, even though he was being rushed from three sides, did not panic. He first drew his .45 and fired at the nearest man, Limerick, hitting him in the head and killing him instantly. Then he spun around and emptied the gun at the other two in turn, shooting first at one, then the other. He hit Franklin in the shoulder and dropped him. When his .45 was empty, he snatched up the rifle and aimed at Lucas. The con stopped in his tracks and put his hands up. By that time, Franklin was back up and rushing him from the other way again. He swung the rifle around and drilled Franklin in the other shoulder, dropping him for the second time. When he turned quickly back again, Lucas still had his hands up and it was all over.

The tower guard was Hal Stites, then forty-two years old, with thirteen years of service. Single-handledly, he had stopped a desperate, organized break.

Now, nearly eight years later, it was his day off and he was lounging in bed, waiting for things to quiet down so he could grab another hour's sleep. The older he got, the more he appreciated his days off. On this particular day, he was very glad he did not have to go to work.

•

In the big cellhouse at the top of the island, in Cell 142, a tense, worried young man paced the short length of his cell. He had been up for more than an hour. Trying to ease some of the tension he felt, he had done twenty minutes of concentrated calisthenics, then, like Bernie Coy, thirteen cells away, had taken a cold sponge bath at the sink. Neither had helped; he was still tense, still worried.

Dan Durando, at nineteen, was one of the youngest men ever committed to Alcatraz. He was serving ninety-nine years for kidnapping. If by chance he was ever paroled from federal custody, the state of Oklahoma had a detainer on him to serve a life sentence for murder. His future did not look very bright this morning.

As he paced, reversing direction every few steps, the muscles in his square, strong shoulders and back rippled like high-power wires. A Chicano, he had eyes like black bolts in a smooth brown face. A tough, experienced fistfighter, he was known to the other cons as the Indio Kid, after his hometown of Indio, Oklahoma.

Pausing in his nervous pacing, Durando looked out the front of his cell and across the corridor. In the north wall of the cellhouse, there were several high windows through which he could see the sky. Daylight had broken clear and bright that morning; it would probably be a pleasant day. Not that it made that much difference to him. Durando was a lock-up prisoner: he was not assigned to a job, and spent most of the time in his cell. Once in a great while he would be taken out as part of a work detail for some cleanup job somewhere in the cellhouse; but for the most part he was kept in his drum, as the cells were called.

This almost constant lockup was beginning to tell on the Kid. He was too high-spirited, too physically active to adjust to the long hours of confinement in the little five-by-eight cubicle. And it did not look as if he would get any relief from the monotony anytime soon. On Wednesday, six days hence, he would have been on the Rock for ten months. He had not been given a job because the classification committee could not find one for which they felt he was suited.

Because he had been in lockup since his arrival the previous July, Durando had not made many friends. One of the few exceptions was Bernie Coy, landscape painter and amateur student of psychology. And it was his friendship with Coy that caused his worry and tension this morning. Coy was planning a little trip. He had invited the Kid to go with him.

Danny Durando could not make up his mind whether to accept or not.

•

Below the windows through which the Indio Kid looked at the sky, another day-watch guard was trudging up the winding road to report for work. As he walked up the paved grade, Officer Bill Miller was pleased that his feet did not seem to be bothering him that morning. He had a strip of moleskin wrapped around each big toe, and it seemed to be preventing the bunion irritation he had been suffering for the past couple of weeks. The moleskin remedy had been given to him by one of the cons, Bernie Coy. Miller was trying to think of some way, within regulations, to show his gratitude to Coy.

As he climbed the next-to-last grade, Miller felt a little guilty because he had not told his wife, Josephine, about his foot problem. Normally, he kept no secrets from her. But he felt that Josephine had enough to worry about already, what with having to take care of their two children, Joan Marie, who was thirteen, and Billy, ten; and she was not yet entirely adjusted to their move to California from Pennsylvania, where they had spent most of their lives. Miller himself was a native of Philadelphia, a first-generation American born of German immigrant parents. Now forty-two, he had transferred to Alcatraz a year earlier from Lewisburg Federal Prison.

Like Cecil Corwin, Miller was considered a "good hack" by most of the prisoners. A good hack on Alcatraz was one who did not go out of his way to harass a con, and did not *look* for infractions of the rules to report. A guard who would report a con for having a homemade knife in his cell, but not for a contraband sandwich from the dining hall, was a good hack. A guard who bent the rules a little, like the Candy Bar Man, was a good hack. Bill Miller was a *con-*

cerned guard. He tried to keep in mind that the men on the Rock were human beings as well as convicts; he went out of his way to deal with them accordingly.

As Miller rounded the curve and started up the last grade, he heard someone call to him from behind. He looked back and saw Cecil Corwin coming up the hill. He had not seen him in two weeks, since the older man went on vacation. He stopped and waited for him to catch up.

"Hello, Ceece," he said as Corwin drew near. "How was the vacation?"

"Couldn't have been better," Corwin said. He was slightly out of breath. "I think this hill got steeper while I was gone."

The two guards continued toward the cellhouse together.

"Got any idea where I'm posted today?" Corwin asked.

Miller shook his head. He had looked at the duty roster the previous night, but had not paid any attention to any assignment except his own. "I did notice that nobody was posted for D Block. I think somebody got sick."

D Block was where the worst inmates in the prison were kept segregated. Working there could be a very easy shift or a very difficult one—depending on the temper of its occupants. Cecil Corwin hoped, if he was assigned to D Block, that it would turn out to be a routine day.

He had no way of knowing that Thursday, May 2, was going to be far from routine.

CHAPTER TWO

7:20 A.M.

As the Alcatraz launch headed for the mainland, the morning watch officers on the prison island were completing the final assignment of their tour of duty: supervising the morning meal of the in-grade inmates. Being in grade was the highest status an Alcatraz convict could attain. It meant that he had full privileges. Full *Alcatraz* privileges. He could send and receive one letter per week. He could have one visitor per month. He could check books out of the prison library. He could spend one hour per day in the prison yard. And he could work at one of the shop jobs in the Prison Industries building.

Inmates not in grade had to do their time the hard way: in lockup, with only occasional work details of the cleanup variety. Work, as many Alcatraz cons had come to learn, was the only antidote for "Rock fever"—the steady, creeping boredom and monotony that had actually driven some inmates mad.

On this second day of May, 1946, of the 272 prisoners on Alcatraz, 202 had in-grade status and were fed in a single long shift in the cellhouse dining hall before going to work for the day. The dining hall was at the west end of the big cellhouse. Its entrance faced the long main corridor that ran the length of the cellhouse. That corridor, running between the two parts of cellblock B and those of cellblock C, had been named Broadway by the inmates. The area at the west end of Broadway, where the prisoners entered the dining hall, was known as Times Square. There were two narrower corridors, parallel to Broadway, which also extended the length of the cellhouse. One of these, separating A Block from B Block, was called Michigan Avenue; the other, between C and D, was officially called the C-D aisle, and unofficially known as Seedy Street.

Broadway was the main avenue in the Alcatraz cellhouse. It was the aisle that contained the four sets of stairs—two at each end— leading to the upper tiers. It was the widest aisle, the lightest— having five more skylights in the high cellhouse roof than the other aisles—and it was the aisle most traveled by guard and inmate alike. It was also the only aisle which had facers: two rows of occupied cells facing each other across the corridor.

It was usually down Broadway that a prisoner walked when he had earned his way off the Rock and was being transferred to one of the other penitentiaries in the federal system. That was the only way a con ever left the island alive—when he was transferred. No one had ever been released from Alcatraz.

As the grade inmates filed down Broadway and across Times Square to enter the spotless, gleaming dining hall, they formed two single lines up the middle of the room. When the lines reached the serving counter, they separated, one going to the right, one to the left, along the counter. Identical menus were served at each of the two counters; having double serving counters merely cut in half the time needed to serve the prisoners.

At the end of each counter, the prisoner turned back into the dining hall with his food and sat in the nearest empty place. There were twenty ten-man tables in the hall, each with two benches. Coffee and water pitchers on the tables were kept filled by inmate dining-hall orderlies. Prisoners ate with spoons and forks only. At the end of the meal, all spoons and forks at each table were counted by a guard. When that was done, the entire table of men was allowed to file out at one time. All prisoners were required to wear pocketless coveralls to meals. This prevented the smuggling of food back to the cells.

The grade inmates were served their meals by inmate kitchen helpers. One such helper passing out food on the morning of May 2 was a quiet, scholarly-looking man who wore rimless eyeglasses to compensate for his extreme nearsightedness. His name was Marvin Franklin Hubbard, Alcatraz number 645. A native of Alabama, he was a soft-spoken, intensely proud man who had become a Depression-era outlaw while still in his teens. Now three months short of his thirty-fourth birthday, he had been on the Rock for one year and seven months. He was serving thirty years for the kidnapping of a policeman during an armed robbery.

•

It had been a sweltering August night in Chattanooga. The year was 1942. In the Roxy Theater on Broad Street, the last showing of the main feature, *Pride of the Yankees,* was on. It was past ten o'clock. Marv Hubbard was slumped down in a back-row seat. He had already sat through the show once. He did not particularly like the picture; he had never cared much for baseball, and the life story of Lou Gehrig was less than inspirational to him. But he liked Gary Cooper. He had seen him the year before in *Sergeant York.* Being a southerner, Marv Hubbard found it much easier to identify with Alvin York than some Yankee ballplayer.

When he reckoned that the last feature was about halfway through, Hubbard got up and went out to the lobby. He fished a toothpick from his shirt pocket, stuck it in his mouth, and ambled back to the theater manager's office, where the manager and cashier were counting the day's receipts.

"Evening, folks," Hubbard drawled, pulling an old break-down .32 revolver from his hip pocket. He handed the manager a paper bag he had used earlier to carry a hamburger into the show. "Keep real still and put everything in the bag," he ordered quietly. "All the change too."

The manager obeyed without a word, but the cashier pursed her lips and said, "You'll never get away with this. The policeman on this street is due here right now to walk over to the night depository with Mr. Sidlow. Isn't that right, Mr. Sidlow?"

"Is that a fact, now?" said Hubbard. He grinned at Mr. Sidlow, who was looking at the cashier in disgust. "I hope you got another job lined up, honey," Hubbard said. Stepping back to the door, he opened it a crack and saw a uniformed Chattanooga police officer leaving his patrol car at the curb and coming into the lobby.

Hubbard was behind the door when the officer entered. He put the gun muzzle against the policeman's spine. "Real still now," he cautioned.

Disarming the officer, Hubbard made the manager and cashier lie on the floor, took the bag of money, and walked the policeman back out to the patrol car. In the car, he gave him directions where to drive. "I usually cut through a few alleys to where I park my truck," he said matter-of-factly, "but no sense walking when you can ride, I always say."

At Hubbard's old pickup truck, parked on a dark street a mile from the theater, Hubbard made the officer open the patrol car's trunk. Inside was a Thompson submachine gun. "My, my, look here, now," the gunman said admiringly. "Just like the city boys use." He jerked his head toward the truck. "Get in. You drive. Take St. Elmo's Highway straight out of town."

"That road goes down into Georgia," the policeman said.

"I didn't figure they'd turned it the other way," Hubbard said dryly. He nudged him with the Thompson. "Get going."

Hubbard had the Chattanooga policeman drive twenty miles into Georgia. There, on a back country road, he abandoned him and drove back to Chattanooga. By transporting a kidnap victim and a machine gun across the Tennessee-Georgia state line, Marvin Hubbard had violated two federal laws. Those violations were the first step on his road to Alcatraz.

•

By an incredible coincidence, the cashier at the Roxy Theater saw Marvin Hubbard walking on a street in Knoxville, 115 miles from Chattanooga, just three weeks later. She had come up by Greyhound to visit her sister. At the sight of Hubbard, she turned white and summoned the police. Hubbard, taken completely by surprise, was arrested without resistance.

"I *told* you you wouldn't get away with it," the woman reminded him loftily. Hubbard could only shake his head wryly at such colossal bad luck.

Hubbard was lodged in the Knoxville jail. The Knoxville law did not have a record on him that first day he was in custody. They did not know that he had been more or less outside the law for fifteen years; had a submachine gun under the seat of his pickup truck parked uptown; was wanted on a federal kidnapping warrant; and had already broken out of two jails during his career. As far as they were concerned, he had simply stuck up a Chattanooga movie house. Small-time stuff. They did not even bother to search him thoroughly.

That night, with a hacksaw blade concealed in the inseam of his trousers, Hubbard sawed through two window bars and was gone. By the time morning rolled around, after his escape had been discovered and his record received, he was all the way to Bolivar, 260 miles across the state.

Bolivar was a bad town for a man on the run to stop in. There was a state asylum in Bolivar, and occasionally one of the inmates would manage to get out and wander around. For that reason, strangers were quickly noticed, quietly observed, and usually remembered. Such was the case with Marvin Hubbard, even though he was in and out of town in an hour, just time enough to have a meal and gas up. Even so, before he reached Bartlett, fifty miles away, he had been identified and had run into a roadblock of federal officers.

Marvin Hubbard was an absolutely fearless man. He had never backed down from a fight in his life, even as a very young boy when his eyesight was so poor he had difficulty seeing his opponent. Now, with glasses and a Thompson submachine gun, he was not about to be taken without a fight. He crashed into the roadblock and came out of his smashed pickup truck shooting. He never had a chance. The trained federal officers, all crack shots, brought him down within seconds. Wounded four times, he fell; but when the officers approached him, incredibly he fought them with his fists and feet. Even with four bullet wounds in him, he had to be beaten into submission.

When he was physically well enough, Marvin Franklin Hubbard was tried in federal court for kidnapping and illegal possession and interstate transportation of a machine gun. He was sentenced to thirty years. Early in 1943, he began his sentence in the federal penitentiary at Atlanta. The following year, he was one of a number of inmates involved in a prison riot. Following that incident, his record was reviewed by the U.S. Bureau of Prisons. It was a sadly unredeeming record: armed robbery, kidnapping, jailbreak, using a machine gun at a roadblock, and now prison rioting. Marvin Hubbard was judged unfit to remain in the normal population of federal prisoners.

In November, 1944, he was transferred to Alcatraz.

•

As Marv Hubbard dished out oatmeal at the serving line on the morning of May 2, a diorama of Depression-era desperados filed past him for breakfast. Some of them Hubbard knew by sight, some he knew by name. Others he knew mostly by reputation.

There were a few men in Alcatraz that day who were known to virtually *all* prisoners on the Rock. One such inmate moving toward the serving line was a husky, pleasant-looking man of forty-five. Well-read, articulate, known throughout the prison for his easy sense of humor, he was a former Public Enemy Number One who had been depicted by the prison bureau and the press as a mad-dog kidnapper and bank robber. In reality, he was the son of a fairly well-to-do Memphis insurance executive, a former university student, the father of two sons who by then were young men, and a man who, by all that was logical, should have taken his place as a respectable member of the business community. That he had not done so was always a puzzle to many who had known him, because he undoubtedly would have been far more successful inside the law than he had been as a criminal. *Why* he had chosen the life he did was a personal matter which he confided to only a few. But it was a choice freely made, and he rarely admitted any personal regret over it.

As he passed Marv Hubbard's place on the serving line that morning, the former public enemy had no way of knowing that the mild-mannered Alabaman who dished out his oatmeal was involved in a plot which, before the day was out, would affect not only him but, in one way or another, every prisoner on the Rock. He took his tray and went to the nearest table with an unoccupied seat. A friend of his, a bank robber from Kansas who was directly behind him in line, sat down beside him and the two fell into conversation as they quickly ate their meal.

The big man's real name was George Barnes, but, to save his respectable family any embarrassment, he had long since adopted his mother's maiden name. He was known to the prison bureau as

George Kelly, Alcatraz number 117. The American newspaper-reading public knew him more commonly as Machine Gun Kelly.

•

In June, 1933, George Kelly had sat at a back table in a Negro speakeasy on Beale Street in Memphis. Across from him was a twenty-nine-year-old West Tennessee bootlegger named James Richmond Howard. In the Mississippi River bottomlands where Howard and his men had their illegal whiskey stills, he was known as Tennessee Slim. At one time he had been a main source of supply for George Kelly, who had been prominently involved in the illegal whiskey traffic in Memphis. Kelly had since given up bootlegging and gone into bank robbing. He and his small, hand-picked gang of men, and his pretty, dark-haired wife, Kathryn, had that year successfully robbed the city banks of Tupelo, Mississippi, and Wilmer, Texas. Now, George Kelly was planning to move into still another area of crime: kidnapping. He wanted young Tennessee Slim Howard to throw in with him.

"I'm not looking to grab any little kids or women," Kelly emphasized. "Kit wouldn't put up with that. The snatch I've got lined up is a rich Oklahoma oil man. We plan to take him in about a month. Kit's folks have a little place in Texas where we can keep him. It's a dirt ranch out in the middle of nowhere. We're going to ask a ransom of $200,000."

Howard whistled softly and smiled. He was a handsome young man, with blond hair that kept falling over his forehead. "That's a lot of greenbacks," he said.

"I want you to join up with me, Rich," Kelly said. "You're smart and I know I can trust you. There'll be plenty of money for everybody."

Howard shook his head. "I can't do it, George. Things has changed since we used to do business. I'm married now and got me a kid. A little boy, just a year old last week. I'm planning to get out of the whiskey business. In another year I figure to have enough money to buy me some kind of legitimate business."

"Come in on this and you'll have enough money in a month," Kelly coaxed.

But the young bootlegger could not be persuaded. He and Kelly parted company, and he drove back to Ripley, Tennessee, fifty miles north of Memphis, where his wife and baby lived. A year later he was captured by federal agents, tried, and sentenced to Atlanta Federal Penitentiary. He never did get his legitimate business.

Machine Gun Kelly went on to pull the kidnapping he had planned. He and his gang kidnapped millionaire oilman Charles F. Urschel in Oklahoma City the following month. They successfully collected $200,000 ransom and released Urschel unharmed.

In September of that year, after a spending spree in Mexico, Kelly and his wife were captured when law officers burst into a bungalow they were renting in Memphis. Kelly, in his pajamas, could not get to his machine gun, but did manage to grab a .45 automatic. Then he realized that double-barreled shotguns were leveled not only at him but also at Kate, who lay in bed beside him. He threw down the automatic.

"Don't shoot, G-Men!" he yelled, little knowing that in using that term for government man for the first time, he was creating an American colloquialism.

The G-Men didn't shoot. Kelly and his wife were arrested, tried in federal court and given life sentences. They saw each other for the last time in October, on Friday the thirteenth, and then Kelly was shipped to Leavenworth and Katherine to the new federal prison in Milan, Michigan.

Kelly was not to remain in Leavenworth long, however. Three months later, the federal government would begin preparing a new prison for public enemies like Machine Gun Kelly. On an island in San Francisco Bay, the new pen would be known as Alcatraz.

CHAPTER THREE

7:50 A.M.

As the grade inmates ate their breakfast, the prison day-watch officers began to report for duty. One of the first to check in was Officer Clifford Fish. A mild, unpretentious man of slight build, Fish was assigned as day-watch armory officer. The armory was located at the opposite end of the cellhouse from the dining hall. It was off a sallyport, the main entrance into the cellhouse.

The sallyport was a short, double-secure corridor connecting the prison's administration offices with the visitors' room and the main cellhouse entry. It was divided into two sections. At the administration end—the first section—was a steel-bar door, a shield plate over its lock. Anyone entering the sallyport had to first pass inspection of the guard at the door. If approved, the guard would signal the armory officer, who would electrically slide the shield plate from the lock, permitting the outside guard to unlock the door. Once the person had entered, the door was relocked and the shield plate moved back over the lock.

When a person was inside the first section of the sallyport, there was no place to go until the sallyport officer unlocked a second barred door eighteen feet away. The space between the two doors was a deadlock area: only one of the doors would ever be opened at a time. If the person in the deadlock area was a visitor, he or she would be passed through the second door to the inner section of the sallyport, and directed off to the left into the visitors' room. If the person was a guard or other official, there would be another pause while the second barred door was closed and locked; then, just past the visitors' room, two more doors, one of solid plate steel and one of bars, would be opened. These two doors, which were only four inches apart, permitted direct access to the cellhouse.

The man who controlled the deadlock doors of the sallyport was the armory officer. He passed everyone in and out of the visitors' room and the cellhouse. He controlled sallyport traffic from within the armory, a totally inaccessible bulletproof room with three windows looking into the deadlock area.

As Cliff Fish stood in front of those three windows on the morning of May 2, the first two officers who entered to be admitted to the cellhouse were Captain Frank Weinhold and Lieutenant Joe Simpson.

"Morning, Captain, Lieutenant," said Fish.

"We'll walk on back to the dining hall, Cliff," the captain said. Weinhold was a tough, white-haired veteran correctional officer. Considered by many of his subordinates as too hard-nosed in his dealings with the inmates, he was not well liked by the majority of the guards. Weinhold was in charge of the Day Watch that Thursday; his second in command was the younger, more easygoing Joe Simpson, highly regarded by guards and prisoners alike.

The officers waited without impatience for the locking and unlocking sequence of the sallyport doors to admit them. Then they entered the big cellhouse and strolled down Broadway, seemingly oblivious of the convicts returning to their cells after breakfast. Some prisoners nodded and spoke respectfully to the two officers in passing, but not many. Few of the men on the Rock were inclined to be unnecessarily friendly toward their keepers. Neither Weinhold or Simpson expected cordiality, and they were not disturbed by the lack of it. On Alcatraz, the only attitude required was obedience; the only environmental essential, security.

•

In the armory, after letting Weinhold and Simpson into the cellhouse, Officer Clifford Fish sat down at the switchboard. Promptly at eight o'clock, he began receiving calls from the island's six gun towers.

"Armory, this is Manderville in the Main Tower, on watch."

"Armory, this is Waldo in the Powerhouse Tower, on watch."

"Armory, this is Metcalf in the Model Tower, on watch."

"Armory, this is Besk in the Hill Tower, on watch."

"Armory, this is Levinson in the Road Tower, on watch."

"Armory, this is Comerford in the Dock Tower, on watch."

The six officers were on duty in tall towers at six strategic locations throughout the island. Each of them was armed with a Colt .45 automatic pistol, a high-powered Springfield rifle, and a Thompson submachine gun.

Of the six towers, three were considered the most secure from possible convict attack. Those were the Hill Tower, manned by Officer Elmus Besk; the Road Tower, manned by Officer Arnold Levinson; and the Dock Tower, manned by Officer James Comerford. Before this day of May 2 was over, however, those three towers would prove to be not the safest but the most vulnerable and dangerous on Alcatraz.

They were the only guard towers which could be seen from the windows of the inmate dining hall and kitchen area.

•

As the tower guards were reporting in to Cliff Fish, other daywatch officers were also coming on duty. At the far end of the cellhouse, Officer Bert Burch was being let into the west gun gallery. Burch was a lean, craggily handsome man with black hair parted in the middle and slicked back. He brought his lunch with him in a metal lunchbox because he would be locked in for an eight-hour shift. The west gun gallery was a two-level, four-foot-wide gun walk overlooking the main floor of the cellhouse. It was situated above Times Square and ran perpendicular to the main cellhouse's east–west aisles: Michigan Avenue, Seedy Street, and Broadway. The gallery was a cagelike affair of waist-high steel plate on each level, with bars above the steel. On the top level, the upper bars extended all the way to the ceiling and curved basket-fashion toward the wall to form a roof. Flat steel cross-braces, spaced eighteen inches apart, held the round bars in place.

From the gallery, Bert Burch could patrol the three main cellblock aisles simply by walking back and forth on either of the two levels. Armed with a rifle and an automatic pistol, his function was to back up and protect the unarmed cellhouse guards on the floor below. Because the gun gallery had no inside doors and could be entered only from a catwalk outside the cellhouse, it was considered to be invulnerable.

Some of the men Bert Burch was covering that Thursday in early May were also just coming on duty at eight o'clock. Ernest Lageson, the cellhouse officer, was a square-jawed, clean-cut guard in his late thirties. His post was at a desk on Times Square, directly below the bottom level of Burch's gun gallery. By way of a curved mirror high on the end wall of the block, the two men could see each other at all times.

Working with Lageson, on walking patrol up and down Broadway, was Block Officer William Miller, who had walked up the hill with Cecil Corwin earlier that morning. Corwin had been assigned to D Block that day.

D Block was the prison's isolation and segregation section. It was not open like the other cellblocks, but was separated by a concrete wall facing Seedy Street. To understand the floor plan of the cellhouse, one should imagine looking down at four cigarette cartons placed flat on a table, side by side, with spaces between them. The carton on the extreme right would be A Block, with B Block next; between them would be Michigan Avenue. Between B Block and the next carton, C Block, would be Broadway. On the left side of C would be Seedy Street. A wall running the length of the cellhouse separated the extreme left carton, D Block, from the other three. Now visualize a large box being placed upside down over all the cartons. The box would be the cellhouse itself: the big building housing the cellblocks. The entire inside of the cellhouse was open, except for the offices at the east end, the dining hall and kitchen at the west, and the one wall enclosing D Block.

The wall isolating D Block also extended into the gun gallery, cutting off the D Block section from the main cellhouse section. A door on each level of the gallery permitted the guard to enter the D Block section of the elevated cage to cover the block officer on duty.

All four cellblocks were three tiers high. Halfway between the sallyport end and the dining hall end, an open passage in B and C blocks, called a cutoff, allowed access from one aisle to another. The block officers who patrolled the corridors and cutoffs between blocks carried no weapons. No guns were permitted on the cellhouse floor for any reason. Any firepower needed had to come from the west gun gallery, where Burch patrolled, or a similar structure just inside the sallyport entry, the east gun gallery. However, because more than 200 of the 272 convicts on Alcatraz were in grade and were taken to the Industries Building to work during the day, and because the other six dozen prisoners were either isolated in D Block or in lockup in their cells, it was not considered necessary to have a day patrol at the armory end of the cellhouse.

Consequently, the east gun gallery was not manned between eight in the morning and four in the afternoon.

•

After the morning meal, the grade prisoners returned to their cells briefly to shed their pocketless coveralls and put on their work clothes. All Alcatraz inmates wore light blue denim trousers and shirts, and dark blue Navy surplus pea coats. Everyone dressed the same. There were no special trusty uniforms, no white caps or white coats indicating trusty privileges. On Alcatraz there *were* no trusties.

When the prisoners had on their work clothes, they left their cells and lined up at the rear cellhouse door to go to the yard. Once there, when it was time to go to Industries, they would form work groups. There was a group for the prison laundry. The brush shop. The blacksmith, or metal, shop. The clothing factory. The dry-cleaning plant. The electrical shop. The shoe-repair shop. The model, or carpentry, shop. And the tailor shop.

One of the men in the tailor shop detail was Miran Edgar Thompson, Alcatraz number 729. Known to his friends as Buddy, Thompson was a twenty-nine-year-old native of Shawnee, Oklahoma, who had grown up in Texas. Dark-haired and handsome, he had a natural innocence about him that often inspired surprise when viewed in tandem with his criminal record. For Buddy Thompson was a confirmed criminal, a lone-wolf outlaw who had left a trail of crime across seven states and made eight successful jailbreaks. He had finally been convicted of kidnapping, armed robbery, and the killing of a police officer. Serving life plus ninety-nine years, he had been sent to Alcatraz the previous November.

Thursday, May 2, was Buddy Thompson's 161st day on the Rock.

•

In the summer of 1945, Buddy Thompson had been making his headquarters in Amarillo, Texas, and pulling armed robberies in New Mexico, Colorado, Kansas, and Oklahoma. It seemed to be a perfect setup. From Amarillo, it was only 66 miles to the New Mexico state line, 105 to the Oklahoma line, 41 miles farther on across the Panhandle to Kansas, and 133 to Colorado. He could pick an area, leave at dusk, hit a few places in a couple of small towns across one of the lines, and be back in Amarillo for breakfast. The scheme had been working nicely for him all year, since January when he had escaped from a Mississippi jail and abandoned that state, along with Alabama and Georgia, as his robbing ground.

On this late July day in 1945, however, Buddy Thompson had something on his mind besides armed robbery. Buddy's brother, Blackie Thompson, had recently been slain by a police officer while a fugitive from the Huntsville Penitentiary. Buddy took the killing particularly hard and was consumed by a desire for revenge. He was in a drugstore across the street from Sam Houston Park in Amarillo, sipping a chocolate soda, waiting for the killer of Blackie Thompson to come in. The officer stopped in every day about that time to buy cigarettes.

When the policeman came in that day, the girl behind the fountain went over to wait on him at the cigar counter. Thompson stayed where he was, directly in the officer's line of sight. Buddy's description was out to every lawman in the southwest; he knew the officer would notice him.

What the officer saw when he looked at Thompson was a pleasant-looking young man of twenty-eight, nicely groomed, neatly dressed in gabardine slacks, a seersucker sports coat, and black-and-white wingtips. A handsome, presentable young fellow. Just like the description of the one who had been sticking up all the filling stations and general stores and A&P markets up and down the northern and western state lines. There was probably not a chance in a million that this boy was the one, but the officer decided it wouldn't hurt to check it out anyway. Besides, there was something vaguely familiar about him—

Cigarettes in hand, the Amarillo officer ambled down to where

Buddy Thompson sat. "Afternoon," he said.

"Howdy," said Thompson, pausing in his soda sipping to smile.

"Mind if I ask your bin'ness?" the policeman said.

"Traveling man," Thompson answered.

"What's your line?"

"Guns."

"Guns?"

"And ammunition," Thompson added. He turned on the stool and let his coat fall open. The butt of an automatic showed prominently above his belt. "You got a gun under your coat," he said coldly. "Use it."

The officer stood there frowning for a few seconds. He could scarcely believe what was happening. This nice-looking young man was actually challenging him to draw. It was like something out of a cowboy movie. "What is this?" he asked. "Do I know you or something?"

"No, and you ain't never going to," Buddy said. "Now you can pull or not, but on the count of three I'm going to blast you. One. Two. Th—"

The Amarillo officer drew.

Buddy Thompson shot him twice before he could level his own gun.

•

Thompson escaped that day in Amarillo. He raced away from the drugstore in his own car, abandoned it on the edge of town, commandeered another vehicle, and forced the driver to take him north across the state line into Oklahoma. There he disappeared.

Buddy Thompson always had notoriously bad luck when it came to getting caught and being put in jail—and extraordinarily good luck when it came to breaking out. He had been arrested eight times and held in small-town jails, and eight times he had successfully escaped. It was only a matter of time until he was arrested again.

Thompson was captured in August, a month after the Amarillo shooting. This time he was not able to escape, because this time he was not charged with a stickup. He was charged with a killing. The Amarillo officer had died.

Thompson went on trial for murder. He was a Texan being tried by Texans for killing a Texan. He claimed that he had tried to avoid the shootout, and that he had intentionally fired low. Somehow the men on the jury could not bring themselves to send the pleasant, handsome young man up to the little red brick house in the Huntsville unit of the Texas Prison System where the state's electric chair was kept. They gave him life instead.

The Texas lawmen were a little upset by the verdict. So much so that they turned Thompson over to the federal courts to be tried for the kidnapping of the motorist. Hopefully, under the Lindbergh law, he would be executed for that. But the kidnap victim had not been harmed, had in fact been treated rather politely, so Buddy Thompson beat the death penalty again. His sentence was ninety-nine years.

Texas let the federal system keep Thompson. He was sent to Leavenworth. Meanwhile, his criminal record was reviewed by the Prison Bureau in Washington. The bureau found him to be a long-time criminal with a history of eight jailbreaks, numerous shootings, and the killing of a peace officer. Leavenworth was not the place for him.

In November of 1945, Buddy Thompson was transferred to Alcatraz.

•

When the men in the cellhouse were lined up and in order, ready to be let into the yard, Cellhouse Officer Ernest Lageson waved to Burch in the gun gallery above Times Square.

"Send down 107, Bert," he said.

Burch turned to a wooden key rack mounted on the wall. He selected a thick, flat, double-grooved key, attached it to a hook on a cord, and lowered it from his cage to the cellhouse floor. Lageson unhooked the key and handed it to Block Officer Bill Miller, so that Miller could unlock the west cellhouse door.

Besides the main sallyport entry, there was only this one other way in or out of the Alcatraz cellhouse: the west door. Located under the gun gallery near the D Block wall, the door—a solid steel panel with a four-by-ten-inch bulletproof observation window—led out of the cellhouse, across a six-by-four-foot concrete porch, and down twenty-three steps to the yard. Because of the accepted invulnerability of the cellhouse's sallyport entry, and because the west cellhouse door was the only other way out, the key to that door—Key 107—was never let into the cellhouse except when it was actually ready to be used. When not in use, it was kept in the key box in the west gun gallery—the only place besides the armory considered one hundred percent secure.

So on the morning of May 2, after Bill Miller had opened the west cellhouse door, let the grade prisoners out, and relocked the door, he immediately returned 107 to Ernest Lageson, who hooked it to the end of the cord and signaled Bert Burch to pull it back up to the gun gallery.

Burch did—and for the moment, Key 107 was again safely in the gun-cage key box.

CHAPTER FOUR

8:05 A.M.

When the lockup prisoners were let out for breakfast, after the grade prisoners had eaten, the husky young Chicano named Danny Durando stepped out of Cell 142 on the bottom tier of B Block and fell in line with the others walking toward Times Square. He walked with a slight strut, just a hint of swagger, of arrogance, as if well aware that he was a tough young kid and knowing that his peers expected him to show it in some way.

The Kid was in an even worse mood now than he had been when he first woke up. Besides worrying about what he was going to tell Bernie Coy that day, he had now started worrying about his people back in Oklahoma, wondering if he would ever see any of them again. They were very poor—dirt poor, Chicano poor. Not much chance they would ever have enough money to come all the way to Alcatraz to visit him. Sometimes, in the big, dark cellhouse filled with the night sounds of other prisoners, he had bad dreams: nightmares about all of his people dying before he ever got to see them again.

Even with the ninety-nine-year sentence, an escape record, the reputation, and the strut, Dan Durando was still very much a boy inside a man's body.

•

When the Kid was fifteen years old, he and another youth walked into the office of a roadside service station in Atoka, Oklahoma. The station attendant was sitting in a straight chair tipped back against the wall, drinking an Orange Crush. He looked up at the two boys, one light-skinned, one dark.

"What you boys want?" he asked in a disinterested drawl.

Dan and his friend looked nervously at each other. "Go on," the friend whispered. Dan pulled an old .25 automatic from his pocket.

"Give us the money," he said almost fearfully.

The attendant looked scornfully at the boys. "You two little piss-ants get out of here before I kick your asses for you," he said.

Durando's eyes flashed anger. "We want the money, mister. You better get up and get it if you know what's good for you!"

The attendant drank the last of his soda pop and let the front legs of the chair fall loudly to the floor. "How'd you like me to whop you over the head with this bottle, you little nigger?" he said coldly. He stood up and took a step toward the Kid.

"You better not try it," Durando warned.

"You got a lot of nerve coming in here and pointing that pea-shooter at me," the attendant said. He hefted the empty pop bottle. "Somebody ought to teach you a lesson."

"Don't come no closer—"

The attendant leaped at Durando, pop bottle raised to strike. The bodies of the man and boy collided. The little pistol went off and the attendant was shot in the heart.

•

The Indio Kid and his youthful partner were captured within blocks of the killing. Taken to the county jail, Durando was charged with first-degree murder. The other boy, who was white, was charged with attempted robbery.

The Kid sat in his jail cell like a trapped animal on the verge of panic. What had started out as a simple little stickup now had him locked up for murder. He could scarcely believe it. The job had seemed so *easy* when they planned it. How could anything that simple go so wrong so quickly?

By the time the jailer came around with his supper, Durando was like a coiled spring forced down to maximum tension. The jailer did not help matters. "You in deep shit now, Mex," he had said matter-of-factly. "They going to fry your ass for killing that white man."

The jailer, like the service-station attendant, had no fear of a Chicano kid, so he opened the cell door and held in a tin plate of beans, side meat, and cornbread. Durando knocked the plate out of his hand, ripped a fist into his stomach, and slugged him unconscious with four rocklike punches to the face. Snatching up the jailer's gun, the Kid threatened his way out of the jailhouse and took off on foot into the hills.

A posse and its bloodhounds caught up with him twelve hours later.

In October of 1943, Dan Durando was convicted of murder and sentenced to life in prison. He was sixteen years old.

At the Oklahoma State Reformatory at Granite, the Kid was put to work in the rock quarry, smashing stone into road gravel with a forty-pound sledge. He worked there for sixteen months, building up back, shoulder, and arm muscles as strong and supple as industrial belting leather. Something else he built up was a reputation as a fighter. In the gravel pit, with guards and inmates looking down like spectators in ancient Rome, he engaged in a dozen brutal fistfights. All of them fights to the finish. Each time he won, the Kid grew a little harder outside and a little more disillusioned inside.

In February of 1945, Durando and two others escaped from the quarry. On a rural road, they waylaid a farmer in an old car and forced him to drive them west across the Texas border to Shamrock. There they let him out, stole his car, and drove away. They doubled back and returned to Oklahoma.

The Kid was recaptured a few days later in Boise City, Oklahoma, only 260 miles from the reformatory he had escaped. This time he faced a kidnapping charge; when he forced the farmer to drive him into Texas, he had violated the Lindbergh Act. The following month, in a federal court, he was convicted of that crime and sentenced to ninety-nine years.

The first federal prison they sent him to was Leavenworth. There, as in Granite, he found himself constantly defending his reputation as a fighter. Within weeks he was classified as a serious disciplinary problem. His record was reviewed in Washington. Armed robbery. A killing. Jailbreak. Assault of a jailer. Escape from a state reformatory. Kidnapping. And now disciplinary problems at Leavenworth.

In July of 1945, Dan Durando, age eighteen, was transferred to Alcatraz.

•

As the Kid walked along Michigan Boulevard to go to breakfast that morning, he saw Dutch Cretzer standing in the open doorway of 152, the fourth cell from the end. Durando knew he was waiting for him. Walking along, he tried to pretend he didn't see Cretzer, but the ploy didn't work; Cretzer called softly to him.

"Kid!"

Durando stopped at the open cell.

"You made up your mind yet?" Cretzer asked. He spoke in a quiet, prison voice, barely moving his lips, so that no one passing his cell would be able to hear.

"I got until noon," the Kid answered.

Cretzer's jaw clenched. "You're sure taking your own sweet time, aren't you?"

"I was given until noon," Durando said doggedly. He moved back into the straggly line and walked away.

Cretzer cursed silently under his breath. He did not like the Kid's attitude, the way he acted like he was as good as anybody else. Especially since he was only one step up from a nigger. If Cretzer had been running the plan, Durando would not even have been in on it. He was too reluctant, too unsure of himself. But there was no point in making an issue of it now, he decided. Not this late in the game.

Sullenly, Cretzer stepped out of the cell and fell into line for breakfast.

•

Joseph "Dutch" Cretzer, Alcatraz number 548, was, like the Indio Kid, a lockup prisoner with few privileges. A stocky, handsome man with black, wavy hair and equally black, penetrating eyes, he was a former Public Enemy Number Four serving life plus thirty years for bank robbery, escape, and the killing of a federal marshal.

A notorious West Coast bank robber, Cretzer had led a gang that laid waste banks from Seattle to Oakland. By the time he was twenty-six, he had climbed to fourth on the FBI's Most Wanted list. Finally captured at twenty-eight, he was convicted in federal court of three bank robberies and sentenced to twenty-five years. In February of 1940, he began serving his term at McNeil Island federal prison in Washington state.

After less than three months on McNeil Island, Cretzer commandeered a prison truck, crashed through the gate, and headed for a boat at the prison dock. He was surrounded and captured just yards from a very good chance at freedom.

In April, 1940, Dutch Cretzer was taken to federal court in Tacoma and tried for attempted escape.

•

The trial in Tacoma was short and uncomplicated. The guards and other prison officials testified in the morning; there were no witnesses for the defense; the verdict was guilty; and Cretzer was returned to court in the afternoon for sentencing.

"Joseph Cretzer, do you have anything to say in your own behalf before sentence is passed in this matter?" the judge asked.

Cretzer shook his head.

"Very well. It is the sentence of this court that, for the crime of attempted escape from a federal penitentiary, you will serve five additional years. This sentence is to be consecutive to any federal sentences which you have outstanding at the present time." The judge's gavel fell. "Remove the prisoner."

A. J. Chitty, a federal marshal, took Cretzer casually by the elbow and guided him toward a door leading to a holding cell behind the court. As they were leaving, Cretzer heard the judge order his court bailiff to look in the hall for an attorney involved in the next case. Cretzer glanced back and saw the armed bailiff leave the courtroom.

When he and Chitty were halfway to the door, Cretzer suddenly whirled and swung his handcuffed wrists at Chitty's face. The steel cuffs struck him in the temple and he staggered back. Cretzer swung again, this time catching the marshal on the cheek. Chitty dropped to his knees. Cretzer reached under the marshal's coat, seized his gun, and pistol-whipped him with it until he fell unconscious. Then the handcuffed public enemy turned to level the gun at the judge. His intent was to take the jurist hostage and use him to escape. Before he could get the judge in his sights, however, he felt the cold muzzle of a pistol against his neck. The bailiff had returned, seconds too soon for Cretzer to take his hostage. Once again, he had barely missed a good chance to make a successful escape.

As Cretzer was being restrained with additional handcuffs until shackles could be brought in for him, the court clerk and several others tried to revive Chitty. Finally the court clerk looked up at the judge.

"Your Honor, I think Marshal Chitty is dead."

•

A. J. Chitty was indeed dead, and Joseph Cretzer faced still another trial—this one for murder.

When the trial commenced, the U.S. Attorney asked for the death penalty. Cretzer's defense counsel argued that a death sentence could not be imposed because the escape attempt had been a sudden, impulsive act brought about by the unexpected absence from the courtroom of the armed bailiff. It had not been planned in advance, therefore the act was not premeditated.

The strongest defense argument for Cretzer, however, was the medical report on the deceased federal marshal. A. J. Chitty had not died from the concussion of Cretzer's blows; he had suffered a heart seizure brought on by the surprise of the sudden assault. Had the marshal's heart been sound, Cretzer's blows alone would not have killed him.

The combined arguments saved Dutch Cretzer's life. He was convicted of murder, but spared the electric chair. His sentence was life imprisonment.

In his cell the night he had been sentenced, Cretzer was visited by Captain Richard Mahoney, a Seattle police detective. Mahoney had known Cretzer since the young public enemy had held up a bank in his city three years earlier.

"Well, Dutch, you finally made the big time," Mahoney said to him. "You'll go to the Rock for sure now."

"If they're smart, they'll keep me away from Alcatraz," Cretzer replied lightly. "I grew up in San Francisco. Having to look at that city every day from a prison cell isn't going to make a model prisoner out of me."

Mahoney chuckled. *"Nothing's* going to make a model prisoner out of you, Dutch. Besides, on the Rock they won't care if you're good or bad. They know how to handle all kinds. They've got Karpis, Kelly, Floyd Hamilton, Whitey Franklin, all the tough ones. You'll look at San Francisco every day whether you like it or not."

Cretzer's handsome face grew serious. "I'm not kidding, Mahoney. If they put me on the Rock, I'll never stop trying to crash out. I'll get off that island no matter what I have to do or who I have to kill. And if I can't make it, I'll get killed trying."

"Keep talking, Dutch," the detective captain said. "That's all you've got left now. Just talk."

"We'll see about that, Mahoney," Cretzer said grimly. "We'll see."

Mahoney had been right. After only a cursory review of Dutch Cretzer's record, the Bureau of Prisons decided there was only one place for him. In August of 1940, Cretzer was taken in chains, under heavy guard, to Alcatraz.

•

On the morning of May 21, 1941, when he had been on the Rock just under nine months, Dutch Cretzer made his first escape attempt. He and a low-intelligence convict named Sam Shockley were working in the mat shop, weaving hemp. From his workbench in the Industries Building, Cretzer could look out the window, beyond the Cyclone fence and barbed wire at the edge of the bluff, to the two-hundred-yard marker buoys that ringed the island. Just a short distance past that marker, two men in a boat were fishing. Or pretending to fish. They were members of Cretzer's gang. The boat was a speedboat. On the deck, under canvas, were four submachine guns.

After the roving Industries guard checked the mat shop that morning and moved on, Dutch Cretzer and Sam Shockley jumped the unarmed shop guard and tied him up with hemp. With Shockley guarding the locked shop door, Cretzer quickly collected the emery wheels from the studding section of the shop. At a far corner window, he plugged in a drill and began to grind away at the curved window bar. The bars were curved basket-style over the lower part of the window, to permit tilting the window in when the weather was good. If just one of those bars could be cut, there would be enough room for a man to squeeze through.

With sweat pouring down his face, Cretzer pressed the spinning emery wheel against the bar. He wore out one wheel and put on another. Then another. And another. Instead of the emery wheels eating through the steel, the toolproof bar was rubbing the wheels smooth. Cretzer worked for forty minutes. He did little more than polish a spot on the bar. Finally, even though he had several wheels left, he threw down the drill in frustration.

"Son of a bitch," he said quietly, as he looked out at the bobbing speedboat waiting to make its quick run to shore. He sighed and turned away from the window.

"Dutch!" Sam Shockley hissed. "The hall screw's coming again!" Shockley was behind the door, ready to jump the roving guard.

Cretzer shook his head. "Forget it, Sam. It's a bust." If the roving guard had a gun, Cretzer might have tried to shoot his way to the shore. But all he carried was a billy. There was no way they could make it now.

Cretzer walked over and put an arm around the slow-witted Shockley. "Next time, Sam," he promised. "Next time, we'll make it."

The roving guard was looking through the observation window now. Cretzer walked over to the shop guard and calmly untied him.

•

It was not the policy at Alcatraz to return lifers like Dutch Cretzer and Sam Shockley to court for attempted escapes unless a guard had been killed or seriously injured. For less violent escape attempts, Alcatraz handled matters in its own way. Cretzer and Shockley were placed in solitary confinement in D Block. Cretzer was to remain in solitary for five years. Shockley, because of his low intelligence and because Cretzer had talked him into the break at the last minute, was put back into population after only three months.

Dutch Cretzer was nearly thirty-five when he was returned to the main cellhouse. He was put back in general population as a lockup prisoner, because there was no job in the prison that he was considered trustworthy enough to be given.

Although few people knew about it, Cretzer was not a well man. For several months he had been waking up in the middle of the night with slight fevers. He had also been suffering intermittent dizziness and severe headaches. But the thing that bothered him the most was his eyes. Along with everything else, Cretzer was experiencing increasing periods of double vision. He suspected that he might be going blind.

Cretzer knew from observation that it would be a long time, perhaps years, before he could expect to be put back in grade. In the meantime, all he had to look forward to were endless hours in a locked cell, Rock fever, and, ultimately, going blind in prison.

Dutch Cretzer refused to accept that future. During the six weeks since his return to population, he had been planning other things.

CHAPTER FIVE

8:10 A.M.

As Dan Durando and Dutch Cretzer crossed Times Square to line up at the dining-hall door, they both glanced over to the extreme southwest end of the square, beyond the Key 107 door to the yard, and watched two kitchen orderlies pushing a steam cart up to the door of D Block. Overhead they saw Burch, in the gun gallery, divide his attention between the orderlies and the lockup cons in the breakfast line. The orderlies halted the steam cart directly in front of the D door—a two-inch slab of steel, mounted in an eight-inch concrete wall. There was a four-by-twelve-inch horizontal vision panel of bulletproof glass at eye level, covered on the inside by a fitted, hinged, metal plate that could be lowered for observation purposes.

When one of the kitchen orderlies knocked on the door, D Block Officer Cecil Corwin opened the hinged plate and looked out at them.

Then he unlocked the door. The D door was set with double locks, one above the other. When opened, it swung out. Durando and Cretzer watched as the steam cart was rolled inside. To Durando, D Block was just another part of the prison that he had never seen. To Cretzer, it was a five-year hell that he had only recently been let out of. Dutch Cretzer considered it the very worst place on the face of the earth. He would gladly die before being put back in D.

•

Situated entirely beyond the wall that ran the length of the cellhouse, D Block was officially listed as the Isolation and Segregation Section. To the guards, it was known as the Treatment Unit. To all, it was the Siberia of Alcatraz. If the Rock could be said to hold the worst of the worst, then D Block held the worst of the worst of the worst. Its occupants were the ones whom the Bureau of Prisons and Alcatraz authorities considered the most dangerous federal convicts in the nation.

When the steam cart was parked at the D Block stairs, the two kitchen orderlies opened its side compartments and quickly began distributing the morning meals to each prisoner. On the top tier, in Cell D-41, a tall, bone-thin man with a bald head and unusually large ears, wearing a green celluloid eyeshade, waited at the food pass opening for his tray to be handed through. A brilliant-dangerous Jekyll-Hyde personality, a psychotic who could suddenly become maniacal, he had already taken the lives of two men—one of them a federal prison guard.

His name was Robert Franklin Stroud, Alcatraz number 594. He was known to the other cons as the Birdman.

•

Thirty years earlier, on March 26, 1916, Robert Stroud had marched in lockstep to the main dining hall of Leavenworth Penitentiary. In the food line, he took his round tin plate of white beans, corn, salt pork, and four slices of bread, and sat with thirteen other men at a wooden table to eat. A meal steward poured hot black coffee into metal cups for every man. There was no water at the table. The men ate without conversation; the rule was silence. Guards in highcollar tunics patrolled the aisles, carrying fifteen-inch wooden nightsticks. Rifle guards walked slowly back and forth along two iron catwalks that stretched across the room. It was a huge room; more than a thousand convicts were being fed.

Stroud, sitting fourth from the end of the bench, nudged the man next to him with his knee under the table. "Watch for Turner," he said in a prison whisper, around a mouthful of bread sopped with bean juice.

The convict next to him, without pausing in his eating, nudged the man next to him and passed the message on. "Watch for Turner." When the con at the end of the bench received the message, he used the toe of his heavy prison hightop to get the attention of the man across from him. "Watch for Turner," he said. The convict facing him immediately glanced up the aisle between tables. Guard Andrew Turner was at the far end of the aisle, talking to another guard.

Stroud sat with his back to the end of the aisle where Turner stood. But he knew that Turner would soon be along the aisle on patrol. The young convict kept eating, waiting patiently.

Stroud was twenty-nine at the time, serving the tenth year of a twelve-year sentence for manslaughter. At the age of nineteen, while working as a railroad construction laborer in the U.S. territory of Alaska, he had gotten into a fight with a local bartender over a woman. Both men pulled knives during the fight. Stroud's knife was the faster; he killed the bartender. After his trial, he began his prison term at McNeil Island. Later he was transferred to Leavenworth.

"Turner's coming," said the convict at the end of the table. The message was immediately passed on. Stroud quickly ate as much of the rest of his food as he could. He knew it would be a while before they fed him anything but slop and scraps again.

Because of the clatter of tin spoons against tin plates, tin cups against wooden tables, Stroud could not hear Andrew Turner's footsteps, but he now knew that the guard was approaching and he was alert for his arrival. Out of the corner of his eye, he watched the aisle for the first sign of the slowly moving blue uniform. Finally it came.

As soon as Turner strolled past his table, Stroud swung around on the bench and stood up. He was now in direct violation of a rigidly enforced rule against rising without permission in the dining hall. The guards on the catwalk did not see him, however. No one saw him in time to stop him—except other convicts. In four quick steps Stroud was in the aisle. Three more and he had caught up with the patrolling guard. Deftly he slipped a prison-made knife from under his shirt.

"Mr. Turner," he said quietly.

The guard turned unsuspectingly. Stroud plunged the knife into his heart.

•

Robert Stroud refused to say why he had killed Andrew Turner. There was much speculation, then and later. Some believed it was because Turner was sadistic and constantly harassed Stroud. Others said it was because Turner had caught Stroud in a homosexual act and was going to report it so that Stroud's mother would find out. The popular view was that Turner had written Stroud a ticket for a minor infraction of the rules, and that because of it Stroud would miss a visit by his mother, who had traveled a long distance to see him. But no one knew for certain, and at his murder trial Stroud remained mute.

Stroud was sentenced to hang. His original trial and subsequent appeals took more than four years, and it was not until April of 1920 that his gallows was finally constructed in a corner of the Leavenworth exercise yard. But while the federal prison system waited anxiously to execute the guard-killer, Robert Stroud's mother was conducting a relentless campaign to have her son's death sentence commuted. That campaign took her finally to the social office of Elizabeth Bolling Wilson, wife of the President of the United States. No one knows the exact conversation that transpired between the two women during their long meeting, but just one week before the scheduled hanging, Robert Stroud's death sentence was commuted to life in prison by President Wilson.

The federal prison system was outraged, but there was no way to appeal the President's ruling. The best it could do was fall back on the original order of the federal judge who had sentenced Stroud. That order had stated that Stroud was to be held in solitary confinement until such time as his execution was carried out. Since his execution had now been voided, the order could be literally construed as one which permitted the prison authorities to keep Stroud in solitary confinement for the rest of his life. That was exactly what they planned to do.

Robert Stroud spent the next twenty-three years in solitary confinement in Leavenworth. In the beginning he passed the time by painting seasonal greeting cards which his mother sold to the outside world. Later, he found an abandoned nest of baby sparrows in the yard where he exercised alone, and began his two-decade study of bird care and diseases. As the years passed and prison administrations changed, the restrictions on Stroud were relaxed. He was eventually given a second solitary cell for a laboratory, and allowed to use surgical instruments and other tools. He was also permitted to write bird-care articles for ornithology magazines, and used that medium to strongly protest the use of round birdcages for canaries. After years of patient study, Stroud had concluded that canaries, like people, often need a corner to which they can retreat. Round cages have no corners.

In 1942, Stroud's massive volume, *The Digest of Bird Diseases,* was being readied for publication. That same year, the Bureau of Prisons, apparently deciding that their already well-known prisoner was on the verge of becoming famous, and undoubtedly feeling vibrations of a pardon, made a sudden and unexplained move. They ordered Stroud transferred to Alcatraz.

On the Rock, Robert Stroud was put at once into isolation in Cell 41 on the top tier of D Block. Unlike at Leavenworth, he was permitted no special privileges; he would be treated like all other D Block lockups. The days of Robert Stroud's experiments with birds were over. Contrary to general belief, and despite his popular nickname, he did no bird research on Alcatraz. Except for being walked twice a week to the shower cell at the end of the tier, Stroud spent all of his time in his cell, writing a history of the federal prison system as he had known it since the age of nineteen.

On this morning of May 2, 1946, Robert Stroud had been on Alcatraz for three years. He had lived in federal prisons for forty years.

•

On the flats of D Block, as the kitchen orderlies began distributing breakfast to the segregated inmates, Officer Cecil Corwin walked over to Cell D-1, the first inmate cell next to the shower cell. He looked up at Bert Burch in the gun gallery, who had walked over to keep an eye on the kitchen orderlies.

"Unlock D-1, Bert," Corwin said.

Burch nodded and moved over to a control box inside the cage. That box controlled all fourteen cells on the D Block flats. Corwin could open the twenty-eight cells on the middle and top tiers, but only the gun-cage guard could open the bottom cells. Burch set the mechanics for D-1 and threw the lever. The barred door of D-1 slid open electrically.

The occupant of Cell D-1 was Louis Fleish, Alcatraz number 574. Diminutive, almost meek, he was a former member of Detroit's infamous Purple Gang. His criminal career had been limited almost exclusively to illegal gambling operations, but he was serving thirty years for possession of a machine gun—a charge Fleish swore was a federal frame-up to help the FBI smash the gang. There was little reason to believe he belonged on Alcatraz, much less in D Block with the prisoners considered most dangerous.

Corwin used Fleish as the block orderly. "Come on out, Louis, and make yourself useful," Corwin said amiably. "Give the orderlies a hand passing out the trays."

"Okay, Mr. Corwin," said Louis Fleish.

Fleish set about helping distribute the breakfast trays. As he worked, he quietly whistled a pleasant little tune he had picked up from Cecil Corwin. He did not know that Corwin had composed the tune.

•

On the middle tier of D, one level down and five cells over from Robert Stroud, in Cell D-22, was perhaps the single most violent and dangerous man on Alcatraz. His name was Sam Richard Shockley, Alcatraz number 462. As he waited at his cell door for the breakfast tray to be handed through the food pass, his lower jaw hung slack, but his eyes were darting and nervous. Thirty-seven years old, known throughout the prison as Crazy Sam, he had an IQ of only 54, roughly that of an eight-year-old. He had been on Alcatraz for six and a half years, and had been in and out of Isolation half a dozen times. Five years earlier, Shockley had thrown in with Dutch Cretzer in his abortive escape attempt. Cretzer, after five years in D Block, had recently been let back into the general population. Shockley, because of his sudden fits of violence and frequent hallucinations, had come back into Isolation three months earlier. This time, because his erratic behavior made him unfit even for routine prison life, it had been decided that he would remain there—permanently.

Ever since his friend Cretzer had been put back in B Block, Shockley had been out of sorts. There was now no one in the cells on either side of him, so he had no one to talk to. He could not sleep at night and often paced his cell like a restless coyote. He chewed his nails —and the skin around them—almost relentlessly. Sometimes his breathing was labored, as if he were asthmatic. Always he was tense, tightly wound: a human electrical outlet that nothing had been plugged into for a long time.

For a month, Crazy Sam had been on his best behavior. He knew he could not afford to have a yelling fit or start throwing his few meager belongings at one of the three block screws. To do so would be to risk being put in one of the dark cells of the flats for a few days' punishment. Shockley had been in a dark cell eight times already. It did not bother him. In fact, there were times when the cool, nearly lightless cells were almost a relief, as if for a few days he had escaped from the Rock.

As tense as he now felt, Shockley would have welcomed a dark cell —and the shouting, throwing fit it would take to be put in one. But he had to restrain himself. Dutch was depending on him. Dutch was the only friend he had in the whole fucking world, and nothing could make him let Dutch down. He just hoped he would not have to wait much longer.

Crazy Sam heard footsteps on the concrete tier range; then a kitchen orderly, accompanied by Officer Corwin, was handing his breakfast tray through the food pass. As usual, no words were exchanged with the food runner. Shockley simply accepted the tray and sat down on his bunk to eat. The compartmented tray contained oatmeal with a circle of Pet milk poured on it, a slice of salt pork the size of an old dollar bill, two pieces of dry toast, six canned grapefruit sections in unsweetened juice, and black coffee. Looking at it, Sam thought of pancakes. Every morning he thought of pancakes, and of the last time he had tasted them.

•

Early one morning in March, 1938, Sam Shockley had hitchhiked into Paoli, Oklahoma, wearing bib overalls, a Mackinaw jacket with holes in both elbows, and badly scuffed hightop work shoes. In the pocket of his overalls was an old .32 caliber revolver with the grips missing from the butt. There were two bullets in the gun. Shockley had fifteen cents in his other pocket. Although there was no significance to the fact at the time, Paoli was only ninety-eight miles in one direction from Shawnee, where Buddy Thompson was born, and ninety miles in another direction from Atoka, where Danny Durando would one day accidentally kill a service-station attendant in his first holdup.

At the Blue & White Cafe, the twenty-nine-year-old low-intelligence farm laborer bought a cup of coffee and a nickel pecan pie wrapped in cellophane. Sitting at the corner of the counter, he watched out the yellowed cafe window as an occasional tradesman walked past the Paoli Bank to open one of the few stores in the little town of three hundred. Just before eight o'clock, a dark green Ford sedan pulled up in front of the bank and parked. A man and a woman got out. The man unlocked the front door of the bank and they entered. Five minutes later, Sam Shockley left the cafe and hurried across the cold, windswept street.

Shockley entered the bank. The man who had unlocked the door, D. F. Pendley, was the bank president. He still had on his heavy camel-hair overcoat and had just finished getting a fire going in the second of two oil stoves that heated the bank. His wife, who had come in with him, had opened the safe and was sorting currency in the drawer. She was the bank's head teller. They both looked up as the ragged farmhand entered.

"Morning," Pendley said with a smile. "Help you?"

"You can give me that overcoat of yours," Shockley said. "I'm cold."

D. F. Pendley laughed. He liked a good joke as much as the next fellow. "Be happy to oblige you except for one thing," he said. "I'm cold too!" He laughed again, louder this time.

Shockley pulled out his gun. "I ain't joking, mister. Take off that coat."

At the sight of the gun, Mrs. Pendley dropped money all over the floor. "Pick it up," Shockley ordered, as he traded coats with her husband. "Put it all in a sack."

"I don't—don't have any sack," the frightened woman told him.

"Give it here, then," Shockley said irritably. He stuffed the bank's money into the belted bib of his overalls. "Out to the car now," he said. "Y'all going to drive me away from here."

"Can't you just take the car and leave us here?" Pendley pleaded. "My wife is very nervous."

"You do what I say!" Shockley snapped. "I can't leave you here 'cause I don't know how to drive. Now get moving!"

They all got in the car and Pendley drove them away from the bank.

"Drive down to Route 19, then head east," Shockley instructed from the back seat. He was headed home, headed back to McCurtain County, and he might as well let the big shot banker take him part of the way there. While he rode, Shockley tried to count the money he had stolen. But he was not very good at figures and kept forgetting his totals.

The car ran out of gas eight miles east of Atoka. By then it was approaching noon and had warmed up some. Shockley made the Pendleys lie on the floorboard of the car out of sight. He put on his ragged Mackinaw again. In a little while, a farm truck came by and gave Shockley a lift. He left the Pendleys there.

In the town of Antlers, twenty-four miles down the highway, Shockley left the farm truck and thumbed a ride south into Choctaw County. He hitched another ride, east again, twenty-five miles to the town of Swink. From there he started walking across the bare, flat, winter fields toward home. Toward a place to hide.

By nightfall, the state police were scouring southeast Oklahoma for the bank robber. Roadblocks had been set up at all county lines. Since the fugitive had been traced to within a few miles of McCurtain County, a posse was formed in Idabel, the county seat, and set out in four cars to look for him. From the description telephoned to the McCurtain County sheriff, they already had a pretty good idea of who they were looking for.

Unaware that pursuit was as close as it was, Shockley stopped at a farmhouse near Millerton, thirteen miles from Idabel, to ask for supper. "I can pay, ma'am," he assured the woman who answered his knock.

It was dark, past suppertime, but people were hospitable in Oklahoma in those days. "No need to pay," the woman's husband said. They let Shockley in and he stood by the kitchen stove to get warm.

"I want to pay," he assured them. "I been working the wells up to Norman, so I got money to pay."

"Better let me see what I can offer you first," the woman said. "Might not be worth paying for."

"I'd like some pancakes if it wouldn't be too much trouble," Shockley said.

The farmer and his wife stared at him. "Pancakes? For *supper*?"

"Yes'am. Buttermilk pancakes. If it's not too much trouble."

"I don't reckon it's too much trouble." She turned toward the stove, muttering. Pancakes for supper. Lord have mercy.

Shockley ate six stacks, as fast as the woman could get them out of the big iron skillet. He was so busy eating that he did not hear the car doors slam outside, did not hear the woman's husband answer another knock at the door. He was not even aware that the sheriff and his deputies were in the house until he saw them in the kitchen door.

"Hello, Sam," the sheriff said, without animosity. Guilty or innocent, he treated everybody decently unless they were wanted for a killing or a sex crime.

"Hello, Sheriff," Shockley replied.

"When'd you get back in the county?" the lawman asked.

"Just a while ago," said Sam. "Thumbed up from Texarkana. Been working at the mill down there."

The farmer and his wife exchanged glances, but said nothing. What was between the sheriff and their visitor was no business of theirs.

"Sam," the sheriff said, "I'm going to have to take you in to Idabel with me. There was a bank robbery up in Paoli this morning. The description of the robber fits you."

"All right by me, Sheriff," the fugitive bluffed. "Be right glad to get the ride."

"You got a pistol on you, Sam?"

Shockley nodded. "Little ol' .32, is all."

"Hand it over."

"Sure thing." Shockley gave him the gun. "Have to pay for my supper before we go," he said, reaching into his bib.

"No need," the farmer's wife said. "It weren't no bother."

"It sure was," Shockley said. "Anyway, we agreed I'd pay a dollar." He pulled out a hundred-dollar bill, folded it small, and pressed it into her hand. "There you go, one dollar, paid in full. I thank you."

He left with the sheriff and his men. An hour later, at the county jail, they found the rest of the bank money in his bib and pockets.

•

On May 16, 1938, Sam Richard Shockley was convicted in federal court of bank robbery and kidnapping. He was sentenced to life in prison.

Shockley spent the month of June in Leavenworth Prison. There he was the object of much discussion and debate. For the first time ever, medical men attempted to find out what went on inside his head. Shockley, who did not like such probing, resisted them. When they persisted, he became violent. He was acutely aware of his mental limitations; he did not need to have his face rubbed in it. The more the doctors pestered him with their tests and tricks and reaction probes, the more Shockley determined to have no part of it. He ignored them, pretended not to understand, cursed them, and, when pressed to the limit of his patience, erupted in a throwing, breaking, yelling fit. Thus the nickname Crazy Sam.

Because he could not be included in any of Leavenworth's inmate classifications, Shockley was deemed incapable of coping with the stress of everyday routine in a normal prison environment. The psychological prognosis was that he would become totally disoriented under stress, and that such disorientation would inevitably result in a violent act. Based on that finding, he was recommended for transfer to Alcatraz.

In September, 1938, Sam Shockley was sent to the Rock.

•

As Crazy Sam thought about pancakes and ate oatmeal on the morning of May 2, he looked out his cell front at the D Block windows. There were nine windows in the block. Each was six feet high, and each set six feet off the floor in the south wall of the cellhouse. As on most of the exterior windows in the big building, the lower bars curved inward basket-style to permit the windows to be opened during fair weather. All cells in D faced the windows across the fourteen-foot aisle that ran the length of the block. Cons on the top tier, like Stroud, could look down on an angle from their cell fronts through the upper window sections and see the entire southwestern shore of the island, the water of the bay, the Golden Gate Bridge, and the ocean horizon beyond. Shockley, and those others on the middle tier, could look out and see the same view, with the exception of the island shore. The view was poorest from the flats; cons on the lower level could only look up, and all they saw, if the day was clear, was the sky and an occasional gull.

There were only eight open-front cells on the flats; the other six were solitary-confinement cells, dark cells, which had solid steel doors. A six-by-fourteen-inch vision panel in each door could be let down by the block guard during the day to allow a half-light to filter into the cell. Inside the steel door, there was a 2½-foot access area into which the block guard could step. Across the back of the access area was a barred cell front. The access area was used to pass food trays to the isolated prisoner, and to push his thin mattress through the bars at night.

On May 2, 1946, there was only one inmate occupying a dark cell. He was Rufus "Whitey" Franklin, Alcatraz number 335, the convict that Officer Harold Stites had shot in a break attempt eight years earlier. A former prisoner on a Georgia chain gang, Franklin had been convicted in 1936 of bank robbery. His sentence was thirty years. After less than three years on the Rock, he had engineered the desperate escape attempt which had begun with the fatal hammer bludgeoning of Officer Royal Cline, and ended with Hal Stites shooting the convicts down as they charged his gun tower. For that escape attempt, Whitey Franklin had been totally isolated in his double-door, half-light solitary cell for seven years and twenty-one days.

The segregated D Block got the last, slanting rays of the setting sun on clear days. The sun going down beyond the Golden Gate was a quiet, sobering, reflective time for men like Stroud, Fleish, even Shockley, and sometimes, if his vision panel had been left open, Whitey Franklin. Even though the end of each Alcatraz day was gut-wrenchingly sad, the men of D Block still retained enough of their independence to scoff at their own sentimentality. Defiantly, they called the D Block aisle Sunset Boulevard.

As they ate breakfast on May 2, none of them knew yet that before the day was over, D Block was to experience a sunset unlike any it had ever known.

CHAPTER SIX

9:00 A.M.

After breakfast, the main cellhouse settled down to its normal morning routine. The grade prisoners were at their jobs, most of them down the hill in the Industries Building. The lockups were black in their cells. The big, honeycombed cellhouse was quiet—a giant steel-and-concrete anthill, with most of its occupants temporarily elsewhere.

In the cellhouse library, Bernie Coy, the landscape painter and amateur student of psychology, waited patiently while two library clerks stacked a wooden cart with books. Coy was the cellhouse orderly; his first job every morning was to deliver library books to the cells. Along his route, he also picked up magazines for redistribution to other cells later in the day.

As he waited for the book cart to be loaded, Coy looked over at the west wall of the library. He pursed his lips thoughtfully. The library was located across Seedy Street from C Block, at the end of the walled-in D Block. The west wall of the library was, on the other side, the east wall of D Block, at the end of Sunset Boulevard.

"Okay, Bernie, you're all set," said one of the library clerks. Coy wheeled the cart through the wire-grille door into Seedy Street. The block officer patrolling the aisle glanced at him. It was a casual glance. Coy and his book cart were part of the morning routine.

Coy's first stop each morning was D Block. As he pushed the cart down Seedy toward the steel-door entry to D, his usual inscrutable expression concealed a tightness in his chest that reminded him of the feelings he had once experienced when he walked into a bank with a sawed-off shotgun under his coat.

A slight, deceptively strong man, Coy had dark, desperate eyes that still reflected his pathetic childhood. As part of a dirt-poor Kentucky hill family, he had been a victim of hunger and deprivation throughout all his formative years. He was only in his teens when his teeth had rotted away with scurvy. For years he had had to wear false teeth which were constantly painful to his crippled gums. It was in desperation, to escape that sub-life of abject poverty, that Bernie Coy had turned to crime.

He had become a Depression-era bank robber.

•

On a cold day in March, 1937, Bernie Coy walked into the Bank of New Haven, Kentucky. He was wearing an overcoat and a gray, snap-brim fedora pulled low over his eyes. There were two customers ahead of him in the bank. He could either wait for them to leave or take the place with them in it. He decided not to wait. Moving to a position where everyone in the bank could see him, he slipped the sawed-off shotgun from under his coat.

"Everybody stand still!" he ordered. "This here's a holdup!"

There were several startled gasps, but everyone did as Coy said.

"That safe open back there?" Coy asked, bobbing his chin at the vault.

"No, sir," answered A. E. Kirkpatrick, the teller. "It's on a time lock. It won't open again until three."

Damn! Coy thought. Seemed like every bank he'd hit in the past year had a time-locked safe in it. Even in little out-of-the-way towns like New Haven. Pickings were sure getting lean.

"All right, empty the cash drawers," he said. "Stack the money on the counter there."

A professional glance at the currency Kirkpatrick pulled out told Coy he would be lucky if there was three thousand there. Not even bothering with a bag, he packed the sheafs neatly in his inside coat pockets.

"Ever'body lay on the floor now," he told them. "Stay there about five minutes, hear?"

Slipping the sawed-off back under his coat, Coy walked briskly out of the bank, got into his car, and drove off.

Before he got two miles out of town, there was a roadblock. It was at the Athertonville crossroads, three hundred yards past the Route 31 General Store and a state sign that read: ABRAHAM LINCOLN'S BOYHOOD HOME, 7 MILES.

Coy pulled off the road and parked next to the store. Slipping a belt across his shoulder under the overcoat, he fashioned a sling that would carry the shotgun out of sight under his coat. Then he went into the store.

"Morning," said the proprietor. "What'll it be?"

"Two packs of Camels," said Coy. At the counter he picked up a punchboard and poked out five ten-cent punches. As he unrolled them, the proprietor put his cigarettes and a free penny box of matches on the counter.

"Win anything?" he asked Coy.

"No," Coy said easily, "I never win anything. What's all the commotion down the road there?"

"There was a bank robbery in town a little bit ago," the man said. "The constable's wife was one of the customers. She knew her husband was out here to my place to get some snuff. I'm the only place around carries Red Cat, that's his brand. Anyways, soon as the feller left, why, the constable's wife saw he was headed this way and got on the telephone and called him. He got right out there and blocked the road."

"Don't look like he's caught him yet," Coy said.

"He will," the proprietor said confidently. "That feller's just plumb trapped now. They's another roadblock behind him at the edge of town. And there ain't no other roads he can turn off on. His tit's in a wringer for sure. Constable thinks it might be that Roger Touhy feller come over from Illinois."

Coy grunted. "More likely it's probably some pore dog looking for a way to get by in life. Listen, you got a tote sack?"

" 'Course. Why?"

"I'm on my way into New Haven to visit some kin. I'd like to take 'em some extra grub. You get the sack and I'll pick out some stuff."

In five minutes, Coy had a burlap sack filled with canned goods and other non-perishable foods. As he took out some money to pay for it all, the proprietor said, "I expect your kin's going to be happy to see you, considerin' the price of groceries these days. That comes to six twenty. Plus another fifty cents for the punchboard. Six seventy."

Coy put the sack in his car and headed back toward New Haven. Half a mile along, when the road was clear in both directions, he pulled over and parked. Slinging the burlap sack over his shoulder, he started off across the fields, as Sam Shockley had done, looking for a place to hide.

•

The cave Bernie Coy found was high on the banks overlooking the Rolling Fork River. As caves went, it was reasonably comfortable. He could not stand up in it, but he could sit, and there was plenty of room to stretch out full-length to sleep. He made a bed of dried moss and slit the burlap bag to spread over it. At night he used his overcoat for cover and kept a small fire going to keep warm. Some of the food he had—beans and stew and chili—he heated in their cans on the fire.

While he was holed up in the cave, Bernie Coy had a lot of time to think. He thought of the four years he had served in the Kentucky State Prison for holding up a hardware store. He thought of his childhood in the Kentucky hills. He was very familiar with the hills he was hiding in, and with the Rolling Fork and the little towns that dotted the western part of the state. Every couple of years, he came back home to drive around and see if anything had changed. Nothing ever did. He usually ended up robbing a couple of banks, then moving on.

Bernie Coy's folks were still around somewhere, sharecropping one place or another, but he never went to see them. The only memories he had of them were ugly and bitter. Another mouth to feed; that had been the sum total of his status in the Coy family. From his father, a brute of a man, he got mostly lashings with a heavy belt; from his mother, a wretch of a woman, little more.

Coy had few friends—few and mostly far between—but he was never lonely. Such had been his upbringing, so remote and distant from his selfish, cruel parents, that he did not have the capacity for loneliness. In that respect, he was fortunate. Had he been able to feel loneliness, he would probably have become a bitter, moody man. As it was, he was simply an American misfit. Like Lincoln, he had grown up dirt-poor in those Kentucky hills; and like Lincoln, he had left the hills for broader horizons. The difference between them, as boys, was that Lincoln knew love, Coy did not.

It was ironic that Coy had come back to the area of his former home to have as close an encounter with the law as the New Haven roadblock. Ironic and, he thought, lucky. If he had been trapped like that in strange surroundings, he might not have made it away as well as he did. But after three days in the cave, he felt relatively safe. The take from the bank had been smaller than he guessed: just a little over two thousand. He had lost his car, but he could always get another one. What he had to do now was get out of the area—and, he decided, stay out. He had made his last trip back to western Kentucky.

Coy knew if he followed the riverbank, it would take him out of the county and eventually east to Danville. From there he could hitchhike up to Frankfort, and from Frankfort he could take the bus into Ohio.

He brushed his clothes off as best he could, divided the money evenly into all his pockets, slung the sawed-off shotgun under his coat again, and made his way down to the riverbank. On the bank, he started hiking east. He had gone less than a mile when two deputized farmers came out of the willows and threw down on him with bird guns.

"Just hold it right there, slicker," one of the farmers said. They patted him down and found the money and gun. "All right now, get to moving," he was told. "We're taking you back to New Haven. By God, we'll learn you city dudes to come down here robbing our banks!"

Coy could not help smiling. He did not tell the farmers he had been born only a few miles away. Because he was no longer one of them, he knew it would have done him no good.

•

At the D Block door, Coy tapped and waited. After careful scrutiny through the bulletproof glass, he was let in by Officer Cecil Corwin.

"Morning, Coy," said Corwin.

"Good morning, Mr. Corwin," Coy replied.

"Looks like it's going to be a nice day."

A flicker of a smile crossed Coy's lips. "It sure does, Mr. Corwin," he said quietly. "It sure does."

Coy parked his book cart next to the steel stairway leading up to the middle and top tiers. He picked up several books and walked up to the top tier. As he walked, he habitually counted the stairs.

Thirteen from the flats to the middle tier. Thirteen more from the middle tier to the top tier. When he got to the top, Coy suddenly wished he had not counted the steps today. Thirteen was unlucky, and he still had enough of the Kentucky hills in him to be superstitious. He would, he decided, have to count something else to banish the number thirteen from his mind.

As usual, he began his distribution of books at the last occupied cell on the top tier, D-41. That was the cell of Birdman Stroud.

"Morning, Bob," said Coy.

The old man got up from his bunk. "Morning, Bernie."

Coy handed him a book through the bars. "Here you are, Bob. *The Little Foxes* by Lillian Hellman."

Stroud grunted and pushed the green eyeshade to the top of his head. "Goddamn if things aren't looking up around this outhouse. It hasn't even been a year since I ordered that one. Seems like only yesterday."

"Well, time flies when you're having fun," said Coy. As Stroud examined the book, Coy counted the bars of his cell front. There were eleven bars in the wall and five in the door. Sixteen. Good. Coy felt better. He tilted his head curiously. "How old are you now, Bob?"

"Old enough," Stroud replied evasively.

"You know, Bob," the frail cellhouse orderly said thoughtfully, "if I serve all my time, I'll be older than you when I get out. I'll be past sixty."

Stroud stepped close to the bars. His eyes narrowed knowingly. "*If* you serve all your time. That's what you said, wasn't it, Bernie?"

Coy stared flatly at the stir-wise old con. "Yeah, Bob. That's what I said."

The eyes of the men remained locked for several seconds. Then Coy moved on along the range, continuing his delivery of library books and magazines. When he finished the top tier, he returned to the flats where his cart was parked. Louis Fleish was just sweeping over his way with a prison-made pushbroom. "How goes it, Barney?" he asked.

"Breaking even, Louie," the Kentuckian answered. "Just breaking even."

Block Officer Cecil Corwin, drinking coffee at his desk, glanced over at the men. Fleish was an Isolation prisoner; he was not supposed to be communicating with any inmate from general population. Corwin knew he had to break up the conversation. As usual, he did it in an inoffensive way. Studying Coy for a moment, he finally said, "Bernie, you look like you're losing weight. Have you been feeling all right lately?"

When Corwin spoke, Louis Fleish knew it was an indication for him to get on with his sweeping. He winked at Coy and moved away as the bank robber turned to answer Corwin.

"My food hasn't been settling, Mr. Corwin," Coy said. "I don't know what's the matter with me."

"Have you seen the doc?"

Coy shook his head. "If I'm not feeling better by tomorrow, I'll go see him."

"You ought to," Corwin advised.

Coy took the books for the middle tier and started upstairs again. His prison shoes sounded heavily on the steel steps. Jesus, he wondered, how many times had he walked up and down steel prison stairs in his lifetime? At the Kentucky State Prison, during his first stretch. Then at the Atlanta Federal Pen, where they first sent him on the bank-robbery conviction. Now here on the Rock. Christ, he was tired of it all. The steel and concrete, the enveloping cold, the fog that came in every night like an asylum blanket: dirty and gray. Fog that made it seem as if the island was wrapped in swirls of cotton that had been smudged by industrial smoke. And with the fog came the foghorns—the incessant goddamned foghorns, sounding in the night like some mournful death call, some eerie signal of a dark world waiting for them all. The foghorns, more than anything else, haunted Bernie Coy.

Working his way back from Cell D-28 at the end of the middle tier, Coy stopped at Cell D-22 and handed a book through the bars to Crazy Sam Shockley. Crazy Sam accepted the book without looking at it. He had never read a book in his life, nor had anyone ever encouraged him to. His eyes, eager and hopeful, searched Coy's face. After a moment, Coy nodded a barely perceptible nod.

"Today," Coy whispered. "Listen for the signal."

Shockley's eyes widened in excitement. As Coy moved on along the tier, Crazy Sam gripped the bars and pressed his face against them. His expression was wild. Saliva collected in the corners of his mouth.

Today!

CHAPTER SEVEN

9:30 A.M.

The morning routine continued.

In his lockup cell on the bottom level of B Block, Dutch Cretzer sat on his bunk with a lined white pad on his knees. His black, usually penetrating eyes were softer, less threatening, as he studied the words he had just written, and pondered those he was yet to write. Thoughtfully, he traced the eraser end of a yellow pencil across his upper lips.

The words on the paper were a poem. The former Public Enemy Number Four had secretly been writing poetry for years. No one knew about it; not even his ex-wife, whom he had nicknamed Eddie and who, now remarried, lived just across the water in San Francisco. Cretzer was extremely self-conscious about his poetry. Other cons knew he *read* poetry, but he would have been mortified if anyone had known he *wrote* it. In his own mind, however, he believed that his work was pretty good.

The rhyme he was working on at that moment was titled "Gray Life." He had just started it. The first stanza read:

> I awaken to gray,
> And gray is my morning sun;
> I live gray, and
> All my days are like one.
> There is no color:
> Only shadows along my way;
> Sometimes I think the blood in my body
> Must also be prison gray.

While he was trying to work out the next lines in his head, Cretzer suddenly became aware that his feet were cold again. "Son of a bitch," he muttered, and put aside the pad and pencil to get his pea coat off the wall stud. His feet had been cold for several weeks, ever since he had been moved from D over to B. In D he had celled on the middle tier. Over here in B, he was down on the lower tier, on what was known as the flats. There was an almost constant draft across the floor of the flats. It was subtle, sometimes unnoticeable, but it was always there, always cold, always making life a little more uncomfortable.

"Goddamn this hole," Cretzer said to himself. He sat down on the bunk again and propped his feet up so he could wrap his pea coat around them. He ignored his lined pad, no longer in the mood for poetry. His black eyes had become dangerous again, his expression grim. "Goddamn this hole to hell," he said tightly. He felt another of his excruciating headaches starting.

Cretzer hated Alcatraz with a passion. He hated all jails, all prisons, but for the Rock he felt a special kind of hatred. It was by far the worst place he had ever experienced. As a prison, it was a classic example of personal deprivation. Cretzer enjoyed the little niceties of life. But here on Alcatraz there were no such things. There was no inmate commissary, which meant no candy, no gum, no soft drinks. No civilian soap could be bought; cons had to use the stone-hard vomit-colored prison soap. There were no newspapers, no radios. No playing cards were allowed. No tailor-made cigarettes; no alternative but to roll your own with the rank, raw tobacco and paper from the dispensers at the end of the block.

Cretzer could understand not having such minor luxuries in D Block; after all, Isolation *was* Isolation. Fair was fair. But to deprive the general population of those things was nothing but calculated, sadistic torture.

Well, he wouldn't have to put up with it much longer, Cretzer told himself. Since he had been back in the open cellhouse, he had been sending out secret messages in coded letters to a lawyer in Oakland. The messages in those letters had been passed on to people he could trust and depend on; answers, also coded, had come back to Cretzer in letters from the lawyer. Everything Cretzer had requested had been done.

By this time tomorrow, he thought, he wouldn't have to do without *anything*.

•

A few yards up the flats, Dan Durando was also in lockup for the morning. As was his custom, he had rested for thirty minutes after breakfast to allow his meal to settle; then he had stripped off his shirt and begun the first of three sets of calisthenics he practiced every day except Sunday. They were simple exercises, based on the Charles Atlas principle of dynamic tension: pitting one muscle against another. Most of the time Durando did it the easy way: he used the bars of his cell. Instead of pushing one wrist against the counterforce of the other, the young Chicano would grip the steel uprights in his cell door and try with all his might to pull them out of their foundation. Or he would grasp them with fists turned outward and try to spread them. Or take hold of a low cross-bar and try to lift it. There was no chance, of course, that he would ever be able to accomplish any of those feats, but over the months he had found that it was great for his body. After his capture in Boise City, while awaiting trial, he had let himself go lazy and soft. Even in Leavenworth, where he had been involved in several actual fistfights, he had still not taken the trouble to stay in shape. But now, here on the Rock, with nothing else to do, the Indio Kid exercised. Three times a day: calisthenics on the bars, pushups on the floor, situps on his bunk, and fifteen minutes of shadow-boxing. After nearly a year on Alcatraz, Dan Durando was trim and fast at 168 pounds.

Danny could not help thinking about all the fights he had been in during his short life. He could not remember how many times some guy had started a fight with him, or he had started a fight with some guy. It seemed like he was always duking it out with somebody for one reason or another. It was odd, the Kid often reflected, how his fists had got him both into and out of so much trouble.

And now, he thought, holding his fists up and looking at them, because of those same fists and what he could do with them, he was being given another chance at life.

Or death.

•

In the kitchen behind the inmate dining hall, Marv Hubbard was working on the tray-washing machine. There was a smile on his face and he was cheerful. The closer it got to noon, the better Hubbard felt.

The timer sounded on the tray-washing machine and Hubbard slid back its aluminum door. With a towel in each hand, he began taking the steam-hot trays out of the washer and stacking them on a tray pass that went through the wall into the dining hall. The clouds of steam gushing out of the machine reminded him of his wife Tola doing the laundry back home on the little place they had in Alabama. She had done their wash in a big cast-iron pot over an open fire pit in the back yard. With a wooden mop handle she had stirred and agitated the clothes in the boiling water, and billows of steam had rolled up at her. Whenever she did the wash like that, Tola had always broken out in sweat across her forehead, her upper lip, and the hollow of her neck just above her bosom. To Marv Hubbard, his wife never looked better than when she was wearing a plain old gray work dress, and sweating in those places where she sweated.

Despite the heat of his work, Hubbard felt his mouth go dry at the thought of Tola. He swallowed and blinked several times. If only he'd been able to make a living during those lean years. He didn't mind working; he was a trained bricklayer, and a good one. But there simply had not been any work. And without work, their lives had been so barren: his, Tola's, and the little girl's. To a proud man like Marvin Hubbard, it was not acceptable to see his family do without. Even if he had to steal to provide for them. But, lord, lord, they would have had a good life if things had been just a little bit different—

Despite his efforts to control them, several maverick tears escaped and streaked down Hubbard's cheek. He stepped back and dabbed at his eyes with a towel.

"You all right, Hubbard?" asked Chief Steward Robert Bristow, the officer in charge of the kitchen.

"Yessir, Mr. Bristow," Hubbard replied. "Just got some steam in my eyes."

Stoically, he went back to work.

•

In the tailor shop, Buddy Thompson, the Texas outlaw who had been on the Rock less than five months, pretended to be sick. At the worktable where he was cutting thick gray canvas, he suddenly put down his work and lowered his face into his hands. Shop foreman Haynes Herbert came over to him.

"What's the matter, Buddy?"

"I don't know, Mr. Herbert. I feel kind of sick."

Herbert looked closely at Thompson for some sign of malingering. But Buddy Thompson, with his handsome, innocent features, fooled him.

"It's a little close in here today," he said at last. "Get yourself a drink of cold water and rest for a spell."

"Yessir. Thanks, Mr. Herbert."

Thompson got up and went across the shop to a shrinkage sink. Turning on the tap, he cupped his hands and took several swallows of water. Then he patted the excess water on his face. He dried his hands on his shirtsleeves. When he came back to the worktable, Herbert pointed to a stack of nine-by-twelve canvas tarps in the storage area.

"Go on over and lie down on those tarps, Buddy," the foreman told him. "If you're not feeling better by noon, go on out for sick call."

"I'll probably be better in a little bit," Thompson said. "Thanks, Mr. Herbert."

He went over to the tarps, stretched out on them, and closed his eyes. So far, so good, he thought.

CHAPTER EIGHT

11:00 A.M.

Throughout the morning, Bernie Coy went quietly and routinely about his job. Numerous times as he pushed his book cart up and down the aisles between cellblocks, he passed the roving block guards who patrolled under the close protection of Bert Burch in the overhanging gun gallery. The guards paid little attention to him; he and his movements were as familiar to them as the rest of the routine of the big cellhouse. Coy had been serving as cellhouse orderly for three of his nine years on the Rock. The block guards were fairly relaxed around him. He was, after all, now well into his forties and had been on good behavior for nearly a decade of imprisonment. Plus they knew that unlike many Alcatraz cons, Coy was not a killer. He had never assaulted a police officer and had no history of violence on his record. Only a few of the sharper guards were leery of him —a few who realized that he was one of the most naturally clever men ever imprisoned on the Rock; a few who knew he used his cell time to study psychology and paint landscapes of the free world he remembered. Perhaps it was this combination of cleverness and creativity that made those few guards apprehensive of him. Perhaps subconsciously they realized that those two traits in Coy were far more dangerous to them than the natural violence of other cons.

The guard who was most friendly with Bernie Coy was Officer William Miller, who patrolled Broadway. The two men were close in age and suffered some common ailments. If no other guards or cons were around, it was Coy's habit to stop and pass the time of day with Bill Miller. He stopped to talk with him at eleven o'clock that morning of May 2.

"Hello, Bernie," said Miller as Coy wheeled the book cart onto Times Square.

"Morning, Mr. Miller." Seeing that Officer Lageson was away from his desk, Coy parked the cart and stopped. "How are your bunions?" he asked.

"Better, thanks," said Miller. "I got some of that moleskin you told me about. It worked just fine."

"That's good." Coy reached up with his thumb and index finger to apply pressure to the inside hinge of his mouth where his gums were constantly sore. Miller noticed him doing it.

"I thought maybe the warmer weather would keep your gums from hurting so much," the guard said sympathetically. "Isn't there anything the doc can do for you?"

Coy shook his head. "He had a dentist come over and look at me. The guy said there was too much damage to the gums; no way to repair it. The only thing he suggested was for me to carry around a bottle of paregoric and rub it on my gums whenever they started hurting. But the doc can't let me do that because paregoric is a narcotic."

"Bernie," Bill Miller said thoughtfully, "I've been thinking I might speak to the warden about your condition. He's a reasonable man, an understanding man. If I explained to him that you were in a lot of pain—"

"I don't think so, Mr. Miller," Coy said, shaking his head. "It wouldn't look good to the other cons. Besides which, it'd probably just get you in dutch with the warden."

"Well, it's not right for you to have to go around in pain all the time. If this was Lewisburg or Atlanta, they'd do something to take care of you."

"Yeah, but it ain't Lewisburg or Atlanta. It's the Rock, Mr. Miller, and you know it as well as I do." Coy grinned a tentative, half-grin. "Jesus, I never thought I'd see the day when a screw would care whether I was in pain or not."

Miller grunted lightly. "Well, I never thought I'd see the day when a con would help me get relief from my bunions."

Just then, the prisoner and his keeper heard brisk footsteps and turned to see Cellhouse Officer Ernest Lageson coming out of the dining hall with a cup of coffee.

"I'll be going," said Coy. He started pushing his book cart toward Broadway.

"Hey, Coy!" Lageson called.

Coy stopped at once. He turned around. "Yessir?"

Lageson crossed Times Square toward him. "Where are you going?"

"Up Broadway, Mr. Lageson."

"Don't you generally do Michigan Boulevard first?" the senior officer asked curiously.

Coy felt ill. He had altered his route today to give the Indio Kid more time to consider the offer Coy had made him. Now Lageson had spotted that deviation from the normal routine and was suspicious. Lageson was a shrewd guard, not easily fooled. If he became the least bit apprehensive about Coy's movements, he would probably have him put in immediate lockup and order a shakedown of all cells receiving books that day.

"Well?" Lageson said, walking closer. "Do you or don't you generally deliver to Michigan Boulevard first?"

"Yessir, I do," Coy admitted. "But the library clerks stacked the books on backwards today. It'll be easier to deliver Broadway first."

Lageson, sipping his coffee, stared thoughtfully at Coy over the rim of the cup. Overhead, Bert Burch moved along the gallery to a point above Lageson. The cellhouse officer said nothing for a moment, but several times flicked his glance at the book cart.

"I can restack the books and deliver to Michigan first, like always, if you want me to," Coy offered.

Lageson finally shook his head. "Forget it," he said. "Go on and do Broadway first."

"Yessir." Coy resumed pushing the cart, being certain not to go too fast.

•

Halfway down the west block of B, in Cell 233, was the last of America's big-time bank robbers: Alvin Karpavicz, better known as Alvin Karpis, age thirty-eight, Alcatraz number 325. Like Machine Gun Kelly a former Public Enemy Number One, he was, ironically, serving a life sentence for kidnapping. Karpis was a short, pleasant-looking man who somehow managed to appear dapper even in Alcatraz denims. He worked in the Alcatraz bakery, under the kitchen.

Because he went to work very early in the morning, he was allowed to come back to his cell to rest after breakfast and to go to the yard for recreation after lunch. On this particular morning he was lying on his bunk thumbing through *Christian Science,* one of the approved periodicals at Alcatraz.

Called by many the most brilliant, daring, and fearless of the Depression-era outlaws—not excluding even the more glamorous John Dillinger—Alvin Karpis had compressed a lifetime of crime into a single ten-year span. At the age of sixteen, Karpis had been a young hobo, riding the rods of the nation's railroads. In Florida he had been caught in one of the south's notorious hobo traps and sentenced to a short term on a chain gang. At eighteen, back in Kansas where he had grown up, Karpis committed his first serious offense: he burglarized a wholesale notions warehouse. Arrested for the crime, he was sent to the Kansas State Reformatory at Hutchinson.

Karpis served three years at Hutchinson, then escaped. He stayed out two years, making his way by holding up small stores and restaurants. In 1930, he was captured in Kansas City, luckily not for a current crime but merely as a wanted escapee. Now twenty-two years old, he was sent to the Kansas State Prison at Lansing to complete his unfinished sentence. While at Lansing, he met Fred Barker, the youngest of three Barker brothers who had been tutored in crime by their mother Donnie, better known as Ma Barker.

After two years in Lansing, Karpis and Barker were discharged just six weeks apart. Barker took Alvin Karpis home to meet Ma. The old lady took to Karpis at once; he was a lot like her own boys: Herman, Doc, and her baby, Fred. From that day on, Alvin Karpis was not only a full-fledged member of the Barker gang, but soon became its acknowledged planner and leader. For unlike Ma's own boys, Alvin Karpis had brains.

For the next two years, the gang successfully committed a wave of major bank robberies in Missouri, Minnesota, Wisconsin, South Dakota, North Dakota, Kansas, and Oklahoma. Then, in 1933, at the urging of Ma, they tried something new, something all the big-timers sooner or later seemed to turn to: kidnapping.

On June 15, 1933, the gang successfully kidnapped William A. Hamm, Jr., the St. Paul brewery owner. Two days later, they collected $100,000 ransom; the following day, they released Hamm unharmed.

The gang split up after the Hamm job. Eventually all of them except Karpis were either captured or killed by the FBI. Karpis, on his own for the first time, was named Public Enemy Number One by J. Edgar Hoover. It was then January, 1935. For the next eighteen months, it was to be cat-and-mouse between the most wanted outlaw and the nation's top crimebuster.

Changing his methods of operation to confuse Hoover, Karpis abandoned bank robbery. Entering new fields, he and several newly recruited gang members stuck up a transfer truck in Warren, Ohio, carrying a $70,000 cash payroll for the Youngstown Metal Company. Then, going even farther afield, they held up the Erie Railroad mail train in the little station of Garrettsville, Ohio, and made off with a money sack containing $40,000. All the while, Hoover's agents were relentlessly stalking, tracking, closing the gap. From his hideout in Hot Springs, Arkansas, the wily bandit leader was traced to Corpus Christi, Texas. Then to Dallas. Oklahoma City. Memphis. Miami. And finally to New Orleans.

Early in the morning on April 30, 1936, J. Edgar Hoover received a call from his agent in charge in New Orleans. Alvin Karpis was living in an apartment house on Canal Street in that city. He had been positively identified.

Hoover issued two orders. Local authorities were not to be notified. And Karpis was to be kept under surveillance, but not arrested.

Alvin Karpis was one arrest the top G-Man intended to make himself.

•

Karpis slept late that morning of the last day in April, 1936. It was nearly noon when he finally got up and went into the living room of the apartment to see if Fred Hunter was up yet. Hunter, an Oklahoma outlaw with whom Karpis had pulled his last two robberies, was lying on the couch reading the paper.

"You been out?" asked Karpis.

"Down to the corner for this here newspaper," Hunter replied.

"How's it look outside?"

"Quiet," said Hunter.

Karpis nodded. He could sense that his time was running out. He knew that Hoover was getting closer and closer to him. For several months now, he had been nervous where once he had been nerve*less;* cautious where he had once been daring; fearful where once he had been afraid of nothing. He knew he was the last of the big-time outlaws and that every lawman in the nation wanted to be the one to get him.

"You eat yet?" he asked Hunter.

Hunter shook his head. "Figured I'd wait for you."

"Okay. I'm going to take a bath, then we'll go eat. I want to look around anyway. I'm not so sure this place is safe."

Hunter, chewing on a stick match, watched thoughtfully as Karpis went back into the bedroom. He knew Karpis was nervous, and he could understand why. But the former gang leader was beginning to make him nervous. Lately they had been moving every week; sometimes just to another neighborhood, often to another city. It was wearing Hunter out. Working with a top man like Alvin Karpis had been great in the beginning. Now Hunter was starting to wonder if it was worth it.

In half an hour, Karpis was ready to go. Freshly bathed, wearing a clean linen shirt and straw hat, he looked cool and as sure of himself as when Hunter first met him. But that was outside. Hunter knew that inside, Karpis was a coiled spring.

"Where's the car?" Karpis asked.

"Where we left it yesterday. I didn't use it this morning."

Karpis loaded a .45 and stuck it in his waistband under his shirt. He looked around the room. "Where's the sawed-off?"

"In the car under the seat."

"Okay," Karpis said, "let's go. I'm hungry."

The two outlaws left the building and walked down Canal Street toward their car. Across the street, coming their way, was a stocky man wearing a dark summer suit and white Panama hat. Karpis, a dandy himself, briefly admired the way the man was dressed; he even had two points of a white handkerchief peeking from his breast pocket.

At the car, Hunter started to go around to the driver's side but Karpis stopped him. "I'll drive," Karpis said. "Where'd you tell me the sawed-off was?"

"Under the driver's seat," Hunter replied, frowning. It was unusual for Karpis to want to drive. Usually, he liked to *be* driven, so that he could keep both hands free for gunplay. Although in all his many armed robberies he had never killed anyone, Karpis was a crack shot; the accuracy of his fire had driven many a peace officer to cover while Karpis and his boys escaped.

As Karpis got behind the wheel, he noticed that the well-dressed, stocky man was crossing the street toward them. Karpis frowned; the man looked vaguely familiar. He glanced at Hunter, starting to say something; then on Hunter's side of the car he saw men emerging from nearby buildings. Looking back at the approaching man in the street, Karpis suddenly realized who he was. The .45 was in his waistband and a sawed-off shotgun under the seat at his feet, but Alvin Karpis wisely kept his hands on the steering wheel. Hunter, now aware of the trap, waited for Karpis to make the first move. But Karpis sat still. The last of the big-timers was simply too tired to fight another fight.

"Alvin Karpis," said the well-dressed man, approaching the rolled-down window on the driver's side, "I'm with the FBI. You're under arrest. Step out of the car with your hands up."

Karpis silently obeyed as federal agents took Fred Hunter out of the car on the other side.

"Are you armed?" Karpis was asked.

"I have an automatic under my shirt. There's also a shotgun under the seat, Mr. Hoover."

The well-dressed man smiled slightly. "How did you know who I was?"

"I saw a picture of you in a magazine after you caught a big sailfish. Your luck is better than mine. I've been trying to catch one for years."

"It's not luck, Karpis," said the G-Man as he took the gun from under the outlaw's shirt. "It's perseverance. The trick is never to give up, never quit trying. If you keep at it long enough, you can catch anything. Sooner or later, anything or anybody will get tired of running."

"You're right about that, Mr. Hoover," Karpis said thoughtfully. "You're sure right about that."

As Alvin Karpis was led away that day, he felt as if a heavy harness had been removed from his shoulders.

•

Karpis was flown to St. Paul, Minnesota, to stand trial for the Hamm kidnapping. Weary and dejected, he entered a plea of guilty in order to avoid a death-penalty trial. Since Hamm had been released unharmed, the court predictably showed mercy for the defendant by sentencing him to a life term.

On August 7, 1936, at the age of twenty-eight, the young Public

Enemy Number One was taken to Alcatraz to begin his sentence. His old partner, Doc Barker, was already on the Rock, having arrived there a year earlier. Doc was a wild one who could not take the mind-dulling routine of prison. Before long, he and four other prisoners had a plan to crash out.

"There's room for one more," he told Karpis in the exercise yard one cold January day.

"I'll pass, Doc," said Karpis.

"Why's that?"

"I just don't want to go back out there, Doc. I don't want to get back in that life again."

"You're a fool," the last of the Barkers told him. "They'll keep you in here until you die."

"I don't think so, Doc," said Karpis. "They'll let me out someday. See, I'm not a killer like you, Doc. They know that. Times change. I'll get out."

Doc Barker grunted derisively. "Good luck, sucker."

Karpis took no offense. "Good luck to you too, Doc."

Within twenty-four hours, Doc Barker was dead, fatally wounded in the Alcatraz surf. The other four men on the break with him were captured. That was the end of the Barker gang. Ma and her youngest, Fred, had been killed by the FBI; Herman had committed suicide while trapped in a bank robbery; and now Doc was dead on the Rock. It was all over; an era had ended.

•

On the morning of May 2, 1946, Alvin Karpis, then thirty-eight years old, was in his tenth year on the Rock. As he heard Bernie Coy coming down the flats, he rose and stood up next to the bars.

"How's it going today, Barney?"

"A hell of a lot like it went yesterday, Ray," the Kentuckian replied. Like a lot of inmates, Karpis had a prison name which was not his own. To other convicts he was known as Ray. Coy handed a Zane Grey novel through the bars and Karpis passed out *Christian Science*.

"Great magazine," he said lightly. "See that I get it every month, will you?"

"You'll have to arrange that with somebody else," Coy said quietly.

Karpis looked steadily at Coy for a long, silent moment. Then he frowned and stepped closer to the bars. He pursed his lips in thought for a moment. "You know, Barney, I had two chances to get in on breaks out of this place. Back in '39 with Doc Barker and again in '43 with Freddie Hunter. I didn't go because I didn't think it could be done." Karpis paused a beat. "I still don't."

Coy shrugged. "You might be right, Ray." Then *he* paused a beat. "You might also be wrong."

"I hope you don't do anything dumb, Barney."

Now Coy smiled. "Christ, Ray, I hope so too!" he said fervently.

Because he knew that both Lageson and Burch could see him, Coy did not linger any longer at Cell 233. He winked at Alvin Karpis and pushed his cart on along Broadway.

When he was finished with the west end of the block, Coy pushed the cart down to the east stairs and delivered to the thirty-nine cells in that section. Then he crossed Broadway to the east stairs of B Block and reversed the routine. He worked all the way back down to Times Square. Pushing the now two-thirds-empty book cart around to the Michigan Boulevard side of B, he parked it and began the last of his deliveries. The only cellblock he had not been in that morning was A Block, and that was because A was empty. Alcatraz prisoners would be regularly housed in A Block only if the country produced enough hardened criminals to fill up B, C, and D Blocks. In the fourteen-year history of the prison, that had never happened. The only time A Block had been used so far was to lock up strikers who staged sit-downs and caused other work problems.

As he moved along the flats of Michigan Boulevard, Coy was aware of his gums hurting again. He thought of what Miller had offered to do for him. He could still scarcely believe it. A *screw* offering to help *him*. That was something. Really something.

When Coy got to Cell 152, Dutch Cretzer unwrapped the pea coat from his feet and stepped close to the bars.

"Steak and lobster tonight, Bernie," he said quietly.

Coy nodded briefly. "You're sure everything is all set in Frisco?"

"Ready and waiting, pal. The hideout's all arranged and the car will be parked on shore with the keys in it. All we have to do is get to it."

"We'll get to it," Coy said confidently. "The prison launch will be at the dock down the hill from two until two-thirty. We'll have between thirty and forty minutes to get from here to there. It'll go like clockwork." Coy handed Cretzer a book through the bars. "Here. The poems of Walt Whitman. Better read them fast."

Coy moved on, placing books on a couple of empty cell doors. When he got to Cell 142, he stopped again.

"Hello, Kid," he said to Dan Durando.

"Hello, Bernie," the Chicano youth answered.

"It's going on noon," Coy said. "Have you made up your mind yet?"

"Yeah, I thought about it, Bernie," said Durando. "No hard feelings, I hope, but I think I'll pass. I been here nearly a year now, you know. Pretty soon they'll move me into grade and I'll probably get put down in Industries. This place won't be so bad once I have something to do." He shrugged. "And I'm still pretty young, Bernie. I'll get out someday."

Coy shook his head. "You're kidding yourself, Dan. You'll end up just like the Birdman."

"Maybe, but I don't think so, Bernie. Anyway, I want you to know I appreciate you considering me."

"I asked you in because I need you, Kid," Coy said flatly. "You're strong and you're tough. You're probably the best fistfighter in the whole joint. I need you to look after the guards for me. We're only going to have one rifle and one pistol. I can't spare either one of them to keep the guards in line. But you, Kid, you could keep them in line with your fists."

Durando grunted softly. "Every time I use my fists, I get in trouble. Every time I do *anything,* I seem to get in trouble. I killed a guy, you know. It was an accident, but the guy is dead all the same. I don't want to get mixed up in no more killings."

"If that's what's worrying you, you can forget it," Coy said firmly. "There won't be any killings on this crashout. We're going out of here clean, Kid, with guards as hostages. Hell, with a little luck there won't be a shot fired."

The Kid's face took on an expression of indecision that made him look almost as if he were in physical pain. "Jesus, I don't know, Bernie," he said in frustration. "I just don't know."

"Think about it for a little while longer, Kid," the older con said. "You don't want to end up like Stroud. I'll check back with you later."

Coy walked away, leaving a frowning, much disturbed Dan Durando in Cell 142.

Coy moved the cart all the way down Michigan Boulevard to the east end and delivered the rest of the block. Then he turned the cart around and pushed it back to the west end of B. Before he pushed it out onto Times Square again, he paused for a moment and knelt to untie and retie one of his shoelaces. Glancing around the corner at the cellhouse officer's desk, he saw Ernest Lageson doing some paperwork. Behind him, at the sallyport end of Michigan, a block guard was casually patrolling. Covertly, Coy raised his eyes to the gun gallery. Bert Burch was on the lower tier, walking slowly toward the D Block wall. Coy's eyes went higher, to the upper tier of the gallery. They followed the steel bars all the way to the ceiling. Just before those bars reached the ceiling, they curved inward toward the wall, forming a barred roof over the top tier of the gun gallery. But they curved back only as *far* as the concrete wall, and there they were fastened to a steel brace mounted *on* the wall. So the ends of the bars were not actually *imbedded* in the wall itself.

In eight years of searching, those bars not being sunk into that concrete wall comprised the only structural weakness Bernard Paul Coy had been able to find in the Alcatraz fortress.

But it was enough.

•

Bernie Coy had known about the structural deficiency of the gun gallery bars for slightly more than a year. He had discovered it one day while sweeping down Times Square after the noon meal. The instrument used to sweep the highly-polished flats was a blanket broom: a mop handle with a cross-bar at the bottom, around which a heavy wool blanket was wrapped. The blanket had come loose one day, and Coy had sat down on the floor, his back against the end wall of B Block, to fix it.

"What are you doing down there, Coy, tearing up government property?" Bert Burch had kidded him from the upper tier of the gun gallery. "Don't you know they can put you in jail for that?"

"Got to catch me first, Mr. Burch," Coy had replied.

Burch had laughed and walked on down the gallery. And Coy, when he glanced back up where Burch had been, had looked straight at the top of the bars. For a moment he could not believe his eyes. Was it possible? he asked himself. Could it be that in this great hulk of a prison cellhouse the toolproof steel bars had been sunk in concrete retainers every place but in the *gun gallery*? Surely to Christ his eyes were playing tricks on him!

But the more he looked, the more he was convinced: the bars at the extreme top of the west gun gallery were not secured in concrete!

The incredibility of it staggered Bernie Coy's mind.

He stayed awake all night that night just thinking about it. The west gun gallery, along with the armory, was one of the two areas in the big cellhouse considered to be totally and absolutely invulnerable. The armory because of its complex double-door deadlock zone; and the west gun gallery because there was no way into it except from *outside* the cellhouse. Because they were considered invulnerable, both contained firearms: the armory a large stock of security and riot-control weapons; the gallery the two weapons carried by the gallery officer: a .45 Colt automatic pistol and a Springfield 30-caliber rifle, plus some riot sticks and gas billies.

Coy thought back to the escape attempts that had been pulled since he had been in the main cellhouse. There had been five of them. Altogether, since he had been on the Rock, there had been eight attempted crashouts, but three of them had taken place while he was in lockup, where he had spent the first two years of his sentence. He knew nothing about those three except that they had happened, and they had failed. But the other five he recalled vividly. They read like a study in frustration.

May, 1941. Dutch Cretzer and Crazy Sam Shockley took over the mat shop and attempted to grind through the bars with emery wheels. The wheels had failed to cut the bars. Result: they had been forced to surrender.

September, 1941. Bank robber Johnny Bayless took advantage of an unexpected opportunity, slipped away from a detail of men working on the landing dock, and went into the water. He had a nine-minute head start before the dock guard missed him. Nine minutes was not enough. The current was against him. He barely got away from the dock area. And the water temperature was only forty-two degrees. Result: Bayless was captured and hospitalized with pneumonia.

For a year and a half after that, there were no escape attempts. Then: April, 1943. Kidnapper Harry Brest, bank robber Jimmy Boarman, mail robber Fred Hunter, and former Bonnie-and-Clyde gang member Floyd Hamilton slugged two guards while working outside the Industries Building on the west end of the island. Working their way through the accordion barbed wire that ringed the island, they dove into the water. Tower guards opened fire and the prison launch was dispatched to cut them off. Result: Brest and Hunter captured by the launch; Boarman killed by tower fire; and

Hamilton, after nearly freezing in a cave, finally came out and surrendered.

Four months later: August, 1943. Bank robber Huron Walters slipped away from an outside work detail and scrambled down a bluff where he had been dropping empty paint cans for several weeks. Lashing the cans to his body in an attempt to turn himself into a human raft, he was surrounded by armed guards before he could get into the water. Result: Walters wisely surrendered.

Following Walters, there was a dearth of escape attempts. Then, in July, 1945, mail robber John Giles came within minutes of accomplishing the perfect Alcatraz escape. Giles, working as a dock helper, was one of the inmates who loaded and unloaded laundry when the Army launch *General Coxe* came over from Fort McDowell. For several weeks he had been methodically stealing clothing from the laundered bundles going back: a pair of socks first, then an undershirt, shorts, trousers, a shirt, a tie. He hid the clothing in a neat bundle in the dock utility shed. Finally he had a complete Army uniform, Eisenhower jacket and all. On the last day of July, while the laundry was being loaded, Giles ducked into the shed, stripped off his coveralls, and put on the uniform. With his coveralls back on over the uniform, he returned to the dock, waited for his chance, and dropped under the pier. Stripping off the coveralls again, he put on his Army necktie and cap, and hopped onto the lower deck of the Army launch. Seconds later, the *General Coxe* left Alcatraz. While Giles sweated out the maddeningly slow trip across the bay, the dock detail officer made an unscheduled head count and found him missing. The Alcatraz launch was quickly dispatched to Fort McDowell. At full speed, it arrived three minutes ahead of the *General Coxe*. Guards were waiting for John Giles when he stepped ashore. Result: an almost perfect scheme foiled by one of the Rock's many unscheduled head counts.

Coy added it all up in his head. In the seven years he had been out of lockup, there had been five attempts involving eleven cons. One killed, ten captured.

Coy decided to pursue his analysis of escape attempts one step further; he set out to learn about the three attempted breaks that took place while he was in lockup, and the one attempt that had taken place before his arrival on Alcatraz in mid-1937. As his source of information, he chose one of the cons to arrive in the first shipment from Leavenworth when the Rock opened in August, 1934: Machine Gun Kelly.

"Sure, I've seen them all," Kelly told him when Coy broached the subject in the yard one Sunday afternoon. "Bowers was the first to try, the year after the joint opened. Joe Bowers, a stickup man. His con number was 210. He made a break over the south fence down toward Industries. Tower bull got him on the second shot.

"Then just before Christmas in '37, a couple of fairies named Ralph Roe and Teddy Cole got out of Industries in the thickest goddamned fog you ever saw. Roe was the daddy of the two; a great big son of a bitch with arms like cable wire. Teddy was a pretty little babyfaced kid, but as mean as anybody you ever saw. Anyhow, they got out of one of the shops in the fog, made it over the Cyclone fence, and jumped off the bluff down to the shore."

"Jesus," Coy said, "they must have had more guts than sense." He was thinking about the Cyclone fence: ten feet high and topped with barbed wire; and the jump from the bluff to the shore: about thirty feet, onto a rough, rocky waterline.

Kelly had shrugged. "Maybe they had guts, maybe they just cracked up, who knows? Like I said, they were queers; they'd been together in McAlester Pen in Oklahoma, and when they finally got sent here for bank robbery and kidnapping, they'd reached the end of the line. This is a rough goddamned place for two guys like that to get together, you know what I mean? Maybe they just couldn't take it."

"Maybe," Coy agreed. "What happened to them?"

Kelly shrugged again. "They went into the drink. Nobody ever saw them again."

"You think they might—just *might*—have made it?" Coy asked.

"Shit, no." Kelly said. "The water was about forty degrees. The tide was running fast that day. It's a mile and a quarter to the nearest Frisco pier; a mile and three-quarters to Angel Island; and two miles to Treasure Island. There's not a chance in the world they made it. Those two chumps went right out to sea under the old Golden Gate. They were food for the fishes."

"What about the two other tries after that?" Coy asked.

"Whitey Franklin, Sandy Limerick, and Jimmy Lucas tried it in '38. They iced the shop hack and got to the roof of Industries. Then they charged the roof tower. Stites was the screw on duty in the tower. He plugged Sandy in the head with his .45 and got Whitey in both shoulders with his Springfield. Lucas crapped out and gave up. Which surprised the hell out of me, 'cause Jimmy Lucas had a pretty tough rep. I remember one day we were all lined up at the barber shop to get clipped, and Jimmy was at the head of the line, see. So old Al Capone gets tired of waiting and walks up and gets in front of him. Now Jimmy's a Texas kid, see, and he didn't like city-slicker big shots. So he says to Capone, 'Hey, lard-ass, get back at the end of the line.' Capone puts on his meanest face and he says to Jimmy, 'You know who I am, punk?' Jimmy turns red because he don't like being called punk. He grabs the scissors from the guy cutting hair and sticks the point of them right up against old Scar-face's fat neck. 'Yeah,' he says, 'I know who you are, greaseball. And if you don't get back to the end of that fucking line, I'm gonna know who you *were.*' "

Kelly chuckled. "Capone got back to the end of the line, all right, and the barber-shop bull took the scissors away from Lucas and had him thrown in the hole. But he'd settled Al Capone's case for good. The big man from Chi learned he was just another con on *this* rock. He never got out of line again, the whole five years he was here. Matter of fact, Bernie, he used to have your job: cellhouse orderly. Only he wasn't allowed in D Block like you. They didn't want him talking to the hard cases."

"There was another break," Coy said, getting back to the subject. "A few months before I got out of lockup. Who was in on that one?"

"Yeah, a week or so after New Years in '39. Doc Barker led that one. Him and Dale Stamphill, Rufe McCain, Hank Young, and a nigger named Will Martin got down to the rocks on the ocean side one night and were trying to put together a raft out of driftwood. The hacks were on them before they'd been there fifteen minutes. When the searchlights were turned on them, they all cut and run. Doc got shot in the head and Stamphill was hit in both legs. The others were caught without being shot. They brought Doc to the infirmary and tried to keep him alive, but it wasn't any use; part of his head was blown off. He kept screaming, 'I'm all shot to hell, all shot to hell!' I think he lived for an hour, maybe two."

Machine Gun Kelly leaned back on the cement bleachers that lined one side of the yard and deftly rolled a cigarette. He studied Bernie Coy with a curious twinkle in his eyes.

"Why the sudden interest in crashouts, Bernie?" he asked. "You getting itchy?"

"Maybe," Coy said. "If I was, would you be interested?"

Kelly shook his head emphatically. "I been on the Rock nearly twelve years, pal. I've seen nine attempted crashouts. Six guys dead and sixteen put in solitary for years. *Years,* Coy. Jesus Christ, look at Whitey Franklin: he'll die in that dark cell; they'll never let him out. Look at Cretzer; he's been in isolation for over four years." He lighted the twisted end of his roll-your-own and sucked in a drag. "If it was any other slam in the country, Bernie, I'd say yes in a minute. But to try a crashout on the Rock—never. It can't be done. Take my word for it. This is one place that *nobody* escapes from."

Maybe, Bernie Coy thought. Just maybe. Because there was one element that had been missing from all of the previous nine crashout attempts. One thing that none of the previous twenty-two men had been able to get their hands on when they made their moves. One thing that Coy was certain would be the difference between success and failure. Just one thing.

Guns.

CHAPTER NINE

11:30 A.M.

At eleven-thirty, the prison whistle sounded, ending the morning work period.

In the Industries Building, at the sound of the whistle, the inmate workers put down their tools and lined up at the door of their respective shops to be searched and counted. Buddy Thompson, who was still lying on the canvas tarps in the corner of the tailor shop, got up and straggled to the end of the line. He was the last one to reach the door where shop foreman Haynes Herbert was doing the counting and searching.

"How are you feeling now, Buddy?" Herbert asked.

"Not so hot, Mr. Herbert," Thompson replied with as much ailing innocence as he could muster. "If it's okay with you, I think I'll go on sick call instead of eating lunch."

"All right, Buddy, you do that," said Herbert.

As Thompson expected, the shop foreman patted him down a little more thoroughly than usual. Buddy Thompson was breaking the normal routine of things and it triggered a subconscious suspicion in Haynes Herbert.

When Herbert was certain Thompson was not smuggling anything out of the shop, he gave him the nod to pass, and the youthful-looking Texas desperado walked out of Industries and fell into the line of convicts trudging up the controlled and heavily guarded path to the recreation-yard wall.

As Thompson moved along in the caterpillarlike line, a slight smile spread across his lips. So long, Haynes, old boy, he thought. If you ever get down to Mexico, be sure and look me up, hear? 'Cause that's the *only* way you'll ever see me again, old pard, unless we happen to meet in hell.

At the top of the path, the movement of the men slowed and backed up slightly. There, at the bottom of a long, very steep set of steps leading up to the rec yard gate, was an electromagnetic metal detector. Referred to by the cons as the "snitch box," it was shaped roughly like a backless, doorless telephone booth. Each inmate had to step inside it, pause, and then, at a word or gesture or nod from the duty guard, pass on.

Buddy Thompson patiently waited his turn, then passed through the snitch box and started the long climb up the steps. There were forty-nine steps up the steep hill, and on wet or windy days it was a miserable journey. This is the last time I'll ever have to climb these goddamned steps to get a meal, Buddy Thompson told himself. In a little while, he would be off this stinking rock. There would be no more steps and no more prison food. Pretty soon it would be sour cream and green cheese enchiladas every night and *chorizo con huevos* every morning. Not to mention all the sweets he wanted.

This time, Thompson promised himself, he was going to play it smart. Even smarter than his Amarillo setup had been. Using Amarillo as a base to hit small towns in adjoining states had been all right, up to a point. But it had still managed to get pretty hectic for him now and then. In the future he wanted to avoid that. He wanted no more running from one hick town to another to get away from the laws. No more hiding out in cheap little motor courts; having to live on Orange Crush and cheese crackers when he had a thousand dollars in his pocket but couldn't risk going into a good restaurant to eat; no more getting arrested by town constables and put in two-cell jails that he had to bust out of before they could try him and send him to a state pen. And no more racing hell-for-leather along unfamiliar back country roads, in stolen, often unreliable cars, only to get caught again in a roadblock on the next highway. His old buddy Clyde Barrow had done it that way for a while, and he and Bonnie had ended up shot to pieces on one of those hick roads. Old Clyde, who was—or would have been—three years older than he, had come out of the Telice, Texas, back country where he, Buddy, had grown up. He could have run with the Barrow gang if he'd wanted to. But Buddy Thompson had always been a lone wolf; a moody, hit-and-run outlaw who trusted no one and believed in nothing except his own cunning and fearlessness. Much like Marvin Hubbard, he was afraid of no man living.

At the top of the steps, the rec yard gate was opened and the line of men filed into the big yard and fell into work group formations at predesignated locations. The gate was locked behind them and the yard guards proceeded to count each group.

Last goddamned formation, Thompson thought. Last of a lot of things, when you came right down to it. Last of the old life, that was for sure. As soon as he got back to Texas, it was going to be straight across the border for him. Some nice little town a little ways in, but not too far. Someplace like Villa Ahumada or Saragosa. Fifty or sixty miles below the border. Close enough to make quick trips into Arizona and New Mexico to hit banks and payroll offices, and then quickly disappear back over the border. Smart, that's how Buddy Thompson intended to play it from now on. Smart and careful.

•

Inside the west cellhouse door, Officer Bill Miller stood and watched through the observation window of the yard door as the formations were counted. As he stood there, he shifted his weight from foot to foot so as not to irritate his bunions. When the men from Industries had been accounted for, the yard officer signaled to Miller. Miller looked down Times Square to Ernest Lageson at the desk near the dining-hall entrance.

"They're ready," he said.

Lageson looked up at Burch in the gun gallery. "Okay, Bert, send down 107," he ordered.

Bert Burch put his Springfield aside and again removed Key 107 from the key rack and hooked it to the cord. He lowered it to the cellhouse floor. Lageson took the key over to Miller, who unlocked the big door and swung it open. The convicts had already been moved from their yard formations to a line at the door. Now, at a nod from Bill Miller, they began filing briskly inside. Like a gray-blue inkblot, they spread out all over Times Square and began streaming down Seedy Street, Broadway, and Michigan Boulevard. For two full minutes the previously quiet cellhouse echoed with the rough brush of denim trouser legs and the slap of shoe leather against concrete. It was a rolling, guttural noise, like stampeding cattle in a Western movie or the rushing of rapids toward a waterfall. As the men began reaching their cells, the noise slowly subsided: the end of a sudden downpour; a few final drops of noise; then a stark return to silence.

As soon as the last man was through the west cellhouse door, Miller closed and locked the entry and handed Key 107 back to Lageson. The cellhouse officer hooked it to the cord and Bert Burch pulled it up to the gun gallery.

All inmates not in the hospital, D Block, or working in the kitchen were now back in their cells. One by one, as the block guards checked the aisles and found them clear, the rows of cell doors would be racked shut. In the cells, the men were stripping off their work clothes, washing in the single-tap, cold-water sinks, and putting on the pocketless coveralls they were required to wear to meals.

Down Broadway from the sallyport walked Captain Weinhold and Lieutenant Simpson, the two officers in charge of the day watch. They joined Lageson at the cellhouse officer's desk and talked idly as the block officers made the noon count.

By eleven-fifty, the count had been completed. All B, C, and D Block inmates were accounted for.

"All right, Ernie," Captain Weinhold ordered Lageson, "let them out for lunch."

The cell doors of the in-grade inmates were racked open and the men filed out and moved toward the dining-hall entrance. Weinhold, Simpson, and Lageson remained standing at the desk, casually scrutinizing them as they passed. Bill Miller and the other block officers patrolled the aisles to keep the lines moving. Above it all, rifle at the ready, Bert Burch watched alertly from the lower tier of the gun gallery.

As the lines crossed Times Square, inmates wanting to go to sick call fell out and waited against the west wall of B Block. There were seven of them. Among the seven, holding a hand protectively over his stomach, was Buddy Thompson.

Prisoners who did not desire to go to the noon meal had the option of remaining in their cells. They would be in lockup for the hour; all cell doors were racked shut after the men had lined up for lunch. One inmate who chose not to go to the dining hall that day was Bernard Paul Coy, the cellhouse orderly.

•

The noon meal on Thursday, May 2, was the fifty-ninth meal Bernie Coy had missed in sixty days. For two months he had been secretly dieting. He had reduced his already lean frame almost to the level of gauntness. During the sixty days, he had lost eighteen pounds. He had managed to maintain most of his deceptive strength, however, by doing arm and wrist exercises taught to him by Dan Durando.

Lying on his bunk, Coy thought briefly of the Indio Kid. He wondered if the young Chicano would decide to come in with them or not. If he did not, Coy's alternate plan was to put the guard hostages he intended to capture into cells and rack the doors shut. He did not like the idea of having to resort to that, because although he was familiar with the cellhouse mechanism that controlled the cell doors, he could not be certain there was not some master control system in the armory that could be used to deactivate the cellhouse mechanism in case of an emergency. If he had to lock his hostages in a cell, and then for some reason was unable to get them out, the break would be a bust. So he hoped he did not have to use the alternate plan. He hoped the Indio Kid would throw in with them.

Coy drew his knees up and turned sideways. His gaze fell on one of his canvases, this one leaning against the wall instead of in the stack on the toilet. It was the Golden Gate Bridge as seen through the barred windows of the prison library. It was a scene he viewed six days a week. The other paintings in the cell were mostly ones that he had done from memory: a Kentucky woods in the fall, a river where he had fished as a boy, the hills near his childhood home. Soon, he thought, I won't have to do everything from memory. Sighing, he closed his eyes and tried to doze. Earlier that morning he had been slightly tight inside, but now he was surprisingly placid —particularly considering that the time had finally arrived, the culmination of all his planning, all his slow and careful accumulation of the men and material necessary for what he was going to make happen that day. As he rested now, his almost haggard features seemed to relax completely for the first time in many months.

It had been a long, tense year for Bernie Coy. Since the day he had discovered the structural weakness in the gun-gallery bars, he had thought of nothing but escape. For several weeks after he first saw that deficiency, he had adjusted his position while mopping Michigan Boulevard and the north end of Times Square so that he could study as closely as possible the design and physical makeup of the gallery. He had to be extremely careful in doing it, for Burch, who constantly roamed the two tiers of the gallery, was a highly alert guard, acutely sensitive to all that went on in the cellhouse. Had he, or any of the block officers, even suspected that Coy was showing too much interest in the gun cage, chances are they would have relieved him of his orderly's job at once. Better safe than sorry was the general rule among Alcatraz personnel. They had not forgotten how Officer Royal Cline had been beaten to death in the aborted break eight years earlier.

After much study of the bars of the gun gallery, Coy concluded that they were of the same specifications as the bars on the cells: round, vertical bars, five inches apart, set in flat, horizontal crossbars eighteen inches apart. The latter measurement—eighteen inches —suited Coy fine. It was the five-inch limit between uprights that worried him.

He went to work on the problem in his cell, designing and redesigning a series of simple jack-type tools that could accomplish what he wanted. His sketches were made on art paper, then painted over. He worked on eleven different designs before he found a feasible one.

Nearly a month after his discovery, Coy approached a lifer who worked in the Industries machine shop. "I need some stuff," he said simply.

"What kind of stuff?" the lifer asked.

"A steel bolt," said Coy. "At least an inch in diameter and just under five inches long. Say, four and seven-eights. With one end notched."

The lifer had looked at him knowingly and disdainfully. Coy ignored the look and continued talking.

"I want a steel nut, three-quarters of an inch thick, to fit the bolt. And I want a steel sleeve four inches long that will just barely slide over the bolt. I want the sleeve notched on one end, too."

"That all?"

"No. I want a one-inch crescent wrench and some axle grease."

"How much axle grease?"

Coy thought a moment. The lifer's accent was Deep South. "About enough to fill a snuffbox," he said.

The lifer thought about it for a moment. "It won't work," he said finally.

"That ain't your worry," Coy pointed out.

The lifer shrugged. "Please yourself. How do you figure to pay?"

"A place in it for you, or the top of the route list for all the magazines as long as I'm cellhouse orderly."

"You going to do the gettin' of the stuff into the cellhouse?"

"Yeah."

"It's going to take quite a spell before you have it all."

"How long?"

"Shit, man, I don't know. Maybe two months, maybe six. But once I start on it, you got to take the whole package, no matter how long. No punking out halfway. Understand?"

"It's a deal," said Coy. "You want a place or you want the magazines?"

The lifer grunted derisively. "You know what you can do with the place. I'll take the magazines."

After arranging for the tool parts, Coy's problems were reduced to three: finding a way to get the parts into the cellhouse; figuring how to get to the top of the gun gallery; and manpower. Because he needed some other form of bribery to arrange the smuggling, he decided to concentrate on the latter and take in his first partner. His choice was the one man on the entire Rock with whom he closely identified and whom he felt he could trust completely: Marvin Hubbard. Both were Southerners, both victims of hardcore poverty, and both were proud, fearless men. There had been instant rapport between them when they had met nearly a year and a half earlier.

"Ever think about going home, Marv?" Coy asked the Alabama holdup man-kidnapper one day.

"Sure," Hubbard drawled. "Who don't?"

"I mean going home early," said Coy.

Marv Hubbard removed his thick glasses and rubbed his eyes. "Once in a while it's crossed my mind," he admitted.

"I think I've found a way."

Hubbard put his glasses back on. "Ol' buddy, you just got my undivided attention," he said.

Coy told him the plan. As he shared it with another person for the first time, the Kentuckian felt an excitement he had not experienced before. Prior to that day, the whole scheme had been only a picture in his mind. Now it was slowly coming to life.

"The magazine route's all I've got to bribe with. I've used that to get the tool-making started in the machine shop. What I need now is something to bribe a laundry worker with."

"How about extra dessert at supper?" Hubbard asked. "They's a couple of guys in the kitchen that are fairy for each other. They've asked me in the past to cover for 'em while they go back behind the ovens together. I usually just tell 'em to get the hell away from me. But if I was to start covering for 'em, why, they'd owe me. Both of 'em works the line. At least three times a week, one or the other is on dessert service. I could probably work a deal for extra dessert for whoever you wanted."

Coy rubbed his nose uncomfortably. "I hate to ask you to get mixed up with fairies."

Hubbard shrugged. "It ain't like I'd be *doing* anything with 'em. 'Sides, it'd be worth it if it worked. If we made it."

"We'll make it," Bernie Coy said evenly.

"Then I'll do it," Marv Hubbard told him.

Coy nodded his silent appreciation. Finally he said, "I figured I could count on you, Marv. You old Alabama boys don't let a feller down."

When Marvin Hubbard's arrangements in the kitchen were made, Coy approached a con who had worked in the prison laundry for nearly ten years. He sat down next to him in the yard. "I'll fix it for you to get extra dessert at least three times every week if you'll bring in four items for me over the next five or six months."

"What kind of items?" the laundry con asked.

"Three pieces of steel small enough to palm. And a small crescent wrench."

"From where? Machine shop?"

"Yeah."

"It can be done," the laundry con said. "There's only one thing: if I get caught, I go to D Block. I don't mind that; it's part of the risk. But what's waitin' for me when I come back to the general pop? Who do I have to be careful of because I fucked up something?"

"Nobody," Coy said. "It's just between you and me. Only thing I want is a fair shake. Do your best."

The laundry con nodded. It was a deal.

From the early fall of 1945 through Christmas of that year, the laundry con would be advised by Coy when the lifer in the machine shop had a piece ready. With Coy coordinating the connection, the lifer would put the piece in a hamper used for dirty, oily rags. The laundry con would collect the hamper and take it to the prison laundry. The piece would be hidden somewhere in the laundry until the next dolly load of clean towels was ready for the prison shower room. Then, concealed deep in the middle of the center stack of towels, it would be smuggled into the basement of the cellhouse. Subsequently it would be passed to Coy during the Wednesday evening or Saturday morning shower and clothing exchange.

There was actually no problem and very little risk connected with the smuggling effort. Except for the crescent wrench, all that the guards would have discovered were three pieces of metal which, taken individually, were harmless. A notched bolt, a hollow steel sleeve no bigger than a cigar, and a thick nut: none of them, alone, would have appeared to threaten the security of the invulnerable Rock. Even the crescent wrench, if intercepted, would not have caused too much of a furor. After all, there was little an inmate could do with a small wrench against tool-proof steel bars set in solid concrete. Provided they *were* set in solid concrete.

The crescent wrench was brought in on a Monday afternoon, which happened to be Christmas Eve, and it passed all guards without even a hint of discovery. By the middle of February, 1946, everything that Coy needed for the break was in the cellhouse. Concealed in his cell were the three pieces of tool he had designed, and a small rubber tube—no bigger than a package of chewing gum —of thick axle grease which the machine shop lifer had brought in himself. The rubber tube was sealed with plumbing tape to keep it from leaking.

During the weeks it had taken to secure those items, Coy had finalized in his mind just how the gun gallery was to be taken and who was to do it. The who, he had decided, would be himself. It was the only logical way to go. Besides himself, he had absolute faith in no one but Marv Hubbard. And Hubbard, with his bull chest and thick arms, was simply too big to do what had to be done. Besides, Coy knew how bad his friend's eyesight was; he secretly feared that Hubbard might get to the top of the gun cage, drop his glasses, and not be able to get the job done.

Coy had certain reservations about taking the gun gallery himself. He would have to diet down considerably and that would take away some of his strength. The climb to the top of the gallery would tax him even further, although in that effort he *had* found an easier way to do it than he had anticipated. A stairwell which led to the basement of the cellhouse had barred, grilled sides with a roof that protruded seven feet above the cellhouse floor. Located near the far north end of Times Square, the stairwell roof reached almost to the bottom of the gun gallery's lower level. Standing on the very peak of that grille roof, a man's head would be just at the top of the waist-high steel plate that protected the gallery guard. By reaching up, it would be possible to grab the vertical bars and pull oneself up. From there the climb to the top would be easy. What would *not* be easy—and what worried Coy more than anything—was the trouble he might encounter with Officer Bert Burch once he got into the cage. Burch was a lean, wiry man, probably fast, probably tough. For that reason it would be more practical to have Marv Hubbard take the gun cage. With his powerful arms and short, damaging punches, Hubbard could finish Bert Burch very quickly.

But, Coy finally decided resignedly, he couldn't have it both ways. So he would have to take the cage himself.

The last decision to be made regarded personnel. He discussed it with Hubbard in the yard one day. "We've got to have somebody with a connection on shore," Coy told his partner. "A *good* connection that we can rely on. I thought of Kelly first, but he don't think it can be done. My next choice is Dutch Cretzer. What do you think?"

Hubbard shrugged. He had little personal use for Cretzer. "I ain't crazy about him," he told Coy. "Them public-enemy types is all full of shit as far as I'm concerned. But if you say we need somebody like that, I guess Cretzer's as good as any. But ain't he still in D Block?"

"He's due out next week. If he can guarantee to make contact with an outside connection for a car, clothes, and a hideout, we'll give him a place. Agreed?"

"Whatever you say, Bernie."

"Okay, now, next we'll need somebody who's still in D Block. I think we'd be smart to leave that choice up to Cretzer. I go in and out of there five mornings a week with the book cart, but I don't really know nobody good except the Birdman and Fleish. The Birdman's too old, and I don't think Fleish would go for it. But Cretzer's been in lockup over there for five years; he ought to know who's reliable and who ain't."

Hubbard sighed. "I hope he don't pick no fruitcake. Half the cons over there are loonies."

"We'll leave it up to Cretzer," Coy decided. "He'll have as much riding on who he picks as we do." Coy looked around the yard and pointed out a new con, stripped to the waist, sunbathing on the concrete bleachers. "Buddy Thompson," he said. "Came in a few months ago. You heard anything about him?"

"Not much," said Hubbard. "Seems to be a loner. Raised a lot of hell before they finally brought him to ground."

"It's always been my thinking that a man who works alone has a little bit extra in the way of guts. The way I figure it, he *has* to have; he ain't got nobody to fall back on except hisself. I think may be this Thompson might make a good backup man. He impresses me as dependable. Why don't you ask around, casual like, and see what kind of general rep he's got. He comes from Texas; if you know anybody from down there, ask about him."

"Check," said Hubbard.

"Okay. I got one more guy in mind; somebody to keep the screws in line after we take them. Somebody who don't need no gun to do it. I was thinking about the Indio Kid."

"Durando?" Hubbard pursed his lips. "Sounds like a good pick to me. He can keep people in line, that's for sure. Ain't many guys in here any tougher'n him." Hubbard glanced up at the guards patrolling the top of the twenty-five-foot wall. "How many we making places for altogether?"

"That's it," said Coy. "Counting you and me, six." He too looked up at the wall guard. "Six men against Alcatraz," he said softly. "Six men against the Rock."

CHAPTER TEN

12:20 P.M.

Captain Weinhold, Lieutenant Simpson, and Cellhouse Officer Lageson were standing outside the dining room as the grade prisoners came out in groups of ten and returned to their cells. Normally, it would have been Block Officer Bill Miller standing there with the two guard officers, but on this particular day Lageson and Miller had done something very rare for them: they had traded lunch reliefs. Instead of Miller relieving Lageson for lunch first, Lageson relieved

Miller. Apparently there was no reason for the change, other than Miller being hungry early and Lageson not. Miller, who always ate in the officers' dining room off the kitchen, had already gone in for lunch. Lageson would eat later in the officers' lounge behind the armory, as was his custom.

The three men were standing near the dining-hall door when Buddy Thompson came back from the cellhouse sick bay. Thompson, holding a sick slip in one hand, approached the three officers near the dining-hall entry and, as regulations required, stopped approximately ten feet away. Weinhold glanced over at him, then pointedly ignored him.

"What is it, Thompson?" Lieutenant Simpson asked.

"I got a sick slip to lay in this afternoon, Mr. Simpson," Thompson said. He stepped forward and handed the slip to the lieutenant. The guard officer glanced at it to verify that it was in order.

"What's the matter with you, Thompson?" he asked.

"Don't know, sir," Thompson replied. "Stomach just feels all messed up. I got pains up in here," he moved one hand to his esophagus. "Doc says I may be getting an ulcer."

Captain Weinhold grunted derisively. "Couldn't be an ulcer, Thompson. Ulcers come from worry. You don't have anything to worry about. Not for the rest of your life—plus ninety-nine years."

Buddy Thompson's youthful, innocent expression remained the same, but inside his whole body clenched. Simpson shot a disapproving glance at his superior officer. One thing the two men had never agreed on: Simpson believed in letting the prisoners do their stretches one day at a time; Weinhold liked to remind them that they had *years* to serve. Simpson, a former Leavenworth officer, believed strongly in rehabilitation—even there on the Rock, where for the most part that aspect of penology was ignored. Weinhold thought it was enough to keep them incarcerated; Simpson wanted to help them.

"All right, Thompson, you stay in lockup this afternoon," Simpson said. "Maybe you'll feel better by dinner."

"Thank you, sir."

"Open up his cell, Bill," Simpson said to Miller, handing him the sick slip. "Log him in lockup and notify his foreman."

Bill Miller nodded for Thompson to go on down to the east C Block stairs, and went over to open the Texan's cell, number 329, on the middle tier.

•

Before twelve-thirty, the lockup prisoners had been let out and had filed into the dining hall. Dutch Cretzer was again in line with the Indio Kid, but made no effort to catch up with him this time. As far as Cretzer was concerned, the goddamned Chicano could throw in with them or not; he didn't really give a damn any longer. It was set for today and it was going to go today—with or without any two-bit punk like Durando.

Again, as the lockup prisoners crossed Times Square, a steam cart was being wheeled into D Block under the watchful eyes of both Officer Cecil Corwin and gun-cage guard Bert Burch. Once inside the Isolation block, the kitchen orderlies again moved quickly along the flats and up and down the two upper tiers, handing trays through the food pass at each occupied cell. The tray for D–14, the cell of Whitey Franklin, was put on Cecil Corwin's desk just before Corwin let the orderlies and their empty cart back out. Then Corwin unlocked the outer solid steel door to Franklin's cell, stepped into the 2½-foot access area, and handed his tray through the food pass of the cell's recessed barred door. Corwin, under strict orders not to speak to Franklin unless absolutely necessary, said nothing as the guard-killer took the tray. Likewise, Franklin accepted the tray in silence. In his early years in the cell, Franklin had talked to himself or sung aloud to break the monotony. For the past two years, however, he had scarcely spoken at all.

While the D Block inmates ate, Cecil Corwin climbed the steel stairs and walked the length of each tier range to make his routine count. The count was made more out of habit than necessity; since D Block inmates remained in lockup except to walk down the tier for their weekly shower, there was actually only one daily count that was important: the second count of the morning, to pick up the razor blades that had been distributed for that day's shave. The real purpose of the second count, besides getting back the blades, which had to be placed in matchboxes on the food pass, was to see if any D Blockers had done themselves any harm. An Alcatraz con could easily commit suicide on any given morning; he had possession of a razor blade for five full minutes every day. The purpose of the Rock was to keep men away from society, not necessarily to keep them alive.

As Corwin checked the middle tier, he noticed that Crazy Sam Shockley was not eating. The brooding, slack-jawed bank robber was sitting on his bunk, staring at the tray of food on his knees as if in a stupor.

"What's the matter, Sam, not hungry?" Corwin asked, stopping at 22. Shockley looked dumbly through the bars at Corwin. He said nothing. Corwin was not disturbed by the prisoner's manner; at best, Sam Shockley's behavior was usually erratic. "You all right, Sam?" Corwin asked conversationally. "Anything wrong?" Shockley continued to stare mutely at him. Corwin finally shrugged and went on his way. "Suit yourself, Sam," he said, half to himself.

As Corwin walked down the range, Sam Shockley smiled craftily.

•

By one o'clock, all lockup prisoners had finished lunch and were back in their cells. The one o'clock count was made by the block officers. Their tallies were given to the cellhouse officer, Lageson. The numbers from B and C Blocks were added to the count Corwin reported by telephone from D. Other figures were also called in from the chief steward in the kitchen and the medical officer in the hospital. Finally, when all figures were in, Lageson added them up.

"Two-seventy-two, sir," he reported to Captain Weinhold.

"Okay, Ernie, rack 'em out for yard time," the senior officer ordered. He turned to Lieutenant Simpson. "Joe, you ready for some lunch?"

"Past ready," said Simpson.

"See you later, boys," Weinhold said to Lageson and Bill Miller, who was now back from lunch. With Simpson, he walked down Broadway toward the sallyport.

As the two men proceeded east along the wide aisle, the cells were racked open and all the grade prisoners who celled on the flats came hurrying out to line up on Times Square to be let into the yard. The ones from the upper tiers moved noisily down their respective ranges to the steel stairs. Again, for several minutes, the big cellhouse resounded with the low, rolling thunder of convict movement.

As the men were coming out to Times Square, Lageson looked in the mirror at the gun gallery.

"Send down 107, Bert," he said.

Key 107 was lowered from the gun cage. Lageson handed it to Bill Miller. Miller crossed to the west cellhouse door and unlocked it. At a nod from him, the first prisoners to arrive began filing quickly into the yard.

When all grade prisoners were in the yard, Miller closed and locked the west cellhouse door and returned the key to Lageson. The cellhouse officer hooked it to the cord and Burch pulled it back up to the gallery.

•

It was now fifteen minutes past one. The only convicts remaining in the cellhouse were the segregated population in D Block; the lockups, who were in their cells; Buddy Thompson, who was lying in on a sick slip; the kitchen orderlies, who were hurrying to get the kitchen and dining hall cleaned up so they could be let out for their yard time; two inmate library clerks; and cellhouse orderly Bernie Coy.

Coy had come out of his cell when the grade prisoners were racked open for yard time. He had gone to the west utility corridor between the back-to-back cells of C Block; Miller had unlocked it for him; and he had removed the long-handled blanket broom. As soon as all the prisoners were out of the cellhouse, he began polishing the wide flats down Broadway.

At one-twenty, Kitchen Officer Joe Burdette walked to the center of the kitchen to line up the first group of kitchen help who had finished their work. They could now be let into the yard. Burdette was the only guard on duty in the kitchen; Chief Steward Robert Bristow had walked down Broadway a few minutes earlier to check with the Administration office on some supplies he had ordered but not received.

As Burdette called the men now to line up for the yard, he glanced around the kitchen and saw that seven men were still working. They would have to be let out singly as they finished their work. One of the men was Marv Hubbard, working at the tray-washing machine.

Burdette walked to the dining room door and gestured to Bill Miller. "All set, Bill."

Miller unlocked the dining hall door and let the orderlies file out. While Burdette stood by, and under the watchful eyes of Burch overhead and Lageson at the cellhouse desk, Bill Miller carefully searched each orderly. One by one, as they passed his scrutiny, he let them line up at the yard door.

"Send down 107," Lageson said to Burch when he saw that the men were ready to go. Once again, Key 107 was lowered. Miller unlocked the door and let the men into the yard.

As Miller walked back toward the cellhouse desk, Lageson said, "Okay, Bill, I'm going on out for some lunch now. Be back in a little while."

Miller bobbed his chin. "Okay."

"Hey, Bert," Lageson called up to the gallery. "I'm checking out for lunch now."

Bert Burch, opening his lunchbox to get out his own meal, looked down. "Roger," he said.

Lageson headed down Broadway. Burdette went back into the kitchen to supervise the seven remaining men. Miller took Lageson's seat at the cellhouse desk. Only after Miller sat down did he realize he still had Key 107 in his hand. He got back up and started to hook it onto the cord. Then he glanced in the mirror and saw that Bert Burch was at the far end of the cage, starting to climb the steel ladder to the top level. Burch always ate his lunch on the upper level, where he could relax a little and still watch the entire west end of the cellhouse. Miller decided not to disturb him. He would be needing 107 to let the other kitchen help out in a few minutes anyway.

Disregarding the standing order that Key 107 was never to be kept on the cellhouse floor, Bill Miller slipped the key into his trousers pocket.

•

Coy had swept from the sallyport end of Broadway to the cutoff and was about to begin doing the west end of the aisle, when he saw Lageson coming toward him. Coy frowned and his dark eyes at once grew troubled. Where in hell was Lageson going? The cellhouse officer was supposed to be back from lunch and Miller, the block officer, was supposed to be leaving. Coy, having remained in lockup during the noon hour, had no way of knowing they had switched lunch hours.

Something's wrong! Coy thought tensely.

He continued pushing the blanket broom. As Lageson passed him, he spoke casually to the officer. "What time you got, Mr. Lageson?"

"What do you care, Coy?" Lageson said easily. "You're not going anywhere." But he glanced at his watch anyway and said, "Twenty-five after one."

"Thanks, Mr. Lageson," said Coy.

The cellhouse orderly pushed on, sweeping the broad aisle unhurriedly as he always did, until Lageson reached the sallyport and was let out of the cellhouse. Then he picked up the blanket broom and started down Broadway toward Times Square.

As he walked, Bernie Coy could feel lines of sweat break from under his arms and run down his sides. Through his mind kept running the same awful thought over and over: eight years of looking for a way, a year of planning and scheming; it couldn't go sour now. Not today. Not just minutes before they were going. It *couldn't.*

As Coy approached Times Square, he saw Bill Miller sitting at

Lageson's cellhouse desk. Other than that, everything else looked normal. A quick glance to the upper level of the gun cage told him that Bert Burch was leaning casually against the upper gallery bars, eating a sandwich and drinking from a thermos. The west end of the cellhouse, as usual, was all but silent at that time of day.

Coy's unscheduled appearance on Times Square, however, alerted both Burch and Miller. Both were experienced keepers of men, ultrasensitive to the slightest deviation from routine. Burch put down his sandwich and picked up his Springfield the moment he saw Coy enter Times Square. Miller, even though he liked Coy, consciously tensed as the convict approached.

"I need to fix this blanket, Mr. Miller," Coy said, pointing to the broom head. "The thing keeps coming loose on me. Okay if I get some more string from the corridor?"

"Sure, go ahead," said Miller. He relaxed and handed Coy the key to the C Block utility corridor. Above him, Burch leaned his rifle against the gallery rail and went back to eating.

Coy opened the utility corridor and got out some heavy brown twine made in the Industries mat shop. Kneeling, he wound some of it around one end of the rolled blanket.

•

Back in the kitchen, in the tiny tray-washing room, Marv Hubbard took the last stack of dirty trays and hid them under the steam-wet washing machine where they could not be seen from the door. Quickly drying his hands, he stepped to the door and looked into the large room of the kitchen proper. Officer Burdette was standing in the center of the room, overseeing the work of the other six orderlies still inside.

Hubbard adjusted his rimless glasses and stepped quietly through the door and over to the wire cutlery tray that held the carving knives. When Burdette was looking the other way, Hubbard quickly took a five-inch stainless-steel knife and slipped it under his shirt. Then he walked directly into Burdette's line of sight.

"Trays are all done and the washing room's cleaned up, Mr. Burdette," he said, just as he said every day at noon.

"Okay, Hubbard, go on out for your yard time," Burdette said. The guard rarely checked Hubbard's work. Marv Hubbard had the reputation of being a reliable, dependable worker.

Hubbard gave Burdette a casual half salute and left the kitchen. Burdette had not searched Hubbard because it was not his job to search the kitchen orderlies; that was the responsibility of the officer on duty at the dining hall entrance. Hubbard, after he had crossed the long dining hall, could see that officer at the desk just outside the door on Times Square. But to Hubbard's surprise, the officer was Bill Miller, not Ernest Lageson, as he expected. Hubbard paused, frowning. Something was not going according to plan. He swallowed and quietly moved nearer to the door. Then he saw Bernie Coy kneeling near the end of C Block, doing something to the blanket broom.

•

As he worked, Coy glanced past Miller and saw Marvin Hubbard peering around the corner of a wall in the dining hall. Coy bit his lip and tried to think of some way to let Hubbard know everything was all right. *If* it was all right.

Finally Coy looked at Miller and said casually, "No lunch today, Mr. Miller?"

"I ate earlier," Miller told him. "I switched lunch breaks with Officer Lageson." Miller looked over and grinned. "Sometimes, Bernie, I think you guys know *our* schedules as well as we know yours."

Coy nodded. "Wouldn't surprise me none, Mr. Miller." He quickly got the blanket tied in place and closed the utility corridor door. "Maybe I can get those flats polished up now," he said, leaving Times Square and heading back up Broadway.

At the cutoff, Coy stepped inside and hurried the few yards over to Michigan. Dan Durando's cell was the second one down from the cutoff. Coy moved quickly to it.

"Kid," he said quietly. The young Chicano came up close to the bars. "It's time, Kid," Coy told him tensely. "One way or the other. In or out?"

The Indio Kid wet his lips. He kept thinking about the Birdman, locked up for forty years, an old man now who would die behind bars.

"In or out, Kid?" Coy demanded. "Last chance."

"No killing?" Durando asked.

"No killing," Coy promised. "I ain't looking to go to the chair."

Durando took a deep, nervous breath. "Okay," he said finally, "count me in."

Coy nodded brusquely. "I'll have you out of that cell in fifteen minutes."

Coy quickly moved back through the access corridor to Broadway, casually swept across the aisle, and hurried through the next cutoff over to Seedy Street. Leaving the broom, he doubled back and ran quietly along the C-D aisle to where it intersected Times Square. He peered around the corner. Miller was still at the cellhouse desk. Two tiers above him, Burch was finishing his lunch.

Coy backed off and knelt down; he wiped perspiration from his brow. He tried to control his breathing, which was becoming labored. He could feel his heart pounding. It had been a long time since he had done anything dangerous and desperate; he knew his blood pressure was shooting up.

After waiting a full minute, he looked around the corner again. Miller was still at the desk. In the gun cage, Burch was tilting his thermos all the way up to drink the last of whatever was in it. Coy pulled back and waited again.

As he waited there at the end of the south side of C Block, Coy was acutely aware of his visibility. Directly ahead of him, across Times Square, was the west cellhouse door with its four-by-ten-inch bulletproof glass observation window. Beyond it were yard guards who might come to the door for something at any moment. To the left of that door and closer to him, in the D Block wall, was the door to the isolation block, containing an even larger observation window. D Block officer Cecil Corwin might walk over and look out at any time. But there was nothing Coy could do until Burch came down from the top tier of the cage.

Another minute. Coy peered around the corner for the third time. This time he saw what he was looking for. Bert Burch had closed his lunchbox, picked up his rifle, and was walking toward the Michigan Boulevard end of the gallery. Coy watched intently until Burch started climbing down the steep ladder to the lower level of the cage; then he sprang up and hurried back along Seedy Street. One of the cons watching him from a cell on the flats was stupid enough to call to him.

"Hey, Coy, what's going on?"

Coy turned on him, livid with anger. "You son of a bitch, keep your goddamn mouth shut!" he said in a voice that turned to a vicious growl. He pointed a threatening finger. "If the screws heard you and come looking for me, you're a goddamn dead man!"

His warning finished, he rushed on down Seedy, paused at the cutoff to grab his blanket broom, then ran to the prison library. A wire grille, extending from the floor to the high ceiling, some thirty feet up, enclosed the entire library area. There were no chairs or study tables in the library, only shelves. At a desk in one corner, the two inmate library clerks were sorting books. They looked up when Coy walked in with the blanket broom in his hand. Just a glance at the grimly determined expression on Coy's face was enough to tell them that something unusual was happening.

"What's going on, Bernie?" one of them asked.

"Nothing that's got anything to do with you," Coy said, his words even, not abusive. "The two of you stay back here at your desk and you won't get in anybody's way. Got that?"

They shrugged in unison. "Sure, Bernie," one of them said.

Coy stepped over to the west wall of the library, the wall that separated it from D Block. With the wooden broom handle, he tapped smartly three times on the concrete.

Then he left the library and hurried back to the cutoff and over to Broadway.

•

In D Block, Crazy Sam Shockley had been listening intently for the three taps on the library wall. As soon as he heard them, his eyes widened and his mouth fell open incredulously. For perhaps thirty seconds he stared out his cell door. Then his childish mind began to function and he became alert and excited.

The signal! he thought. *That was the signal!*

Shockley picked up his tray of food, still untouched, and hurled it violently at the cell door. It struck the bars and clattered loudly to the floor. Shockley at once retrieved it and began pounding the bars with it.

"Let me out of here!" he screamed wildly. "It's after me, it's going to get me! Help me! Somebody help me!"

D Block Officer Cecil Corwin was up from his desk at the first sound of the tray hitting the bars. He had looked up from his paperwork at the sound of the three taps, and had quickly decided that they were probably repairing a shelf in the library. But when he heard the tray hit the cell bars and then clatter to the floor, he leaped to his feet. He had walked to the middle of the flats, his eyes searching the cells, when Shockley started screaming.

Corwin quickly ran up to the middle tier. "Sam, calm down," he said. "What's the matter with you?"

"Let me out, let me out!" Shockley screamed.

"Take it easy, Sam. Calm down. Tell me what's wrong."

"It's after me!" Shockley yelled, wide-eyed and wild. "It's going to get me!"

"Nothing's going to get you, Sam," Corwin said patiently. "Stop your screaming now."

Shockley put an arm through the bars and threw the food tray at Corwin. The guard easily sidestepped it.

"I could put you in a dark cell for that, Sam," said Corwin, his voice taking on an edge for the first time. "Now why don't you calm down before you get into real trouble."

"I'll burn this fucking place down!" Shockley screamed. He dragged the linen from his bunk and piled it in a heap on the cell floor. Standing back in the cell, he began lighting stick matches and throwing them onto the pile.

"Shockley, I'm ordering you to put those matches down!" Corwin said firmly. Crazy Sam paid no attention to him.

Corwin hurried along the range and back down to the flats. He picked up a phone on the wall under the gun-cage overhang. Cliff Fish answered in the armory.

"Cliff, connect me with Bert in the cage," said Corwin. "I'm having trouble with Sam Shockley."

"Right away," Fish said. Corwin heard a buzz and then Burch answered.

"Bert, this is Ceece," said Corwin. "Come over here and cover me, will you? Shockley is having some kind of fit. He's setting fire to his bed linen. I may have to open his cell to restrain him."

"Be right there," Bert Burch replied.

•

Bernie Coy, back on Broadway, was pushing his blanket broom toward Times Square. His face was set, his mouth a tight line, dark eyes almost glowering. Under his shirt, nervous sweat was popping from his pores. He was roughly thirty feet up the aisle from Times Square when he heard the phone ring in the gun cage and saw Bert Burch answer it. *It's working,* he thought with a wild exhilaration. *Goddamn, it's working!*

He watched Burch hang up the phone. The gun-gallery guard looked in the mirror at Bill Miller at the cellhouse desk. "I'm going into D, Bill. Ceece is having a problem with Shockley."

Miller grunted. "Have fun," he told Burch. Burch walked to the south end of the gallery and went through a wooden door into the D Block section of the cage.

As the door closed behind Burch, Bill Miller glanced up and saw Coy mopping toward him down Broadway. Unlike his earlier reaction, Bill Miller experienced no unusual sense of alertness at Coy's appearance this time. Miller knew that it was just about the time Coy should be finishing up with Broadway. The cellhouse orderly was usually mopping down Times Square when Miller, taking his noon break at the normal time, returned from lunch.

As Coy mopped along, Miller looked over toward the D Block door. Idly, he wondered what the problem with Shockley was. There was never any way of telling what was going on in D. The concrete separating wall and the thick steel door effectively soundproofed one side from the other. Captain Weinhold himself had once commented that a small war could be conducted in D Block without ever disturbing the rest of the cellhouse.

As he stared over at the D Block door, Miller's thoughts were interrupted by someone calling his name. He looked around and saw Marvin Hubbard standing inside the locked dining hall door.

"Excuse me, Mr. Miller," the Alabaman drawled, "but Mr. Burdette said I could go to the yard now."

"Okay, Hubbard," said Miller, getting up and looking through Lageson's keys for the one to the dining-hall door.

As Miller flipped through the keys, Coy worked to the end of Broadway and leaned his blanket broom against the wall. Looking at Bill Miller's back, he briefly wished it was not Miller who was on duty. Coy had planned the break to begin when Cellhouse Officer Lageson was on duty. Seeing Lageson get taken down by Marv Hubbard would not have bothered him at all. But for some reason, he hated to see Bill Miller get hurt. He refused to allow himself to think that it was because he *liked* Miller. That, to him, was ludicrous. Alcatraz cons simply did not like their keepers. It was unheard of.

Bernie Coy shook his head slightly. He didn't know how the hell to figure it. But there was one thing he *did* know: today was the day, and now was the time, Bill Miller on duty or not.

At the dining hall door, Miller found the right key and opened the door for Marv Hubbard. As he did so, he thought that it was a good thing he had held on to Key 107 and put it in his pocket. Otherwise, with Burch over in the D Block section of the cage, Miller would not have been able to let Hubbard into the yard.

Hubbard stepped out of the dining hall and stood next to the door to be searched. Miller began patting down the kitchen orderly's arms and sides. Hubbard did not mind; the carving knife was now under his belt in the middle of his back. Behind Miller, Bernie Coy moved as quietly and quickly as he could across Times Square.

Miller finished patting down Hubbard's front. "Okay, turn around," he said.

Marv Hubbard did not move.

"Turn around, Hubbard," the guard repeated.

Behind Hubbard's thick, rimless glasses, his eyes narrowed slightly. For the second time, he failed to obey Miller's order. The block guard parted his lips to speak again, to issue a harsh command this time; but suddenly he sensed that something was wrong. By then, it was too late.

Coy leaped the last few steps to Miller's back and pinned the guard's arms to his sides. Before Miller could muster any resistance, Marv Hubbard stepped forward and drove a heavy fist into his face. Miller's head snapped back and he groaned. Hubbard drove his other fist into the guard's face. Blood gushed from Miller's nose. Hubbard hit him again. Coy felt Miller's legs buckle.

"That's enough," Coy said tightly to Hubbard as the weight of Miller's slack body sagged back against him. Coy gently lowered the unconscious guard to the floor. Then for a gripping, heavy moment, Bernie Coy and Marv Hubbard looked starkly into each other's eyes. Each of them felt as if he were in a hazy, muted, slow-motion world. They seemed to be standing off to the side, watching something of which neither of them was a part. Oddly, as they stared at each other, they seemed to sense that their strange feelings were mutual. Each of them *knew* that to the other, what they had just done seemed like a dream. Neither of them could believe for several seconds that it was really happening.

But it was.

The time was 1:40 P.M.

The break had now begun.

CHAPTER ELEVEN

1:40 P.M.

"Okay, we're moving!" Bernie Coy said. He slapped Marv Hubbard stingingly on the arm muscle. "Get him around on Seedy Street and find an empty cell."

Without a word, Hubbard grasped Bill Miller under the arms and dragged the unconscious guard across Times Square to the flats of the C-D aisle. Hubbard's knuckles throbbed like hell from the punches he had thrown. It had been a long time since he had hit a man. He dragged Miller around the corner, dropped him to the floor, considerably less gently than Coy had, and quickly searched for an empty cell.

Coy, meanwhile, had grabbed Miller's club and the ring of cellhouse keys from Lageson's desk. At the end of the block, he unlocked the control panel containing the switches that operated the cell doors. Then he looked around the corner at Hubbard.

"I'll put him in 403," Marv Hubbard called quietly.

Coy racked open 403. He had no trouble with the controls; working as the cellhouse orderly for so long, he had been in a position to constantly observe the block officers opening and closing individual cells. He could work the controls as well as any guard on the island. Closing the control panel, he hurried around to where Hubbard was already dragging Miller into the cell. Hubbard started to leave the unconscious guard on the floor, but Coy grabbed Miller's feet.

"Lift him onto the bunk."

"What for?" Hubbard said. He did not know that Coy and Miller were friendly.

"Come on, Marv, do as I say," Coy told him urgently. Hubbard helped him put Miller on the bunk. "It'll be easier for you to get his coat off this way," Coy said, quickly thinking up an explanation. "Now put on his coat and cap and go sit at Lageson's desk."

Hubbard started unbuttoning Miller's uniform coat as Coy stepped over to the cell door. Cautiously, he peered out and looked up at the gun gallery. It was deserted; Burch was still in D Block. Coy hurried from the cell. Making no effort to be quiet, for there were now no guards in the main section of the cellhouse to hear him, he ran furiously across Times Square to the B Block control panel. Unlocking it, he worked the controls to rack open his own cell and the cells of Dutch Cretzer and Dan Durando. That done, he hurried around the corner of the block to his cell. Rushing inside, he tossed the ring of keys onto his bunk and dropped to his knees in front of the lidless porcelain toilet. Rolling up one sleeve, he reached into the bowl and felt around in the water for the edge of the closed trap. Finding it, he forced it down a quarter of an inch and slid his fingers back to its hinge. The water began gurgling as it seeped down into the big main pipe. Presently, Coy's seeking fingers found the hump of a knotted shoelace forced into the joint of the trap hinge. He held it firmly with two fingers while he used his thumb and knuckles to push the trap open a little farther. Quickly then he looped the shoelace around his fingers to keep it from slipping from his grip, and with his other hand he pushed the flush knob of the toilet and opened the trap completely. The bowl water rushed down over his hand, but as it did Coy drew the shoelace out of the pipe and pulled with it a homemade cloth sack tied securely to its other end.

Not even bothering to wring the water out of the dripping sack, Coy snatched up the keys and rushed back out of the cell. He looked around the corner at the gun gallery; it was still empty. At Lageson's desk near the dining-hall entrance, Marv Hubbard now sat, wearing Bill Miller's cap and coat.

As Coy stood there at the end of B Block, Dutch Cretzer and Dan Durando ran down the flats of Michigan Boulevard to join him. The two men faced him tensely for a second. The Kid's face was as stolid as an Aztec mask; he did not even blink. Cretzer's dark eyes were wide; there was a nervous grin on his lips.

"Come on," said Coy. The three men trotted across Times Square to the desk where Marv Hubbard sat. Coy looked through the cellhouse keys and selected one. "We ain't got much time," he said, "so let's move. Kid, you go around on Seedy to 403 and watch Miller; he's knocked out right now but he could come to any time." Durando hurried off. "Come on," Coy said to Cretzer. He led the way to the control box at the end of C Block. "I'm racking open Buddy Thompson's cell. It's 329 on the middle tier of C. Pick him up there, then the two of you go through the cutoff and over to A." He handed him the key he had taken from the desk. "This is the A Block key. Go up to the east end and watch the sallyport from there. If a screw should come back from lunch before I get the gun gallery, the two of you lay for him at the cutoff. Got it?"

"Got it," said Cretzer. He hurried to the east C Block stairs. Coy set the control panel to open just the one cell, and threw the lever. Then he closed the box and crossed back to the cellhouse desk. Marv Hubbard, the calmest, coolest member of the break gang, looked steadily at him. "You going to have enough time, Bernie?" he asked emotionlessly.

Coy wet his lips and looked up at the still-empty gun gallery. "If Crazy Sam can keep Burch over there another three minutes, we'll have it made," he replied.

Coy began stripping off his clothes.

•

In D Block, Bert Burch was standing with his rifle trained on the middle tier of the isolation cells. From Cell 22, a few wisps of gray smoke trailed through the door bars onto the range. Inside the cell, Sam Shockley had created in the pile of linen on his cell floor a near-fire that would not burn but was smoldering persistently. Shockley himself was standing on his stripped bunk, yelling at the top of his lungs.

"Burn them out! Burn them alive! They can't get you if you set fire to them!"

When Burch first came in from the main cellhouse section of the gallery, Cecil Corwin had started toward Cell 22 to go in and restrain the wildly screaming Shockley. Burch had cautioned him against opening the cell.

"There's no back-up officers in the cellhouse, Ceece," he said from the cage. "Why don't you leave him in lockup until some of the block officers get back from lunch?"

"I'd like to calm him down before he hurts himself," said Corwin. "Besides, that stuff he set fire to is starting to smoke."

"I still think you ought to leave him in until you get some backup," Burch advised. "Use the extinguisher on the smoke."

"All right, I guess you're right," Corwin said, reconsidering. He could tell that Burch was nervous about his being alone in the block. Corwin was sure he could handle Shockley and calm him down; but there was always that outside chance that something would go wrong. And Cecil Corwin was far too humane and compassionate a man to take even a remote chance of being the cause of Bert Burch's shooting an inmate. Particularly a pathetic person like Shockley.

Corwin returned to the flats and went over to a locked cabinet in the guard's lavatory under the gallery overhang. Opening it, he lifted out a large fire extinguisher. Returning to the middle tier, he stood back on the range from Shockley's cell.

"Get back out of the way, Sam. I'm going to have to wet down that stuff you set fire to."

"No! No! You're not going to put it out!" Shockley yelled. He danced back and forth in front of the cell door.

"Move out of the way, Sam," Corwin warned. "If you don't, you're going to get wet."

"Fuck you!" Shockley shouted.

Corwin sighed quietly. His patience was running out. "Suit yourself, Sam," he said finally. Corwin triggered the extinguisher, directing a hard blast of water into the cell. He tried to miss Shockley, but Crazy Sam jumped right in front of it. The convict's shirtfront was drenched.

"You cocksucker!" he screamed at Corwin. He jumped up on his bunk.

Corwin turned the extinguisher on the smoldering pile of linen on the floor. He laced the pile with enough water to terminate the smoke entirely; as a precaution, he also wet down Shockley's mattress, as the convict jumped to the back of his cell. Then he turned off the extinguisher.

"I'm afraid you're going to have to spend some time in a dark cell, Sam," Corwin said gravely.

Corwin walked to the end of the range and stood in front of Cell 15, which was closest to the gun gallery. Bert Burch came over to talk with him across the fifteen feet of space that separated them.

•

Beyond the D Block wall, on the flats north of B Block, Bernie Coy had stripped down to his shorts and socks. Looking at him, Marv Hubbard could not believe how skinny and bony his friend was. Hubbard knew that Coy had been dieting, but he had no idea the lean Kentuckian had become so emaciated. Coy looked like a winter twig, weak and brittle. Silently, Hubbard prayed that Coy would be able to take Bert Burch out quickly, by surprise. He feared that if Burch was able to put up a fight, the gallery guard would break Coy in half. And without the gallery, the break would be a bust.

Hubbard watched in fascination as Coy tied the cloth bag around his neck with an extra shoelace. Then, without pausing, the frail-looking convict gripped the grille of the stairwell and quickly climbed to its narrow, peaked roof. As Coy balanced himself on the point of the roof, Hubbard knew the narrow steel bar at the top was probably pressing painfully into the bottoms of his feet; but glancing up, he saw no expression of pain in Coy's face. All he saw was a look of rigid, intractable determination.

Coy, balancing precariously on the stairwell roof, reached above his head and grasped the top edge of the waist-high steel shield that ran along the lower gallery tier. Straining with the weight of his own body, he managed to pull himself far enough up to reach the first of the flat horizontal crossbars through which the round vertical bars ran. Gripping the crossbar, he held with one hand for a split-instant while he threw his other hand up and grabbed the same bar. Quickly then, while he still had the breath to do it, he pulled his bare knees up and got them over the top of the shield. The cold, hard metal dug painfully against his kneecaps and caused him to blink back tears.

He paused five seconds to get some new breath, then brought his feet up to the top of the shield and began to move upward. The hard part of the climb was over. For the rest of the way, it was a simple matter of using the vertical and horizontal bars as steps to make his way upward and over. He worked his way almost to the very end of the cage, past the gallery ladder; then he finished climbing up: a human spider moving up a steel web. He got to the upper tier, easily pulled himself past the waist-high shield on that level, and followed the bars all the way up to where they curved inward to form the roof of the gun cage. Once on top, he dropped his legs through the bars and locked his feet together to hold himself in place. He was now balanced on top of the gun cage, thirty-eight feet above the flats.

As he untied the sack from around his neck, Coy for the first time saw at close range the structural inadequacy he had discovered a year earlier. The curved bars that formed the roof of the gun gallery ended at the concrete wall instead of being imbedded. They were simply held in place by a steel brace bolted to the wall. Incredible, Bernie Coy thought for perhaps the hundredth time since his discovery. But he did not waste any precious seconds in wonderment.

Opening the homemade bag, Coy quickly assembled his bar-spreading tool. The three-quarter-inch-thick nut was already threaded onto the notched end of the one-inch-diameter steel bolt. Using his teeth, Coy quickly bit a corner off the small rubber tube of axle grease. He squeezed the grease up and down the length of the bolt, rubbing it into the threads with his thumb and forefinger. When it was sufficiently greased, he slipped the hollow steel sleeve over the bolt. The notched end of the sleeve and the notched end of the bolt were at opposite ends of the combined apparatus.

Coy held the tool in the five-inch space between two round bars and turned the nut with his fingers. As the nut turned, it moved up the threads of the bolt, pushing the hollow sleeve ahead of it. After only a few turns of the nut, the tool had expanded far enough so that Coy could seat each notched end securely against one of the round bars. He seated the two ends equidistant between two flat crossbars which were eighteen inches apart. With thumb and forefinger, he turned the nut until the tool was firmly set. Then he adjusted the crescent wrench snugly on the nut and began turning it around and around.

The bar opening with which Coy was working was eighteen inches long, between flat crossbars; and five inches wide, between the vertical round bars that curved over the top of the cage. With each turn of the crescent wrench, the five-inch width expanded. It became five and one-eighth inches, then five and one-quarter, then five and three-eighths, spreading the bars an eighth of an inch each time Coy turned the crescent wrench and its captive steel nut one full revolution.

In a matter of seconds, Coy had turned the wrench sixteen times and spread the opening from eighteen by five inches to eighteen by seven inches. He continued turning.

With each revolution, the steel nut became harder and harder to turn.

•

On the middle tier of C Block, the former Public Enemy Number Four and the lone Texas outlaw who had been on the Rock only 161 days met for the first time. Buddy Thompson, following Coy's instructions, was waiting outside his racked-open cell when Dutch Cretzer came trotting up.

"Dutch Cretzer," he introduced himself, sticking out his hand.

"Buddy Thompson," said the Texan, shaking hands. "I've heard of you, Dutch."

Cretzer smiled his handsome smile. "You're going to hear of me a lot more when I get off this rock," he promised. "Come on, follow me."

Cretzer shunned the stairs and slipped through the pipe railing to drop onto Broadway. Thompson did the same. Cretzer led Thompson to the cutoff. As they crossed to Michigan Boulevard, he said, "Bernie's getting into the gun cage now. We're going to stake out around the corner on A Block and watch the sallyport entry."

A Block, on the extreme right of the sallyport entryway, was unoccupied. Its aisle was separated from the rest of the cellhouse by a ten-foot grille fence, with a gate to which Coy had given Cretzer the key. Cretzer unlocked the block; then he and Thompson made their way quietly to its east end. They found the east end sealed off from the sallyport aisle by a six-foot grille similar to the fence they had just passed through at the opposite end. There was no way to peek around the corner because of the grille. In order to watch the sallyport entrance, Cretzer determined at once that they would have to stand nearly halfway out in the ten-foot-wide aisle. That would expose them to the view of the sallyport guard through the four-by-twenty-three-inch observation panel in the steel sallyport door.

"This is no good," he told Thompson. "The first screw coming back from lunch could glance through that glass and see us." He looked around quickly, wetting his lips. "Wait here," he said.

Ten feet back from the grille was a spiral stairway—fourteen steel steps set in a rising circle around a steel pole—that led up to the middle tier. Cretzer quietly climbed the stairs and moved to the front end of the range. Lying on his stomach, he peeked around the corner of the end cell with one eye. He had a clear view of the sallyport entry, with a bare minimum of exposure to himself. Rolling over, he whispered down to Thompson.

"It's perfect. Come on up."

As he waited for Thompson, Cretzer looked up at the unmanned east gun gallery and thought of Coy. He hoped to hell Coy didn't have any trouble getting into the west gallery. They were going to need the gallery screw's rifle and automatic before the guards started coming back from lunch. He began to consider the guards. When they reentered the cellhouse after lunch, they automatically turned to the left, toward Broadway, which was twenty-two feet away. Since they had to log in at the cellhouse officer's desk upon returning to duty, almost without exception they walked directly down Broadway to Times Square, where that desk was located. An occasional guard might make the walk by way of Michigan Boulevard, ten feet to the right of the sallyport door, if that was his watch patrol area and he wanted to check on a lock-up prisoner for some reason. But no guard, for any reason, had ever been known to go all the way over to the A Block aisle, thirty-five feet away, unlock the door in the screen, and walk down that way. So unused and ignored was A Block that its aisle, facing the north wall of the cellhouse, had never even been given a nickname: it was simply the A Block aisle. It was extremely rare for it to be used. With that in mind, Dutch Cretzer felt reasonably safe lying on the middle tier of A.

As Cretzer lay there, Buddy Thompson stretched out beside him, slightly back. "Think Bernie will make it into the cage all right?" Thompson asked, after they had lain there quietly for several moments.

"He will if he don't get interrupted," Cretzer replied.

Just then, as if it had been timed to Dutch Cretzer's words, the main cellhouse door opened and Chief Steward Robert Bristow was let in. As expected, Bristow did not even glance toward A Block, where the two convicts watched. He walked over to Broadway and headed directly for the dining-hall entrance.

Sitting at the cellhouse officer's desk just outside that entrance, wearing a guard cap and coat, was Marvin Hubbard, who worked for Bristow in the kitchen.

Atop the gun cage, Bernie Coy was using both hands to force the crescent wrench around for its twenty-sixth revolution. He had spread the round bars three and one-quarter inches, opening the space he was working on to eighteen by eight and one-quarter inches.

Sweat was pouring down Coy's face now, filtering through his brows, running into his eyes. His mouth had gone bone-dry, and he could barely swallow. The palms of both hands were slick with sweat; he had wiped them on his shorts so much that the shorts now stuck wetly to his bony thighs.

Breathing heavily from the exertion of forcing the nut, he left the wrench in place in an upright position for a moment and reached down to take off one of his socks. He used the sock to wipe the stinging sweat out of his eyes and to dry his hands. Stuffing the sock into the waistband of his shorts, he reached back for the wrench. His hand moved too quickly and knocked the wrench loose from the bolt. Coy's heart stopped as he dove with both hands to catch the tool. He grabbed it inside the bars, against one calf, and held it there, stock-still, until he was certain it was not going to slip away from him. For a terrible split-instant, he had pictured the wrench falling noisily to the steel floor of the gun gallery's top tier, completely out of his reach. He sucked in a gasping breath and carefully worked the wrench up his leg until he had it in a firm grip again.

Coy put the crescent on the nut and with both hands forced it around a twenty-seventh time. The bars spread to eight and three-eighths inches. He gritted his teeth and forced it again. Even with the axle grease, it took every ounce of Coy's strength to pull the handle all the way around. But finally it was upright again. Twenty-eight times. Eight and a half inches.

Grimly, he closed his hands around the handle and began forcing it for the first of four more turns. He needed nine inches between the round bars.

•

"I'll get you for this, Corwin!" Crazy Sam Shockley, drenched from the waist up, was screaming from his D Block cell. "You cocksucker, I'll get you! I'll get you!"

Corwin, at the end of the range talking to Burch, shook his head. "The only thing he's going to get is a dark cell again and four slices of bread a day. Weinhold will keep him in solitary for a month this time."

Burch nodded agreement. "I can't figure why they don't ship him off to Springfield and stick him in a violent cell. Keeping him locked up here isn't doing any good. One of these days he's just going to hurt himself. Or somebody else."

"That's for sure," said Corwin. He rubbed his chin uncomfortably. "In a way I hate to see him go to a dark cell. He's just not *responsible*, Bert."

Burch shrugged. "It's not up to us, Ceece. The captain has to decide that. And you know as well as I do what he'll decide."

Corwin nodded resignedly. "The hole."

"That's it," said Burch. He shifted the rifle to his other hand. "Well, I guess I'll wander back to the big room so Bill Miller don't get lonesome."

"Miller?" said Corwin. "I thought Ernie Lageson was on now."

"Bill and Ernie traded lunch times today," Burch said. He started back for the door leading into the main gallery. "See you later, Ceece."

•

At the east end of A Block, Cretzer and Thompson just watched Chief Steward Bristow come in through the main cellhouse door and start down Broadway. Cretzer, not wanting to leave the sallyport unobserved, rolled over and bobbed his chin at Thompson.

"You take him, Buddy," he said. "Get behind him at the cutoff. That way he'll be caught between you and Hubbard."

"Check," Thompson replied. He shimmied back, quietly descended the spiral stairs, and hurried down the A Block aisle.

Cretzer, frowning slightly, watched him go. He was a little worried about the men Bernie Coy had picked for the break. This guy Thompson, a Texas gunny who might or might not be reliable; the Indio Kid, a goddamned Mexican who *definitely* wasn't to be trusted with any important moves; and that hillbilly Hubbard, who had a reputation for getting himself all shot up every time he turned around. It was Coy's break, Cretzer realized, and Coy had the right to pick his men. That was fine—as long as everything went according to plan. But the first time something went wrong, the first time one of Coy's selections doped off and didn't carry his weight, then he, Dutch Cretzer, would have to step in. Cretzer had a lot riding on this break; he wasn't about to let it be screwed up by some punk.

As he watched Buddy Thompson disappear around the far end of A, Cretzer thought how much better he would feel when they got into D Block and let Sam Shockley out. Sam wasn't that bright, Cretzer knew. Maybe he was even a little bit crazy, like they said. But Cretzer had been in on one break with Shockley, and he had celled next to him off and on during his five years in Isolation. There was one thing about Shockley that Cretzer knew he could count on. When it came to doing exactly as Dutch Cretzer told him to do, Sam Shockley was as dependable as they came.

Cretzer was not going to feel that the crashout was completely under control until he had Crazy Sam at his side.

•

Chief Steward Bristow walked casually down Broadway past the cutoff. Ahead of him he could see the cellhouse desk with a blue-coated, blue-capped figure seated behind it, bent over as if doing paperwork. Bristow did not look too closely at the figure. He was thinking about the supper menu already, as usual trying to think of some way it could be improved. The food on Alcatraz was already far and away better than that served in Leavenworth or Atlanta or any other federal penitentiary. And it was not simply because of the calorie allowance either, although that certainly was a major asset. Each inmate on the Rock who was not on a restricted diet as punishment was allowed 3600 calories per day, which was roughly one-third more than the allowance in other prisons. The extra calorie ration had been put into effect under the same theory as the unlimited roll-your-own tobacco ration. That theory was that well-fed convicts who had enough cigarettes were subconsciously more content and less liable to cause trouble than if they had daily complaints about the food and lack of smokes.

Bristow was a conscientious steward. He took pride in his work and constantly made an effort to improve not only the quality but the variety of prisoner meals. For the most part, he succeeded. Alcatraz inmates, whether they ever admitted it or not, generally were well satisfied with and enjoyed the meals they were served. It could be said that in the severest, most restrictive prison in the country, mealtime was the one small pleasure remaining. Only for chronic malcontents like Dutch Cretzer, mental deficients like Sam Shockley, and those few like Bernie Coy whose desire for freedom was a relentless pressure, were the meals not important. Bristow was well aware as he walked down Broadway that some inmates would never appreciate his culinary efforts; but he was also convinced that for many, the meals he served were a small contribution to their ultimate rehabilitation.

So engrossed was Bristow in his own thoughts, that he was not aware of Buddy Thompson stepping out of the cutoff behind him and slowly moving closer to him. He did not become aware that anything was wrong until he reached Times Square and saw that it was a convict instead of a guard at the cellhouse officer's desk.

Bristow froze in his steps and started to turn back. As he did, Marv Hubbard rose and came around the desk.

"Hold it, Chief," Hubbard said calmly.

Bristow heard footsteps behind him. He looked around and saw Buddy Thompson dangerously close, his hands closed into fists.

"I wouldn't do nothing dumb if I was you, Chief," Hubbard warned. "You been square with me in the kitchen, so I don't want to see you get hurt."

Bristow turned sideways in a slight crouch so that he could see both convicts with a minimum movement of his eyes. A quick upward glance told him that the gun gallery was empty. In the course of that sweeping glance, he saw what appeared to be a naked Bernie Coy doing something high atop the upper tier of the cage. Bristow closed his own hands into fists as Marv Hubbard came a step closer.

"You know you ain't no match for both of us, Mr. Bristow," Hubbard said rationally. "How about just walking nice and easy around to 403 to join Mr. Miller? That way you keep from getting all beat up."

Evaluating the situation, Bristow concluded that Hubbard was right. There was no way he could come out on top resisting the thick-armed kitchen orderly on one side and a second con ready to jump him from the other. It was better to surrender without violence and perhaps be able to do something intelligent later on. Bristow put his hands down and nodded.

"Okay, Hubbard."

As Hubbard and Thompson led him along Times Square, Bristow

glanced up at Coy again. What the hell was he doing up there? he wondered. And more important, where was Bert Burch while all this was going on?

•

Above the upper tier of the gun gallery, Bernie Coy was also thinking about Bert Burch.

Coy now had the round bars spread to nine full inches, giving him an elliptical opening measuring eighteen by nine inches. Twisting and squirming, he was relentlessly forcing his body through that opening. It was a grueling, painful ordeal. Despite the thinness of his dieted frame, despite the natural lubrication of his sweat-covered body, the toolproof steel scraped his skin raw in more than one place as he literally *drove* parts of his body through the restricted opening. With the weight of his torso, he punished his hips for agonizing seconds until they were through. Then he kicked and jerked with his dangling legs as the rough steel dug some of the hair out of his chest and lacerated one of his nipples until it seeped blood. Finally, choking, almost strangling for breath, his eyes streaking tears, his whole being so wracked with pain that for the first time in years he was unaware of his ruined gums aching, Coy battered first one shoulder, then the other, down past the brutal bars. He dragged a layer of skin off one collarbone, but it was worth it. At last, he soundlessly dropped nine feet into the top tier of the gallery.

The floor was ice cold on the bottom of his one bare foot, and the sudden termination of all the tension and strain caused him to experience a quick chill and shiver. He was breathing so heavily that he had to exert conscious effort not to pant audibly. His lower lip trembled uncontrollably. With shaking hands he put back on the sock he had taken off. Then he untied the crescent wrench he had hung down into the cage with the shoelace from his tool bag.

His whole physical and mental being was shot with anxiety, pain, and dread fear as Coy padded silently down the gun gallery ladder to the lower level. He held his breath all the way, until he could peer through the rungs into the lower tier. The enormous relief he felt when he saw that the gallery was still empty almost made him cry out. He had to muffle a half laugh, half sobbing sigh, to keep from making a noise.

Stepping onto the four-foot-wide gun range, Coy instinctively fell into a crouch and moved down-tier. His eyes were wide, his jaw slack, the crescent wrench held at the ready. As he moved, he was acutely aware of the abuse to which he had just put his body. The muscles of both arms felt strained from the effort of turning the nut on the bar spreader. His hips and shoulders felt as if he had been beaten and kicked. His ribcage and collarbone ached mercilessly; his scraped nipple throbbed. And the incredible part of it, he thought, was that he had done all that to himself in just over three minutes. To Coy, it seemed as if at least an hour had passed.

Jesus, he told himself, *if I can just get out, if I can just make it this one last time, I'll never do anything to get put back in prison again. I swear it. I'll find some other way to live. I'll—*

His thoughts dissolved to cold fear again as he saw the D Block gallery door beginning to open.

CHAPTER TWELVE

1:54 P.M.

The break, astonishingly, was only fourteen minutes old when Bert Burch returned to the main cellhouse from D Block. As he unsuspectingly pushed open the door to the main section of the gun gallery, he was thinking what a pity it was that nothing could be done for poor, pathetic misfits like Sam Shockley. Nothing, that is, except keep them in permanent lockup. If only doctors could devise a way to repair crippled minds the way they did crippled bodies. Maybe then places like Alcatraz would not be necessary.

With that contemplative thought, Burch strolled back through the D Block door. He was alert but not wary; observant but not cautious. And no reason to be. The very last thing to enter Bert Burch's imagination was that a con could penetrate his gun gallery.

But at that very moment, Bernie Coy, having covered the last twenty feet of the cage in a frantic, desperate dash, was behind the door as it opened.

As the self-closing door pulled shut behind Burch, Coy swung at his head with the crescent wrench. Ordinarily, a well-placed blow to the head with such an instrument would have rendered a man unconscious. But Coy's reflexes were slowed by his strained and aching muscles; he swung with determination, but that was all. It was a clumsy blow.

The wrench struck Burch a glancing rap across the side of the head. He stumbled forward, dropping his rifle, surprised more than stunned. Whirling around, he faced his attacker in wide-eyed disbelief.

"Coy! What the hell—?"

Coy moved forward and swung the wrench again. Burch, alert now, grabbed Coy's wrist, jerked him forward, and drove his fist into the convict's face. The crescent wrench clattered to the floor. With the heel of his free hand, Coy clubbed Burch in the eye. The guard and the convict stood toe to toe then, slugging it out in the narrow cage, trading punch for punch like two contenders for a vacant title.

In seconds, their faces and fists were red with blood.

•

On the flats below, Marv Hubbard and Buddy Thompson had just turned Chief Steward Bristow over to the Indio Kid to be held in Cell 403. Coming back onto Times Square, they saw Coy and Burch locked in combat in the cage above them. They stood and watched helplessly as Coy fought furiously for control of the gun gallery.

"Come on, Bernie," Hubbard said tightly, not even aware that he was speaking. "Come on, Bernie, take him. Take him!" Beside Hubbard, Buddy Thompson alternately watched the fight and the nearby D Block door with its observation window. Accustomed to working alone and having to cover every danger spot himself, Thompson was acutely aware that D Block officer Cecil Corwin not only could look out and see them, but also was safe from them in the isolation block and could use the block telephone to sound the alarm.

It'll be a miracle if we pull this goddamned thing off, he thought edgily.

•

At the east end of A Block, Dutch Cretzer was still lying on his stomach, peering around the corner of the middle tier at the main cellhouse entrance. Every twenty seconds or so, he kept looking behind him at the spiral stairway. Thompson should be back by now, he thought. He wondered if Hubbard and Thompson had run into trouble with Bristow. Surely to Christ the two of them could handle one lousy screw. Jesus. He wondered too if Coy had been able to take the gun cage yet. I should have stayed back on Times Square, he thought, so I'd know what was going on. Somebody else could be up at the end of A, watching the sallyport. Hubbard could be doing it; hell, it didn't take any brains.

The cellhouse door opened and Cretzer tensed. He heard brief, muted voices, and then Ernest Lageson, the cellhouse officer, came through the door. Cretzer gritted his teeth.

Goddamn! Of all the hacks who could have walked in at that moment, Lageson was the *last* one Cretzer wanted to see. There was no telling where the hell Thompson and Hubbard were. He himself was alone; if he left the A Block lookout, a dozen screws could breeze in unannounced at any time. Now in walks Lageson, one of the sharpest guards on the Rock. Son of a *bitch!*

Cretzer waited until he saw Lageson turn into Broadway. Then he rolled over, sat up, and quickly pulled off his shoes. Jumping to his feet, he held the shoes in one arm like a football, hurried down the stairs, and ran as fast as he could down to the cutoff aisle leading to Michigan Boulevard.

Once on Michigan, ignoring the excited faces of the lockup cons who were watching him, Cretzer continued his frantic dash to get to Times Square before Lageson did.

•

In the gun gallery, Coy and Burch, still punching with wild abandon, suddenly connected with accidentally accurate, simultaneous punches, and went falling back away from each other. Burch bumped the back of his head on the hard floor and sat up groggily. Coy slammed back against the gallery wall and bounced to the floor, scraping the skin off one elbow. He too sat up, his nose bleeding, choking momentarily on blood he had swallowed.

Burch shook the cloudiness from his head and saw Coy sitting several feet away. He seized the opportunity to reach for his pistol. During the struggle with Coy, his holster had slipped around to his back. He twisted a hand behind him to pull it back. He was aware that Coy, spitting blood, was watching him with wide, terrified eyes. As Burch clawed awkwardly at his holster, he found himself wondering in almost detached fashion if he would shoot Coy or merely apprehend him. There had never been a shot fired inside the big cellhouse. The noise, especially of a .45, would be ear-splitting.

Burch did not have to make the decision. He got the holster back around to his side and was just pulling the flap open, when Coy, with what he was sure was the absolute last ounce of energy in him, threw himself forward and snatched up the guard's fallen rifle. Just as Burch's fingers touched the checkered walnut grips of his pistol, Coy smashed the stock of the rifle against his head. Burch dropped like a waterlogged rope.

Panting and bleeding, Coy clawed his way to his feet and leaned against the vertical bars. He saw Hubbard and Thompson staring up at him. Coy raised the rifle over his head and smiled a bloody half-smile. He had captured the gun gallery!

Hubbard and Thompson exchanged excited grins. It was written in each of their faces what they were thinking. *We're going to make it! We've got guns!*

At that moment, Dutch Cretzer hurried onto Times Square from around the corner of B Block. He saw Coy with the rifle, saw Hubbard and Thompson at the end of C.

"Watch it!" he called softly to all of them. "Lageson's coming down Broadway!"

Coy immediately dropped out of sight behind the waist-high steel of the gallery. He crawled over to the unconscious Burch and took the automatic pistol from the guard's holster. Crawling down to where he would be out of the approaching officer's line of sight, he cautiously stood back up in the cage. His eyes swept Times Square. Hubbard and Thompson were flattened against the end of C Block, both poised to strike. On the other side of Broadway, Dutch Cretzer was flattened against the end of B Block, holding up one of his heavy shoes as a weapon. Coming very close, almost to the end of Broadway, were Officer Ernest Lageson's steady footsteps.

Cretzer looked up at Coy, thinking: Jesus, he looks like he's been run over by a Mack truck. But it was obvious that Coy, as always, knew exactly what he was doing. He bobbed his chin at Cretzer and hooked his right arm through the bars. Cretzer, seeing what Coy was going to do, smiled.

Coy tossed the .45 down and Dutch Cretzer, dropping the shoe, deftly caught it. Flipping it over in his hands, Cretzer jerked back the slide and threw a round into the chamber. The click of the gun's action corresponded exactly with Ernest Lageson's last two steps as he walked onto Times Square.

"Hold it right there, screw," Cretzer warned coldly. "One funny move and you'll be a dead son of a bitch!"

•

Hubbard and Thompson took Lageson and shoved him roughly around the corner onto Seedy Street to Cell 403.

"Here's another one for you, Kid," Hubbard said to Durando with a grin. "They're really biting today." He paused and looked at the three guards they now held captive. "Just so you'll know, Kid," he said for the benefit of the guards, "Bernie just took the gun cage— and the guns."

Inside the cell, Bristow and Lageson exchanged fearful glances. Bristow, with Dan Durando's permission, was holding a cold, wet handkerchief to the unconscious Bill Miller's forehead.

"Me and Buddy got to get back, Kid," Hubbard said. "Can you handle them okay?"

"Yeah, go on," the Indio Kid replied.

Hubbard and Thompson joined Dutch Cretzer on the Times Square flats. They all looked up at the gallery as a bloody-faced Bernie Coy choreographed their next moves.

"Buddy, you get back over to A where you can watch the sallyport. Marv, you man that desk again so you can see anybody coming down Broadway. Dutch, you get over by the D Block door with that rod. I'm going into the D side of the cage and throw down on Corwin. When he opens the door, take his keys and give him to the Kid to put in 403. Then I'll tell you how to work the panel to let Shockley out."

Thompson and Hubbard hurried off as soon as Coy told them what to do. Cretzer waved the .45 in acknowledgment and headed for the D Block door.

After checking again to make sure Burch was still unconscious, Coy threw a round into the chamber of the Springfield and went down to the D Block gallery door. The sweat was beginning to dry on his near-naked body now, and he shivered slightly and sneezed twice. He rubbed his watery eyes on the back of one hand, then pulled open the door and moved cautiously into the other area of the gallery. Down on the flats he saw Cecil Corwin sitting at his desk. Louis Fleish was leaning back against one of the steam radiators, talking with him. Coy trained the rifle on Corwin.

"Hey, Corwin," he said in a normal tone.

The men looked up at him; their eyes widened in stunned surprise. "Coy—?" Corwin said, as if he did not believe what he saw.

"Yeah, it's me, all right, Corwin," the convict assured him. "This rifle is cocked and ready to fire, so do like I say. Get your keys and open the door over there."

From the middle tier, Shockley started yelling. "Bernie! Bernie, you made it, you made it!"

"Yeah, I made it, Sam. We'll have you out in a minute." He bobbed his chin at the guard. "Come on, Corwin, move."

"There's no way you'll get away with it, Coy," the D Block guard warned.

Louis Fleish, always the gambler, had already calculated the odds on their predicament. "Better do what he says, Mr. Corwin," he told the guard. "He's got you cold."

"Wait'll I get my hands on you, Corwin, you cocksucker!" Shockley yelled at him.

"Goddamn it, Sam, shut up!" Coy ordered. "Corwin, get that door open or I'll drill you!"

The guard glanced apprehensively up at Shockley, then back at the rifle Coy held. The thought of Shockley being let out frankly terrified him; but the more imminent threat came from the rifle. If there had been an open cell, or anyplace else in the block where he could have ducked for cover, Corwin would have chanced it. But he was caught in an open area, on the flats. There was no place to hide except behind his wooden desk. And at such close range, in the face of the high-powered Springfield, that would have been like taking cover behind an open newspaper. So Cecil Corwin did as Coy told him to.

As soon as the D Block door opened, Dutch Cretzer grabbed Corwin and dragged him into C Block. "All right, screw, you're *taking* orders now!" he growled.

Louis Fleish hurried over to the door. "Take it easy with him, Dutch," he said.

"You mind your own goddamn business, Fleish," Cretzer snapped. He manhandled Corwin down to Cell 403. "Get your ass in there!" he said, shoving him roughly into the cell. The Indio Kid threw Cretzer an annoyed look. It wasn't necessary to push Corwin around like that. But the Kid said nothing.

As Cretzer ran back into D Block, he could hear Crazy Sam yelling. "The dirty cocksucker got me all wet! I'm going to kill him!"

"Shut up!" Coy ordered from the gallery. "You ain't going to kill nobody!" Coy looked down as Cretzer ran in. "Dutch, you got to keep him under control. I don't want no guards hurt. We'll need every one of them as hostages to get down to the dock."

"I'll handle him. Just tell me how to get him out."

"Open that second control panel," Coy instructed. "The one closest to the door."

Cretzer hurried to the end wall of the block and opened the panel door. The first thing he saw was a plate which read: DOOR OPERATING LOCKING AND INDICATING SYSTEM. CENTRAL RAILWAY SIGNAL CO. ROCHESTER, NEW YORK. "What now?" he yelled to Coy.

"Move that indicator from the word *Group* to the word *Individual.* Then find the switch under Number 22. Flip it from *Close* to *Open.* Now push that bottom lever down."

Cretzer followed instructions and heard Shockley yell gleefully, "I'm out! I'm out!"

"Watch him, Dutch," Coy warned again.

Then he hurried back into the main gallery.

•

By now, Bernie Coy's aching, bleeding body was wracked by relentless shivering. Jesus, I'm freezing, he thought. He sneezed three times in quick succession. Got to get warm.

Back in the main gallery, he laid the rifle down and stripped off Bert Burch's uniform trousers and coat. Putting them on, he immediately felt less chilled. Although Burch, like Coy, was lean and rangy, the guard's clothes were too large for the convict. But they were warm, and that was all that concerned Coy.

"Marv," Coy called quietly down to the flats, "grab this stuff as I toss it down."

Hubbard got up from the cellhouse desk and moved over so that he would be out of sight of anyone coming down Broadway. When Hubbard was ready, Coy began dropping the gun gallery's supplies to him: Burch's rifle and gunbelt, the extra ammunition, three billy clubs, and the all-important key rack.

"Okay, I'm coming down," Coy said, when the gun cage was stripped.

"What about Burch?" Marv Hubbard asked.

"There's nothing I can do but leave him here. But it don't matter. We'll be long gone by the time he comes to."

Coy picked up the crescent wrench and returned to the upper tier. Retrieving the bar spreader, which he had rested across an unspread section of bars, he quickly screwed it down to five inches and seated it near one cross-bar of the spread section. With the wrench, he moved the nut around and around until the end of the bars had moved an inch. Then he did the same thing with the spreader at the other end of the section. The work took him less than ninety seconds; but they were a precious ninety seconds that he could not have spared getting into the gallery.

The extra inch at each end of the elliptical opening made all the difference in the world. Even wearing Burch's clothes, Coy was able to get back through the bars with very little strain. In less than two minutes, he was climbing back down to the flats of Times Square.

•

There were now four prison officers in Cell 403. Lageson and Corwin, the two most recent captives, were standing near the door.

Bristow was on his knees next to the bunk, still applying a cold, wet handkerchief to Bill Miller's forehead. Presently, Miller began to come around. He swallowed and blinked several times. When his eyes focused on Ernest Lageson, he forced a wry smile. "Last time I ever trade lunches with you," he said quietly.

Lageson felt bad about it. "I'm sorry, Bill. I know it should be me lying there."

"Forget it. I was only kidding."

Lageson glanced at Cecil Corwin, who looked the most apprehensive of all of them. He and Corwin, both scholarly types, were close friends. Lageson himself was studying nights to become a teacher. He often discussed Shakespeare with the older guard. At the moment, he had no way of knowing that Corwin was thinking of Crazy Sam Shockley. "Take it easy, Ceece," Lageson said. "We'll get out of it okay."

The cellhouse officer took a step toward the open door. Danny Durando eyed him suspiciously.

"Just stay right there, Mr. Lageson," the young Chicano warned.

"You don't have a gun, Danny," said Lageson. "What would you do if I came out?"

"You know what I'd do, Mr. Lageson," Durando replied.

"Think you could handle all of us, Dan?" Lageson asked.

The Indio Kid grinned. "You have to come out that door one at a time, Mr. Lageson. I wouldn't even work up a sweat."

Lageson raised his eyebrows. "Know something, Dan? I believe it."

"That's good," said the Kid, nodding. "Makes it easier on both of us."

Lageson pursed his lips and looked thoughtfully at Dan Durando for a moment. "You know, Kid, I never would have expected you to be in on a fool thing like this."

The young Chicano shrugged. "I'm doing the book, Mr. Lageson. If I don't crash out, I'll probably end up like the Birdman."

"That's nonsense, Dan," the cellhouse officer said easily, but with obvious sincerity. "Hell, you're just a kid. You'd do maybe fifteen years, maximum; then they'd turn you loose on parole. You'd be in the prime of your life, barely past thirty."

"Yeah, but I got no guarantee I'd get out," Durando argued. "This way, at least I got a chance."

Lageson shook his head in pity. "Do you really believe you can get off the Rock, Dan?"

The Kid smiled a brilliant smile. "We ain't doing too bad so far, Mr. Lageson," he pointed out.

As Durando spoke, he heard a commotion across the flats, near the now open D Block door. Looking over, he saw a convict in a soaking wet shirt, pulling away from Dutch Cretzer and heading toward the cell where Durando was holding the guards. Inside the cell, Cecil Corwin's face drained of color. "I knew it," he said in cold dread. "I knew he'd come for me." Lageson and the others looked at Corwin curiously. He edged as far away from the door as he could.

Shockley stalked up to Durando, whom he had never met, never even seen before. "You got Corwin in there?" he asked angrily.

"Yeah, he's in there," Durando said.

"Get him out here!" Shockley ordered.

Durando, standing directly in front of the cell door, said, "What for?"

"Because he got me all wet, that's what the fuck for!" Shockley spat. "Now get him out here, I'm gonna stomp his fucking face in!"

Durando shook his head. "Coy don't want no guards hurt, pal."

Shockley put his face close to Durando's. "I want Corwin, you brown-skinned nigger! Get the fuck out of my way!"

Durando glanced over at Cretzer, who was coming toward them. "Dutch, you better get this guy away from me before I have to hurt him—"

As Durando was speaking, Shockley jumped him. The D Block convict closed his hands around Durando's throat and lunged against him, throwing him back against the adjoining cell. In 403, Lageson moved tentatively toward the open cell door, contemplating a dash down the Seedy Street flats to the sallyport entry. Before he could try it, Dutch Cretzer came up.

"Get your ass back in there, Lageson," he snapped, leveling Burch's automatic at him. "You two fools cut it out!" he shouted at Durando and Shockley, who were struggling against the front of Cell 402.

Dan Durando had his back to the bars, with Shockley choking him angrily. Putting his two fists together, the Kid brought them up hard, like a wedge, and broke the maddened convict's stranglehold. Opening his hands, he slammed his palms against Shockley's shoulders and pushed him back two feet. Then, when he had made room, he dug a vicious fist into Crazy Sam's stomach. Shockley blanched, doubled up, and pitched to the floor.

"That's enough, Mexican," Cretzer said to Durando, half turning the gun toward him.

At that moment, Bernie Coy came running up. He was wearing Bert Burch's uniform, had a billy stuck in his belt, and was carrying the Springfield and his convict clothing. His face had begun to puff up from the fight he had with Burch. "What the hell's all the racket?" he demanded.

"He wanted me to give him one of the hacks," Durando said, bobbing his chin at the fallen Shockley. The Kid was clenching and unclenching his fist. Jesus, it felt good to hit a man again!

Coy stepped over and pulled Shockley to his feet. "These guards ain't going to be hurt, Sam," he said evenly, his dark eyes fixing Shockley in a flat, warning stare. "I mean it. They're the tickets we need to get on that boat. I'm *telling* you not to touch any of them, understand?"

"That cocksucker Corwin got me all wet," Shockley whined. He hugged his shoulders. "I'm cold."

Coy handed the rifle to Durando and took off Burch's uniform coat. "Get out of that wet shirt and put this on, Sam," he said, handing him the coat.

Shockley's eyes brightened at the thought of wearing a guard coat. "Thanks, Bernie!" he said with delight.

Coy put his convict shirt back on and stepped over to 403. His eyes settled on Lageson. "What time you got now, Mr. Lageson?" he asked wryly.

Lageson looked at his watch. "Two o'clock, straight up."

Coy held out his hand. "I'll take the watch. You see, I *am* going somewhere, Lageson. And I'm on a time schedule." He snatched the watch from Lageson and strapped it onto his wrist. "All right now, everybody listen," he said crisply. "We're running five or six minutes behind schedule, but that's okay because I had an extra ten minutes built into the plan just in case. We've still got plenty of time to make it, but we ain't got no time to *waste*. I want to be ready to head for the wall in five minutes." He looked at Shockley, who had pulled on Burch's coat. "Sam, go over to the east end of A. You'll find a guy there named Buddy Thompson. Tell him we're getting ready to go and the two of you get back here quick."

"Okay, Bernie," he said meekly. He hurried toward the cutoff.

"Dutch," said Coy, "you go out to the desk and tell Marv to get Key 107 off that rack. Get it and meet me at the yard door."

"Check," said Cretzer.

"Kid," Coy turned to Durando, "you keep these gentlemen in the cell until I tell you different. Use this if you have to," he handed him the billy from his belt. "I'm going into D and check the south side from the windows in there."

Before he left, Coy looked over at the cell bunk. Bill Miller was fully awake now and sitting up on the bunk. His bottom lip was badly swollen where Marv Hubbard had hit him.

"You okay, Miller?" Coy asked. It was the first time he had ever addressed the block officer without calling him mister.

"I'm okay, Coy," the guard answered. It was the first time Miller had ever called Coy by his last name.

The two men stared at each other for a moment, each realizing with new perspective the futility of any feeling between them. Each in his own way was a little sorry.

"Be back in a couple of minutes," Coy said finally to Durando, and trotted off.

•

After Coy left, the Indio Kid stepped across Seedy Street and leaned against the D Block wall, facing 403. Restlessly, he shifted the unfamiliar billy club from hand to hand. Idly, he wondered exactly what he would do after they got off the Rock. There would be a getaway car and a hideout: Coy had told him Dutch Cretzer had arranged that for them. So all six of them would probably be together for a while, at least until the heat was off. But then they would start splitting up—and that was what worried the Kid. He had no idea what he would do or where he would go when that happened. Coy and Hubbard, he knew, were real tight and would probably throw in together. The same was true of Cretzer and Shockley. Cretzer had friends waiting for him, but he would more than likely take Shockley along with him; they had been in on one other break together, and had celled side by side in the D Block lockup.

The Kid wondered about Buddy Thompson. He was the only one left who didn't have a partner to throw in with. He was tough and he was smart; a man could do worse when it came to picking a partner. But the more Durando considered the possibility, the more he decided it probably wouldn't work out. Thompson had a rep as a lone wolf; he had never worked with a partner. Besides, the Kid thought with a quiet sigh, Thompson was a Texan. He'd never throw in with a Chicano.

•

In Cell 403, as Dan Durando pondered his future, the four captive guards had a few brief moments of privacy.

"Do you think we should try rushing the Kid?" Bristow asked Lageson.

The cellhouse officer shook his head. "Not with that billy in his hand. He's as strong as an ox, that boy, and his hands move like a snake's tongue. We'd be clubbed to the floor before we could land a punch. Besides, Coy and Cretzer are armed now. Either one of them could come back at any time."

"I wonder if they killed Bert," said Cecil Corwin.

"I don't know," said Lageson. "There's a good chance they did."

"I don't think so," said Bill Miller. "Bernie Coy is too smart for that. Why do you think he's got the Kid protecting us from maniacs like Crazy Sam? He knows he has to keep all of us alive or he's got no chance at all of getting off the island."

"You may be right," Lageson allowed. "I hope you are. I hope Bert's just tied up or knocked out up there in that cage."

"If they use us as hostages," said Cecil Corwin, "what do you think is going to happen when we get out in the yard?"

"Yeah," said Bristow. "What about the men in the towers? Will they fire as long as the cons are holding us?"

"I don't think the tower guards will have to make that decision," Bill Miller said quietly. He got up and reached over to the sink to rewet the cold handkerchief which he was now holding to his swelling lip. Glancing back to make certain that the Indio Kid was still out of hearing range, he leaned closer to Lageson and said, "I've got 107. It's in my pants pocket."

Lageson's eyes widened slightly and his lips parted incredulously. Bristow and Corwin both looked at Miller in disbelief. "It's against regulations for that key to be in the cellhouse except when it's actually being used," Lageson said in little more than a whisper. "What in hell are you doing with it?"

"Burch was in the top tier of the cage when I got ready to send it back up. So I just held onto it to let the kitchen orderlies into the yard."

"Jesus," said Bristow, "that could cost you your job, Bill. Keeping that key in the cellhouse is about the worst rule you could have broken."

"Right now you ought to be damned glad I *did* break it," Miller whispered. "Without 107, they can't haul us out into the yard and use us as shields."

"That's right," Lageson said thoughtfully. "Without that key, they can't leave the cellhouse. They'll be trapped."

Lageson looked at each man in turn, his trained custodian's mind racing as he weighed the convicts' chances in the yard against their chances in the cellhouse. He swiftly concluded that the best tactic was to keep them in the cellhouse, keep them contained.

Turning his back to the cell door, Lageson held out his hand. "Give it to me."

Miller slipped Key 107 out of his pocket and passed it to Lageson.

•

In D Block, Coy stood near the center of the top tier, looking out at the southwest side of the island compound. There was no sign of unusual activity of any kind. Below him, Louis Fleish watched from near Corwin's desk. Presently, Coy returned to the flats.

"So you went and did it, Barney," he said in the neutral tone of a card player.

Coy walked over to him. "I think I can make it, Louie. We've got two guns and four screws as hostages."

Fleish raised his eyebrows, impressed. "That's a good start," he admitted. For a brief instant he felt a tinge of regret that he was not going along. Then he thought about the final odds and was satisfied not to be a part of it.

"Gotta be going, Louie," Coy said.

"Good luck, Barney."

Coy nodded and started back for the C Block door. Before he got there, someone called to him.

"That you down there, Bernie?"

Coy recognized Robert Stroud's voice from the end of the top tier. "Yeah, Bob, it's me. What do you want?"

"How about racking me out?" the Birdman said. "I haven't left this tier in more than three years. Be nice to take a little unscheduled walk."

Coy thought about it for a moment. He looked at the faces watching him from the upper tiers. All the Isolation cons were standing at their cell doors, staring excitedly at Bernie Coy and the rifle he held. Poor bastards, Coy thought. Locked up all day, all night, all the time. Let them out? Goddamned right he would!

"Okay, Bob," he announced from the middle of Sunset Boulevard,

"I'm going to rack you open. As a matter of fact, I'll rack you all open!"

A rousing cheer went up from the D Block cons. Coy grinned and held up his hand to quiet them down.

"Just one condition," he said loudly. "Nobody leaves the block. Nobody, understand? We've got guards we're holding on the other side, and I don't want nobody in my way when me and my boys take them out and head for the dock. So everybody stay in D Block."

Coy went to the control box that operated the middle and top tiers. He threw the indicator to *Group*, flipped all the switches to *Open*, and pushed the control lever down. It unlocked all but the eight segregation cells and the six dark cells on the flats. From D-14, the most isolated of the dark cells, came a fervent plea.

"Hey! Hey, whoever's out there! Somebody let me out of here!"

As the D Block cons started straggling down the stairs onto the flats, Coy trotted over to D-14. He used Corwin's keys to open the outer solid door of guard-killer Whitey Franklin's cell. Beyond the access area just inside, Franklin clung to the barred front of his cell with a wild, desperate expression. Coy stared at him. He had not seen Franklin in nearly eight years, since Franklin and his two partners had tried their break. Few cons had *ever* seen him. Some of the old-timers, like Coy and Machine Gun Kelly, vaguely remembered him, but Coy doubted if anyone would have recognized him. He was thirty-four, but looked a dozen years older. His hair, which had been thick and full, had fallen out in scattered patches. His skin was dry and parched, and was a doughy color from his long years of lockup. His eyes, unaccustomed to much light, were in a constant squint. Because he spoke so rarely, his vocal chords were tight, his voice strained.

"Who are you?" Franklin almost demanded, as Coy came into the access area.

"Bernard Coy," the escape leader said. "I'm from Kentucky. In for bank robbery."

Franklin nodded. "Yeah. Yeah, I think I remember you." He blinked several times, looking puzzled. "I'm Rufus Franklin," he said after a moment.

"I know."

"You're crashing out, huh?"

"Yeah."

"Take me with you?"

"Can't, Whitey," said Coy. He nudged the inside cell door with his toe. "This door is controlled from the gun gallery. I was in the gun gallery but I didn't think to open the dark cells."

Whitey Franklin stared at him through his pathetically squinted eyes. With an oddly purplish tongue, he wet his flaky-skinned lips. "How many going out on the break?" he asked.

"Six, including me," said Coy.

"Of the six, who's been on the Rock the longest?"

"I have," Coy answered.

"When'd you get here?"

"July of '37."

Whitey Franklin's expression turned glacier-hard. "Do you know that except for my trial, I've been in this fucking cell all but ten months of your whole time on the Rock?"

"I know, Whitey."

Franklin pressed his desperate face to the door. His hands were gripping the bars so tightly that his knuckles had squeezed white. His voice was hoarsening. "Go back up to the cage, Coy," he pleaded. "Let me out."

Coy looked at Lageson's watch. "I wish I could, but I ain't got time," he said self-consciously. He wished to hell he had never come over to Franklin's cell. "I'm sorry, Whitey."

Whitey Franklin stared at him for a moment. Then he nodded in reluctant understanding. He turned away from Coy and lowered himself slowly to the floor of his empty cell and sat on the cold, hard cement he had been sitting on for nearly eight years. He hung his head. Then his shoulders began to jerk with sobs.

Coy stepped out of the access area onto the flats. Face pale, mouth a thin line, he moved through the silent, staring D Block prisoners, blinking his eyes rapidly. He hurried toward the door back to C Block.

•

As soon as he stepped into the main cellhouse, Coy forced Whitey Franklin from his mind.

"Okay, Kid, time to go," he called tensely to Dan Durando as he ran down Seedy Street. He waved the rifle at the four guards in 403. "Move out of there in single file and head for the yard door," he ordered. "Kid, go see what's keeping Cretzer with that key."

Durando trotted on ahead as Coy herded the four guards across Times Square to the yard door. Glancing down the flats, Coy saw

Hubbard and Cretzer at the cellhouse officer's desk. They appeared to be arguing. Coy's face tightened in a slight frown. Beyond the desk he saw Shockley hurrying back from A Block with Buddy Thompson.

Lining the guards up at the door, Coy yelled across the flats at the others. "Get a move on!"

At the sound of Coy's voice, Dutch Cretzer turned from the cellhouse desk and jogged over to him. Cretzer's expression as he came up to Coy was tense, bordering on anger.

"Hubbard says 107's not in the key box," he said.

CHAPTER THIRTEEN

2:11 P.M.

Bernie Coy's frown deepened as Cretzer's words registered. Cretzer's voice had an abrasive edge to it, and he was handling the .45 automatic as if he were only a fraction away from using it on someone. Coy knew that Cretzer had a short fuse when things did not go as planned.

"Take it easy, Dutch," he said in as calm a tone as he could muster. "The key's there somewhere. I'll find it. You watch these guys. And relax, Dutch. Okay?"

"Okay, okay," Cretzer replied shortly. "Just find the goddamned key and let's get out of here!"

Coy ran over to the desk. Hubbard, Durando, Shockley, and Thompson were all standing there, looking helpless and indecisive.

"The key ain't here, Bernie," Hubbard said weakly, as if it might conceivably be his fault.

"I'll look for it," Coy said.

"I've checked every one of them, Bernie."

"You could have missed it, Marv," Coy told him with a trace of irritation. Seeing them all standing around like dummies made him nervous. He bobbed his head down the flats. "Go over to West B and look out the window. See if you can see the pier from there. Look for the launch." He turned to the others. "Buddy, you and Sam beat it up to the cutoff and each take a side of Broadway in case somebody else comes in. Here," he tossed the rifle to Thompson. "Kid," he said to Durando, "go over and help Dutch keep those screws in line."

Everyone departed and Coy sat down at the cellhouse desk. Beginning to sweat again, acutely aware of their rapidly diminishing time schedule, he began a careful, systematic examination of all the keys on the rack he had dropped from the west gun gallery.

•

Back in the cellhouse kitchen, Officer Joe Burdette glanced at his watch and wondered what was keeping Bristow. Burdette's lunch was in the officers' lounge behind the armory and he could not go get it until the chief steward returned. Burdette was a big, husky man; he got hungry all over, and he had very little patience when it came to waiting for his meals. He could have found something to eat back there in the kitchen, but he did not want to; he wanted his own lunch, that his wife had prepared for him.

Glancing at the six orderlies who were still at work, Burdette went over and picked up the kitchen phone. Cliff Fish answered in the armory.

"You seen Bristow out there anywhere?" he asked Fish.

"I let him back in the cellhouse a few minutes ago," Fish said.

"He's probably out on Times Square talking to Miller and Lageson," the kitchen guard said, "while I'm back here starving to death."

"How can a man starve to death in a kitchen full of food?" Fish asked.

"It ain't easy," said Burdette.

"Relax," said Fish. "Bob will be back there in a minute. And you can take some time to eat today; the Old Man isn't in." The Old Man was the warden.

"Oh? Where is he?"

"He wasn't feeling well this morning, so he stayed over at the house," Fish said. The house Fish was talking about was a three-story mid-Victorian structure situated directly across the broad front plaza from the main cellhouse entry, close to the warden's office and the various administrative offices across the sallyport from the armory.

"Never thought I'd see the day when the Old Man would admit to not feeling well," Burdette said.

"He didn't admit it this time," Fish replied. "It was his wife who said he wasn't feeling well."

"Hope he didn't hear her say it," Burdette commented wryly.

Fish laughed. "See you when you come up to eat," he said. He unplugged the line.

Burdette, hanging up the kitchen phone, decided to go see if Bristow was on Times Square.

•

At the west end of B Block, Marv Hubbard climbed up on a steam radiator, holding on to the inside bars covering the windows, and looked out on the northeast side of the island, where the dock lay. Hubbard could not see the dock itself, but he did see the prison launch just making its turn to approach the landing pier.

Hubbard dropped from the window and ran around to the A Block aisle. Climbing up on another radiator, he managed to get a view of the dock itself. He watched the dock guard check several people who debarked: two women, probably wives of guards, a man with a briefcase who was probably coming to see the warden or associate warden, and one guard in civilian clothes coming back from a morning in town. When they had left the dock, the pilot of the launch stepped ashore and offered the dock guard a cigarette. The two men lighted up and stood talking.

Hubbard hopped off the radiator. If the boat was in, it was past two o'clock. Hubbard swore softly. Bernie's schedule had called for them to be in the yard long before this. The mix-up with Lageson and Miller switching lunches had thrown them off; it had caused Coy to have to come down to Times Square pretending to have to fix the blanket broom in order to check out the situation. Then Burch had put up a hell of a fight in the gun cage. Now the goddamn 107 key was lost. Everything seemed to be going wrong.

Hubbard hurried back over to the cellhouse desk. "The boat just got here, Bernie," he reported.

As Hubbard spoke, both he and Coy heard the distant slap of footsteps coming across the big dining hall. Coy's heart skipped a beat. He had completely forgotten about big Joe Burdette back in the kitchen.

"Get out of that doorway, quick!" he hissed.

•

Joe Burdette, just approaching the dining-hall door from the inside, saw someone move away from the cellhouse officer s desk; for a second it had seemed like a guard wearing mismatched trousers. But that was ridiculous, he told himself. It must have been a con wearing his dark pea coat. He wondered idly why a con would have on a winter coat on such a nice day.

As Burdette stepped out of the dining hall onto Times Square, he suddenly came face to face with Bernie Coy and Marv Hubbard. The big guard tensed, crouched slightly, and froze.

"Just stay where you are, Burdette," said Coy. He picked up one of the billy clubs. Next to him, Marv Hubbard pulled out the carving knife.

"Lay that knife down, Hubbard," Burdette said evenly. "That's an order."

"You ain't giving orders no more," Hubbard retorted. He took a step toward the guard.

"I'll break you in two, Hubbard," the big officer threatened. "Knife or no knife. You better put it down."

Just then, another voice spoke. It came from down Broadway. "Hold it right there, hack."

Burdette spun around and faced Buddy Thompson, holding a rifle. Standing near him was Sam Shockley. Burdette's mouth dropped open, and he stared at the two convicts.

"Stand real still or I'll plug you," Thompson warned.

Thompson and Shockley moved quickly onto Times Square. Coy tossed the club to Shockley. "Put him with the others."

Shockley raised the club threateningly. "Give me any lip and I'll split your skull with this," he warned. The billy was the first weapon Shockley had held in many years. It gave him an instant feeling of elation. He wanted desperately to use it on someone.

As Thompson and Shockley shoved Bristow toward the yard door, Coy gave Thompson a billy also and took back the rifle. Then Coy went immediately back to searching for the 107 key.

After a long two minutes, Coy finally looked up grimly at Hubbard.

"It's not here," he said quietly, puzzled. "The 107 key's not here."

"You think maybe it's still in the gun cage?" Hubbard asked.

Coy shook his head. "I stripped that gallery clean. Every key that was on that key rack is right here on this desk." A thought suddenly occurred to Coy. He turned and stared for a moment at the guards being held at the yard door. He pursed his lips and his eyes narrowed slightly. "Bring Miller over here," he said quietly.

Hubbard went over to the yard door and brought Officer Bill Miller over to Coy. Miller's face, with a badly swollen lower lip and a large, ugly bruise coloring the left cheek, looked almost as bad as Coy's. The escape leader had a puffy left eye with a small, drying cut in the eyebrow, a split in one corner of his mouth, dried blood around both nostrils, and a slanted, one-inch cut on the point of his chin.

When Hubbard delivered Miller to the desk, Coy said, "Go over to the end of C and keep an eye out down Broadway, Marv." Hubbard left the desk, leaving Coy and Bill Miller alone. Miller, studying Coy's marked-up face, spoke first.

"Looks like you and I have gotten the worst of it, Bernie. So far, anyway."

Coy ignored the attempt at conversation. "Where's 107, Miller?" he asked without preliminary.

Miller shrugged. "It should be there with the other keys."

"I know where it *should* be," Coy replied. "I also know where it ain't. It ain't in the gallery, it ain't on the rack, and it ain't in this desk. The only other place it could be is on you."

"If that's what you think," said Miller, "search me." He nodded at Hubbard. "And search him; he's got on my coat."

Coy called to Hubbard. "Go through that coat you're wearing, Marv. The cap, too. See if 107 is stashed anywhere." Then to Miller, "Turn your pockets inside out."

Miller did as he was told. When his pockets were out, Coy turned him around and expertly patted him down. He checked the underside of Miller's shirt collar, his necktie, waistband, under his belt, the tops of his socks.

"You do a good job of frisking, Bernie," said Miller.

"I ought to," Coy replied. "It's been done to me enough over the years. Take off your shoes."

Miller sat back against the desk and removed his shoes. There was no key. Hubbard whistled softly and Coy looked over at him.

"Not in the coat or cap, Bernie," he called.

"Sure?"

"Sure, Bernie."

Coy turned back to Bill Miller. His expression was threatening, inflexible. "I want 107, Miller."

"I haven't got it, Bernie."

"If you don't have it, then you know where it is. Tell me."

Miller remained silent.

Coy raised the barrel of the rifle and leveled it at Miller's face. "Tell me where 107 is or I'll blow you apart."

Miller shook his head knowingly. "No, you won't. Not you, Bernie. Cretzer, maybe; Buddy Thompson or Crazy Sam; even the Kid. But you're no cold-blooded killer, Bernie."

"I'm about to become one if you don't tell me where that key is," Coy warned solemnly. He and Miller locked eyes and held each other's stare. Coy waited a long moment for Miller to change his mind. When it became obvious he intended to say nothing more, Coy slowly tightened his finger on the trigger. But he did not fire. Finally he lowered the rifle. "Shit," he said, mostly to himself.

Suddenly, from the direction of the yard door, a yell and the sound of a scuffle attracted Coy's attention. He looked over and saw Crazy Sam clubbing Cecil Corwin with the billy he had given him. The Indio Kid was trying to pull Shockley off the fallen officer, while Cretzer and Thompson held the other officers at bay with the automatic and a club.

"Marv, get over here with Miller," Coy ordered. Hubbard hurried over to the desk and Coy ran down the flats to the yard door. He ran up to where Shockley had Corwin down; roughly, he stuck the muzzle of the rifle against Crazy Sam's ear. "Let him alone! Let him alone or I'll blast you!"

Shockley leaped off Corwin. Eyes wild, saliva drooling from his mouth, he swung the club at Coy. Coy pulled his head back, feeling the air move as the club cut an arc in front of his face. Then he stepped in and slammed the butt of the rifle against the side of Shockley's face.

Shockley screamed and pitched to the floor. He rolled over and looked up, blood gushing from his nose. "He hit me, Dutch! He bloodied me up! Kill him! Kill him, Dutch!"

Coy pivoted to face Cretzer. The former public enemy had instinctively turned the automatic on Coy. For an electric moment, the two armed convicts faced each other with guns ready to fire.

"Sam's one of us, Bernie," Dutch Cretzer snarled. "You didn't have to mess him up like that!"

"I said I didn't want any screws hurt, goddamn it!" Coy snapped back. "He's lucky I didn't blow his goddamn head off!"

"You're not the only one that can blow heads off around here!" Cretzer reminded him, hefting the automatic. "Sam's my friend. If it wasn't for him keeping Burch occupied, you'd never have got into the goddamn gun cage. Maybe you've forgotten that!"

Coy, breathing heavily, kept his eyes and the rifle steadily on Cretzer. Off to the side, he saw Shockley stagger groggily to his feet. Thompson still held a club threateningly against the other three officers. Dan Durando had knelt to see what he could do for Corwin, whose scalp bore a gash from Shockley's clubbing.

As Coy and Cretzer continued to face each other down, Marvin Hubbard walked up, guiding Miller ahead of him with a firm grip. "Bernie," he said quietly but urgently, "the boat's already at the dock. We ain't got much time left."

Without taking his eyes off Cretzer, without even blinking, Coy delivered an ultimatum. "Well, what about it? Are we still crashing out or do we start gunning each other?"

There was a final flash of anger in Dutch Cretzer's eyes, a final clenching of his handsome jaw, and then he lowered the .45 and stepped over to help Shockley steady himself.

"All right," Coy ordered, "all screws back in the cell. Kid, help Corwin get back to 403. We've got a key to find. Come on, let's move!"

Coy, with the rifle, herded Lageson, Miller, Bristow, and Burdette back down Seedy Street. Hubbard and Thompson, with clubs, flanked the line of men. Cretzer helped Crazy Sam along. The Indio Kid helped Corwin.

As the group passed the control panel at the end of C Block, the bleeding Cecil Corwin suddenly broke loose from Durando and lunged for the block phone, five feet along the wall. Durando, surprised at the quick move of the injured man, yelled, "Hey—!" Cretzer, just ahead of them, turned quickly to see what was happening. Along with Durando, Cretzer grabbed for Corwin, but both men were a split-second too late. The D Block guard, functioning on desperate instinct, snatched up the receiver.

Cretzer moved in quickly. He raised the .45 and viciously whipped Corwin over the head with it. Coy ran back just as Corwin fell unconscious to the floor and Danny Durando quickly hung the phone back up.

Cretzer, eyes dangerous, glared at Coy. "We should have let Sam kill the son of a bitch. If somebody tried answering that phone at the other end, we're all washed up."

Coy wet his lips. "The Kid probably got it hung up in time," he said. His words lacked conviction. Cretzer grunted derisively. Coy ignored him and mustered himself to command again. "Come on, we've got to find that key. Marv, Buddy, line these screws up and shake them down, *good*. Dutch, you and the Kid drag Corwin into 403 and search him."

"You're sure as hell good at dishing out orders, Coy," Cretzer said evenly, not moving to obey. "The only thing is, things aren't going so hot with your orders so far."

Coy, who had started to move away, turned back then and raised the rifle muzzle slightly. Cretzer did the same with the automatic. For the second time, the two armed prisoners confronted each other with unconcealed hostility.

This time it was Danny Durando who tried to prevent a battle from erupting between them. "I can handle Corwin by myself, Bernie," he said, dragging the unconscious officer between them and into Cell 403. The ploy did not work. Coy and Cretzer still faced each other.

"It's *my* break, Cretzer," Coy said when Durando was out of the way. "If you want to argue that, do it now!"

Dutch Cretzer, flushing red with fury, flexed himself to answer Coy's challenge.

Before they could clash, the two men were stopped by the chilling sound of the C Block phone ringing.

CHAPTER FOURTEEN

2:19 P.M.

Captain Henry Weinhold, a toothpick in his mouth, walked into the armory after lunch to see if he had any phone messages from the warden, the tower guards, or Burch in the west gun gallery. As he entered, he saw Armory Officer Clifford Fish staring perplexedly at the switchboard.

"What's the matter, Cliff? It talking back to you?" Weinhold asked easily.

Fish nodded his head slowly. "I could have sworn that the light for the C Block phone came on a minute ago. But when I plugged in, the line was dead. Now I just tried to call it back and there's no answer."

Weinhold grunted softly. "Those chowhounds Lageson and Miller are probably back in the kitchen sampling one of Bristow's apple pies. Ring the dining hall, you'll get them." Weinhold grinned mischievously. "Tell them I'm on my way back there, making my rounds early; that'll get them back to their posts."

Weinhold sat down at a desk and opened the early edition of the *Examiner*. He began reading a story about an argument that Secretary of State Jimmy Byrnes had the previous day with Soviet Foreign Minister Molotov at the Big Four Conference in Paris. Byrnes had been so upset about it, he had called President Truman via trans-Atlantic telephone.

Working the toothpick around in his mouth, Weinhold snorted irritably. Politicians! They always ended up acting like kids in a sandbox.

At the switchboard, Clifford Fish was frowning slightly. What the captain said really had not made sense. If Lageson and Miller were in the kitchen, who took the C Block receiver off the hook?

Frowning, Officer Fish pulled up a cord and plugged into the dining-hall phone.

•

On Seedy Street, the confrontation between Coy and Cretzer had again reached an impasse. Both of them had run down to Times Square when the C Block phone started ringing. Like wary jungle animals they had checked the flats as if the ringing of the phone might somehow be connected with an assault by guards. But the flats were as deserted as they had left them. And after a moment the C Block phone stopped ringing.

"That tears it," Cretzer said tightly. "They'll be onto us in a matter of minutes."

"We've still got time," Coy said. "If we can just find that goddamned key!"

They hurried back down Seedy Street. As they neared Cell 403, Marv Hubbard came over to them. "None of them have the key, Bernie," he said glumly. "We've searched them all." Coy's shoulders sagged and he sighed inaudibly.

"It's a bust!" Crazy Sam Shockley shouted wildly. "The whole fucking thing is a bust!"

Coy turned on him lividly. "Shut up, you goddamned moron!" he stormed at Shockley. "Shut up or I swear I'll kill you!"

"Don't let him hurt me again, Dutch!" Shockley shrieked, cringing toward Cretzer.

"Don't worry, Sam," Cretzer said ominously, "He's not going to hurt you." Cretzer was once again hefting the .45 restlessly, as if wanting desperately to use it on someone. Preferably Coy.

Coy, feeling a different kind of desperation, ignored Cretzer and

Shockley. Time, he kept thinking nervously. Time was running out on them. But they could still make it. Barely.

"Buddy," he crisply ordered, "get that box of keys off the cellhouse desk. Take it over to the yard door and start trying every key in that lock. There may be a duplicate with a dummy number on it." Thompson nodded and trotted off. Coy turned to Hubbard and the Kid. "You two stand watch at the end of Broadway."

"Right," they said in unison, and dashed after Thompson.

As Thompson reached the desk and Hubbard and Durando hurried toward Broadway, they all heard the phone in the dining hall begin ringing. They froze and stared in the direction of the sound. For several seconds they stood like that, listening to the shrill, grating sound echo throughout the cellhouse. After six rings, Hubbard snapped them out of it. "Come on, let's go, Kid," he said, slapping Durando smartly on the back. "Buddy," he snapped at Thompson, "do like Bernie told you." The three men started to move again.

On Seedy Street, Coy and the others also heard the persistent ringing. "That's the dining-hall phone," Cretzer said. "They're onto us."

Coy began to pace up and down in front of Cell 403. His lips moved as he muttered silently to himself. From time to time he cast hostile glances in at the captive guards. His gums had begun to ache, his punched-up face was throbbing, and the nipple he had lacerated getting into the gun cage was hurting constantly. Jesus, how could so many things go wrong at once? he wondered. Then he grunted softly to himself. Hadn't that always been the way, though? All his goddamned jinxed life? Hell, if he had half-sense, he would have known that no matter how well he planned it, something would happen to foul it up. The old Bernie Coy luck: all bad.

As Coy paced and thought his bitter thoughts, the dining-hall phone stopped ringing.

•

"No answer in the dining hall either, Captain," Officer Fish said.

The veteran guard captain lowered the newspaper he was reading and thought for a moment. They could have *been* in the dining hall and were now on their way back to the cellhouse desk, he decided. Lageson and Miller were both good officers; neither would stay away from his post for long.

"Ring Burch in the gun gallery," he instructed Fish. "He'll know where they are."

And Burch *had* to be there to answer the phone; he was locked into the gallery from the outside.

•

Bernie Coy stopped pacing as soon as the dining-hall phone stopped ringing. As if his thinking had been suspended with the ringing, and had returned with the silence, an expression of realization suddenly spread over his face. He whirled around and faced the guards.

"Everybody out!" he ordered. "Come on, out! Quick! Get out of that cell! Pick Corwin up and bring him with you! Move!" As the officers came out onto the flats, Coy looked over at Cretzer. "If it's not too much trouble, Cretzer, would you mind keeping an eye on them for a second?" His voice was heavy with sarcasm.

Coy dashed into 403, stood the Springfield in a far corner where neither Cretzer nor Shockley could grab it, and began a thorough search of the cell. As he had seen the guards do many times over the years, he began with the bunk. First he removed the bare mattress and carefully felt along all seams on both sides and at both ends. Then he ran his fingertips along both surfaces and around all sides looking for small slits through which a key could have been slipped. He examined the mattress thoroughly. When he was convinced it was not concealing the key, he rolled it and stood it at the end of the bunk out of his way.

Next, Coy dropped to his knees and ran his fingers along the underside of the bunk frame, the edges, the hinges, the sides of the steel wall mounts. As he was searching, another telephone began ringing somewhere. Coy was aware of Cretzer speaking to Shockley, of Crazy Sam running down the flats, then returning almost at once. The psychotic bank robber said something to Cretzer, and Cretzer came over to 403.

"That's the gun cage phone," he said.

Coy ignored him. He stood up. Another thought had just occurred to him. He turned toward the back of the cell and with narrowing eyes looked at the lidless porcelain toilet. The very place he himself had hidden the bar spreader in his own cell.

Jesus Christ, Coy, he chastised himself, I ain't sure you even *deserve* to escape.

•

Officer Clifford Fish was now visibly nervous.

"Captain Weinhold, there's no answer to the gallery phone," he said anxiously.

Weinhold pursed his lips and stood up. As he did, his second in command, Lieutenant Joseph Simpson, and another Alcatraz guard, Officer Carl Sundstrom, entered the armory from outside.

"What's up?" Simpson asked, noticing Fish's anxiety.

"I think there may be something the matter with the phones in the cellhouse," Weinhold said. "I'm going to walk across the flats and check with Lageson. Joe, you take over here while I'm gone."

"Yes, sir."

Weinhold walked out into the deadlock. The door guard let the captain into the cellhouse. The senior guard captain entered the captured cellhouse and walked briskly down Broadway.

In Cell 403, Bernie Coy had shoved his diet-skinny arm as far into the cell toilet as it would go. His face was set tensely, his lips drawn into a dry line. He was breathing heavily again. Deep in the neck of the bowl, Coy's fingers searched the inside surface of the closed aluminum trap. Suddenly his eyes widened and his lips parted excitedly. He struggled briefly, gritting his teeth, then triumphantly twisted and wiggled his dripping arm out of the bowl. In his hand was a key. Coy quickly checked the number. It was 107.

"I found it!" he yelled, and began to laugh. He snatched up the rifle and dashed out of the cell. Pausing, he held up the key for the guards to see. "Thought you were smart, didn't you, you bastards?" he scorned. "Well, you weren't smart enough. I found it! I found the goddamned key!" Coy spun around and faced Cretzer and Shockley. He could not resist sneering at them. "Watch the screws," he ordered, "while I get the yard door open. We're back to the original plan now; *my* plan."

Coy ran up Seedy toward Times Square.

•

Marv Hubbard and the Indio Kid were flattened against the end wall of B and C, one on each side of Broadway, listening to brisk footsteps becoming louder and louder. Each man had a billy club at the ready, and they looked tensely at each other across the open space between them. The footsteps came closer and closer; then a figure walked out onto Times Square. Hubbard and Durando jumped out to confront the latest arrival with raised clubs. They were momentarily surprised to see that it was Captain Weinhold, the highest-ranking guard on the island.

"Jesus," said Hubbard. He lowered the club and held up a tense hand. "Take it easy, Captain," he warned. "Don't do nothing dumb."

The Indio Kid took a tentative step closer to the senior guard. "You ain't going to try anything, are you, Captain?" he asked in a half-plea. "You know we can take you down quick with these billies."

Weinhold stared at the two convicts for a moment. From his almost total recall of Alcatraz prisoners, he quickly summed them up in his mind. Hubbard: bank robber, hostage taker, never-surrender type. Durando: two-time escapee, hostage taker, deadly fistfighter. Both men extremely tense at that moment; each a little nervous about capturing him. Both still somewhat intimidated by his rank and authority. Obvious that neither of them wanted to hurt him.

Other bits of data also surfaced in Weinhold's finely honed mind. The convicts had two clubs, which must have somehow come from the gun cage. Durando was a lockup prisoner, not supposed to be out of his cell, so they had the keys to the control boxes. That meant they had Lageson and Miller. Burch was nowhere to be seen in the gun gallery, a fact which Weinhold found incomprehensible. The D Block door was open; also incomprehensible. Across the flats, his back to Times Square, a convict whose face Weinhold could not see was trying various keys in the yard door.

It was a break—probably a well-planned one.

"All right, Hubbard, Durando," the captain said authoritatively, as if he were doing them a favor, "I won't resist you at this point. Where are my men?"

"The other side of C Block," Hubbard said, jerking his head toward Seedy Street.

"Come on, Captain," said the Kid, "we'll take you there."

With Durando leading the way and Hubbard following behind Weinhold, the convicts escorted the captain along the C Block end of the flats and around the corner into Seedy Street. There they encountered Bernie Coy hurrying toward the yard door.

"I've got the key, Kid," Coy said excitedly to Durando. "I've got 107!" Then he saw Weinhold, directly behind Durando, and stopped short. His lips parted. "Well, Captain, this is an unexpected surprise," he said.

"It's a surprise for me too, Bernie," Weinhold said. As much as he tried, the captain was unable to keep a hint of stiffness, of marked disapproval, out of his voice. He glanced at the rifle Coy held and immediately knew that his initial evaluation had been correct. With Coy in on the break, it would definitely be well planned. The rifle could have come from only one place: the gun cage. Weinhold glanced down the C-D aisle and saw Dutch Cretzer, with a pistol in his hand, and Sam Shockley, who was supposed to be in segregated lockup in D Block. The captain's jaw clenched as his eyes met Coy's again. "I thought you were smarter than this, Bernie," he said reproachfully. "You must realize there's no way in the world for you to get off this island."

"No?" Coy replied, raising his eyebrows. He knew every second was valuable now, but he could not resist the opportunity, just once, to rebuke the lofty Captain Weinhold. "Two hours ago, you wouldn't have believed we could take the gun gallery either. But we did. You wouldn't have believed we could get our hands on a rifle and a pistol. But we have. You wouldn't have thought we could capture five guards; make that six, now that we've got you. And"—he held up 107—"you'd never have believed we could grab the one key that can get us out of the cellhouse. But we did all that, Weinhold! We did all that and we're going to do more. We're going all the way, *Captain.* We're going to crash off this island. For once in our lives, we're going to be the winners!"

"You're a fool, Coy," the captain said.

"No, *you're* the fool, Weinhold. If you weren't a fool, you wouldn't have come strutting in here all alone like some kind of god. You and your big-shot attitude: like you're so great and all us cons are dirt for you to walk on. Well, fuck you, mister; we're all equal now. You're no better than we are, and I'm going to prove it to you. Take off that big-shot captain's coat."

Weinhold did not move.

Coy pointed the rifle directly in his face. "Take it off or I'll kill you where you stand."

Slowly, without taking his eyes off Coy, the captain unbuttoned his coat and removed it. Coy snatched it out of his hands. "Now you look like everybody else, *Captain,*" the escape leader said. He threw a curt nod at Danny Durando. "Put him in with the others, Kid. Marv, go over to that window and see how many people are on the boat so far."

His orders given, Coy turned and dashed across the flats toward the yard door, which Buddy Thompson was frantically trying to open with all the keys from the gallery rack. Coy, having told off Weinhold, now felt a surge of elation rush through him. As he hurried over to Thompson, he wiggled into the coat he had just taken from Weinhold.

"Buddy, I've got the key," he said exuberantly. "I found 107!"

Thompson turned around in distress. "Bernie, there's a goddamned key jammed in the lock."

The elation evaporated.

•

Down Seedy Street, the Indio Kid guided Captain Weinhold to Cell 403. As they approached, Dutch Cretzer stared at the officer in surprise. "I'll be a son of a bitch," he muttered.

Shockley, seeing the captain, immediately went berserk. "It's Weinhold! It's the head screw! He's the cocksucker who put us in D Block, Dutch!" Crazy Sam turned beseechingly to Cretzer. "Give me the gun, Dutch, please. Let me kill him, Dutch, please."

The Indio Kid cringed inside. "You give him that rod, Cretzer, and he's liable to kill us all," Durando warned.

The Kid urged Weinhold forward, wanting to get him into the relative safety of the cell as quickly as possible. But before Weinhold could enter 403, Shockley leaped forward and threw a punch at him. Although twenty years older than his convict attacker, Henry Weinhold was smarter and a great deal more alert. He was also generally scornful of convicts. Deftly avoiding the blow, he brought up his right hand and stingingly backhanded Shockley across the mouth. Crazy Sam stumbled back, shocked.

"Don't try that again, Shockley," Weinhold warned. "Gun or no gun, you'll not manhandle me."

"We'll see about that, you son of a bitch!" yelled Dutch Cretzer. "Sam's been pushed around enough for one day!" He charged up and shoved Durando away from Weinhold. Then he viciously slugged the guard captain over the head with the automatic. Weinhold groaned and sagged to the floor.

Durando, closing his deadly fists, dropped into a fighting crouch and moved toward Cretzer. The former public enemy, expecting it, quickly turned the gun on him.

"I'll blast you, you goddamned Mexican punk," he warned coldly. "Crashout or no crashout, I'll blow your goddamned head off!"

Durando pulled up short, inches from the black hole of the muzzle. He wet his lips and slowly straightened, unclenching his fists.

"Okay, Sam," Cretzer said, bobbing his chin at the fallen Weinhold, "you can have him now. Let him have it for me too. Five years in D Block was a long, long time."

Shockley, wild-eyed, rushed over and began kicking Weinhold.

•

At the yard door, Bernie Coy was working furiously to get the stuck key out of the lock so that he could use 107 to open the door. His expression was grim and determined, his brow running with lines of perspiration as he wiggled and twisted the foreign key, trying to extract it from the lock.

Behind him, Thompson watched, tight-lipped and anxious. Thompson, like Coy, knew that their time schedule was all shot to hell; but like the escape leader he also knew there was still an outside chance they could make it. Having Weinhold as a hostage would give them much better bargaining power once they got as far as the yard. But Thompson knew that getting into the yard was crucial to the escape. Once in the yard with their six hostages, they would have a definite psychological advantage. They could parade Weinhold and the others around to intimidate the tower guards and the warden. With the guns and clubs they had captured, and the hostages to use for human shields, they could take over the whole goddamned island.

But first they had to get out of the cellhouse. As long as they were still in the cellhouse, they were still prisoners. No matter what they did *inside* the cellhouse, Buddy Thompson knew the break would really begin only after they got *out* of it.

Coy slumped back against the wall and let his hands fall to his sides. "My arms feel like they're made out of lead," he said, taking a deep breath and wiping his sweating face. "You try it again. Real gentle, so you don't jam it worse."

Thompson began working the key very easily from side to side, moving it up and down slightly, and pushing it forward in an attempt to then pull it out of the lock. He tried a wide variety of moves in an attempt to hit on a single combination that would release the stuck key. Like Coy, Buddy Thompson failed. Coy watched him work at it for about four minutes, then nudged him aside.

"Let me have it again."

Thompson moved aside and let Coy back at the lock. Coy renewed his previous efforts with intense concentration, seeming to pursue with his entire mind and body the goal of extracting the key. So complete was Coy's attention to the key that he did not see Marvin Hubbard as his friend walked slowly across the flats and stood silently at his side for a moment. When Coy still failed to look up,

Hubbard finally put a hand gently on his shoulder.

"It's gone, Bernie," Hubbard said when Coy finally turned to him. "The boat's gone."

Coy's thin shoulders slumped and he shook his head wearily. "Hell," he said in a barely audible voice.

CHAPTER FIFTEEN

2:30 P.M.

In the armory, Lieutenant Joe Simpson and Officer Carl Sundstrom were exchanging uneasy glances as Armory Officer Cliff Fish stared vigilantly at the silent switchboard. Finally, after fifteen minutes, Simpson decided they had waited long enough.

"We should have heard from the captain by now," he said, as much to himself as to Sundstrom or Fish. He motioned to Sundstrom and the two men walked out of the deadlock and into the administration offices. Simpson looked around and called to the first guard he saw, Mail Officer Robert Baker, at a nearby desk. "There may be a problem of some kind in the cellhouse," Simpson told Baker, without explaining further. "The three of us are going in to check it out."

Simpson had Fish pass three riot clubs out the weapons window; he handed one each to Sundstrom and Baker, then led the way through the sallyport. "Open it up," he ordered the guard. "We're going in."

"Yes sir, Lieutenant." The guard passed the men through the second sallyport door, then opened the solid steel entry door, and the barred door beyond that, and let them into the cellhouse.

The entry door was closed and locked behind them. "We'll stay together until we get a line on what's going on," Simpson said. Baker turned toward Broadway, but Simpson put a hand on his arm and nodded in the opposite direction. "We'll go down Michigan Boulevard."

Quietly, the men crossed the entry flats and moved down the aisle between A and B blocks.

•

Bernie Coy left Buddy Thompson slumped desolately by the yard door and, with Marv Hubbard, trudged wearily back to Cell 403.

When he got there, he found Danny Durando on his knees with some wet handkerchiefs furnished by the other guards, cleansing the blood from Captain Weinhold's open scalp where Cretzer had slugged him, and his battered, torn face where Crazy Sam Shockley had kicked him.

"What happened?" Coy asked the Kid.

"Cretzer held the gun on me while that maniac friend of his worked him over."

"Weinhold hit me first, you cocksucker!" Shockley yelled defensively.

"You're goddamned right he did," Cretzer confirmed. "I saw the screw backhand Sam." Cretzer turned toward Durando, brandishing the automatic. "You better make up your mind which side you're on, Mex."

The Indio Kid sneered. "You can stick that gun up your ass, Cretzer. You don't scare me none with it. I've seen tougher guys than you in reform school."

Cretzer's nostrils flared and he moved toward the kneeling Durando. Coy stepped between them with the rifle.

"All right, that's enough, for Christ's sake!" Coy yelled. "Let's everybody calm down for a goddamn minute. We've got bigger problems to worry about."

"Oh Jesus," said Cretzer. "What now?"

"Buddy got a key jammed in the yard door," Coy said quietly. "We can't get it out." He sighed a weary sigh. "And even if we could get the key out, the launch has already left. It won't be back for an hour. By that time, every hack on the island will have us surrounded."

"That's just peachy," Dutch Cretzer snapped. "Terrific plan you had, Coy. Not one goddamned thing has gone right from the very beginning!"

"It would have worked perfect if the 107 key had been where it was supposed to be," Coy said, in a voice almost sad.

"*If!*" Cretzer sneered. "That's a goddamned big word. *If* I'd been born a lousy Rockefeller, I wouldn't be here watching everything go wrong. Face it, Coy: your plan's a bust!"

Coy stared solemnly at his antagonist, but he did not have the energy left to argue with him. Cretzer was right. It looked as if the plan—and the break—*was* a bust.

•

Sitting on the floor, leaning up against the wall next to the yard door, Buddy Thompson was silently cursing himself for ever joining in on the crashout. He should have continued to follow the lifelong pattern he had set for himself: that of working strictly alone; never joining a gang of any kind. It had always—at least, *nearly* always—worked fine for him in the past. He made his own plans, picked his own time to execute those plans, and did not have to worry about or depend upon anyone but himself.

It was Alcatraz, he knew, that had caused him to change. He had been on the Rock less than six months, but already he had recognized it as a kind of hell which he was not at all certain he would survive. Life plus ninety-nine years was the book, no matter how you looked at it, and Buddy Thompson knew without conscious thought that he would have to escape. What he was not prepared for was the high degree to which Alcatraz lived up to its escape-proof reputation.

Since arriving on the island the previous November, Thompson had acted the part of a subdued prisoner, resigned to his fate. To the guards who observed him, he seemed almost to enjoy the unchanging, peaceful routine, the relative tranquillity of prison after his wild, running, hiding, shooting, outlaw days. In the tailor shop, he became a model worker and a good cloth handler.

"You got the makings of a good tailor, Buddy," his shop foreman, Haynes Herbert, had told him. "You cut a nice, proper line." Herbert, also a Texan, took an extra interest in Thompson and showed him several ways to improve his work.

All the while, Buddy Thompson had been looking for a way out. A flaw in the routine, a careless habit on the part of one of the guards, a way to get down to the dock—anything with a little possibility, a little hope, attached to it. But in five months of looking, he found nothing. Then one day, while sunbathing during his yard time, two men had come up and introduced themselves. Coy and Hubbard. They had checked him out and they had a proposition for him. He listened. Then he checked *them* out. At first he had been ready to dismiss the puny-looking, older Coy, and the half-blind, bandy-legged Hubbard; but in short order he had learned that their reps were solid, and that Coy, particularly, was held in high regard as a man who never acted unless he was absolutely sure of what he was doing. It irritated Thompson that Coy had been able to devise a workable escape plan, when he himself, in five months of trying, had not. But he soon found out why when he asked Coy how long it had taken him to discover the structural weakness in the gun gallery bars.

"Eight years," Coy had answered. "I looked for a way out for eight years before I spotted that place where the bars would spread. And I been putting the actual plan together for nearly a year now."

Almost nine years, Buddy Thompson had thought to himself. After that, Thompson had a great deal more respect for Bernie Coy.

Now, he shook his head in disgust. Everything had gone down the drain. His in-grade status, his job, his privileges: all gone. It would be D Block for him, probably for five long years. Constant lockup except for a trip down the tier to the shower every week. He would be spending nearly every waking hour in a cell: living in it, eating in it, day after day after day. By the time he got back into the main cellhouse, he would be nearly forty, and they would forever watch every move he made. He would rot away the rest of his life on Alcatraz.

All because of a lousy jammed key, he thought. He reached up without thinking and tapped the key angrily but lightly with one knuckle. Then he stuck the tip of his little finger into one of the three holes in the head of the key and unconsciously fidgeted with it. Presently he pulled with that little finger—and the jammed key slipped easily out of the lock and bounced once on the cement floor next to him.

•

In front of 403, Cretzer, Shockley, Durando, and Hubbard were wondering what to do next. There was no alternate plan, so the lock-jammed yard door had all but suspended the escape. Cretzer and Shockley stood together, talking softly. Hubbard and the Indio Kid were standing near each other, but not saying anything. Coy had walked away from everyone and was standing alone.

In Cell 403, Lageson and Burdette were ministering to Weinhold, who was stretched out on the bunk. Bristow was sitting on the floor of the cell, holding the unconscious Cecil Corwin's bloody head in his lap. Bill Miller was rinsing and wringing out blood-soaked handkerchiefs as they were passed to him by Burdette.

Coy, off to himself, was standing in front of Cell 396, halfway down the aisle to the cutoff. His back was braced against the bars and he cradled the rifle in his arms Indian-style. His face was solemn as he stared at an imaginary spot on the flats and, like the others, wondered what to do next. Coy could not bring himself to believe that they had reached the end of the line, that all the work and planning had only brought them this far. There *had* to be an alternative.

As Coy stood deep in thought, Marv Hubbard, still wearing Miller's uniform coat and cap, came over and sat down across the aisle from him, leaning his back against the D Block wall. He said nothing, so as not to interrupt Coy's thinking, but sat in sight so his friend would know he was there if needed.

The Indio Kid, who had wandered by himself up Seedy Street toward Times Square, was the first of the convicts to see Buddy Thompson running down the aisle toward them. *That's it,* the Kid thought. *The guards are coming after us.*

"Where's 107?" Thompson asked anxiously as he ran up to them. "Come on, where is it? I got the jammed key out of the yard door!"

"What the hell difference does it make?" Cretzer said flatly. "It's too late now: the goddamned boat's gone. And once they know we're loose in here, they won't let it dock again."

"We can *make* them let it dock again," Thompson argued. "With those screws as hostages, they'll have to do whatever we say."

"Like hell," Cretzer scoffed. "If the boat was still here, they might let us *get* to it; but nobody's going to take the responsibility of ordering it back." He shook his head emphatically. "Face it, Thompson, the break's a bust."

"Hold it a minute," said Bernie Coy, his face alive with hope again. "You say the jammed key is out of the yard door lock?" he asked Thompson. "Completely out?"

"Completely, Bernie," Thompson assured him. "That lock's just waiting for 107."

Coy removed 107 from his pocket and bounced it in his hand a few times. "There may still be a way," he said thoughtfully. Hubbard and Durando walked back over now. Coy glanced at each man in turn, wondering how they would react to his idea. "Once we get into the yard and out the yard gate," he said, speaking quietly so the guards in 403 could not hear him, "instead of heading for the dock, we can go the other way, toward the apartments where the screws and their families live. If we can grab a few wives and kids as hostages, they'll get that boat back here as fast as it can turn around."

"Wives and kids," Cretzer said, his face lighting with interest. "Yeah, that might work."

"Jesus, it's perfect, Bernie," Buddy Thompson said enthusiastically.

"Sounds good, Bernie," Marv Hubbard allowed.

Coy glanced at Durando. The Kid looked at the floor, saying nothing. Shockley, next to him, merely frowned stupidly.

By then, Cretzer was rubbing his chin. "Yeah, screws are one thing, but wives and kids are something else. We could make them give us a goddamned luxury liner if we wanted one!"

Shockley smiled moronically at his protector. "Are we gonna get us some women, Dutch? And some little girls?"

Cretzer patted him on the shoulder. "Go sit over there by the wall, Sam," he said gently. "I'll come over in a couple of minutes." Turning to Coy, he said, "Let's you and me go in the dining hall, have a talk, and see what we can work out."

Coy nodded. "Marv, you and the Kid watch out for the screws. Keep Shockley away from them. Buddy," he tossed Thompson the 107 key, "take this and wait by the yard door. Keep an eye out the observation glass in case any guards try coming up on us through the yard. And don't unlock the door yet." To Cretzer, he said, "Okay, Dutch, let's go talk."

The two armed convicts walked down to Times Square and the dining-hall entrance.

•

Lieutenant Simpson and Officers Baker and Sundstrom had made their way down Michigan Boulevard as far as the cutoff. Carefully crossing over to Broadway, Simpson removed his cap and peered around the corner down the wide main aisle. He studied the flats, Times Square, the deserted cellhouse officer's desk, the empty gun gallery, and the dining hall entry for a full sixty seconds. He saw no sign of life, except along Broadway where the lockup cons were standing at the front of their C Block cells looking out.

"Deserted," he said to the two officers when he drew his head back and put his cap on again. "The whole area down there is completely deserted. But all the lockup cons are at the front of their cells looking out. Something's definitely up."

"What the hell could be going on?" Baker asked.

"Hard telling," said Simpson. "Some of the cons might have grabbed the cellhouse officers. They may be holding them to negotiate for something."

"But why hasn't Burch thrown down on them from the gun gallery?" wondered Sundstrom.

The lieutenant shook his head. "I don't know. They may have managed to keep a cell open and holed up in it. They may even be in D Block; Bert could have them pinned down somewhere, which would explain why he couldn't get over to answer his phone. But whatever's going on, we've got to move in and break it up. There couldn't be more than three or four of them, because it looks like all the lockups are still in their cells. Whoever's in on it, we'll talk to them if we can; if not, we'll use our clubs, fast and hard. Carl," he said to Sundstrom, "you keep going down Michigan. Bob and I will go down each side of Broadway. Double back and catch up to us if you see anything. We'll do the same."

The guards separated. Sundstrom cautiously and quietly continued alone down the A-B aisle. Simpson and Baker moved warily onto the B-C aisle, each taking a side of the wide thoroughfare, and began walking slowly toward Times Square.

•

While Lieutenant Simpson was giving instructions to Officers Sundstrom and Baker, Bernie Coy and Dutch Cretzer had walked casually across Times Square and into the dining hall. They were through the dining hall and out of sight in the kitchen by the time Simpson and Baker came out of the cutoff.

In the kitchen, Coy and Cretzer found the six convict orderlies waiting for Officer Burdette to come back. The eyes of the men widened in fear and surprise at the sight of the guns Coy and Cretzer were carrying, and the captain's coat that Coy was wearing.

Coy studied the men for a moment, biting his lower lip in thought. He looked around the kitchen and located the stairs leading down to the bakery in the basement. "You guys beat it downstairs," he said, waving the rifle. "Don't come back up." When they were gone, he found a key in Bristow's desk and locked the door.

Coy and Cretzer went into the officers' dining room. In the pastry cupboard, a very hungry Bernie Coy found a whole apple pie. He took it out, sat down, and began eating it. Cretzer went to a nearby urn and drew them each a cup of coffee, using the heavy porcelain mugs reserved for the guards.

"Been a long time since we drank out of anything that wasn't tin, hasn't it, Bernie?"

Coy stared at him for a second, not really understanding the significance of the remark. To Coy, it was what he was drinking and how much of it he had; not what he was drinking it *from*. But he shrugged and said, "Yeah, I guess it has."

Cretzer watched Coy ravage the pie for several moments. Then, in an even, rational tone reminiscent of his days as a gang leader, he said, "Bernie, we aren't going to be able to get over to the guards' living quarters without shooting the tower screws."

Coy shook his head, disagreeing at once. "We got six hostages, including the top guard captain. The tower screws won't fire on us."

"Wrong, Bernie," said Cretzer patiently. "They wouldn't fire on us if we headed for the dock to get the boat. But the minute they see that we're heading for the apartments where the wives and kids are, they'll cut us *and* the hostages down. Believe me, Bernie, they *won't* let us get to their families, no matter who they have to shoot."

"I don't want any killing, Dutch," Coy said adamantly. "If we ice one screw, they'll never stop hunting for us."

"They never will anyway," Cretzer replied with infallible logic. "Don't you realize what a slap in the mouth it's going to be to the feds when six cons bust off this rock? It won't be like your pal Hubbard breaking out of that Tennessee pen, or Thompson and his eight jailbreaks down in the sticks, or even me crashing out of McNeil. We'll have beaten *Alcatraz*, Bernie! The goddamned Rock! That's like spitting right in the government's face. Hell, every copper in North America will be after us."

Cretzer finished his coffee and walked over to get some more. The .45 was stuck snugly in his waistband. He hoped Coy would listen to reason. If he did not, Cretzer had decided he would have to kill him and give the rifle to Buddy Thompson. He had decided on Thompson rather than his friend Shockley, because he did not trust Sam with a gun. Anyway, Thompson was a Texas outlaw; all those cowboys knew how to use a rifle. Marv Hubbard could probably handle the Springfield too, but Hubbard was very tight with Coy, both of them being hillbillies and all. It was very possible, Cretzer knew, that if he killed Coy, he would have to kill Hubbard also. Which he was fully prepared to do. If it came down to that, then he would put the Indio Kid back in a cell and continue the crashout with only Thompson, Crazy Sam, and himself.

"Look, Bernie," he said, turning back with his fresh mug of coffee, "I don't particularly want any killing either. Hell, I've already faced the chair once; I don't like to think of facing it a second time if I ever get caught again. But I'm convinced that we won't get ten feet past that yard gate unless we take out the tower guards."

Coy stuffed the last of the pie into his mouth and wiped his lips on the sleeve of Weinhold's coat. Cretzer glanced away in distaste. Coy got up and went over to glance out the window at one of the three towers that could be seen from the dining hall area. At the window, Coy was careful to keep Dutch Cretzer in the periphery of his vision, and to keep his finger close to the trigger of the rifle. Coy knew that this was the last disagreement between himself and Cretzer. Unless they could reach some kind of compromise on how best to resume the escape, one of them was not going to leave the kitchen alive. And that one, Coy was reasonably sure, would be Cretzer. There was not much doubt in Bernie Coy's mind that he could drill Cretzer two or three times with the rifle anytime Cretzer reached for the pistol in his belt.

But Coy did not want to kill Dutch Cretzer. If he killed Cretzer, he would also have to kill Shockley. Unlike Cretzer, he harbored no plans of depleting their number and strength. When the time came for negotiation with the warden, Coy knew that the more of them there were, the better it would be. So for the sake of the break, he wanted to keep all of them together. But he still did not want to kill any guards.

"There might be another way, Dutch," the Kentucky outlaw said, turning from the window.

Cretzer shook his head. "There isn't," he said doggedly.

"There might be," Coy insisted. He walked back and faced Cretzer across the table. "Suppose we take out the tower guards without killing them? Suppose we just wound them, put them out of commission?"

Cretzer grunted. "Sure, that would be great if we had Buffalo Bill or somebody with us. But who do you know that can shoot that good?"

"Me," Coy answered flatly.

"You?"

"That's what I said. I can shoot that good. Back home in the hills I used to be able to bring down jackrabbits on the run with an old single-shot of my daddy's. How to shoot a rifle was the only thing I ever got from my old man besides a kick in the ass three times a day. Maybe being his kid is finally going to be good for something. With this baby," he hefted the modern Springfield, "I can take a man's ear off at a thousand yards."

Cretzer was unconvinced. "It sounds awful damned risky to me."

"It ain't any riskier than killing them and having all the rest of the screws after your ass for doing it. This way we're keeping the killing in reserve. It's something to hold over their heads."

Cretzer turned and paced up and down while he considered it. Coy slipped the tip of his finger over the inside edge of the rifle's trigger guard. He watched Cretzer closely, half expecting him to whirl and pull the automatic. But Cretzer's hands did not move toward the gun; instead, while one hand held the mug of coffee, he shoved the other deep into the pocket of his prison trousers. Although he hated to admit it, even to himself, Dutch Cretzer was impressed by Coy's last remark. It made sense to keep the *threat* of death hanging in the air. After they killed the first guard, most of the shock value would be lost. Killing a second and a third one would only make the warden and his other screws that much more immune to—and angry about —subsequent kills. Much better, he decided, to hold it over their heads for as long as possible before using it.

Cretzer stopped pacing and faced Coy again. "Okay, Bernie, I'll play along with you. One last time. I just hope your way works this time."

"It will," said Coy. "I'll take out the tower guards—and I'll do it without killing them." Coy lowered the rifle a fraction, but not much. "Come on, let's get the screws out and get ready to hit that yard."

The two convicts headed for the door leading to Times Square.

•

Approaching Times Square from the opposite direction, Lieutenant Joe Simpson and Officer Robert Baker had reached the west end of Broadway. Their clubs at the ready, they had covered the distance from the cutoff still having no knowledge of the exact situation in the cellhouse. So intently were the two officers concentrating on what they might face around the respective corners of B and C blocks, that neither of them paid much attention to the open, deserted flats directly in front of them, or the dining hall entry across those flats. And it was through that entry that Coy and Cretzer now hurried.

The encounter between the two pairs of men was sudden and surprising. One moment Simpson and Baker were cautiously stepping out onto Times Square; the next, Coy and Cretzer came swiftly out of the dining hall and they met. All four men were momentarily petrified.

It was Coy who had the presence of mind to react first. He quickly leveled the rifle at the two guards. "Drop those clubs!" he ordered.

Simpson and Baker dropped their billies to the floor. Cretzer stepped over and kicked them out of the way. At that moment, Officer Sundstrom stepped partway around the corner of the A-B aisle. Seeing the two convicts holding guns, he quickly jerked back —but not quickly enough to keep Coy and Cretzer from seeing him.

For a split instant there was silence in the big cellhouse. Coy primed himself for a possible gunfight if a cadre of guards suddenly burst onto the flats from Michigan Boulevard. But none did. Expression tense, he aimed the rifle at Baker. "Who's over there?" he asked quietly. "Tell me or I'll kill you."

"Sundstrom," Baker replied without hesitation.

"Just him?" Coy's voice was a hiss.

Baker quickly nodded. "Yeah."

"Any other screws come in with you?"

"No."

Coy wet his lips. "Cover these two, Dutch," he said. Without warning, he burst into a run down Broadway, holding the rifle in front of him with both hands. His leather soles beat a brisk tattoo on the cement floor.

On Michigan Boulevard, Sundstrom had paused indecisively after ducking back out of sight. Simpson and Baker had been taken. It was clear that something was seriously wrong in the cellhouse. He knew his smartest move would be to hurry back to the armory to sound a general alarm. But he hesitated to leave Simpson and Baker like that. While he was trying to decide what to do, his mind was made up for him. He heard the echoing slaps of running feet heading down Broadway, and he knew instantly that they were trying to cut him off. All indecision dissolved and Carl Sundstrom broke into a fast run down Michigan Boulevard.

Lockup prisoners stood tensely at their cell doors as the two men ran madly down the parallel aisles. On Broadway, Coy was desperately pumping his legs, his forty-six-year-old body responding with a super burst of energy, like that of the person who lifts the weight of an automobile off a trapped loved one. And on Michigan Boulevard, precious seconds behind him, Carl Sundstrom, still gripping his billy club, ran just as furiously, just as frantically, because by then he was convinced that he was running for his life. Sundstrom could not hear Coy's footfalls now that his own were echoing in his ears, but he knew that the running convict was ahead of him and would try to intercept him at the cutoff. He hoped fervently that the convict would not shoot him as he dashed past that intersecting aisle.

As for Coy, he had no intention of firing the rifle that close to the sallyport. He would have drilled Dutch Cretzer back in the kitchen, because he was fairly certain that the shot would not have been heard all the way up to the opposite end of the cellhouse and through the big cement wall that separated the cell blocks from the administration section. But firing a shot as close to the sallyport as the cutoff was unthinkable. If the sallyport guard was as far inside as the cellhouse entry door or even the second deadlock door, he would almost surely hear the report. Coy had to stop Sundstrom. But not with a bullet.

Coy reached the cutoff ten feet ahead of Sundstrom. He executed an almost unbalancing turn and raced through the cutoff toward Michigan. Halfway through, he saw Sundstrom speed past the Michigan side of the cutoff, tossing him a frightened look as he ran on toward the sallyport. Coy careened into the A-B aisle mere steps behind the running guard. He tried to force himself to run faster, to close the distance between them so that he could swing the rifle like a club and bring Sundstrom down with a quick blow. But Coy's body had reached its maximum of performance. His breath was coming in bursts; he could run no faster.

As Sundstrom neared the east end of the A-B corridor, Coy realized he would not be able to catch him before he was within sight of the sallyport entry. There was one last, desperate gamble that Coy could take: he could use the rifle. Not to fire, but to throw. It was a chance he hated to take; the thought of letting the rifle out of his hands scared him; but Sundstrom *had* to be stopped.

With no more time left to make up his mind, Coy hurled the rifle forward like a softball pitched underhand. It cut straight through the air spear-fashion, knee-high from the floor. Flying, it hit Sundstrom behind the knees and sent him flailing forward—directly into the cross-corridor in front of the sallyport.

For a split-second, everything stopped. Sundstrom lay stunned, half in and half out of the cellhouse entry corridor. Coy was frozen where he stood, afraid to step into view of the entry. The rifle had slid out of the immediate reach of either man.

•

In the armory, Cliff Fish was anxiously watching the switchboard, hoping for some word from Lieutenant Simpson. Fish looked nervously at the armory clock. Simpson, Baker, and Sundstrom had been in the cellhouse about ten minutes. That was more than enough time to reach Times Square and get to one of the block phones. Fish toyed with one of the switchboard cords. He was not sure exactly what to do. Normally he would have called the captain, Weinhold, or his next in command, Simpson; but they were both in the cellhouse. The associate warden, he knew, was around on the north side of the island inspecting some work done earlier by an inmate paint crew. Fish's eyes kept flicking anxiously to a plug in the switchboard marked *Warden.*

After several moments, he swiveled around and spoke to the sallyport guard. "Take a look in the cellhouse and see if you can see anything."

The guard opened the second deadlock door and passed through to the main cellhouse entry door. He peered through the vision panel.

•

Twelve feet on the other side of the door, Bernie Coy decided to take still another gamble. Having heard no sound of entry from the sallyport door, he rushed up to the fallen Sundstrom and grabbed him by his ankles. He began to pull him out of the cross-corridor. Sundstrom, feeling himself dragged, shook off the grogginess of his violent fall and looked up to see Coy holding his feet. Mortified at being handled by a prisoner, Sundstrom reddened with anger and jerked one of his feet free. With a strong knee-flex, he kicked Coy solidly in the chest. Coy pitched back, lost his balance, and fell to the floor. Struggling to his feet, Sundstrom made a dash for the sallyport door; he slipped briefly, then regained his footing and ran into the cross-corridor. Coy no sooner hit the floor than he was back up again. Exerting all of his now rapidly diminishing strength, Coy leaped after the guard and managed to hook a bony arm around his throat before Sundstrom could reach the door. Gritting his teeth, he simultaneously choked and dragged Sundstrom back into the A-B aisle, toward where the rifle lay.

They were out of sight of the cellhouse entry door.

•

The sallyport guard, looking through the vision panel, scanned the cross corridor just inside the cellhouse. Having missed by seconds seeing Coy and Sundstrom fighting, he now saw nothing at all. He watched the corridor for perhaps a minute, then went back to the deadlock door.

"It looks all clear in there," he reported to Fish.

Cliff Fish drummed his fingers indecisively on the sill of the armory window.

•

In the A-B corridor, Coy finally managed to force Sundstrom to the floor and throw him against the wall. Then, nearly spent, he dove for the fallen rifle and managed to snatch it up before Sundstrom could right himself. Panting, almost choking for breath, Coy quickly covered the still-strong guard.

"Get on your feet, screw," Coy ordered in a forced voice. He snapped out the words between gulps of air. "Back to—the cutoff. Then—over to Broadway. No—funny moves—or I'll—drill you. Get going—"

Sundstrom, finally surrendering, moved obediently down Michigan Boulevard, with Coy behind him.

•

In the armory, Officer Clifford Fish finally decided that something *had* to be seriously wrong in the cellhouse. He was not certain just what to do, but he knew he had to do *something*.

Sitting back down at the switchboard, Fish first attempted to call the residence of the associate warden, in the island's personnel compound. He let the phone ring for what seemed like a very long time, but there was no answer.

Finally, Cliff Fish did what he had suspected all along that he would have to do. He pulled up a switchboard line, and plugged it into the warden's residence.

CHAPTER SIXTEEN

2:48 P.M.

When Coy arrived back at the end of C Block with Carl Sundstrom, Cretzer and the others turned to him anxiously. "Did he tip us?" Cretzer asked.

Coy shook his head. "I got him just in time. I had to fight him right by the goddamned sallyport door. It was close." Coy saw that Simpson and Baker were standing with their hands over their heads in front of Cell 402. It was impossible to fit any more officers into 403.

Coy nudged Sundstrom with the rifle. His chest hurt where the guard had kicked him. "Get over there," he said irritably, nodding toward the other two. "Watch them for a second, Dutch."

Coy went down to the control box, quickly set the mechanism, and racked open Cell 402. Then he shuffled back down the aisle to where the others waited. He was almost totally exhausted now; every inch of him ached, every nerve in his body screamed for rest, relief. When he got back to the cells, Cretzer came over to him.

"Are you ready to take out the tower guards now?" he asked in a voice too low for the captured officers to hear.

"In a minute. I got to keep a promise first." Coy looked over at Danny Durando. "Come here, Kid."

Durando came over and Coy took him down the flats to the end of the block where they could be alone.

"Kid," said Coy, "I'm going to give you a chance to pull out. I promised you there wouldn't be no shooting, but I can't keep that promise no more. We missed the prison boat, so we're going for the guards' apartment building. We're gonna see if we can get some wives and kids for hostages to force the warden to deal with us. I know you don't like that; I seen the look on your face when I came up with the idea. Just between you and me, I don't like it either; but the way things done fell, it's the best chance we got. The only thing is, in order to go for the apartment building, we first got to take out some of the tower guards. I'm the one that's going to do that, with this baby here—" He held up the Springfield. "I'm going to try just to wing them, and I'm pretty sure I can do it; I'm a good shot. But there's always the chance it won't turn out the way I want it to. If one of them should move at the wrong time or something—well, he'll probably be a dead man and there's nothing I can do to help it."

Durando looked pained. "If you kill a guard, Bernie, they'll put you in the chair for sure." He wet his lips in a quick, nervous movement. "Why don't you call it quits right now, Bernie?"

Coy shook his head emphatically. "Too late for me, Kid. They'd give me another ten for attempted escape and assaulting Burch and Sundstrom. I'd probably have to do at least five in an isolation cell like Whitey Franklin. Then—" Coy shrugged. "Well, I don't want to end up like Stroud either."

"Better to end up like Stroud than go to the chair," Durando said soberly.

"For you maybe," said Coy. "That's why I'm giving you a chance to pull out."

"What are the others going to say?" the Kid asked.

"They've got no say," Coy told him flatly. "It's still my break, and this is between you and me. Make your choice."

The Indio Kid sighed and slowly nodded his head. "Okay, Bernie, I'm out." He handed Coy the billy club he had been carrying. A slight resigned smile spread over his lips. "I guess I'll go over and sit in D Block. That's where they'll put me when it's over anyway."

"Your cell is still racked open in B," Coy said, "in case you want to go back there later."

Durando nodded. "Thanks."

Coy punched him lightly on the arm. "Luck, Kid."

"Luck to you too, Bernie."

The Chicano youth walked across the flats toward the D Block door.

Coy went back to where Cretzer, Shockley, and Hubbard waited.

"Okay, let's get organized," he said. "First of all, just so you'll know, the Kid's out of it now, so that just leaves five of us—"

"What do you mean, the Kid's out of it?" Dutch Cretzer asked suspiciously.

"That yellowbellied Mex!" snorted Crazy Sam. "You should have shot the cocksucker!"

"The Kid ain't yellow," Coy said. "He came in on the break only because I promised there wouldn't be no shooting. I *told* him he could pull out. And," he added with narrowed eyes, "I don't want no goddamned arguments about it! Now let's get on with our business." Coy jerked his head back toward Times Square. "Buddy's waiting by the door with the key that'll let us out. Marv, I want you and Sam to stay here and keep these screws in the cells. Dutch will be right up the flats at the corner of the block with the .45 in case you need help. I'm going into the kitchen and take out the tower guards south of the yard. As soon as I take care of that, I'll signal Dutch and he'll help you and Sam herd the screws to the yard door. Then we go!"

Coy nodded to Cretzer and the two of them hurried down Seedy to Times Square. Cretzer dropped off at the end of C Block, where he could watch the Square and Seedy at the same time.

"Good shooting, Coy," he said tonelessly.

Coy nodded. "Thanks, Cretzer." He could not be sure whether

Cretzer was ridiculing him or not. But he had no time to dwell on it. He continued across Times Square and ran through the dining hall.

In the kitchen there were three large, barred windows facing southwest, and a fourth window, in the corner, which faced west. Coy ran first to this latter window. He poked out a piece of glass with the rifle barrel and rested the rifle on the sill between two bars. Steadying the weapon, he squinted and sighted in on the guard in the Hill Tower.

Holding his breath, he slowly squeezed off the first shot.

•

In the Hill Tower, Officer Elmus Besk was standing in the open doorway. Before he even heard the sound of the shot, a .30-caliber slug tore into his right thigh and threw him violently to the floor of the tower.

Coy could not resist a smile of satisfaction as he saw Besk drop in the Hill Tower. It had been a good, clean leg shot.

Wetting his lips, he turned to his left, to the trio of windows which faced southwest. At the one nearest the corner, he punched out another window pane, and aimed the rifle at the blue-uniformed figure in the Road Tower.

Carefully, he squeezed off a second round.

•

In the Road Tower, Officer Arnold Levinson had a frown on his face. Seconds before, he was certain he had heard a gunshot. It had sounded as if it came from the direction of the Hill Tower, but as Levinson looked up there now he could see no one who might have fired it. Besk, the Hill Tower guard, was the only person in that vicinity who was armed, and he was nowhere to be seen. Levinson frowned even more deeply at that. The Hill Tower looked empty. Where in the hell had Besk gone to?

As he was wondering, Arnold Levinson felt a bullet rip through the sleeve of his uniform coat and plow into the ceiling of the tower. The sound of the shot reached his ears a split-second later.

Levinson, with superb reflexes, dropped immediately to the floor and began crawling toward a submachine gun in the corner.

•

Coy, smiling confidently again, certain that he had wounded Levinson with a clean shoulder shot, ran back into the dining hall and took up his third position. The dining hall had eight tall, barred windows on each side of the room. Coy checked the windows in the northeast wall until he found one which gave him a clear line of fire to the Dock Tower. It was the next-to-last window near the rear of the hall. He broke the window, knelt, aimed carefully, and sucked in his breath.

For the third time, Coy fired.

·

In the Dock tower, Officer James Comerford had taken a moment to stare out at the sparkling, sunlit waters of the bay. His back was to the big cellhouse and he was standing half in and half out of the tower. As he stood there, he felt something slap violently at his trouser legs; heard the far-off crack of a rifle shot; and in the same instant was startled by the extremely loud whine of a slug ricocheting off a steel gun port inside the tower.

As Levinson had done, Comerford instinctively dropped back inside the tower and to the floor. He could hardly believe what had happened, but wasted no time wondering about it. One thing was abundantly clear: someone had just fired a shot at him.

Reaching up, he dragged the tower phone down to the floor and clicked the button frantically for the armory switchboard to answer.

·

Below the Dock Tower, on the winding road that went up to the cellhouse, Associate Warden Edward J. Miller had been inspecting some painting done the previous day. He too heard the muted crack of the rifle shot that hit the tower, and immediately whirled around to see where it had been fired from. Squinting his eyes, he quickly scanned that part of the big cellhouse visible to him. He saw nothing.

Turning back to the tower, he saw Jim Comerford peek up over the steel siding. Miller waved to him. Comerford rose up a little farther, cautiously.

"You hit?" Miller yelled.

"No," the guard yelled back. "I tried to flash the armory but I didn't get an answer."

"Stay down," the associate warden told him. "Keep trying the armory. I'm going up the hill." He turned and started trotting up the winding road.

As associate warden, Edward Miller was second in command of the prison operation. No relation to Officer Bill Miller, he was a strong, beefy man, tough and unyielding as a keeper of men. Among the majority of Alcatraz inmates, he was, along with Captain Weinhold, one of the most disliked officials. The convicts had nicknamed him Meathead.

Running, a dozen demanding thoughts exploded in Miller's head at once. He could not even remotely imagine where the shot had come from, or who could have fired it. It was inconceivable to him that an inmate could have a gun; but it was also inconceivable that an officer would have fired the shot. But inconceivable or not, someone had definitely thrown a shot at Comerford. And he was damn sure going to find out who.

•

In the master bedroom of the warden's house, a stocky, gray-haired man was resting on a large, fourposter bed that had been beautifully crafted in the furniture shop at Leavenworth. Because he was an older, very formal gentleman, and even though he had not crossed the plaza to his office at all that day, he was nevertheless fully dressed in starched white shirt, necktie, and vest. His suit coat hung neatly on the back of a nearby chair. His one concession to comfort had been to remove his shoes and put on of a pair of green felt slippers. A sheet of plain brown wrapping paper had been placed under his feet to keep from soiling the white chenille bedspread that had been in his wife's family for three generations. He rested with a spotless linen handkerchief spread over his face; it moved slightly with the flow of his steady, even breathing. When the telephone rang on the night stand beside him, he reached over without removing the handkerchief and answered it on the second ring.

"Yes?"

"Warden, this is Clifford Fish in the armory," the caller said in a nervous voice. "Sir, I think we may have trouble in the cellhouse. No one has been answering any of the phones for the past half hour or so. Captain Weinhold went in to investigate, and didn't come out again. Then Lieutenant Simpson took two officers in to find him, and they haven't come out either. And no one is answering any of the cellhouse phones."

"What about the gun gallery officer?" asked the warden, moving his thoughts at once to the cellhouse's main line of invulnerability. "Are you able to contact him?"

"No, sir," said Fish. "I've rung the cage several times. There's no answer."

"I'll be right over," said the warden. He hung the phone up and removed the handkerchief from his face. Sitting up on the side of the bed, he removed his slippers and began putting on his business shoes.

Warden James A. Johnston was seventy years of age. He had been a penologist for nearly forty of those years. Holder of a degree in law, he had served as warden of both Folsom and San Quentin prisons, and had ultimately been appointed director of the California Department of Penology. One of the most respected men in his field, he had, six years earlier, been elected president of the American Prison Congress.

In 1934, the United States Department of Justice had asked Johnston to take on the task of establishing and running the new maximum-security–minimum-privilege federal prison on the island of Alcatraz. It was an exciting, challenging offer, and Jim Johnston, then fifty-eight, had eagerly accepted.

From its inception, Alcatraz had been *his* prison. He controlled it every step of the way, from personally designing the cellblocks, to drafting the most rigid set of regulations ever used in an American prison. The prisoners who subsequently did time there came to call Alcatraz "the Rock." And because it was so completely governed by its warden, they called him "Saltwater" Johnston.

In his bedroom, only a minute after the phone had first rung, the warden had on his shoes, coat, and glasses, and was ready to leave. He went into the dining room, looking for his wife. Instead, he found a note: *Gone down the hill to the store.* Johnston uncapped a fountain pen taken from his vest pocket and scribbled under it: *Gone to the office.*

●

Associate Warden Miller ran through the main entrance of the prison building and hurried to the armory window. A very worried Clifford Fish looked out at him.

"What the hell's going on up here?" Miller demanded. "Somebody just fired a shot at Comerford in the Dock Tower!"

"I don't know what's happening, Mr. Miller," Fish replied. "Nobody's answering any of the phones in the cellhouse. The captain and Mr. Simpson and some others went in to investigate and haven't come back out—"

"Give me a gas billy," Miller ordered. Fish passed the associate warden a billy club with a tear gas cannister that could be fired from one end of it. "Open the deadlock! I'll find out what the hell's going on in there."

Miller was passed quickly through the sallyport and let into the big cellhouse. He walked briskly down Broadway, gas billy held ready.

•

Bernie Coy, satisfied that he had successfully wounded the three tower guards, started to leave the dining hall and go back onto Times Square, when he saw still another uniformed guard coming down Broadway.

Jesus Christ, he thought, they just keep coming and coming. When he planned the break, he had counted on four hostages: Lageson, Corwin, Bristow, and Burdette. Now they had nine, and here came another one. What the hell was wrong with them anyway? Were they stupid or what? They already knew that nobody was answering the goddamned phones back here, so they must at least *suspect* that something is wrong. Yet they still kept walking in. Like pigs in a slaughter pen. It was crazy.

Coy peeked around the dining hall entry at the approaching officer. The man reached the cutoffs and was close enough for Coy to see who it was.

I'll be goddamned, the convict thought. Miller. Old Meathead himself.

Coy buttoned up Captain Weinhold's coat, hitched up Burch's trousers a bit, and concealed the rifle behind him as well as he could. Lowering his head, he stepped out of the dining-hall entry and crossed Times Square. He started down Broadway toward Miller. Rolling his eyes up, he could see Miller take another step, then stop and study him. When it became obvious that Miller was suspicious, that he did not intend to come any farther, Coy raised his head and looked directly at him.

Miller was shocked. "Coy—?"

Coy brought the rifle around and leveled it. "Make one move, Meathead, and you're a dead man."

With most guards, the warning would have worked. But Associate Warden Ed Miller was tougher than most. He had been in armed conflict with inmates before; the situation was not new to him. During his long career as a custodial officer, he had been assaulted with homemade knives, lead pipes, kitchen utensils, even a broken prescription bottle from a prison pharmacy. His reaction in every case had been instant retaliation. When a con threw down on him, Miller never hesitated to respond in kind. He did not hesitate now.

Almost before Coy had finished delivering his warning, Miller acted. Stepping sideways toward the nearest cell, in order not to present a silhouette target for Coy, the associate warden hurled the gas billy in the direction of the convict. Because he had moved too far to the side of the aisle, however, the billy did not clear the overhang of the second-tier range. It hit the under edge of the overhang and bounced back in Miller's face.

As the billy exploded, its combustion burned the right side of the associate warden's face from just below the eye to his collar. Then it spewed tear gas across the wide aisle.

Miller reeled back, covering his eyes. Incredibly, he was not blinded by either the explosion or the gas. Knowing that his counterattack on Coy had failed, he whirled and ran as fast as he could back down Broadway.

Coy could not see Miller clearly through the haze of tear gas. The running officer was a blur of motion, undefined in the swirling white cloud. Raising the rifle to fire, he hesitated, still reluctant to kill anyone. And he was not sure he could merely wound the running guard. But he was even more reluctant to let Miller get back to the armory. For some reason, despite the unanswered phones in the cellhouse, no assault squad of guards had yet been sent in to investigate. And no escape siren had been sounded. It was just possible, Coy thought, that the element of surprise was still on their side.

With that thought in mind, Coy quickly decided he at least had to try to stop Miller. He brought the rifle to the offhand position, pulled it back hard into his shoulder, and sighted in on the running blue blur. He fired. The bullet hit the east cellhouse wall. The blur kept moving. Coy fired again. Again he missed. Miller by then was dangerously close to the east corridor. Coy tried one last time. And missed. He saw the running figure disappear around the end of the block.

That tears it for sure, he thought tightly.

•

Warden Johnston had left by the front door of his residence and walked across the flatstone square, past the tall flagpole. Johnston carried himself erect, seeming taller than he actually was. There was a spring to his step that belied his threescore and ten years.

Instead of going around to the north side of the building where he had a private entrance into his office, he went directly to the Administration Section's main entrance and proceeded immediately to the armory. Cliff Fish looked up with relief when the warden entered.

"Any word from anyone?"

"No, sir, Warden. Mr. Miller just took a gas billy and went in to investigate."

"All right. How many officers do you personally know to be in the cellhouse?"

"Let's see," said Fish, counting them off on his fingers, "there's Bill Miller, there's Bristow and Lageson. There's Corwin, who's on duty in D Block. And Burdette, he didn't come out for lunch. Then Captain Weinhold went in to see why nobody was answering the phones."

"Did the captain go in alone?"

"Yes, sir."

Johnston's jaw tightened slightly. "Continue."

"Then Lieutenant Simpson took Baker and Sundstrom in to see what happened to the captain. That's it, Warden. Except for Burch in the gun cage, of course."

"I don't see any possible way anyone could have got to Burch," Johnston said, as much to himself as to Fish.

Just then the sallyport guard shouted, "Mr. Miller's running toward the door! It looks like he's been shot!"

With the deadlock area secured in front of it, the east cellhouse door was swung open and Associate Warden Miller, one side of his face blackened and burned, plunged into the sallyport. "Lock it, quick!" he ordered in an explosion of breath.

When the big steel door was locked, the deadlock was opened and Miller rushed into the armory.

"It's Coy, Warden! He's loose in there with a gun! He shot at me!"

Johnston turned calmly to the armory officer. "Mr. Fish, kick on the siren."

•

On Broadway, Dutch Cretzer came running up to Coy. "What the hell happened?"

" Meathead Miller came in," said Coy. "He shot a gas shell at me and beat it back out front. I tried to get him but I missed."

"How hard did you try?" Cretzer asked scornfully.

Coy looked at him steadily. "It don't really make a hell of a lot of difference now, does it?"

Cretzer shook his head in disgust. Along the flats of Broadway, the tear gas had diffused into the cells of the lockup cons, and they began to yell and cough and curse. "You going to let them out?"

Cretzer asked Coy. The Kentucky outlaw looked at him in near revulsion.

"Hell, no! That's all we need is twenty or thirty lockup cons wandering around getting in our way. We ain't got enough problems already. Besides, that tear gas ain't going to kill them. Couple of minutes and it'll all blow away. Come on, let's get out of here!"

"Did you get the tower screws?" Cretzer asked as they hurried to Seedy Street.

"You bet I did," Coy said. "Got 'em one-two-three, like ducks in a shootin' gallery."

When they got to the corner of Seedy, Coy waved down to Hubbard and Shockley. "Get the screws out! We're on our way!" He turned and looked across the flats where Buddy Thompson waited at the yard door with 107.

"Okay, Buddy, open her up!"

Hubbard and Shockley herded the nine captive guards toward the yard door. Coy stood on the flats, urging them on with the rifle. Suddenly Buddy Thompson turned from the door, looking panic-stricken.

"Bernie, it won't open! The 107 key won't work!"

"Jesus Christ, I don't believe this," Dutch Cretzer said.

Coy ran across the flats to the door. "You're crazy! It's got to work!" After all their trouble getting 107, Coy could not conceive of it not working. Roughly, he pushed Thompson aside. "Let me see the goddamned thing." Thompson's eyes flashed anger; he was not accustomed to being pushed.

Coy, the rifle on the floor at his knees, carefully and patiently began working the 107 key in the lock. It moved in and out of the lock with ease, but would not revolve to drop the cylinders. His face like a death mask, Coy moved the key relentlessly, never forcing it but never pausing in his slow, continuous jiggling and twisting. Behind him on the flats, the others, guards and convicts alike, watched silently. Captain Weinhold had regained consciousness now and was staying on his feet with the help of Lieutenant Simpson and Officer Baker. Officer Cecil Corwin was also awake, and being steadied by Bristow and Burdette. Both Weinhold and Corwin had dried blood on their faces. Bill Miller, the only other officer who had suffered any physical damage, had managed with a cold compress to get the swelling in his lip reduced. His feet were beginning to bother him, and he wondered briefly how Coy's gums were feeling.

At the yard door, Coy's hand began to sweat. He wiped it on the guard coat he was wearing. Then he resumed working the key, patiently, doggedly, his dark eyes half frightened, half sick, as if he already knew that all his work had been for nothing.

After a long, frustrating attempt to turn the key, Bernie Coy finally shook his head and sighed a deep, helpless sigh. Wearily he leaned his forehead against the cold steel of the door and closed his eyes.

"It's jammed," he said quietly, to no one in particular. "Trying all them other keys must have messed it up somehow."

As Coy finished speaking, almost in emphasis of his helplessness, the Alcatraz escape siren began its terrible shriek.

CHAPTER SEVENTEEN
3:05 P.M.

In the armory Warden Johnston began to issue orders.

"You four men get down to Industries as quickly as you can. Advise all shop officers that the grades are to be kept in their respective shops until further notice." He turned to the next man. "You wait out front. As soon as they hear the siren, all the off-duty officers will be reporting. Direct them into the Admin office and have them stand by." He turned to Fish. "Mr. Fish, notify the FBI, the San Francisco police, the California Highway Patrol, and the Coast Guard that we have an armed break on our hands here."

Johnston then strode across the sallyport, through the Admin offices, and into the small office occupied by his male secretary. Sitting down next to the desk, he wrote a terse message on a lined pad. "Get this on the teletype to Washington at once."

"Yes, Warden." The secretary swung his chair around to the teletype. He keyed the machine into operation and quickly sent the first word of the break to the Bureau of Prisons.

3:10 P.M. ALCATRAZ. URGENT.
PRISONER LOOSE IN CELLHOUSE
WITH GUN. SITUATION SERIOUS.
MORE LATER. STAND BY.

In Washington, it was 6:10 P.M. A night-duty clerk received the teletype message. His eyes widened as he read it. Nervously he opened his bureau telephone book and looked up the number of the director. When he called, the director himself answered.

"Teletype from Alcatraz, sir." The clerk read it. The director had him read it a second time.

"I'll be there in a few minutes," the director said and hung up.

The director of the Bureau of Prisons was James V. Bennett. Son of an Episcopal minister, he was a former air cadet in the Army Air Corps who after his discharge had worked his way through law school at George Washington University. Entering federal civil service, he had worked first for the U.S. Bureau of Efficiency. While there, he had been assigned to the Justice Department to conduct a study of America's prison system to determine whether then idle federal prisoners could usefully be put to work. He later transferred to Justice, and was assigned to its bureau overseeing government prisons. Now fifty-two years old, Bennett had been with the bureau for sixteen years. Nine years earlier, in 1937, he had been appointed its director by President Franklin Roosevelt.

It was Bennett who had selected James Johnston to head the Alcatraz project and become its warden. He had personally approved Johnston's plans and specifications for the island prison's big cellhouse. As he prepared to go back to his office on the evening of May 2, he could not imagine how a gun could possibly have got into that cellhouse.

At that time, Bennett probably did not even remember a convict named Bernard Paul Coy, whose record he had reviewed nine years earlier. As assistant to the former prisons director, Bennett had been one of the bureau executives who recommended Coy's transfer from Atlanta to Alcatraz.

•

Across the bay from Alcatraz, at the Presidio, headquarters of the U.S. Sixth Army, a thin, slightly stooped man with a craggy face, silver spectacles, and white crewcut hair stood staring out the window of his office. He was looking at the rockbound prison and listening curiously to the steady, relentless wail of its siren.

The man was Lieutenant General Joseph "Vinegar Joe" Stilwell, hero of the Burma Campaign in World War Two. Former commander of two Chinese army divisions, he had, early in the war, been driven into India by vastly superior Japanese forces. Only a forced march of twenty days had saved his men from total annihilation. But in December, 1943, Vinegar Joe had come back. Launching an all-out counteroffensive from the Indian border, he had forged a path of jungle victories that took him all the way to the famed Burma Road and a linkup with other Allied forces. Now, with the war behind him, he was commander of the Sixth Army.

After scrutinizing the Rock for several minutes, Stilwell turned back to his desk and flipped an intercom switch.

"Yes, General?" said the pretty WAC lieutenant who was his secretary.

"Maggie, what's going on over at Alcatraz?"

"I don't know, sir. I've been looking out the window; everything seems normal. Maybe their siren is stuck."

"See if you can find out, will you?"

"Yes, sir."

Stilwell went back to his paperwork, a duty which was boring as hell to the old warhorse and which he detested so much that it often gave him psychosomatic headaches. He was looking forward to a short respite from routine, however; that evening he was going to San Diego for a speaking engagement the next day before a veterans' organization. He always enjoyed getting back with the boys again.

His secretary buzzed him a few minutes later. "Sir, I've called several federal offices downtown and no one seems to know what's the matter on Alcatraz. Would you like me to try calling the prison directly?"

"No, I don't think so. But ask my chief of staff to step in, please."

Several minutes later, another general entered Stilwell's office. This man, wearing two stars less than his commanding officer, was Brigadier General Frank Merrill. He had known Stilwell intimately during the war. As leader of the famed long-range penetration regiment known as Merrill's Marauders, he had won fame throughout the China-Burma-India war zone. When Vinegar Joe had led his Chinese divisions to the linkup at the Burma Road, Frank Merrill and his jungle-tough raiders had been there to meet him. Theirs was a unique friendship.

"What do you think's going on over at the prison, Frank?" Stilwell asked his next in command.

"I don't know, Joe," answered Merrill. Both soldiers went to the window to look out. The siren continued unabated. "I've never heard that siren before," said Merrill. "It must mean trouble."

"Likely," said Vinegar Joe. He rubbed his craggy chin. "See if you can get hold of the warden on the phone. Call personally. Don't insinuate that he needs our help, but let him know it's available. Get back to me as soon as you know something."

"Right."

Merrill went back to his own office.

●

At the U.S. Coast Guard station at Yerba Buena Island, a lieutenant serving as officer of the day was making up the next patrol's duty roster when he was interrupted by the seaman first class who was assigned to the operations desk.

"Lieutenant, a call just came in from some guy named Fish over at Alcatraz. He says they're having a prison break over there."

The lieutenant looked dubious. "Did the call sound legitimate?"

The seaman shrugged. "The guy sounded excited, sir."

The lieutenant rose and walked out onto the headquarters porch. The seaman followed. They stood quietly, listening. Their station was on the south side of the Bay Bridge, around the corner of San Francisco from Alcatraz. It took them a moment to tune in to the distant siren, but they finally heard it.

"It's legitimate," the lieutenant said urgently. "Get on the phone and locate the captain. Tell him about the call, and tell him I'm putting two armed cutters in the water to circle the island."

●

At San Francisco police headquarters, Clifford Fish's call was put through to Captain of Inspectors Bernard McDonald. Although McDonald could not personally hear the Alcatraz siren, he had already received calls from four divisions advising that radio cars all over the waterfront were reporting the alert. McDonald, unlike the two army generals at the Presidio, knew full well what the siren probably meant. He was a longtime police officer in San Francisco; he had heard the Rock's siren before.

On the chance that it might be a false alarm, he had done nothing when the first report was received, except to note the time. When the second call was received, four minutes later, he had started preliminary planning, making a few notes on a memo pad. Three minutes later, the third call came in, and immediately after that the fourth. When the Alcatraz siren had been on for eight minutes, McDonald called the inspector in charge of patrol units and ordered a deployment of radio cars. When the call came in from Clifford Fish, Mc-Donald had a report ready for him.

"We're aware of your emergency, Officer Fish," he said after Fish had officially reported the escape attempt. "Please advise the warden that we are presently assigning two radio units and four officers to every pier, dock, and wharf on the waterfront. If we can assist, please call us at once."

When he finished talking to Fish, the captain of inspectors put on his coat and went upstairs to Chief of Police Charles W. Dullea's office. "There's a break on the Rock, boss," he said. "Phase One deployment has been put into effect."

"Any details yet?" Dullea asked. He was sipping iced tea at his desk, where he had been going over the crime statistics for his city for the month of April. They were depressing figures. There was no getting around it: the crime rate was definitely rising now that the war was over and the men overseas were coming home. Adjusting to peace after fighting a war must be pretty difficult for some men, he had concluded.

"No details yet, boss," said McDonald.

"One of these days," Dullea said almost absently, "there's going to be a *real* break on that goddamned island, and our streets are going to be crawling with mad dogs like Kelly and Karpis and the rest of those killers. I don't know why they couldn't have put their prison somewhere else. There's a perfectly good island in Hawaii that used to be a leper colony. Be perfect for a federal prison." He sighed and shook his head. "Okay, Mac, keep me posted. And keep our boys on the waterfront alert, just in case this is the one where they make it to shore."

"Will do, Boss."

Bernard McDonald went back downstairs.

•

Along the waterfront, and even up the hill as far as Washington Square, the prison siren had begun to attract attention. A few tourists on Fisherman's Wharf paused to look curiously out at the bay. Some longtime residents of nearby Bay Street came to their windows to look out, wondering why the siren was sounding so *long* this time.

Up Powell Street, at the North Beach playground, a mixed group of Anglo and Oriental boys from Saints Peter and Paul Church were playing softball and paid no attention at all to the intruding noise. A priest in a sweatshirt, who was supervising the game, hoped the siren would stop before four o'clock, so that it would not distract from the church's afternoon chimes.

Still farther up the hill, on the bay side of the park at Washington Square, a group of young Chinese mothers had their children out to play. They ignored the siren completely. Alcatraz meant nothing to them. None of the guards—or inmates, for that matter—was Oriental; and if any of the prisoners *did* manage to escape and get to shore, none of them would be foolish enough to try to hide in Chinatown. They would be safer in the sea end of the bay with the sharks.

Beyond Washington Square, very few people heard or paid much attention to what was happening on Alcatraz. Yet.

•

After Warden Johnston sent the first teletype to Washington, he took a moment to step into his office and telephone his wife. He knew she would be back in the house by then; the siren would have immediately driven all women and children indoors. His wife answered the phone on the first ring.

"There's trouble," Johnston said. "It's very serious. Lock all the doors and stay inside."

"Yes, Jim," his wife answered.

The warden hung up and went into the Admin office. About two dozen guards were waiting there. Johnston's trained eyes flicked over them once and then returned to a man who stood near the center of the group.

"Lieutenant Boatman, step forward, please."

George Boatman, a quiet, efficient guard officer with prior service at Atlanta and Leavenworth, moved up beside the warden.

"You're assigned as operations officer until this emergency is over," Johnston said. "All right, men," he addressed them all, "here's the situation. At least one inmate is loose in the cellhouse with a rifle—" A shock wave of conversation rumbled through the group. "All right, quiet down," Johnston ordered. "I know it's hard to believe, but nevertheless it's true. And we don't have time right now to try to figure out *how* he got it. Our main goal right now is to regain control of the cellhouse. There are at least ten of our officers in there—maybe alive, maybe dead, we don't know yet. So let's get organized. Lieutenant Boatman, have automatic weapons issued to all men and start handing out assignments. Keep an accurate list of where everybody is stationed. Make sure all strategic locations are double-guarded, and put triple reinforcements on the road between the wall and the personnel living quarters. Also get a couple of men on the catwalk outside the D Block windows. Maybe they can see what's going on inside. Use all due caution."

"Yes, sir," Boatman replied briskly.

Just then, Johnston's secretary stuck his head in the door and said urgently, "Warden, Fish just got a call from Besk in the Hill Tower! He's been shot in the leg and he's bleeding heavily!"

"I'll handle it, sir," Boatman said quickly.

Johnston walked briskly out of Admin, across the deadlock area, and into the armory. "Is the line still open to Besk?"

"Yessir," Fish said.

"Tell him help is on the way."

"Yessir. And I've got a call holding, sir. Warden Duffy of San Quentin."

"Plug it in over here, Cliff." Johnston picked up the phone at the desk where Weinhold had been reading the newspaper an hour earlier. "Hello, Clint," he said tensely.

"The highway patrol called us, Jim," said Clinton Duffy. "What's up?"

"We've got a con loose in the cellhouse with a rifle," Johnston said. "Nine of my guards have gone in there and haven't come out. And I can't contact my gallery officer."

"Do you think they're dead?"

"I don't know, Clint," Johnston said almost fearfully. "I hope to God not. But it doesn't look good."

"Are most of your inmates still in their shops?" Duffy asked.

"Yes."

"Let me send you some help, Jim. I can spare a dozen men; have them there in an hour. Just one thing: use them to guard the shops and relieve your own men to do the shooting. Try to keep my boys out of the line of fire. If one of them should get shot, the people down at the state house who don't like my policies would have me drawn and quartered."

"I know it, Clint. I'll keep them in the background. And thanks."

As Johnston hung up, Cliff Fish swiveled around from the switchboard. "Warden, General Merrill just called from the Presidio. He said to tell you he can have two platoons of Marines over here to assist you anytime you give the word."

"I don't really think we need the Marines in on this," Johnston replied. "Thank General Merrill anyway."

A lieutenant came hurrying in. "Warden, a man just reported back from the catwalk outside the D Block windows. All the Isolation prisoners have been let out. They're wandering all over the block. And he saw Dutch Cretzer through the door that leads into the main cellhouse. Cretzer was carrying a .45."

The elderly warden paled and one of his hands began to tremble. He crossed back into Admin, went to his secretary's desk, and scribbled another message to Washington. His secretary put it on the wire at once.

ITS CRETZER. HE HAS A
FORTYFIVE. RIOT CALL SOUNDED.
MOBILIZING ALL OFFICERS.
STAND BY.

Johnston walked back into the big Admin office and stood there indecisively for several moments. There was a pained look on his face. He could scarcely believe what was happening. Convicts with guns. Ten officers captured in the cellhouse. The isolation prisoners —the very worst in his keep—let out of their cells. He shuddered slightly at the thought of what might happen next.

Quickly, as if driven by his thoughts, he returned to the armory. "Call General Merrill back," he instructed Fish. "Tell him I will be grateful to accept his offer to send over Marines."

As Johnston walked back into Admin, he noticed Associate Warden Miller being given first aid for his badly burned face before being taken to a mainland hospital for treatment. It suddenly occurred to Johnston that he had not reported to Washington what had happened to Miller. For the third time, he went to his secretary's desk and composed a message to the Bureau of Prisons.

COY ALSO LOOSE WITH RIFLE
AND TRYING TO PICK OFF TOWER
OFFICERS. HAS WOUNDED TOWER
OFFICER. DEPUTY MILLER ALSO
WOUNDED. SITUATION CRITICAL.

CHAPTER EIGHTEEN

4:15 P.M.

In the cellhouse, the nine hostages had once again been herded back into Cells 402 and 403.

In 403, Captain Weinhold was stretched out on the bare mattress of the bunk, with Ernest Lageson attending him. Weinhold's head and face wounds had finally stopped bleeding. Lageson was applying wet compresses to the side of Weinhold's swelling face, being careful not to disturb the stanched blood. Weinhold kept waking up and then lapsing into unconsciousness again.

While Lageson took care of the guard captain, Joe Burdette was sitting on the floor holding Cecil Corwin's bloody head in his lap. Corwin was awake and in such intense pain that he could not keep his eyes open; but his gashed scalp, like Weinhold's, had stopped bleeding. Now and again Corwin would groan softly and Burdette would pat him gently. Bill Miller, his punched lips and left cheek swollen and purple, stood near the front of the cell and watched Bernie Coy and the remaining four cons holding a tense conference a few cells down Seedy.

Next door, in 402, Lieutenant Simpson and Officer Bob Baker also stood near the cell front, watching. Carl Sundstrom, who had fought Bernie Coy in sight of the main cellhouse door, was slumped on the bunk, dabbing at his cuts and bruises with a wet handkerchief. "Another few feet," he was muttering angrily to himself. "Another few lousy feet and I could have got help."

"Take it easy, Carl," said Simpson. "You did your best. Anyway, help will be coming in soon." He bobbed his head at the conferring convicts. "It was all over for them the second that siren kicked on."

"That son of a bitch Coy," Sundstrom said. "If I ever get my hands on him, I'll kill him."

Simpson looked curiously at his fellow guard. "If I were you, Carl, I'd be glad I was alive. Coy *could* have killed you, you know."

Sundstrom looked away and did not reply.

•

On the flats, the five convicts assessed their situation.

"They could be coming in here in force any second," Buddy Thompson said nervously.

"Nobody's coming in here in force," Coy said quietly. He glanced briefly at the Texas loner, deciding that Thompson wasn't as smart as he had thought. "Marv, check the rifle ammo. Dutch, how many slugs you got for the .45?"

The two men counted the bullets. "Twenty-one," Cretzer said.

"Sixty-five for the rifle, Bernie," said Hubbard a moment later. "Plus whatever you got in it."

"Four left in it," said Coy. "That's sixty-nine. Plus Dutch's, gives us ninety rounds."

"That won't be much if they rush us," Thompson said solemnly. "Sam and Marv and me don't even have guns."

"I already told you they ain't going to rush us," Coy said with a trace of irritation. "Not as long as we've got those nine friends of theirs in here. With hostages, these guns, and all the food in that kitchen, we can hold out in here forever. And they know it. We may not be off this goddamned rock, but we ain't beat yet either."

"What do you have in mind to do next, Bernie?" asked Hubbard.

"I'm thinking about having a little chat with the warden. I'm wondering what he'd be willing to give us in exchange for the nine screws."

"An airplane!" Crazy Sam said gleefully. "Make him give us an airplane!"

"Shut up, Sam," Cretzer said sharply. To Coy he said, "We can't settle for anything less than a boat, Bernie. You know that, don't you? The only chance we've got is to get to that car on shore. Unless we get a boat, we might as well cash in our chips right now."

"For once we see eye to eye, Dutch," said Coy. "That'll be our deal. Nothing less than a boat." He nodded toward the Times Square end of the aisle. "I'll call him. You keep everything under control here."

"Check."

As Coy trotted down Seedy, Cretzer looked over and saw Crazy Sam sulking near one of the empty cells. Feeling guilty, he went over and put an arm around him.

"Hey, why the long face, Sam?" Cretzer asked. Shockley turned away and would not look at him or answer. "Ah, come on now, Sam—"

"You told me to shut up," Shockley accused. "You're just like everybody else: never pay no attention to anything I say. Making them give us an airplane was a good idea."

"Sure it was, Sam. I didn't say it wasn't."

"Then why'd you make me shut up?" Shockley pouted.

Cretzer started to explain that there was no place on the island for a plane to land; but he decided that that might make his friend feel even worse for not having thought of it himself. "It'd just take too long to get a plane, Sam," he said instead. "We want to get out of this dump as quick as we can, don't we?"

"I guess so," Sam answered sullenly.

"Well, they can get us a boat a lot quicker than they can a plane." Cretzer wrestled his friend about playfully. "Hey, I'm sorry I told you to shut up. Come on, we're still pals, aren't we? You and me, the old D Block boys. Come on, Sam, what do you say?"

Shockley grinned sheepishly. "Okay, Dutch."

"Fine," Cretzer said, smiling. He kept his arm around Crazy Sam. "Tell you what, as soon as Coy gets back, you and I will go in the kitchen and raid the bakery!"

Sam Shockley's eyes lit up like a child's might have.

•

At the end of C Block, Bernie Coy had the phone to his ear. One of the men now helping Cliff Fish in the armory answered at the switchboard.

"This is Coy, screw," the convict leader said. "I want to talk to Johnston."

The guard at the switchboard caught his breath slightly. It was the first time he had ever heard the head of the prison referred to without a "Mister" or "Warden" preceding his name. Even in casual conversation, the guards did not speak of him like that. The closest they came was when they called him the "Old Man," and even that was said respectfully. Now to hear a convict simply call the warden by his last name was a minor shock.

The armory guard plugged into the warden's office. "It's Coy, Warden. He wants to talk to you."

"Thank you," Johnston said calmly. He heard the guard make the connection. "This is Warden Johnston."

"This is Coy, Warden. We're ready to talk some business if you are."

"Before we go any further, Coy, I want to know the condition of my officers," Johnston said firmly.

"You're entitled to that," Coy replied reasonably. "I'm going to level with you. We had to beat up Miller a little when we first jumped him. And we had to slug Corwin over the head when he made a grab for the phone." Coy paused, thinking about Shockley's attack on Weinhold. And about his own fights with Burch and Sundstrom. Johnston caught the pause at once.

"What else?" the warden demanded.

"That's all," Coy lied. Johnston would have no way of knowing about the other three, he decided. It would only complicate matters to mention them. "Other than Miller and Corwin, they're all okay."

"You understand," said Johnston, "that any arrangements we make will be predicated on my speaking to each officer on the phone to assure myself that they're all alive. Is that clear?"

"Clear. Now let's get down to business. We want a boat and safe passage to shore."

"Where on shore?"

"You don't need to know that," Coy drawled. "All you got to do is clear the bay and make sure nobody tries to stop the boat. We'll take the guards with us until we figure we're safe; then we'll let 'em go."

"I'll have to get approval from Washington before I can say yes or no," Johnston told him. "I'll call you back. Which phone will you be near?"

"I'll call *you* back, Warden," Coy replied. "Me and the boys are moving around a lot. And we're moving these hacks of yours with us. I'll ring you back in a while."

Coy hung up.

•

In his office, Warden Johnston sat looking at the dead receiver. A boat and safe passage to the mainland, he thought. He shook his head solemnly. Never.

Johnston depressed the phone button several times.

"Yes, Warden?"

"Where was Coy calling from?"

"C Block, sir."

"All right," Johnston thought for a second. "Please put through a call to the Director of Prisons in Washington."

"Yessir."

"And send Lieutenant Boatman in here."

Boatman came in a moment later and Johnston motioned him to a chair.

"What I want to do now, George, is put together an assault team to get into the west gun gallery," the warden said. "Who's our best shot?"

"It would probably be a standoff between Phil Bergen and Harry Cochrane, Warden."

"Bergen has the rank, doesn't he?"

"Yes, sir. He's a lieutenant."

"Get him in here," said Johnston.

As Boatman left, the phone on Johnston's desk rang. It was Fish. "Sir, the line to Washington is open, but Mr. Bennett says to wait until he can get the call tied in to the attorney general's home. He wants it to be a three-way call."

"All right, Cliff. I'll hang on until they're ready."

Johnston swiveled around in his chair and looked out a wide bay window at what was conceivably the most panoramic view of the bay that existed. From the middle of the bay his eyes could sweep both coasts and the entire length of the Bay Bridge. If there had been prisoners in A Block, they would have had essentially the same view, disrupted to some degree by bars; but since A was not occupied, Warden Johnston was the only resident of the island able to enjoy the spectacular scene.

The warden rested his head back and briefly rubbed his temple. A headache was slowly settling on him. His lower back was aching, too. And his stomach was in dire need of a nice glass of warm milk. I'm getting too old for this sort of thing, he thought. I'm seventy. I should be off somewhere fishing or pitching horseshoes or doing some of the other things old men do. I shouldn't be sitting here on top of a powder keg like some damn *young* man.

Sighing, he looked around his big private office. It was a nice office, very nice indeed. Large. Airy. Comfortable. With its own fireplace and a private bathroom. And, of course, the view. Johnston grunted quietly. Hell, he didn't even *like* fishing.

"Hello," said a staticky voice through the receiver at his ear, interrupting Johnston's thoughts. "Are you there, Jim?"

"Here, Mr. Director," Johnston acknowledged.

"Jim, I've got the attorney general on a party line," said prisons director James V. Bennett.

"Hello, Warden Johnston," said a second voice, that of U.S. Attorney General Tom Clark. A forty-seven-year-old Texan, Clark had been appointed to the cabinet after his friend Harry Truman succeeded Franklin Roosevelt to the presidency. In three more years, after Truman's upset victory over Thomas Dewey, the President would appoint Clark to the Supreme Court of the United States.

"What's the situation out there, Jim?" asked Bennett.

"Joseph Cretzer is loose in the cellhouse with a pistol," said Johnston. "Bernard Coy is also in on the break; he has been seen carrying a rifle. One of our tower guards has been shot in the leg. There are at least nine officers, including a captain and a lieutenant of guards, who are being held hostage. I have extra help coming over from San Quentin and the Presidio."

"Besides the cellhouse, is the rest of the island secure?" Bennett asked.

"Yes. The key to the yard door is in the cellhouse somewhere, but either they haven't found it or they tried to use it improperly. The lock is designed to jam if an attempt is made to force it."

"Warden," said the attorney general, "have you had any communication from the convicts who are in on the break?"

"Yes, we have, sir," Johnston replied. "Coy called from a cellhouse phone. They want a boat and guaranteed passage to shore in exchange for the hostages."

"That's out of the question, of course," said Bennett. "Don't you agree, Mr. Attorney General?"

"Absolutely," Tom Clark said firmly.

"Jim," said Bennett, "do everything possible to get our men out alive, but under no circumstances are any prisoners to be let off the island. Are you evacuating any wives and children?"

"Not at this time. The dock is within range of that rifle Coy has. I'm not certain whether any of the A Block windows would afford him a clear shot at anyone getting on the boat or not, but I don't want to chance it unless there's no alternative."

"All right, whatever you think best," said Bennett. "I'll call Leavenworth, McNeil Island, and Englewood, and have the wardens each send you a cadre of selected officers to supplement your own forces. Can you think of anything else I can do for you, Jim?"

"Not at the moment, no," Johnston replied.

"All right. Good luck, Jim."

"Yes, good luck, Warden," said Tom Clark.

"Thank you, gentlemen. I think I may need it."

•

Johnston hung up the receiver and looked up to see Lieutenant Boatman waiting at his office door.

"Lieutenant Bergen is here, sir," Boatman said. Johnston motioned them inside.

Lieutenant Philip Bergen was a tall, square-jawed, handsome man who looked as if he could have been the hero of every Saturday movie serial ever made. He had cool, direct eyes and a natural fearlessness. On Alcatraz, Bergen was considered a "high-risk" guard. He was a daredevil who thought nothing of plunging head-first into danger. In addition, he was a deadly shot.

"Phil," said the warden, "I presume you've been briefed on the situation inside, as much as we know of it. What I want now is a team to enter the west gun gallery. I want to know what's happened to Burch, and if possible I want to know where the rest of our men are being held. Can you do it?"

"Yes, sir," Bergen replied at once. He looked at Boatman. "I'd like to take Harry Cochrane with me."

Johnston shook his head. "It's not a two-man job, Phil. We've got nine men being held hostage now because they went in there in twos and threes. Take Cochrane if you like, but I want at least five more men to go also. We know that Dutch Cretzer and Bernie Coy are both in on this. Cretzer is a killer and Coy is just about as smart as they come. Let's not underestimate them any more than we apparently already have. Make it six men plus yourself. Draw whatever weapons you want from the armory."

"Yessir."

Bergen and Boatman left the warden's private office. In the big Admin office, Harry Cochrane was waiting for Bergen. Cochrane, shorter and stockier than Bergen, was a nerveless Irishman who, like his friend, was also a crack shot and considered a high-risk officer. "What'd we pull?" he asked Bergen, knowing that whatever assignment Bergen had been given, he, Harry Cochrane, would be a part of it.

"The west gun gallery," said Bergen. "But he wants five more men to go with us."

"Five more!" said Cochrane. "That's too many, Phil. We'll be like sardines in that gun cage. Hell, we won't be able to aim!"

"The warden said five more," Bergen told him firmly. "Get me some volunteers, will you, George?" he said to Boatman. "Have them meet me in the armory."

Bergen and Cochrane walked out into the deadlock, Cochrane still complaining about the size of the assault team.

•

In his office, Warden Johnston sat at his desk, drumming his fingertips soundlessly on the arm of his chair. He was staring at his desktop, not sure exactly what to do next. From the drawer of his desk, he had taken a large binder containing numerous contingency plans for the handling of various emergencies. The book covered everything from fires and earthquakes to riots in the dining hall and work strikes. What it did *not* cover was the possibility of inmates getting their hands on guns in the cellhouse.

By now, Johnston had concluded that the guns must have come from the west gun gallery. All that had been seen was one pistol, being used by Cretzer, and one rifle, in the hands of Coy. Those were the weapons carried by the gun gallery officer.

But *how?* Johnston asked himself over and over. *How* had those guns gotten from the elevated cage down into the cellhouse? After a dozen years of invulnerability, how had the gun gallery at last been neutralized and its weapons seized?

As Johnston pondered, his secretary came to the door. "Warden?" Johnston did not respond.

"Warden?" the man said again, louder. This time the elderly prison head looked up.

"Yes? What is it?"

"The siren, sir. Can we turn it off now?"

"Turn it off?" the warden said. He blinked his eyes rapidly behind his rimless glasses, as if he had not quite understood the question.

"The siren's been on for an hour and a half, sir. It's making some of us nervous. Is it all right to turn it off?"

"Of course. Give the order at once," Johnston said.

Moments later, mercifully, the shrieking siren was silenced.

CHAPTER NINETEEN

5:00 P.M.

The assault team preparing to storm the west gun gallery was assembling with their weapons on the plaza between the cellhouse and the warden's residence. Besides Lieutenant Philip Bergen and his friend Harry Cochrane, the team included Officers Fred Richberger,

Herschel Oldham, Fred Mahan, and Joe Maxwell. The last man to join them was Officer Hal Stites, who that morning had felt so good knowing he did not have to go to work that day.

Stites came out of the armory, a Thompson submachine gun cradled in one arm, and walked outside to join the others. Harry Cochrane saw him coming. "Our worries are over, boys," he said loudly. "We're being joined by Harold Stites, the fastest draw on Alcatraz."

Stites smiled his easy smile. He was the guard who had shot down Limerick and Franklin, and captured Lucas, in their escape attempt eight years earlier. Since then he had taken a lot of kidding from Cochrane and some of the other marksmen on the Rock. But it was all in the spirit of camaraderie that most of the Alcatraz guards enjoyed, and Hal Stites, one of the most easygoing of the lot, never let it bother him. As he approached Cochrane now, he looked wryly at the other guard's .45 pistol.

"Hello, Deadeye," he said. "What's the matter, wouldn't they give you a tommy gun?"

"With an eye like mine, lad, they could give me a slingshot and I'd get the job done."

Phil Bergen went to the front of the group. "Everybody set?" he asked. The men stopped talking and faced him. No one spoke. "Okay, let's go," he ordered. "Stay close to the building. Remember, we'll be right under the windows of D Block."

With Bergen leading the way, the men moved in single file around to the south side of the cellhouse. They followed a path that led to a steel sidewalk extending the entire length of the outside wall of D Block. Halfway along the wall, the ground under the walk sloped down into a hill; the steel walk continued in the form of a catwalk attached to the side of the building. Seven feet above the walk were the nine lower windows of D Block.

At the corner of the D Block wing, the catwalk turned and extended along the west end of the block some twenty-eight feet to the double-doored outside entry into the west gun gallery.

Bergen led the assault team around the outside corner and quickly along to the gun-gallery door. Harry Cochrane was right behind him. Then Hal Stites and, in order, Hersh Oldham, Fred Richberger, Fred Mahan, and Joe Maxwell.

Of the seven, only two would *walk* back along the steel sidewalk.

•

Inside D Block, Birdman Stroud was sitting on the flats talking with Louis Fleish.

"Think they've got any chance of making it, Bob?" Fleish asked.

Stroud shook his head emphatically. "They'll be dead before midnight," he said. He grunted softly. "So might the rest of us."

"What makes you say that?"

"Because Coy's got the gun-cage screw's rifle. And somebody else has got his pistol. They probably had to kill him to get those guns. When the screws come charging in here, they're going to shoot anything that moves."

"Then what the hell are we sitting down here on the flats for?" Fleish asked edgily.

Stroud smiled his old man's smile. "Why not? You don't want to live forever, do you?"

"I want to live long enough to get off this Rock," Fleish said.

Stroud chuckled quietly. "Relax," he said. "There's still time before they come in. Prison hacks ain't like other people. They're slower; take longer to do things."

"You know, I've noticed that," said Fleish with sudden interest. "I wonder why that is."

"Because they're lazy," Stroud told him. "Only a no-account, lazy son of a bitch would take a job where he didn't have nothing to do all day except walk up and down and watch. Hell, back in Leavenworth when I had my bird lab, I used to accomplish more good in one week than a goddamned prison hack does in a year. They're worthless, all of 'em."

Fleish leaned forward on his knees and deftly rolled an almost symmetrically perfect cigarette. "You think you'll ever get out, Bob?" he asked casually. "You think they'll ever turn you loose?"

"Shit no," Stroud answered. The tone of his voice implied that he really did not give a damn.

As the two men sat there, they saw Danny Durando come into the block from C and look around. The dark young Chicano seemed uncertain exactly what to do next.

"Who's that?" Stroud wondered.

"I think it's that Mexican who came in last year. They call him the Indio Kid."

"He on the break with Coy?"

"Could be," said Fleish. "He's acting kind of nervous."

"He looks lost," said Stroud. He studied the young man for several moments. "Hail him over," he said finally.

Fleish called to Durando. "Hey, Kid!" When Durando looked, Fleish motioned him over. The Kid walked up to them. Fleish handed up the cigarette. "Have a smoke, Kid."

"I don't smoke," said Durando.

"Looks like a good time for you to start," Fleish said. "What are you so jumpy about?"

"Nothing," the Indio Kid said quickly. "I ain't jumpy."

"What's your name, boy?" Stroud asked.

"Dan Durando," the Kid answered.

"Well, sit down over here, Dan, and relax. You a friend of Bernie's?"

"Yeah," said Durando. He sat down next to Stroud, wetting his lips, his dark eyes darting.

"Ease up, Dan," said Stroud. "You're among friends. Were you going on Bernie's trip?"

The Kid nodded.

"What happened?"

"I canceled out. They're going a different route now." Durando looked closely at Stroud, and it suddenly dawned on him who the old convict was. "You're the Birdman, ain't you?"

"That's me," Stroud said wryly. "This here is Louie Fleish."

"Here," Fleish said, offering the cigarette again. "Try a smoke, Kid. It'll help you to loosen up."

"Okay," said the Kid. He took the cigarette, lighted up, and coughed a little as he tried smoking for the first time. Stroud and Fleish looked away so as not to embarrass him. Fleish bobbed his head at the twenty or so D Block cons who were milling around on the flats. He grunted softly.

"For them this whole thing is like a holiday."

"Before it's over, it could turn into a nightmare," Stroud said.

•

Former public enemy Alvin Karpis and four other men who were in the yard for late recreation had been near the outside of the west cellhouse door when Coy fired at the tower guards from the dining-hall windows. Even though the siren had not yet sounded, it was obvious to them all what was beginning.

"I don't know about you boys," Karpis said, "but I think I'm going to make myself scarce. I've never been shot yet and I don't want to start now." He rose and walked toward the cellhouse door. The others followed.

Just outside the cellhouse door was the six-by-four concrete slab porch, with twenty-three steps leading up to it from the yard walk.

Under the steps, with a door directly beneath the side of the porch, was a storage area where the yard cleanup men stored brooms and sweepers, and where the prison's limited recreational equipment was kept. Except for the door, the room was protected on all sides by concrete.

Karpis went in and flopped down on some old canvas yard cushions that had been made in the Industries mat shop. They were used on the eight wide slab bleacher steps that formed one side of the yard, up against the kitchen and dining-hall end of the cellhouse. The four men who followed Karpis into the storage area all found places to sit and made themselves as comfortable as possible. One of the men was Harold Brest, serving life plus fifty years for kidnapping and bank robbery.

"Why aren't you in on this one?" Karpis asked Brest. "Getting mellow in your old age?"

Brest grinned. "Once was enough for me, thank you kindly."

Two years earlier, Brest had attempted a break with three other men, one of them Fred Hunter, who had been sitting in the car with Karpis in New Orleans when J. Edgar Hoover arrested them. Hunter had subsequently been charged with harboring Karpis as well as robbery of a cash mail transfer. He had ended up on Alcatraz with a twenty-five-year sentence.

When Brest, Hunter, and the other two had made their escape try two years earlier, one man was shot to death in the water and the other three were hospitalized. Brest himself, shot in the elbow, was fished out of the bay by the prison launch. That night, when Warden Johnston went up to the hospital to see him, Brest said, "Well, I'm sorry I didn't make it, but I'm sure as hell glad to be alive."

The men in the storage area passed around the makings and rolled cigarettes. From time to time, one of them went over to the door and peeked out at the very limited area of the yard bleachers that was visible.

"Who do you think's in on it, Ray?" one of the men asked.

"Beats me," Karpis said. He knew that Bernie Coy was a part of it, but that was something other people would have to find out for themselves. Alvin Karpis did not talk about things that were none of his business. Just as he avoided trouble on the Rock, avoided controversy and discipline, so also he abstained from gossip. He still hoped, fervently, that someday, by serving his time and paying what they said was his debt to society, he would be paroled.

"Whoever's in on it has a gun," one of the others said admiringly. "That's a step up from any other break that's been pulled in this shithouse."

Karpis nodded soberly. "Maybe it's a step up," he reflected. "And maybe it's a step down. We'll have to wait and see about that."

A man looking out the door heard footsteps above. "Screws," he said tensely to the others. "Just over the lip of the wall there."

"That's where the outside door to the gun cage is," Karpis said. "They must be getting ready to go in."

Karpis thought about Coy, wondering just how long the Kentucky bank robber had to live. Silently, he guessed about two hours.

•

Outside the west wall of D Block, Lieutenant Phil Bergen was unlocking the outer barred door to the gun-gallery entrance. He swung the door out and pushed it back against the wall. Then he quietly unlocked the solid steel inner door. He pushed the door open a fraction, then waited. Nothing happened. Bergen swallowed dryly. He glanced to his left, where Harry Cochrane stood poised with a cocked .45 at the ready. And to his right, where Hal Stites held the submachine gun. "Okay," he whispered. He slowly pushed the door all the way open.

Still nothing happened. Beyond the door was a narrow room that extended along the end of D Block. The long wall of the room, facing the door Bergen had just opened, separated the room from the block. There was no other entry to the room. There was nothing in the room except, to the right of the door, a narrow, steep flight of steel stairs leading up to the gallery's lower level.

Bergen motioned for four of the men to remain behind as back-up. He picked Cochrane and Stites to go in with him. Drawing his own .45, he stepped quickly into the room and flattened himself against the wall where he could fire on anyone coming down the stairs. Cochrane and Stites, coming in one at a time, followed him. Inside the dimly lighted room, the three officers waited tensely, their eyes fixed on the stairs, ears straining for sound. Each of them doubted that they would encounter any convicts in the gun cage; they had yet to admit the possibility that the gallery could be entered from inside. They knew that Bert Burch had not responded to persistent attempts to reach him on the gallery phone; they knew that Coy and Cretzer had a rifle and a pistol—weapons that could only have come from the cage. But in the backs of their minds they all suspected that somehow Burch had been slugged from *outside* the cage and his weapons fished out through the bars. Without exception, they all believed the gun gallery to be entryproof from the cellhouse side. But they were nevertheless alert to the *remote* possibility that the stairs leading to the lower level of the cage represented a danger to them.

Bergen approached the stairs first, cautiously, every nerve in his trained body and mind alert. He held the .45 pointed toward the ceiling, its chamber armed, hammer back. Bergen could lower the weapon and fire in the blink of an eyelid, and he had never been more prepared to do so.

Peering up the stairs, the lieutenant saw nothing. From within D Block, his ears picked up the sounds of muted voices. He already knew that the Treatment Unit cons had been let out, so the voices did not surprise him or cause him to hesitate. Slowly, as soundlessly as possible, Bergen climbed the stairs and moved in a crouch into the section of the gun gallery that overlooked Sunset Boulevard. Behind him came Cochrane, his own automatic held high and ready. And then Hal Stites, a toothpick in his mouth, a submachine gun in his hands.

One by one, the three guards moved in low, tight crouches along the D Block section of the elevated gun gallery.

•

In C Block, Buddy Thompson, who had missed lunch to go to sick call, had waited until Coy returned from calling the warden, and then he had gone up the flats and into the kitchen for something to eat. In Chief Steward Bristow's private refrigerator, Thompson found half a bologna sausage, a basket of fresh tomatoes, and a jar of homemade mayonnaise. He cut himself a thick piece of the sausage and sliced up a tomato. Taking bread from a bakery cupboard, he spread a great gob of mayonnaise on it and made himself a large sandwich. To wash it down, he took a pitcher of milk from the dairy case.

As he ate, Thompson wandered back into the big empty dining hall. He saw the windowpane Coy had broken to draw a bead on the dock-tower guard. With the sandwich in one hand and the pitcher of milk in the other, he strolled over to see what kind of shot it had taken. The window was in the north wall, on the same side of the cellhouse as A Block. If Thompson had been attracted to something on the other side of the room and had gone over to look out a window of the south wall, he would have seen Phil Bergen and six other guards hurrying along the catwalk to the gun-gallery entrance.

Buddy Thompson had once again changed his mind about the possibility of the break succeeding. In the beginning he thought there was a very good chance the plan would work; everything seemed well thought out, and they would have guns to clear their path to the dock. Then, when Key 107 could not be found, when guards kept coming in one after another, and when the boat finally left, he decided it was a bust. He changed his mind again when Coy found 107 and altered the plan to include knocking out the tower guards and taking wives and kids as hostages. That would have meant sure escape. Now, with 107 jammed in the yard-door lock, no possible way out of the cellhouse, and that goddamned siren screaming for an hour and a half to alert practically every cop on the West Coast, Buddy Thompson had decided once again that the break was a failure. There was no way on God's green earth that Johnston was going to give them a boat or any other goddamned thing. Anyone who hoped differently was a fool. The situation was hopeless.

At least, *their* situation was hopeless; Coy's and the others. As for himself, he had always been a loner, and now he was again *thinking* like a loner. The way he looked at it, he had only one good chance of coming out of this fiasco in good shape. If Coy, Cretzer, and the others killed the hostage guards, and shot it out with the screws that rushed the cellhouse, then he—if he laid low, hid out somewhere during the gunplay—might be the only one to avoid either getting killed or facing a murder rap. If everyone but him got killed, there would be no one to connect him with the break. The Kid wouldn't squeal, or any of the lock-up cons who had seen him out of his cell. He would be in the clear. On the other hand, if some of the others were taken alive, he could testify against them. That might give him an opportunity for a courtroom escape. Or facilitate his transfer to a less restricted pen like Leavenworth or Atlanta, from which he could plan a future escape. He had to start thinking about tomorrow, that was certain. Today was sure shot to hell.

Thompson's plan of betrayal was not yet firm in his mind, but there is little doubt that an embryo plan *was* there. His natural lone-wolf tendencies were dominant again—brought back into play by the obvious failure of the escape plan, by his disenchantment with the leadership of Bernard Coy (for whom *nothing* had seemed to go right), and probably by the fact that Coy had pushed him bodily away from the yard-door lock: a physical insult for which Thompson forgave no man.

It would teach that son of a bitch Coy a lesson to get shot up by the screws or have to go to the chair for killing their hostages, Thompson thought as he finished eating. He drank the last of the milk, wiped his mouth on the sleeve of his shirt, and set the empty pitcher on one of the shiny dining-hall tables. Looks like it'll be a while before I get any of that good Mex food I been thinking about, he told himself resignedly. Or any of that hot Mex snatch either. Goddamn piss-poor luck, that's what it was.

Thompson left the dining hall and walked across Times Square toward Seedy Street. On his way he glanced at the yard door with 107 jammed in its lock. "You son of a bitch," he said quietly to the door. He started down Seedy, glancing as he did through the still-open D Block door. He saw a flash of movement in the gun gallery above D. Catching his breath, Thompson leaped against the wall next to the door and stood stock still. After a moment, he lowered himself to a kneeling position and peered around the edge of the doorframe with one eye. He saw more movement and heard a faint shuffle of leather soles on the gallery floor.

Thompson jumped up and ran down Seedy. "Bernie, Dutch!" he said urgently. "Screws are coming into the gun cage in D!"

Coy and Cretzer both started for the D Block door.

"Hold it, Dutch!" Coy said, stopping. Cretzer stopped also. "You stay with the screws we already got. I'll stop the ones coming in."

Cretzer sneered knowingly. "Still afraid some screw is going to buy it, Bernie?"

"I'm interested in dealing my way off this rock, Dutch," Coy replied flatly. "I ain't looking to start no bloodbath." He nodded his head back toward the hostage cells. "Stay here."

"Whatever you say, Bernie." Dutch Cretzer made up his mind at that moment that he had just taken his last order from Bernie Coy. He fixed the escape leader in a cold, dangerous stare.

Coy grinned slightly. "You sure look mean, Dutch," he said easily. Then he turned and hurried on, leaving Cretzer behind.

In the D section of the gun gallery, Bergen, Cochrane, and Stites raised their heads just enough to peer over the waist-high steel shield into the isolation block.

"Every con in the unit is out," Cochrane whispered. "Just like Boatman said."

Bergen nodded. "But none of them seem to be in on the break. They're just standing around, talking. I don't see any guns."

"Isn't that the Indio Kid down there with Stroud and Fleish?" Hal Stites asked. "What's he doing over here in D?"

"Maybe Coy and Cretzer let all the lock-up cons out," Bergen said. "The Kid might have come over here to stay out of trouble." Bergen looked at the door leading into the main section of the gallery. "I'm going to see if I can find Burch. Cover that open door down on the flats."

Bergen started toward the gallery door on his hands and knees. Harry Cochrane rose from behind the steel plate shield just enough to draw a bead on the open block door. As he aimed his gun, a rifle shot exploded from the doorway. The bullet tore into Cochrane's exposed shoulder and slammed him back against the wall. He dropped to the floor. Four more shots immediately laced the gallery. Bergen and Stites, staying low, scurried over to the bleeding Cochrane and started dragging him toward the narrow stairs.

●

On the flats below, the D Block convicts dashed for cover when the first shot was fired. There was general confusion as men raced for any cell that was open. Louis Fleish and Danny Durando jumped up and hurried to the nearest dark cell. It was empty. They took cover in the access area between the barred cell front and the solid steel door. After they were safe, Durando looked back and saw the elderly Stroud having difficulty getting up off the floor. The Kid left the cover of the access area and rushed back out to help him.

"Come on," he said, pulling the old con to his feet. He hurried Stroud across the flats to the dark cell.

"Thanks, Kid," the Birdman said, slumping back against the wall. "I owe you one."

"Skip it," Durando said. He turned to Fleish. "How's about another smoke?"

●

In the gallery, Bergen and Stites hauled the wounded Cochrane down the steep stairs. As they carried him out onto the catwalk, Bergen jerked his head toward the stairs. "Get up there!" he ordered three of the backup guards. Hersh Oldham, Fred Richberger, and Fred Mahan rushed into the room and up the stairs. Bergen and Stites started carrying Cochrane along the narrow catwalk. "Stay here for backup," Bergen yelled back to Joe Maxwell. "We're going to get Harry out of here!"

Bergen and Stites carried the limp, moaning guard around the corner of the D Block wing and hurried toward the front of the cellhouse with him.

•

In the gallery, Oldham, Richberger, and Mahan had spread out facing the length of the D Block aisle. They were crouched behind the steel plate, each with a submachine gun at the ready. Oldham was farthest into the gallery; the open door to Seedy Street was below and a few feet to his left.

"Where was he shooting from?" Mahan asked quietly.

"I don't know," said Oldham.

"Could be anywhere," Richberger whispered.

Oldham looked down at the open door. "I'll blast the doorway," he said. "You two spray the aisle." He wiped his sweaty right hand on his trouser leg. "Ready?" Richberger and Mahan nodded. "Now!" said Oldham.

The three guards rose in tandem and began firing. Oldham strafed around and through the open doorway to Seedy Street. Richberger and Mahan raked Sunset Boulevard with simultaneous fire.

The thunder of the combined attack was deafening.

•

Bernie Coy, kneeling on one knee behind the open, double-thick steel door in C Block, cringed as a downpour of .45 slugs ricocheted past him. He knew he was safe behind the door; the rain of fire alternately whined down Times Square or skipped off the concrete end of C Block as the machine-gunner moved the muzzle back and forth. Because of the angle of fire, all ricochets continued forward; none came back toward Coy.

Have fun, you sons of bitches, Coy thought smugly. Shoot up the whole goddamned place! But when you stop, that's when you get it.

He gripped the now familiar Springfield and waited, calmly and patiently, for what seemed like long minutes but was actually closer to fifty seconds. Then, like the sputtering of a dying engine, the firing stopped.

Coy swung from behind the steel door, took quick aim, and fired. His first shot tore into Richberger's leg and threw him back. Hersh Oldham, who had been strafing the open doorway, instinctively turned to the right to aid his comrade. As he did, Coy fired again. The slug caught Oldham in the left arm and he dropped.

Mahan, who was closest to the stairs, yelled down, "Two men hit up here! Get me some help!"

Officer Joe Maxwell, the only backup guard at that moment, dashed up the stairs. At the top, he found Mahan trying to drag a wounded and bleeding Richberger to safety. Maxwell scurried into the gallery to help him. Together they got Richberger to the stairs. Mahan went down first and Maxwell lowered the wounded man to him. As he did so, Maxwell stood up too far. Coy's rifle sounded again. The bullet ripped open the top of Maxwell's shoulder and splattered his face with blood. He fell to his knees. Wiping the blood from his eyes, he continued helping Mahan until they had Richberger out of the cage. Then he struggled down the stairs and fell dizzily to the floor below.

Bergen and Stites, hurrying back from taking Harry Cochrane out, rushed in with four reserve guards as Maxwell fell. At a signal from Bergen, the reserve guards quickly got Richberger and Maxwell out onto the catwalk and carried them around the corner to safety.

Mahan, breathing heavily, yelled, "Oldham's hit too! He's still up there!"

Instantly, Bergen and Stites ran in to the stairs and back up to the cage. Having already been in the gallery once, they were now extra cautious and stayed well below the steel shield at the bottom of the cage. Almost crawling, they got over to Hersh Oldham, whose entire left torso was now saturated with blood. As carefully as possible, they pulled and tugged their way back to the stairs with the last wounded guard.

Bernie Coy, still in the open C Block door, could hear the noise of movement in the D Block section of the gallery, but he was unable to see anyone. They're getting wise, he thought. Staying low. Clenching his jaw, he estimated approximately where along the width of the cage the noise was coming from. For psychological effect, he raised the rifle and he fired four quick shots directly against the steel shield. The bullets ricocheted off the armor plate and plowed through the high D Block windows.

Bergen and Stites instinctively ducked as the four bullets crashed against the shield just inches from where they were struggling with Oldham. "Whoever that son of a bitch is, he knows how to shoot," Hal Stites said tightly.

"Might be Coy," Bergen said. "He's the one who was spotted with the rifle."

Stites reached the stairs and started down. Two reserve guards, back from carrying Maxwell out, hurried in to help bring Oldham down. Then Phil Bergen came down. With Stites, Bergen went out onto the catwalk and sat down, breathing heavily. Fred Mahan was there, slumped against the wall. Presently, the other reserve guards returned from carrying Richberger to safety.

Bergen wiped his face. His expression became set and determined. He looked up at one of the reserve guards. "Get word to the warden that the four men who were hit were shot from Seedy Street. Tell him we still haven't been able to locate the captured officers. Ask him if he can slip a man into the east gun cage and fire some tear-gas grenades down Broadway to draw their attention over there. Tell him that Stites, Mahan, and I will go back into the west gallery and then try to find out where our men are being held." To the other reserve officer, Bergen said, "You stay down here for backup." Then to Stites and Mahan: "Let's go."

The three guards, each with a submachine gun now, moved once again toward the gun-gallery steps.

•

Inside the C Block door, Bernie Coy checked his rifle and discovered that it was empty. He quickly felt in his pockets but found no more ammunition; Marvin Hubbard still had the rest of it. Coy cast a quick, searching glance up at the now-quiet D Block section of the gun cage, then trotted back down the Seedy Street flats.

"What's the story?" Dutch Cretzer asked as soon as Coy ran up.

"I winged four of them," Coy said. "Then I ran out of lead." He tossed the empty Springfield to Marv Hubbard. "Fill 'er up, bartender," he said with a grin.

"You're pretty goddamned cheerful, considering our situation," Cretzer remarked almost accusingly.

"Hell, we're in good shape, Dutch," the Kentuckian replied. "Good shape."

"I don't see how you figure that. Unless you know something I don't."

"We've got old Johnston over a barrel, is how I figure it," said Coy. "Look, I've picked off three tower screws plus four other guards who tried to rush the gun cage. The warden's going to be doing some sober thinking about that. We offered him a deal and he tried to pull a fast one on us instead. It didn't work. And it cost him those last four guards. He knows if he tries anything funny again, one of his men is liable to get it permanently. He's going to have to make a deal with us to keep that from happening."

"Here you go, Bernie," said Hubbard, handing the rifle back.

"I hope you're right this time," Cretzer said. "It would be a refreshing change, believe me."

"Give me some extra shells," Coy said to Hubbard. Then he turned to include Shockley and Thompson in what he was going to say. "Now listen, all of you. I'm going to get up on the top tier of C in case some more screws are still coming into the gun gallery. If they are, I can get a clear shot at any of them who come over into this side. We'll wait about fifteen minutes. If nothing else happens, then I'll call Johnston back. I want everybody to just hang on, stay right here out of trouble, and don't let anything happen to our friends there," he bobbed his chin at the nine guards in 402 and 403.

With his reloaded rifle and an extra handful of shells, Coy hurried back up Seedy. Earlier, to get to the middle tier, he had jumped up, grabbed the pipe rail, and pulled himself up to the range. Now he was too tired, and aching too much, for any more acrobatics. When he ran around onto Times Square and cut over to Broadway to the tier stairs, he found that it was even a chore to walk up the two flights.

If we don't get out of here soon, he thought, I'm going to need a stretcher to get me to that boat.

•

After Coy left, Dutch Cretzer started wandering up Seedy toward Times Square.

"Where you going?" Hubbard called to him.

Cretzer stopped and looked back. "What's it to you?"

"Bernie said for everybody to stay here," Hubbard reminded him.

Cretzer walked slowly back to where Hubbard stood. "I don't take orders from Bernie," he said coldly, his face so close that Hubbard could feel his breath. "I don't take orders from *anybody*. You understand that?"

Hubbard glanced down at the .45 in Cretzer's belt. Goddamn public enemies, he thought. They were all the same, every goddamn one of them. Glory boys. Junior John Dillingers. Hubbard grunted softly. Full of shit, all of them.

"I asked if you understood me," Cretzer repeated.

"I understand you," Hubbard said. "Do what you damned well please."

"I intend to," Cretzer told him.

Turning, Cretzer again walked up Seedy. He went to the end of the block, paused, looked cautiously around the corner, then stepped out onto Times Square. He looked at some of the chips in the floor made by the submachine-gun bullets. Looking around, he found two of the flattened slugs. He slipped them into his pocket for souvenirs.

Wandering back toward Seedy again, he quietly crossed over to the D Block door. Getting behind the open door where Coy had hidden, he slowly put his head around and peeked into the isolation block.

•

In the gallery above D Block, Bergen, Stites, and Mahan had again worked their way along the narrow walk behind the steel shield. Bergen had put down his submachine gun, drawn his .45, and was edging slowly toward the gallery door that led into the main cellhouse. Mahan and Stites were separated on the gallery: Mahan at the end near the stairs, looking straight down Sunset Boulevard, his eyes flicking and darting from tier to tier, cell to cell; Stites in the middle of the cage, his eyes locked unmovingly on the open door leading into C Block. Both men were on their knees, caps off, only the tops of their heads up past the shield. Their submachine guns were held down but ready.

It was Hal Stites who moved first. He saw the convict face the instant it came into view peeking into D Block. The face triggered him; he leaped to his feet, swung the submachine gun up and over the rail, and sprayed the doorway with bullets.

"Who was it?" Bergen asked tensely when Stites ceased fire and ducked behind the shield again.

"Dutch Cretzer."

"Did you get him?"

"I'm not sure." Stites removed the toothpick from his mouth and tossed it on the gallery floor. "We'll probably know in a minute."

"Blast away again if you see Cretzer or Coy or any other con with a weapon," Bergen ordered.

The guard lieutenant continued inching toward the gallery door.

•

On the flats, Cretzer had ducked back just in time to avoid being hit by any of Stites's fire. As Coy had done, he cringed back behind the steel plate door and listened to the deadly .45 slugs chip and graze the floor and walls, then ricochet and whine away in the echo of their own explosion.

"You sons of bitches," he cursed under his breath. "You dirty bastard hacks!" He was outraged that they should shoot at him unexpectedly like that, without warning of any kind. They hadn't even called to him to give up! The lousy pricks. Trying to shoot him down like a dog with not even the benefit of a warning!

Try to blast me like that, will you! Cretzer thought, enraged. All right, big shots, I'll show you who you're dealing with! This isn't any Kentucky hillbilly or Texas gunny or halfbreed Mexican nigger you're shooting at! This is Dutch Cretzer!

He quickly stripped off his prison coat and held it loosely in his left hand. With his right he drew the already cocked .45 automatic and thumbed the safety off. Smiling coldly, he waved the coat into the open doorway. Instantly a hail of machine gun fire spat from the gallery again. The coat was torn from his hand, held suspended in the air for a split second, then shot to the floor and chewed to pieces by the deadly volley of bullets.

Cretzer waited until the fire ceased. The instant he knew that the gunner's trigger finger had relaxed, he sprang into the doorway and fired six shots at the figure still standing in the D Block gallery.

All of Cretzer's bullets missed except one. That one ripped into the body of Hal Stites and lodged in one of his kidneys. The force of the slug threw his body the entire length of the gallery. He landed headfirst at the top of the stairs. Bergen and Mahan immediately moved to his aid.

•

Bernie Coy, on the top tier of C, was lying on his stomach, covering the gun-gallery doors with the rifle, when the shooting started. He pushed himself to his knees and started to get up; then several of the ricocheting slugs whined up toward the roof, and he flattened himself on the tier walk again.

When the first burst of gunfire ceased, Coy leaped to his feet and looked down on Times Square. He saw Cretzer pressed back behind the D Block door. What's that son of a bitch doing now? he wondered irritably. He checked the gallery doors on both tiers to be sure no one was trying to slip in; then he hurried to the stairs and started back down to the flats.

When Coy reached the middle tier, he heard another long burst of machine-gun fire. He stopped on a stairway landing and crouched down in a corner as once again there was a hail of whining ricochets. When the second burst stopped, Coy leaped up to look over at the gallery doors again. Still closed. At that instant, he heard six quick shots from an automatic. He looked over the rail and saw Cretzer jump back from the D Block doorway. Jesus! he thought tightly.

Coy bounded down the rest of the stairs to the flats and ran over to a still coldly smiling Dutch Cretzer. "What the hell happened?"

"The lousy bastards tried to get me with a tommy gun," Cretzer replied angrily. "But they missed. Then I gave the pricks a taste of their own medicine!"

Coy stepped over to the open door and carefully peered around it through the doorway. He could hear movement in the D Block gallery, but there was no one in sight. He listened for sounds of someone who might have been hit. There were none. He glanced apprehensively at Cretzer. "You get anybody?"

"I didn't stand out there to find out," Cretzer replied indignantly.

Coy listened again. After a moment, he decided that Cretzer had probably *not* hit anyone. There was none of the yelling and groaning such as he had heard when he had picked off the four guards earlier.

"I think it's about time to call the warden again," he said.

"Sure, why don't you do that?" Cretzer said sullenly. The former public enemy dropped the magazine out of the .45 and started pushing blunt-nosed bullets into it. He watched Coy walk away. As his fingers worked, Cretzer gritted his teeth and little knots stood out at each hinge of his jawbone. He was almost certain he had dropped the machine-gunner in the gallery.

•

Outside the gun-gallery entry, Hal Stites was stretched out on the steel catwalk. His face was chalk-white. A puddle of blood was spreading beneath him. Phil Bergen and Fred Mahan were kneeling beside him. Their lips were parted in disbelief, their eyes fixed unblinkingly.

Several backup officers came around the corner of the building and stood over them. "Lieutenant?" one of them said.

Bergen did not respond. Like Mahan, he continued to stare at the body of Hal Stites. Neither of the men could believe he was really dead.

"Lieutenant?" the guard said again.

Bergen looked up, almost absently. "What?"

"The warden wants to know your situation here, sir."

Bergen nodded slowly. He saw that the guard was carrying a cased walkie-talkie. "Where'd that come from?" he asked in a detached voice.

"The Marines are here, Lieutenant. They brought them. Sir, the warden wants—"

"I know," said Bergen. "Our situation." He swallowed dryly. "Tell the warden that Officer Harold Stites is dead. He was hit with a .45 slug in the stomach. We think the con who fired it was Dutch Cretzer."

The guard moved several feet away and began relaying the message to Warden Johnston.

Still kneeling, Phil Bergen looked at Stites again and felt a tear streak his cheek. He put a hand on the dead guard and shook his head sadly. "A wife," he said quietly. "Three boys still at home."

"Take it easy, Phil," said Fred Mahan, even though tears were streaking his own face. "They'll pay for it."

"No," Bergen said, "no matter what we do to them, they can't pay for this."

The guard with the walkie-talkie came back up to Bergen. "Lieutenant, the warden says to remain at this position but do not attempt to enter the gun gallery again until it gets dark. He says he'll send more men and weapons over and cut all power in the cellhouse. Then we'll try to take the gallery under cover of darkness."

Bergen nodded. Then he sat down on one side of Stites and leaned back against the wall. Mahan sat on the other side of the dead guard.

The two men did not say anything else.

CHAPTER TWENTY

6:20 P.M.

It was becoming apparent by now that this was not just another short-lived escape attempt, but possibly the prelude to a major crash-out.

Ninety minutes after Armory Officer Fish's initial call to Captain of Inspectors Bernard McDonald, the San Francisco Police Department received a second call from the island. This time it was Warden Johnston calling Chief of Police Charles Dullea.

"Chief, my news isn't good," Johnston said without preliminary. "We've got an armed uprising on our hands out here. My men are attempting to regain control of the cellhouse but haven't been able to do so. I've had five guards shot and one killed so far, and another nine are being held hostage. It is possible that as many as three dozen men are in on the break. At this point I am not able to say for certain that we'll be able to contain them in the cellhouse. We're also faced with the problem of having more than two hundred inmates presently outside their cells. We're going to try to isolate them in the yard, but that entails moving them all up the hill from their shops. They've heard the siren and they've heard the shooting. I don't think it would take much to touch them off. If that happens, we'll have a mass rebellion to deal with. It's not inconceivable that we could have convicts swarming all over the island within the hour."

"How can I help, Warden?" asked Dullea.

"The thing that worries me is boats," said Johnston. "The Navy and Coast Guard are sending cutters to patrol the island's perimeter, but they'll be letting our own launch through as well as Army craft and possibly some kind of hospital craft. It occurred to me that friends of someone like Dutch Cretzer might try to slip a small speedboat or something through the blockade under cover of darkness, either to liberate prisoners or bring in more weapons. I don't have full confidence in the Coast Guard and Navy to prevent that. They're military, not law-enforcement; their standards and suspicions are different from ours."

"Would a heavily manned police boat ease your mind, Warden?" the chief asked.

"Immensely," Johnston replied.

"It'll be in the water in thirty minutes," Dullea promised.

When he finished talking to Johnston, the chief called Captain of Inspectors Bernard McDonald. "Mac, I want a police boat in the water at once to patrol the Rock. Have Sergeant Hanlon get hold of the eight best sharpshooters we've got and put them on board. You'll be in charge. Your job is to keep all unauthorized craft from slipping through the Coast Guard blockade. Keep your searchlights flashing constantly and don't hesitate to fire at any boat that doesn't properly identify itself. Don't go ashore unless the warden summons you, but in that event put yourself and your men entirely at his disposal. Any questions?"

"No questions, boss," said McDonald. "I ought to brief you on our crowd-control problem, though. Our patrol units are reporting fairly large assemblies of people who have begun to notice the activity in the water around the prison. That's going to get worse."

"I'll take care of that, Mac. Thanks. Now get going."

There were now five Coast Guard cutters constantly circling the island. Lookouts on every deck scanned the rocky shore with binoculars for escapees or unauthorized boats.

The blockade had opened up shortly after six o'clock to pass through two Navy landing craft carrying thirty U.S. Marines dressed in full battle gear. The Marines had gone ashore at the Alcatraz dock and double-timed up the winding hill to the plaza in front of the main building. There, after a brief discussion with Lieutenant George Boatman, a Marine officer had given them their orders.

"All right, people, listen up! Some of you are going to be taken down that road yonder and stationed at strategic locations behind the Cyclone fence that stretches between that large shops building down there and the wall that you can see back behind you. The rest of you are going to be taken up *on* that wall and assigned sentry posts at various locations around the top of the wall. A couple of hundred convicts are going to be herded up that road, through a gate in the wall, and into the yard. There will be prison guards on the road and in the yard. They will have charge of the convicts. You people are there to back them up. The guards will not be armed; you people will be. If there is any altercation between the convicts and the guards, you will interfere at once and stop it as quickly as you can. You are all expert riflemen. If you are called upon to fire, I expect you to demonstrate your skills accordingly. That is all. Now unsling your weapons, lock and load!"

Five minutes later, the battle-ready Marines had been divided into two platoons and marched to the Industries road and the high wall catwalk.

•

In the shops, as Warden Johnston had surmised, the convicts were restless and edgy. The pressure was building up. It had been started by the long, nerve-wracking wail of the escape siren; added to by the echo of gunfire that resounded clearly from the gun-gallery entrance; and further compounded by the fact that the men were being kept in their shops long after they should have been marched back to the cellhouse for supper.

In the Prison Industries office, Machine Gun Kelly, the chief clerk, was slowly and laboriously typing a production report on an old Underwood typewriter. As a younger man, Kelly had picked up some office experience in his father's insurance agency. Using it, he worked well as the Industries clerk.

Most of the men in the shops had already stopped working, but Kelly pragmatically went on with his typing. He had learned long ago that on Alcatraz there was no truer maxim than the one about idleness breeding discontent. Kelly liked to keep his hands busy.

One of the other clerks came over and sat down next to the desk. "What do you think's going on up there, George?" he asked.

Kelly grunted. "Suicide, that's what's going on up there."

"Who do you think is in on it?" the clerk asked.

"I don't think; I *know* who's in on it. At least I know who's running it. Bernie Coy. He's been working on something for a good year now. More than likely this is it."

While Kelly and the other clerk were talking, three cons from the shop next door came into the office. They were shorttimers: men who had been on the Rock only a couple of years. Kelly, who had been there since the prison opened, barely knew them. But like everyone else on Alcatraz, they knew who Machine Gun Kelly was.

Kelly and the other clerk stopped talking the instant the trio walked up. "Something I can do for you boys?" Kelly asked.

"We got a plan," one of them said.

Kelly raised his eyebrows. "Yeah? A plan for what?"

"For going over the fence when they start us back up the hill."

"What's the plan?"

"That's it. We go over the Cyclone fence when they're marching us back to the yard."

"Great plan," said Kelly. "Take you long to think of it?"

"We figure it'd be a perfect time," said one of the others. "Most of the screws will be concentrating on whatever the hell's happening up in the cellhouse. Nobody will suspect a second crashout down at this end. We figure we'd have a good chance of getting to the water and putting together a floater out of driftwood. When it gets dark, we can sneak past them patrol boats."

Kelly shook his head. "I think I'll pass. But thanks for thinking of me."

"Don't tell me the great Machine Gun Kelly is yellow," said the man who had spoken first.

"Jesus Christ," Kelly sighed. He shook his head. "Look, sonny, the people who run this place aren't stupid. Not like you and me. We're stupid, or we wouldn't be here. But they're smart, take my word for it. They know that there's two hundred cons down here that are all getting very nervous right about now. The last thing they're going to do is walk us back up that hill without a heavy guard on us."

"They ain't got a heavy guard," the other man argued. "All of the reserve screws will be stationed at the cellhouse."

"Have it your own way," Kelly said. "Just deal me out."

"He's yellow," the first man muttered. Kelly turned his back on the trio. After a moment they went away.

Grunting quietly, the other clerk said, "I think they're looking to get their pictures in the paper with the great Machine Gun Kelly."

"They're looking to get killed is more like it."

The other clerk studied Kelly for a moment. "You're getting mellow in your old age, George. That little creep just called you yellow and you let him get clean away with it. How's come?"

"Because I'm tired of it all, that's how's come. I'm tired of having to live up to that goddamned Public Enemy Number One title. From now on, anybody can call me anything they want to. I'm not going to be put in a goddamned dark cell just so some asshole can say he fought Kelly."

Kelly's friend grinned. "I'll pass the word around. From now on we'll call you Pop Gun Kelly."

"That's fine with me."

Later, when the in-grades were marched up the hill to the yard, they saw for the first time that the island had been reinforced with Marines. As Kelly and his friend hiked along, they passed the straggling, uncertain trio who had offered Kelly the escape plan.

"Hey, sonny," Kelly said to the con who had called him yellow, "when you go over that fence, be careful not to get one of them bayonets up your ass."

•

Machine Gun Kelly had no way of knowing that his refusal to participate in a second escape attempt had probably prevented the possible mass rebellion that Warden Johnston was worrying about. It would have been a bloody rebellion, to be sure, because the thirty Marines were combat veterans and clearly primed to kill. At the same time, it is more than probable that at least *some* of the two hundred-plus in-grades would have managed to gain at least the limited freedom of the island. What havoc would have resulted from that can only be guessed.

The Marines were not the only reinforcements detailed to the island that night. Warden Clinton Duffy's twelve San Quentin guards had also arrived, and Director Bennett had issued orders which were already being carried out to furnish additional federal guards. Five Leavenworth guards had boarded an Air Transport Command plane at Topeka, Kansas, and were due to arrive in Oakland by 8:30 P.M. Ten others were on their way down from McNeil Island, Washington, and twelve more were coming from Englewood, Colorado. And much closer, the San Francisco police boat ordered by Chief Dullea was preparing to cast off from the Van Ness pier.

Sergeant Richard Hanlon, who was in charge of the eight police snipers, was being pressed by a reporter, Ed Montgomery, to let him join the expedition. Montgomery, who wrote for the San Francisco *Examiner,* was to gain fame eight years later with his involvement in the case of Barbara Graham. Convicted along with two male companions in the robbery-murder of a wealthy Pasadena widow, Barbara Graham would be sentenced to die in California's gas chamber. Montgomery, at first believing her guilty, would later change his mind and conduct a personal investigation which would convince him that she was innocent. His attempts to help her avoid the gas chamber would be futile, however, and she would ultimately be executed.

On the evening of May 2, 1946, with the Barbara Graham case still well in the future, all Ed Montgomery was interested in was getting as close as he could to the Alcatraz story.

"Look, I promise I'll stay out of everybody's way," he pleaded.

"Montgomery, there's a *Captain of Inspectors* aboard," Sergeant Hanlon said patiently. "This is no joyride; it's an *armed patrol.* The department couldn't be responsible for your safety."

"I don't *want* the department to be responsible for my safety," Montgomery replied. "I just want to get a *story*! Look, haven't I always been good to you guys? Don't I always see that the boys with the badges get an even break in my paper? Is this the way you show your gratitude?"

"Gratitude has nothing to do with it. Are you trying to get me fired?"

Montgomery reared back in indignation. "They wouldn't *dare* fire you for trying to help the press! Why, my paper would crucify them! Now look, Hanlon—"

"All right, all right!" the policeman finally conceded. "Get on board. If Captain McDonald sees you, tell him you're a stowaway. And *please,* try not to get shot."

"You can depend on me," Ed Montgomery promised.

The reporter slipped aboard and minutes later the police boat headed out toward the Coast Guard blockade.

•

The sun was now going down behind a cloud bank beyond the Golden Gate Bridge. Dusk was settling over the west and southwest slopes of the island. The last rays of sunlight struck the green and lavender ice plants growing wild above the rocky shore, and made them look as cold and shiny as their name implied. For a little while, as daylight ended, it was calm and quiet on that side of the island.

On shore, however, the excitement was mounting. Rumors were rampant—most of them outrageous, frightening. Hundreds of mad-dog convicts had captured the island prison and were systematically slaughtering all the guards and raping their wives. The children were being hurled into the bay. As soon as the carnage on the island was over, it was certain that the bloodthirsty killers would launch an attack on San Francisco itself. Further, U.S. Navy battleships were being summoned to bombard the island's shores, while Army Air Corps planes would momentarily be flying over to bomb the summit cellhouse.

To see all this, huge crowds began to gather. They sought vantage points atop Telegraph Hill and Russian Hill, and along the North Beach, Marina, and Presidio waterfronts. There were already thousands of people settling down to watch the expected spectacle, and city police were experiencing the beginning of a growing crowd-control problem. The first serious situation was with vehicular rather than pedestrian traffic. Automobiles jammed the hills from all directions, and motorists at the top found that they—or at least their cars—were trapped. Along the Embarcadero, traffic was measured as moving twenty-nine *inches* per hour in a hopeless snarl that caught the disinterested along with the curious. Hundreds of persons lined the bay side of the Golden Gate Bridge, some of them hanging precariously over the rails for a better view. At the Hyde Street and Van Ness piers, there was a massive traffic jam involving several hundred cars that had all driven in one direction at the same time—right up to the water's edge, from which there was no retreating and no advancing.

Atop Telegraph Hill, a slight man of about fifty moved through the crowd with a pair of binoculars. "Ten cents for two minutes," he chanted. "See it up close for two whole minutes for only a dime. More shooting could start at any second. Here you go, two minutes for ten cents!"

Before the sun came up the next morning, he would earn more than thirty dollars in dimes.

CHAPTER TWENTY-ONE

6:44 P.M.

In the armory, another call was received from the C Block phone. It was immediately plugged into the warden's office. "It's Coy again, sir."

Johnston, his face cold and set, picked up his phone. "What is it, Coy?"

"Have we got a deal, Warden?" Coy asked. "Are you going to get us our boat?"

"There'll be no deal, Coy, and no boat," Johnston said with icy firmness. "You don't kill one of my officers and then bargain your way out of it."

"Kill? What the hell are you talking about?" Coy demanded. "Nobody's been killed. I plugged every one of them guards personally. They were only wounded!"

"Wrong, Coy. They just carried the body of Officer Harold Stites down to the dock. He was killed by a .45 slug in the stomach."

Coy's mouth dropped open. He stared incredulously into space.

"You'd better surrender, Coy," Johnston said angrily. "This is the only chance you're going to get. You either give up right now or we're going to come in and get you. We'll kill you and we'll kill Cretzer. We'll kill every goddamn con that had a hand in this. Do you hear me, Coy?"

Coy slowly hung up the phone. He turned trancelike and looked across Times Square to where the others were waiting at the cellhouse officer's desk. Coy had finally consented to racking closed cells 402 and 403, so that no one had to stand guard there. Now Cretzer, Hubbard, Thompson, and Shockley were waiting to hear what the warden had said. While they waited, Marv Hubbard began sweating and removed Bill Miller's uniform coat. It lay tossed across the Seedy aisle, next to the D Block wall. Of the four, only Shockley, in Burch's coat, still had on part of a guard's uniform.

Coy walked over to them. He ignored everyone except Cretzer. His dark eyes, once desperate but now empty of hope, fixed menacingly on the former public enemy.

"You goddamn gun-crazy punk," he said in a strained voice.

"What's eating you?" Cretzer snapped, frowning.

"You weren't happy pulling off a nice clean crashout, were you? You *had* to show everybody what a goddamn big shot you are!"

"What the hell are you talking about?" Cretzer's face reddened.

"You know what I'm talking about, you son of a bitch!" Coy suddenly erupted. "You fixed us all good! You killed a screw!"

Cretzer's mouth tightened. He flexed his stomach muscles slightly to reassure himself that the .45 was still in his waistband. He realized he was being watched, not only by his friend Crazy Sam and the others, but by some nearby lockup prisoners as well. Almost as if he had been given a cue, he shrugged off Coy's accusation and assumed his public-enemy role again. "If I killed a screw," he said indifferently, "he had it coming."

Coy's nearly nine years on Alcatraz flashed through his mind like a terrible kaleidoscope. He glared at Cretzer, infuriated. It was too much. Cretzer had doomed them all—and the son of a bitch didn't even care. Coy felt the blood rushing to his head. Livid with rage, he leaped forward and raked the rifle barrel across Cretzer's face. Cretzer pitched back against the wall. His right hand instinctively jerked the .45 from his waistband. Before he could level it, Coy swung the rifle butt around and knocked the gun from his hand. It went sliding along the polished flats. Cretzer's friend Shockley moved to retrieve it, but Marv Hubbard stepped to the middle of the flats between him and the gun, and raised a billy club threateningly. As long as Hubbard was around, no one was going to interfere with Bernie Coy.

Cretzer, holding his mouth while blood seeped through his fingers, closed his free hand into a fist. "Come on then!" he challenged Coy. "Come on, you two-bit hillbilly bastard! I'll take you on without a gun! Come on!"

Coy prodded him back with the muzzle of the gun, then viciously swung the butt into Cretzer's side. Cretzer clutched at his middle and doubled over. Coy put a heavy shoe in his face and shoved him brutally against the concrete wall. Cretzer collapsed face-down on the floor. Coy stood over him, not even breathing heavily.

"I ought to finish you off right now, you dirty bastard," he said tightly. "But I want the screws to have the pleasure of doing it!"

Coy turned and stalked away, heading into the dining hall. Marv Hubbard forgot about the automatic and followed him immediately.

Sam Shockley hurried over and snatched up the gun. He rushed over to Cretzer, who was struggling to a sitting position.

"I got your gun, Dutch," Shockley said proudly. He helped Cretzer sit up. "Here, Dutch, here's your gun back."

"Where's Coy?" Cretzer asked thickly. "I'll kill him. Where'd he go?"

Buddy Thompson, sensing that the time was right to put his own plan into action, came over to Cretzer. "I wouldn't worry about Coy, Dutch," he said evenly. "What you better worry about is the guards. If you want to kill somebody, you better kill those screws. If just one of them gets out of here alive, we're all going to the chair."

Cretzer got to his feet, wiping the blood from his face. He stared thoughtfully at Buddy Thompson for a moment, then walked somewhat unsteadily across Times Square and down Seedy Street. Thompson and Shockley followed him.

In the aisle in front of 402 and 403, Dutch Cretzer stopped. He stared at the captive guards. "Do you know how to rack open these cells?" he asked Thompson.

"Sure," the Texan answered.

"Do it," Cretzer ordered.

Thompson went to the end of the block and opened the two cell doors.

"Miller, you son of a bitch, get out here," Cretzer said.

Officer Bill Miller pushed his way to the front of 403 and stepped into the aisle. As soon as he was out of the cell, Cretzer slugged him in the face with the .45. Miller pitched to the floor. "You're the one who fucked up this whole break, Miller!" Cretzer raged. Holding the gun up to keep the other guards in the cell, he began kicking Miller in the side. "You dirty bastard! If you hadn't hid that fucking key, we'd have made it out of here!" He kept kicking the helpless guard. Miller groaned once and rolled over. Cretzer began stomping him in the face and chest. "Dirty bastard!" he said over and over again. Once he slipped and said, "You dirty bastard, Coy!"

As he kicked Miller half to death, he was probably wishing it was

Bernie Coy on the floor instead of the guard.

"All right, get him back in there!" Cretzer ordered when he was finished. Steward Bob Bristow dragged the unconscious Miller back into 403. Cretzer stood back from the door, breathing heavily. Again, Buddy Thompson pressed his plan.

"Better finish them all, Dutch," he urged. "It'll only take the testimony of one of them to put us all in the chair."

Dutch Cretzer stared thoughtfully at Thompson again.

"Kill 'em, Dutch," the Texas outlaw urged. "Kill 'em all, right now."

•

In 403, Cellhouse Officer Ernest Lageson's jaw tightened as he listened to Buddy Thompson urge his and the others' execution. They've killed somebody, he thought. He assumed it was Burch. But after the beating he just took, Miller might now die also. Lageson knew without thinking that Thompson's argument was entirely valid. Without guard witnesses, it might indeed be impossible to convict anyone but Coy of any killings that had taken place. Coy was the only one who had been in contact with the outside. Coy was probably the one who had killed Burch; but Cretzer was the one who had kicked Miller so brutally. And the others in on the break were just as guilty under the law. As far as Lageson was concerned, they all deserved equal punishment. But if Dutch Cretzer killed all the guards, as Thompson wanted him to, and if Bernie Coy was subsequently killed, either by guards or by Cretzer, then there was a very good chance that the rest of the attempted escapees would never be identified. Lageson, who had no way of knowing that Hal Stites, not Burch, had been killed, and that Cretzer had already been identified as the killer, shuddered at the prospect of *any* of the convicts escaping punishment.

Lageson slipped a pencil out of his jacket pocket. "Bob, step over in front of me," he said to Bristow. Captain Weinhold raised his head slightly, saw what Lageson was going to do, and nodded brief approval.

Lageson leaned over in the corner of the cell and began to scribble names on the cement wall. He wrote "Cretzer" first, then "Coy." Then he remembered Durando. The Indio Kid had guarded them, kept them prisoner, when he could have let them go. Lageson wrote "Durando." Looking out, he saw Buddy Thompson still urging Cretzer to kill them. And Shockley supporting Thompson. But he also remembered someone who was not there: Marvin Hubbard. He continued writing.

When he was finished, Lageson had inscribed on the wall in broken, slanted, but entirely readable script, the six names:

> Cretzer
> Coy
> Durando
> Hubbard
> Thompson
> Shockley

Lageson put his pencil, which was nearly chewed up, back in his pocket. Somebody, he thought, would surely find the names after it was all over. Lageson just hoped it would not be a convict.

•

On the flats outside the cells, Buddy Thompson, his loner's mind racing at full speed, continued to preach death. "You've got to get rid of them, Dutch," he urged. "Right now, before it's too late."

"Yeah, Dutch," Crazy Sam shrieked, "kill 'em!" The Oklahoma retard began to drool. "Kill 'em all! Kill Corwin first, Dutch!"

"Go to it, Dutch," said Thompson. "We ain't gonna get out of this place. The screws are going to take us sooner or later. With one screw dead, we'll all get the chair if there's anybody alive to testify against us."

"Kill 'em, Dutch!" Crazy Sam continued to rant. "Do it! Do it!"

"Shut up, both of you!" Cretzer stormed. "Give me a minute to think, for Christ's sake!"

"What the hell's the matter with you, Dutch?" Thompson said, issuing an open challenge. "Give me the goddamn gun if you ain't got the guts to do it!"

"If *I* don't have the guts!" Cretzer snapped indignantly. He turned to Shockley. "Listen to him! A two-bit holdup man!" Back to Thompson, he said, "Who do you think was Public Enemy Number Four, you punk? Who do you think crashed out of McNeil Pen? Who do you think iced that federal marshal? Who's already tried to break out of this fucking place once already and spent five years in lockup for it? No guts, huh? You just watch me, junior! I'll show you killing with a capital K!"

Cretzer stalked across the flats, gun leveled.

"Go to it, Dutch!" Crazy Sam shrieked in delight. He leaped and danced alongside his friend.

Buddy Thompson, eyes darting nervously, watched from across the aisle.

Cretzer stood in front of Cell 403 and aimed the gun through the open door. Captain Henry Weinhold, very weak from his earlier beating by Shockley, pushed himself to a sitting position on the bunk and motioned to Lageson to help him to his feet. When he was up, he faced Cretzer and his gun with defiance and unconcealed scorn.

"You're an animal, Cretzer," Weinhold said coldly. "A ruthless, mindless animal. You don't belong with human beings."

Cretzer's lips curled into a sneer. "Fuck you, Weinhold." He squeezed the trigger and shot the captain squarely in the chest.

Weinhold pitched back against the other guards. Lageson leaped to help him. Cretzer fired again. Lageson's face exploded in blood. Bristow and Burdette were pinned to the back of the cell by the lurching bodies. Cretzer fired once at each of them and they went down. Miller was already on the floor, unconscious. Cretzer aimed the gun at him and fired. His body bucked when the slug hit him. Cecil Corwin was the last of the six to remain standing. Already bloody from the pistol-whipping Cretzer had given him earlier, Corwin stared incredulously at Dutch Cretzer. He looked directly into the convict's eyes and could not believe what was about to happen. Cretzer calmly shot him almost point-blank in the face.

"Good, good!" Crazy Sam yelled. "You got Corwin! He's the cocksucker who got me wet! Good for you, Dutch!"

Cretzer, his eyes like the bullets he was firing, ejected the automatic's magazine and shoved a full one in place. He worked the slide and readied the weapon to fire again. Then he stepped over to the next cell. Lieutenant Joe Simpson was waiting for him.

"You son of a bitch!" Simpson snarled. He lunged at Cretzer. The convict shot him in the stomach and Simpson was thrown back onto the bunk. Baker and Sundstrom also leaped toward Cretzer. He fired twice more. Both men went down.

Cretzer stepped back and looked into both cells. No one moved in either of them. He paced back and forth in front of the two cells several times. After a few seconds he heard a moan from 402. He went over and saw Joe Simpson on the bunk, holding his stomach, grimacing in pain.

"You son of a bitch, what does it take to kill you?" Cretzer raged. He leveled the .45 again and shot Simpson squarely in the chest.

Simpson slammed back flat on the bunk and did not move.

Cretzer began his insane pacing again.

•

An eerie silence followed the carnage.

Buddy Thompson, wide-eyed, visibly frightened by what he had seen, moved quietly and fearfully down to the cutoff and disappeared from Seedy Street.

Crazy Sam, grinning idiotically, looked into both cells as Cretzer had done. He nodded his head in satisfaction at the nine bodies that lay so still. Then he saw the bloody mess that was now Cecil Corwin's face. He shuddered in revulsion.

The aisle was full of gunsmoke. The smell of cordite reached Dutch Cretzer's nostrils and made him sneeze. He sneezed several times and his eyes began to water. "Goddamn it," he muttered.

Shockley looked back at his friend. Dutch appeared to be getting angry. Crazy Sam glanced around and saw that Buddy Thompson was gone. Cretzer was cursing and sneezing sporadically. Shockley wiped the drool of spittle from his mouth with the back of his hand. "I'm gonna go tell everybody in D that the screws are dead, Dutch. Okay?"

"I don't care what you do, you fucking halfwit!" Cretzer yelled at him. "Leave me alone!"

"Sure, Dutch, sure," Shockley said quickly, backing away. He shuffled up Seedy Street, toward Times Square. On the way, his stupid grin returned. "The screws are all dead." He began repeating the singsong phrase. "The screws are all dead, the screws are all dead!" He went skipping toward the open D Block door.

Just inside the D Block door, Danny Durando stood watching. The shooting from the gun gallery had stopped some time earlier, and the Kid had come curiously back onto the D Block flats. When he heard the gunfire from C, he had hurried over to see what was going on. He had seen Cretzer fire part of a magazine into 403, reload, and fire three shots into 402. "Holy Jesus," the young Chicano whispered under his breath.

As Durando stood there, Crazy Sam came prancing through the door. "You missed the fun, Kid," he said gleefully. "Dutch shot all the screws!"

Durando's eyes flashed angrily as he looked at Shockley. "You get away from me, you fucking creep," he said coldly. "Get away from me and stay away." He pointed a warning finger at Shockley. "If you come near me again, I'll break your back."

Shockley glared at him resentfully. "Big talker, ain't you, Mex?" he said, in what he imagined to be an imitation of his friend Dutch. Durando took a threatening step toward him. Shockley turned and ran.

When Crazy Sam was gone, the Indio Kid looked back into C Block again. He saw Dutch Cretzer blotting his eyes on the sleeve of his shirt. He watched quietly as Cretzer looked around Seedy Street and suddenly realized that he was all alone. Then Cretzer looked up and saw Durando watching him.

"Come over here, Mex," he said.

Durando did not move. Cretzer leveled the gun at him.

"Come over here," he said again. It was clear from his tone that he would not say it a third time.

The Kid crossed the flats to Cells 402 and 403.

"All you spiks are good with a knife, Kid," Dutch Cretzer said. "Go in and cut their throats. Make sure they're dead."

"I don't have no knife," Durando said quietly.

"I said make sure they're dead!" Cretzer raged, brandishing the big Colt.

"Sure, Dutch, sure," the Kid said at once. It was clear to him, looking into Cretzer's wild-eyed face, that he was dealing with an insane man.

Durando stepped as far as he could into Cell 403 and bent to examine the heap of tangled, bloody bodies. The sight almost sickened him. Corwin's face was a swollen, grotesque blob of bloody flesh. Weinhold was white and still. Lageson's face was bathed in blood. Looking closely, he saw no conscious movement, but there were definitely some signs of breathing. He backed out of the cell.

"They're all dead, Dutch," he said.

"Check out the other cell," Cretzer said, waving the gun toward 402.

The young Chicano went into 402. Baker was obviously alive, and he thought Sundstrom was too. The lieutenant, like Weinhold next door, was very pale, very still.

"All dead in here too," he said. He came back out.

"Okay, you did a good job, Kid," Cretzer said in an almost friendly tone. "Go on now, beat it."

Dan Durando did not have to be told twice. He hurried back to the D Block door.

Cretzer hefted the .45 and headed for Times Square. Then he

stopped and reversed direction, heading for the cutoff. But he could not make up his mind and stopped again. He looked around almost frantically, his anxious eyes darting to the execution cells; then up to the ever-threatening gun gallery; then down past the cutoff to the east end of the big cellhouse, where by now he knew there must be scores of other guards getting ready to come in and kill him.

Cretzer whimpered once, almost inaudibly, and finally hurried down to the cutoff and, like Buddy Thompson, disappeared.

•

Later, when Seedy Street was still and silent, when only a hint of dull gray light remained against the darkness, a shadowy convict figure stepped through the D Block door and removed his shoes. He left them by the door and padded lightly down the C Block flats to 403. He moved in among the fallen guards, lightly touching one and then another. Suddenly, one man's eyes opened. He looked up fearfully at the convict. The convict touched his lips for silence.

"Don't say nothing," he whispered, bending low. "Cretzer could come back any time. If he does, you play dead. I'm going to get some stuff for bandages. See if you can figure out who's still alive."

The convict hurried along the flats, reaching through the bars of empty cells to fling blankets off bunks so that he could snatch up the sheets. At the occupied cells he said, "Give me your towel," to the lock-up con inside. No one argued, no one refused. In less than a minute, he was back in 403.

"Who's hurt the worst?" he asked.

"I can't tell," the conscious guard whispered. "The captain got it in the chest, but I don't know if he's alive or dead. And Corwin's face is half shot off."

The con handed the guard a towel. "Make a compress of this here and put it on the captain's chest. Maybe it'll stop the bleeding." He reached over and soaked a second towel at the sink. "I'll wrap this around Mr. Corwin's face," he said. He pulled Cecil Corwin into a sitting position.

The convict worked for ten minutes, administering crude but effective first aid to Weinhold, Lageson, Miller, and Corwin. As he worked, he did not know whether the men he was treating were alive or dead.

While he was folding a sheet into a new compress to replace the blood-saturated towel on Weinhold's chest, the con heard a moan come from the next cell. "I better go tell them to quiet down," he said to the guard. "If Cretzer hears that moaning, he'll come back to finish the job."

The convict crept into 402. Carl Sundstrom, unharmed except for the superficial wounds sustained in his fight with Coy, jumped up and closed his fists to fight.

"Take it easy," the con whispered. "I'm trying to help. Who's making the noise?"

"The lieutenant," Sundstrom said warily, still keeping his distance from the convict. "He's hit in the stomach and the chest. I think he's dying."

"Try to keep him quiet," the convict said. "I'll get something to make a compress for his wounds. If Cretzer comes back, play dead."

The convict left 402 and once again hurried along the cellfronts collecting towels and sheets. As he neared the cutoff, he wondered if he should try running past the cross-aisle and trying to get to the main cellhouse entry. If he could get to the sallyport door, there would probably be an army of guards there that he could bring back to help the hostages. Getting past the cutoff would be risky, however. Cretzer might be hiding there, just waiting for someone to shoot at. And even if Cretzer wasn't there, even if he got past the cutoff and all the way to the sallyport door, how did he know the guards wouldn't gun him down? After all that had happened, they were probably itching for a shot at a con. I'll just do what I can for them in the cellhouse, the convict decided.

He trotted on shoeless feet back to 402 to see what he could do for Lieutenant Joe Simpson.

CHAPTER TWENTY-TWO

8:20 P.M.

After leaving Seedy Street, Bernie Coy had stalked across Times Square and through the dining hall into the kitchen, with Marv Hubbard following quickly behind him. Coy had no particular reason for going into the kitchen; all he wanted to do was get out of the sight of Dutch Cretzer before he lost control of himself and killed the son of a bitch. Coy was blind with anger at Cretzer's having killed

Hal Stites. As he went through the dining hall, Hubbard, following, could hear him cursing steadily and without pause. He had never seen a man so angry.

In the kitchen, Coy slammed the rifle down on a baker's table. He paced back and forth across the room, his face now streaked with tears as he cried openly at the frustration of it all.

"We could have made it!" he wailed in an agonized voice. "We could have got out of here! We could have beaten the Rock!" He stopped to pound a table with both fists. "Now I'm going to die here! I'll never get out! Never get out!"

Hubbard hurried over to him. "Take it easy, Bernie. Come on, calm down. It ain't the end of everything—"

Coy jerked away from him. "What the hell do you know about it, Marv? What are you: thirty, thirty-two? I'm past *forty-six,* for Christ's sake! I'll end up like Stroud!" Coy started pounding his fists on the table again. Hubbard grabbed his wrists to keep him from hurting himself. "Let go of me, goddamn it!" Coy screamed. But Hubbard held firm with his tree-trunk arms and pulled his friend away from the table. Coy shook his head violently, tears streaking his face. "Goddamn Cretzer! Let me go, Marv! Let me go back and drill him! Marv! Marv—"

Suddenly Coy's mouth dropped open and his eyes opened very wide. His eyeballs rolled up and the irises disappeared. Marv Hubbard stared at him, frightened and confused. "Bernie! What's the matter? Bernie?"

While Hubbard had hold of his wrists, Coy collapsed and fell up against him. Hubbard lowered him to the floor and put an ear to his chest. He heard Coy's heartbeat and saw that he was still breathing.

Hubbard quickly grabbed the rifle and ran over to a storage pantry near the north side of the kitchen. It was not locked because nothing was kept there that the kitchen cons would steal. Flipping on the light, Hubbard tossed the rifle onto a pile of burlap sacks filled with beans. Then he ran back to where Coy lay and, without a great deal of effort, lifted him into his arms and carried him to the pantry. Hubbard made a crude but not uncomfortable bed out of the bags of beans, and laid Coy on it.

Looking down at his friend, Hubbard shook his head sadly. Coy's left eye was puffy and purple, his nose red and swollen, the corner of his mouth split and bloody, the point of his chin cut and angry-looking. And underneath the loose-fitting guard uniform, there was no telling how many more aches, cuts, and bruises the Kentuckian was suffering. At that moment, Bernie Coy was the most completely gutted human being Marv Hubbard had ever seen.

"You rest, good buddy," Hubbard said quietly.

He took the rifle and sat with it on his lap, facing the door.

•

Buddy Thompson had left Seedy Street via the cutoff. He ran through to Broadway, looked up and down without seeing anyone, then trotted through the next cutoff to Michigan Boulevard. He carefully checked that aisle, again without seeing anyone.

Thompson was looking for Danny Durando. He suspected that the Kid might still be in D. He had seen him go into the isolation block earlier, and guessed he was probably still in there. Thompson wanted badly to find the Kid, but he hated the thought of going into D Block to look for him. D had already been shot up twice. It was not a healthy place to be.

Thompson's eagerness to locate the Indio Kid was connected with his plan for personal survival. He wanted to throw in with Danny Durando to establish an alibi in case Coy was captured instead of killed. Coy, as far as Thompson knew, was the only one who was definitely known to be a part of the break. With the hostages now dead—or so he thought—only Coy could identify the other participants in the escape plan. If Coy *was* caught, and if he *did* inform on the others, Thompson wanted to have an alibi and a partner to back up that alibi. He wanted to be able to say that Coy let the Kid and himself out of their cells and invited them to join the break; that they refused; and that afterward the two of them went to Thompson's open cell, where they remained for the duration of the break. If both he and the Kid stuck to that story, there was no way they could be tied in with the break and the killing of Stites and the hostages.

The only problem, apparently, was going to be in finding the Kid to work out the plan. Goddamn greaser, Buddy Thompson thought. Irritably and reluctantly, he started down Michigan toward Times Square, to cross over to D Block.

•

Sam Shockley, after being run off by Danny Durando, climbed the D Block stairs and shuffled down the middle tier to Cell 22. He looked inside. It was a filthy mess. Soggy, burned cotton and wool all over the floor; the mattress smelling putrid from being soaked;

dried food on the bars that Corwin's stream of water had missed. Cruddy, the whole place. Sam Shockley did not even consider going back into the cell. Despite his low intelligence, he was personally a very clean individual. His fingernails, teeth, hair, everything, were always kept as clean as Alcatraz's limitations would permit. The condition of Cell 22 disgusted him.

Looking at the dirty cell made Shockley think of Cecil Corwin; he shuddered at the memory of Corwin's destroyed face. Sweating, he wiped his face on the sleeve of the coat he was wearing. Then he suddenly realized it was a guard's coat: the one Coy had given him down on Seedy Street. At once he felt ill. After what had happened over on Seedy, if the screws caught him wearing a guard's uniform, his life wouldn't be worth shit.

Shockley quickly removed the coat and rolled it into a ball. He walked down to the end of the range and threw it over the rail, onto the flats near the gun-cage overhang.

Not knowing what to do next, Shockley went into 23, which until a few weeks earlier had been Dutch Cretzer's cell, but was now unoccupied. He unrolled the mattress and sat down on the bunk. He tried to think of some kind of alibi for himself, in case he was tied in to the break. But the more he tried to think about it, the more his mind kept drifting back to C Block. Back to Cell 403. Back to Corwin's grotesque face.

•

Dutch Cretzer had found himself alone on Seedy Street, and after a terrible moment or two of fear and indecision, had finally hurried up to the cutoff and run over to Broadway. He had not noticed which way Thompson or Crazy Sam had gone, but he did not really care. It no longer mattered where any of them were. The crashout was a bust. They were all dead men, no matter what.

Cretzer crossed Broadway as Thompson had done a few minutes earlier. He cut through to Michigan and walked down to his cell, fourth from the end. It was still racked open. He went in and sat down heavily on the metal seat that was bolted to the wall. Taking the .45 from his waistband, he placed it on the small metal table that was attached to the seat. Dropping out the magazine, he thumbed all the bullets onto the table and took out the few he had left in his pocket. He counted them. Twelve. Slowly and deliberately, he pushed half of them back into the magazine and snapped it into the gun's handle again.

From behind him on his bunk, Cretzer got his lined pad and pencil. Almost without thinking about it, he began to write his last verse. He called it *Death*. It read:

> There has been death this day,
> And there will be more.
> Many men will come
> Across the prison floor.
> They will kill me;
> Of that there is no doubt.
> There are many ways in,
> But no way out.
> My life has reached its final span.
> There is nothing left but to do what I can.
> They won't kill a convict; they'll kill a man.

He tore off the page, folded it neatly, and put it in his shirt pocket. Leaving the cell, he walked around on Broadway to the cellhouse officer's desk. He put down the .45 again, and began looking through the keys that were still spread out on the desktop.

By the time Cretzer sat down at the desk, Hubbard already had the collapsed Coy safely in the storage pantry; Buddy Thompson had crept into D Block and was looking around for Durando; the Kid was nowhere to be found; and Shockley was sitting in Cretzer's old cell in D trying to figure out how to keep from being involved in what had happened. None of the men crossed each other's path again that night.

Cretzer found the key he was looking for. It was tagged "UC-C," which meant Utility Corridor–C Block. Taking the key, Cretzer crossed Broadway to the end of C Block. On the way, he saw Bill Miller's uniform coat, which had been discarded by Hubbard. He went over and picked it up, then returned to the end of C Block.

In the middle of the end wall of C was a steel door six and a half feet high. Cretzer unlocked the door and pulled it open. Beyond it was a dimly lighted corridor, thirty inches wide, that extended all the way to the top of the cellblock and opened onto its roof. As with A and B blocks, the cells in C were constructed back-to-back, with a utility corridor separating them. The corridor contained a maze of intertwined water pipes, steam ducts, and electrical conduit—a deep, narrow, cluttered trench between the back walls of the cells. At the top of the trench it divided the cellblock roof into two even sections, one facing north, the other south. There was a ten-foot space between the top of the cellblock and the overhead roof of the cellhouse. Bars extended from the outer edge of the cellblock roof up to the underside of the big cellhouse roof. Their presence turned the block roof into a large, empty cage with a deep slice—the corridor—down its middle. Light shone onto the roof from the nearby overhead skylights above Broadway and Seedy. It was an indirect, filtered light that did little except emphasize the emptiness of the top area, the dust that hung in the air up there, and the starkness of the tall bars that surrounded nothing.

Entering the corridor, Cretzer pulled the door closed behind him and began climbing. He used the maze of pipes and conduit as his ladder. They would take him all the way to the top. To the big cage.

As he worked his way up, Cretzer thought about the twelve bullets he had left. Won't be much of a battle, he told himself.

Below and behind him, the door to the corridor, which he thought he had closed all the way, silently opened an inch.

•

Outside, in the high-walled prison yard, all the Industries prisoners had finally been herded into the corner farthest from the back of the cellhouse. They were crowded together like cattle, some standing, some sitting, others milling about in the limited space allowed. They were unhappy—with everything: the cool air beginning to settle over the bay, the fact that they had not been fed, and the mistake of having allowed themselves to be herded into the yard when they could have revolted and remained in the comparative comfort of the shops with no one able to do a damn thing about it. But mostly they were angry about the Marines on the wall; Marines who kept them bathed in the harsh glare of big searchlights, and under the constant threat of ugly M-1 and Browning automatic rifles. The Marines were young, tanned, and fit. They were also tough and respected—two attributes that all cons secretly cherished. They moved along the top of the wall with a confidence honed in the jungles, and the knowledge that they had earned their place in the elite corps the hard way. Unlike the men in the yard, who had become a part of *their* elite through failure.

"Hey, you got your mamma with you, junior?" one of the cons yelled up at a particularly young-looking Marine above him. That started it.

"Hey, sonny, send your old lady down here! We've got something for her!"

"If she ain't here, come down yourself!"

The taunts soon became bitter.

"Go back where you came from, you fucking punks!"

"Go suck some Navy cocks, you bastards!"

"Come on down in the yard, you motherfuckers! Let's see how tough you really are!"

The challenges were hollow; the cons knew they would not be accepted. The vulgar insults angered the Marines, but they were trained, under orders, and did not respond. It was obvious that most of what the cons yelled up from the yard was generated by the discomfort of being where they were, by the frustration of not being able to extricate themselves from the situation, and by a deep-seated jealousy of the tough young men on the wall who eventually would return to the lights, music, drink, and women of San Francisco. The taunts and insults became cruder, more vociferous, and harder for the Marines to take as the night wore on.

"Hey, kid! Is it true you fucked your mother and then refused to pay her?"

Only rigid Marine Corps discipline prevented a response. The Alcatraz guards attempted several times to quiet the men, but they were ignored. Because of the congestion in the corner-penned body of lookalike men, it was impossible to single out any one person for later punishment. The convicts had all the representatives of authority at a name-calling disadvantage, and they were making the most of it.

It was going to be a long night.

•

In his office, Warden Johnston asked the Marine sergeant stationed with him to contact Lieutenant Phil Bergen on the walkie-talkie. The sergeant made contact with the guard on the catwalk outside the west gun-gallery entrance. "Warden Johnston calling for Lieutenant Bergen," he said. "Over."

There was a long moment of silence, then: "This is Bergen. Over."

"Phil," said Johnston, "I think it's time to have another try at securing the gun gallery. I'm going to cut the lights in the cellhouse. Then we'll sweep all A and D Block windows with searchlights from the outside. That may drive those killers into a hole somewhere. I want to send rescue teams in through this end to try and get our captured officers. I'd like to have them located first. Maybe you can do that from the gallery. Take the walkie-talkie with you. If you hear any sound or detect any movement, let me know at once. Clear?"

"Clear, Warden," said Bergen.

"How many men do you have now?"

"Twelve, counting Fred Mahan and myself."

"Give them a good briefing, Phil. Let's try not to have any more men hit."

"Yes, sir."

"All right, Phil. Good luck." Johnston handed the walkie-talkie back to the sergeant and picked up his phone. "Cliff," he said when Officer Fish answered, "call the powerhouse and have them kill all lights in the cellhouse. I want everything out."

"Yes, Warden."

Johnston rose and walked out to the Admin area. An emergency coffee bar had been set up against one wall and several pots were percolating on hotplates. Johnston glanced about the room for two lieutenants he had on standby, Isaac Faulk and Fred Roberts. He motioned them into his office.

"I want some volunteers," the warden said when they were facing his desk. "Five volunteers for each of you. I want men who are willing to enter the cellhouse and look for our captured officers. I'll want them to go in unarmed."

"Sir?" Isaac Faulk said. He was not sure he had heard right.

"Did you say *un*armed, sir?" asked Fred Roberts.

"That is correct. The security design of that cellhouse is to keep guns off the cellhouse floor. That is why floor guards carry no guns, and that is why the galleries are elevated. No guns have been taken onto the cellhouse floor since this institution opened. We must continue to operate within that principle."

Faulk and Roberts exchanged glances but said nothing. It was obvious that the warden had made up his mind on the subject. To debate the matter with him would simply result in being relieved of the assignment and replaced by someone else. Neither Faulk nor Roberts wanted that. The nine men being held inside the cellhouse were friends of theirs. They dreaded the thought of entering the cellhouse unarmed, but they would have gone in naked if it meant a chance to get Weinhold and others out.

"Get your volunteers and report back to me," Johnston ordered.

The two lieutenants left, feeling slightly ill.

•

When the cellhouse lights were extinguished, Phil Bergen and Fred Mahan again made the climb into the gun gallery, this time leading four of the new guards who had joined them. All was quiet as they moved into the narrow cage; very quiet and, at first, very dark. Duck-walking or crawling on their hands and knees, the six men lined the D Block section of the gallery. When they were all in, Bergen contacted the warden on the walkie-talkie.

"We're in the gun cage, sir," he said, keeping his voice as low as possible.

"Can you see anything or anybody?" Johnston asked.

"No, sir. Everything's black."

"All right, Phil. Stand by. I'm going to have the searchlights hit the D windows." Johnston got Fish on the line again. "Cliff, call the road tower. Have them turn the searchlights on the south wall. Tell them to concentrate on the seven D Block windows between the library wall and the west cage."

"Yes, sir."

Bergen and his squad waited in a void of dark silence. In less than a minute, several strong, penetrating beams of silvery-gray light burst into D Block. From the cage, Bergen and his men heard the sudden eruption of muted, frightened voices from the still-open D Block cells. They peered over the shield at the now ghostly-looking block.

"Phil? Does that give you any visibility?" asked the warden.

"Yes, sir."

"All right. Keep under cover. I'll get back to you when the rescue teams are ready to come in."

Just as Johnston hung up, his secretary hurried into the office. "Warden! Cliff Fish has been trying to ring you. There's a call from Bert Burch in the gun gallery!"

Johnston snatched up the phone.

•

It was now almost 11:00 P.M. Bert Burch had been lying on the lower tier of the main gun gallery in his underwear for nearly nine hours. His face, as a result of the hand-to-hand battle with Bernie Coy, was cut and puffy. The left side of his upper jaw was swollen grotesquely where Coy had hit him with the rifle butt. He had been unconscious off and on until eight o'clock.

When Burch finally came completely out of his unconsciousness, he had experienced head pains so severe he could barely open his eyes; his body was cold and very stiff; and he felt urgently sick to his stomach. By lying still and sucking in deep breaths of cool air, he had managed to overcome the nausea. Then, quietly sitting up, he had spent the better part of an hour rubbing warmth and circulation back into his numb limbs. For the swelling on the side of his face, he had leaned his jaw gently against the inside of the steel shield. Its icy coldness relieved the pain a little, but Burch was certain his jaw was broken.

When he had finally worked himself in shape to function, he got to his knees and peered over the shield. The cellblocks were still and quiet, with only an occasional creak or muted voice to remind him that he was not alone in the big room. The door to D was standing open. There were keys all over the cell-house officer's desk. The air smelled faintly of gunpowder.

Quietly, Burch sat down and assessed his situation. His coat and trousers were gone; more importantly, so were his rifle and pistol. The gallery had been stripped of billy clubs and ammunition. Burch visually examined the cage from the north end to the D Block door. There was no sign of a way Coy could have got in. Yet he *did* get in. Through the top tier somehow, Burch decided. Apprehensively, he looked up at the underside of the top tier. For all he knew, there could be cons up there right then.

Burch looked at the gallery phone. It was down in the middle of the cage, mounted on the wall, a good two feet above the top of the shield. As he was trying to decide whether to try and get to it, he heard footsteps on Times Square. He quickly took off his shoes and twisted himself around to peer over the shield again. He saw a con walking quickly into D Block. Burch could not see his face, but from the back he looked like Buddy Thompson. The gallery guard remembered that Thompson had gone to sick call at noon and stayed in lockup after lunch.

Just as he was about to sit down again, Burch glanced up Seedy Street and saw Officer Carl Sundstrom step partway out of a cell on the flats. Burch parted his lips to call out to his fellow guard; then he saw a shadowy con come out of an adjoining cell. Burch quickly ducked his head. He did not see the con hand a bundle of sheets and towels to Sundstrom for fresh compresses.

A while later, after sitting quietly again, Burch heard footsteps a second time. They stopped somewhere in the center of Times Square. Extra cautiously, he looked over the shield. His eyes widened at the sight of Dutch Cretzer, a .45 next to him, searching through the keys on the cellhouse officer's desk. Burch ducked back down. Several minutes later, he heard a key being used to unlock something. It sounded as if it was being done at the west end of C. Burch surmised that Cretzer was opening the control box in order to rack open some cells. It did not occur to him that the former public enemy might be unlocking the door to the C Block utility corridor.

The cellhouse was again quiet for a while. Burch decided finally that he should make a try for the phone. He was convinced by now that there were no cons in the gallery with him; the upper tier had been silent since he woke up. Slowly he began to inch his way toward the middle of the cage. He could not help recalling all the times he had mentally complained about the restricted space in the gallery; how he often seemed as trapped and caged as the men he guarded. Now, traversing it by inches, the gun tier seemed uncommonly long.

Before he got to the phone, Burch heard footsteps for the third time. He stopped and peered down again. It was Buddy Thompson; no mistaking him this time. The Texas outlaw was heading down Broadway, walking briskly. Burch watched him turn quickly into the C Block stairs and walk uprange on the south side of the middle tier. He disappeared into a cell.

Just as Thompson passed from view, the cellhouse lights went out. Burch dropped to the floor of the cage and lay flat. Something was about to happen; he *felt* it. He stayed absolutely still, straining his ears to listen. Except for the same occasional creaks and muted voices, he again heard nothing. The big cellhouse was pitch dark; it reminded Burch of a tremendous tomb, the door of which had just been pulled shut. The void was complete, total, frightening. Burch swallowed and tried to quiet his breathing, which suddenly seemed inordinately loud.

Moments later, light returned. A *kind* of light, at least: frosted, moving, teasing the darkness without really challenging it. Burch got to his knees to see what kind of light it was. It seemed to be coming intermittently through the three high windows in the cellhouse library, and filtering down Seedy Street from there; and some of it appeared to come from the open D Block door. Searchlights, Burch thought, recognizing the texture of the light the instant he got a close look at it. Something was *definitely* about to happen. He *had* to remind someone that he was still in the gallery.

Feeling relatively safe in the almost total darkness of the gun cage, Bert Burch stood up for the first time since Coy had knocked him out, and shakily jiggled the telephone hook to flash the armory.

•

On the phone, Johnston listened as Burch related to him every-thing he had observed from the gallery since regaining consciousness: the movements of Thompson, Cretzer, and Officer Carl Sundstrom. Johnston asked a few quick, pertinent questions, some of which Burch was able to answer and some of which he was not. After a two-minute conversation, the warden instructed Burch to remain where he was. "I'll have Lieutenant Bergen and some more men in there with you in a few minutes."

Johnston then got on the walkie-talkie to Bergen. "Phil, we've just heard from Bert Burch," he said, with obvious relief in his voice. Earlier, Johnston had guessed that Burch was already dead. "He's right next to you in the main section of the cage. Get in to him with a coat if you can; they've taken his uniform. Try to get him out of there as quickly as possible; apparently he's been beaten up."

"Yes, sir," Bergen acknowledged. He turned to Mahan, next to him in the gray-lighted D Block gallery. "Burch just called. He's in the main cage. Pass the word to the other men to stand by. You and I will go in."

"Right."

After the word was passed, Bergen and Mahan eased over to the gallery door. Bergen pressed his ear to the door and listened. He heard nothing. In the back of his mind was the thought of a trap: Burch forced at gunpoint to call the warden. But that presupposed the presence of one or more convicts in the gun gallery—a condition Bergen still could not bring himself to believe.

Bergen slowly opened the door. The main cage was dark. He would be a silhouette for the split-instant he was in the doorway. He moved fast: a half step, half jump; then he was through the door and crouched on the floor next to the wall. With his automatic ready, he moved toward the middle of the gallery. As he neared the phone, he sensed the presence of someone very close to him. He pointed the .45 toward where the person's head would be.

"Who's that?" he asked tensely.

"Burch," a dry voice replied.

Bergen expelled a held breath. "Phil Bergen here, Bert. How badly are you hurt?"

"Just beat up a little, Lieutenant. My jaw might be broke. I was in a fight with Bernie Coy. He bashed me in the head with my rifle. Mostly I'm just cold right now."

Bergen took off his uniform coat and gave it to Burch. "Coy was *inside* the cage?" he asked incredulously.

"Big as life. Came out of nowhere. Took me completely by surprise."

"How the hell did he get in?"

"I don't know. I looked over this tier pretty good before the lights went out. Didn't see anything down here, so it must be up above."

"You think there are any cons up there now?"

"I don't know. I haven't heard anything. But I don't know."

"Okay," Bergen said. "You slide over to the door. Fred Mahan's there. Tell him I'm going to check the top tier."

Bergen moved quietly along the cage to the steep metal ladder that led up to the top tier. With his gun ready, he climbed the ten steps and moved in a crouch along the tier. He held the .45 at gut level and walked straight ahead with his left arm stretched out to touch the bars above the shield. He kept his feet wider apart than usual, so that if anyone were crouched next to the shield, his knee would touch them. He had decided coming up the stairs that he would fire at anyone he found in the gallery, immediately and without warning.

Bergen checked the entire length of the main gallery, then went on into the upper D Block tier. The grayish light up there made it possible for him to check it visually without going all the way in. He quickly saw that it was empty.

Bergen went back down to the lower level and returned to where Burch was waiting with Fred Mahan. "The cage is clear," he said quietly. "Fred, take the walkie-talkie and go downstairs. Send three of the back-up men up here to man the top tier. Then notify the warden that the gun gallery is secure. Bert, you go with him and we'll get you to the first-aid room."

"I'd like to stay here, Lieutenant," Burch said.

Bergen shook his head. "Your jaw needs looking after."

"It's not broken," Burch said. "I've been examining it while you were upstairs."

"I think I'd better relieve you, Bert."

"Look, Lieutenant," Burch said, "Mahan told me what happened to Hal Stites. That had to be my .45 that he was killed with. I'd like another crack at the con who took that gun away from me."

Something about Burch's voice overruled Bergen's better judgment. To Mahan he said, "Have somebody get some clothes and a gun for Officer Burch."

"Thanks, Lieutenant," Bert Burch said quietly.

•

Across Times Square, lying on his stomach on top of C Block, Dutch Cretzer lay listening to the hushed voices of the whispering guards. He had seen Bergen's silhouette when the guard lieutenant first entered the main gallery; had listened to him climb to the top tier and search it. If the visibility had been better and the line of fire less awkward, he would already have blasted at least one, probably two, of the screws in the cage. But with only twelve bullets left, he had to be very conservative in selecting his targets. The more hacks he took out with him, the bigger the headlines would be when they finally got him. And that was all he had left.

In the dark at the top of the cellblock, Dutch Cretzer smiled. Tomorrow, when the light was good, he would make it a bloody day.

PART TWO

FRIDAY, MAY 3, 1946

CHAPTER TWENTY-THREE

12:05 A.M.

It was just after midnight when Warden Johnston came into the Admin office to brief the two rescue teams. Lieutenants Isaac Faulk and Fred Roberts each had their five volunteers. They had encountered no resistance in getting men for the job, although the men they got expressed unanimous disagreement with the warden's order that no guns be carried on the assignment. There had been considerable bitching during the quarter-hour that it took the men to turn in their weapons at the armory and assemble in Admin. Even as the warden was coming out of his office, there were some remarks made about suicide missions and the fact that Johnston was known to have a gun in his *office,* where there was no danger at all. The warden heard none of the comments, of course. If he had, the guards making the remarks would have been relieved.

"Men," Johnston said, "I am happy to tell you that we have had a call from Bert Burch and that he is not seriously injured. At this moment, he is being rescued from the west gun gallery by Lieutenant Bergen and his men. The gun cage has been secured; there are officers with machine guns on both levels."

Johnston paused and studied the twelve men facing him. Except for the two lieutenants, he found that he could not think of any of their names. All of their faces were familiar, but the names escaped him completely. But no matter, he thought.

"Now then, to the business at hand," he continued. "We know that two convicts are armed: Coy and Cretzer. We don't know where

225

Coy is. Cretzer was last seen on Times Square shortly before the lights went out. I urge you to be particularly careful in that area. And remember you will be covered by the men we now have in the gun gallery.

"There are two other convicts who may or may not be in on the break. One is Buddy Thompson, who has been observed out of his cell, roaming in and out of D Block. Incidentally, I want that D Block door closed; we must try to keep the Treatment Unit prisoners isolated. It is essential that they not be allowed to have contact with any of the general population. The men in D have all been isolated for a reason, and we must uphold the principle of—of, uh—"

"We'll see to that door first thing, Warden," Isaac Faulk said. *Jesus, get on with it!*

"Very good, Lieutenant. Now then, where was I? Oh yes, one other convict was observed coming out of a cell near the west end of the C-D aisle. He hasn't been identified. Officer Sundstrom was also observed in the same area. The convict may have been helping Sundstrom in some way; we don't know. However, the convict must be a lock-up prisoner and he should not have been out of his cell. There is no provision for any lock-up prisoner being out of his cell like that—"

"Sir," Lieutenant Roberts interrupted, "would you let the men in the gun cage know we're on our way in, so they don't mistake our movement for convicts on the loose?"

"Yes, of course. I'll do that now—"

The warden turned to the Marine sergeant with the walkie-talkie. As he did, Faulk and Roberts seized the opportunity to get their teams moving. "All right, men, line up in the deadlock!" Faulk ordered briskly. "Let's get going!"

The two lieutenants managed to hurry their volunteers out of Admin before Johnston could resume the briefing.

•

In the deadlock, the twelve guards paused while the sallyport guard locked the outside door and Cliff Fish moved the shield plate over the lock. Then the inside deadlock door was opened and the men passed through to the cellhouse entry. The inner solid steel door was unlocked and pulled open. The barred door on the other side of it was unlocked and pushed open into the cellhouse.

Faulk and Roberts had already made their plan and briefed their teams before Johnston's talk. There was no hesitation now as they filed quietly into the dark cellhouse. They knew exactly what they were going to do. Their job was to rescue the captured officers. The only way to do that was to move as rapidly and quietly as possible down to the hostage cells, and try not to get shot while doing it. The cells were probably near the end of Seedy, where Burch had observed Sundstrom and the unidentified convict.

Inside the cellhouse, the teams separated. Faulk and his men moved over to Seedy and, beginning with Cell 376, briefly examined every cell along the flats. The light from the searchlights flashing through the library windows, directly across Seedy, gave them good illumination, so it was not necessary for them to use the flashlights they carried. As they started their search down Seedy, they were twenty-six cells away from 402 and 403.

Roberts and his men had gone over to Michigan Boulevard. Beginning with Cell 127, they moved west toward Times Square. There was almost no light at all down Michigan, so Roberts was forced to shine his flashlight into each cell in order to see who or what was in it. He and his team knew that at any moment the on-off beam of the flashlight could draw gunfire from either or both of the armed convicts. In spite of that, they moved relentlessly on.

•

In Cell 402, Carl Sundstrom heard the sound of footsteps down Seedy Street. They were coming from the same direction in which first Buddy Thompson, then Dutch Cretzer, had run away after Cretzer's insane shooting spree.

Sundstrom pulled himself up off the floor where he had been sitting holding a thick compress on Joe Simpson's stomach. Sundstrom did not know whether Simpson was dead or alive. The convict who had made the compress was gone now; he had run away when the searchlights started flashing.

At the open cell door, Sundstrom stood very still and listened. There was definitely someone down near the cutoff, and that someone was coming his way. There was residual light along Seedy from the searchlights outside, but Sundstrom did not want to look out into the aisle. If the footsteps were being made by Cretzer or Coy, they might see him. He had a better chance of coming out of this nightmare alive if he took the convict's advice and played dead. But before he stretched out on the floor like a corpse, there was something he wanted to do. Just in case Dutch Cretzer was taken alive, and the other hostages and himself were killed.

Sundstrom took a small spiral notebook and pencil from his pocket. Bracing the notebook against the wall, he wrote:

> Cretzer killed or shot Joe Simpson in the stomach and chest twice. He missed me so far.
>
> Carl Sundstrom

Tearing out the page, he folded it and put it into his trousers pocket. Then he went to the back of the cell, stepped over the still form of Bob Baker, and lay down on the floor. He listened helplessly as the footsteps came closer.

•

High above the flats, Dutch Cretzer was also listening. He could hear the quiet shuffling of Fred Roberts and his men as they finished checking the cells down Michigan Boulevard and came around the end of the block onto Times Square.

Cretzer was on the north side of the cellblock roof; through the bars he could look directly down onto Broadway. He flattened himself on his stomach and waited. Then the shuffling noise came off Times Square and turned up Broadway. Cretzer saw the first flash of light as Lieutenant Roberts checked Cell 238 on the Broadway side of B.

I wonder how many of them there are? he thought, rolling over and picking up the automatic.

•

On Seedy, Faulk and his men had passed the cutoff and methodically worked their way down the west half of the cellblock. When they got to 402, they found the cell door racked open. Faulk squinted at the ghostly-looking figure lying on the bunk. Quickly he shined his flashlight in.

"Good God, it's Joe Simpson. He's got blood all over him—"

There was movement at the back of the cell. Faulk and his men tensed. "Don't shoot," a voice said urgently. "It's me, Carl Sundstrom."

Don't shoot. That was a good one, Faulk thought. He moved to the back of the cell and helped Sundstrom up. "Are you hurt?"

"No. But Lieutenant Simpson's been shot twice. And Bob Baker's on the floor there; he may be dead."

"Where are the others?"

"In the next cell."

Faulk turned to his first two men. "Get Simpson out of here, quick. Carry him up to the sallyport." To a third man, he said, "You help Sundstrom get Baker out. You last two come with me."

Faulk went next door. He shined his flashlight onto the red slaughter scene in 403. "My God," he whispered.

"Who's there?" a voice asked hoarsely from inside.

"Lieutenant Faulk. Who's talking?"

"Bristow. Burdette and I are okay. We've been playing dead."

"I'm alive too," another voice said. "Lageson. But I've been hit. My face is all swollen and bloody."

"Hold on," said Faulk. "We'll get you out one by one."

•

Above Roberts and his men, Dutch Cretzer waited until they were up to Cell 232. There, in the quick flash of light that the guard lieutenant shone into the cell, Cretzer could tell that there were at least four or five other guards grouped around him.

That's it, you stupid idiots, he thought. Keep all bunched up like that, so there won't be any way for me to miss.

Cretzer had been unwilling to risk shooting in the dark at the guards moving into the gun gallery, because they were spread out and the light and angle of fire were poor. But now the circumstances were different. Now there was a group he could fire into; the angle of his shot would be almost straight down; and the momentary flash of light at each cell was a perfect beacon at which to aim.

Cretzer hung his arm through the bars, thumbed off the safety, and waited. As soon as the flashlight flicked on again, he fired two quick shots.

Both bullets hit Lieutenant Roberts and sent him sprawling onto the flats of Broadway. He knocked down two of his men as the impact of the slug sent him reeling.

In the gun gallery, the double orange burst of fire was clearly visible. Phil Bergen, Bert Burch, and one other officer on the lower tier, plus the three officers on the top tier, all opened fire and raked the top of C Block with a sheet of fire.

On the flats, Roberts's men rushed to him and dragged him back around the corner onto Times Square.

•

Over on Seedy, Isaac Faulk heard the first two shots, then the barrage that followed. "Come on, men, step lively," he said. "Let's get the rest of them and get the hell out of here!"

Simpson, Baker, and Sundstrom were safely in the deadlock, and the three guards who had helped them were now back. Faulk's other two men had carried Captain Weinhold out. Bristow and Burdette had carried Cecil Corwin out. When the first three guards returned, Faulk had two of them pick up Bill Miller and start back with him. The third steadied Ernest Lageson and helped him down the aisle.

As the last of the hostages were taken past the cutoff, Faulk walked quickly up to the end of C and closed the door that opened into D Block. There was a sharp click as the lock engaged automatically.

CHAPTER TWENTY-FOUR

1:00 A.M.

In the deadlock, Warden Johnston watched tightlipped as his rescued officers were brought out of the cellhouse. Captain Weinhold and Lieutenant Simpson were unconscious and looked dead, their bodies and clothing saturated with blood. Cecil Corwin, also unconscious, looked as if a tractor had run over his face. Ernest Lageson's face and neck were a mass of pulpy, half-dry blood. Bill Miller was semidelirious, Bob Baker feverish, from arm and leg wounds. The floor of the deadlock became slick with blood. But incredible as it seemed, not one of the nine men in the two execution cells had been killed.

Just before the inner deadlock door was secured, the second rescue team returned with a wounded and unconscious Lieutenant Roberts. He was put with the other wounded. Then the inner door was locked and the outer deadlock opened. A team of U.S. Public Health Service doctors, led by Dr. Louis Roucek, the prison doctor, was waiting in the Admin area. As the wounded were brought in now, the doctors quickly went to work. Weinhold and Simpson were stripped to the waist. "They're both alive," said Dr. Roucek as he quickly examined them. Johnston and the others in the room could barely believe it. The doctor gave them each an injection and had them wrapped in blankets. "Stretchers!" he called, and four Navy corpsmen hurried over. "These two. Down to the dock and over to Marine Hospital emergency!"

Another doctor had unwrapped Corwin's face. "Christ," he muttered. He removed the blood-stiff towel and put an ice bandage in its place.

A sheet folded over numerous times was taken from around Lageson's neck and shoulder, and the blood sponged from his face. Bill Miller and Bob Baker were given injections of morphine and temporary splints were put on their wounded arms and legs. Lieutenant Roberts had two bullet holes in his right shoulder, going all the way through. He was still unconscious when his wounds were cleansed.

As they worked, Dr. Roucek remarked, "It's a damn good thing the men had the presence of mind to use these towels and sheets for compresses. If they hadn't, we'd have a room full of dead men here."

By one-thirty, all of the wounded had been taken down to the dock, put aboard Navy launches, and rushed across the water to the Marine Hospital.

•

Warden Johnston returned to his office and summoned his secretary. He began to compose what was to be his last teletype message of the break to Washington. After his first three messages, Johnston had kept in periodic touch with Director Jim Bennett throughout the night. He had informed him of the arrival of the Marines; the successful movement of the Industries prisoners into the yard; the death of Hal Stites and the wounding of Maxwell, Cochrane, and Oldham. For some unknown reason, he had failed to mention Fred Richberger's wound. Later, he had teletyped Bennett that Officers Bergen and Mahan had retaken the gun gallery. Now he wrote his final message:

> ALL HOSTAGES NOW RELEASED.
> PRISONERS WITH GUNS HAVE
> BEEN DRIVEN TO COVER.
> DOOR TO D BLOCK CLOSED.

"Get that off at once," Johnston instructed his secretary. "Where are the three hostages who weren't wounded? What are their names?"

"Bristow, Burdette, and Sundstrom, sir. Sundstrom was beaten up by Coy; he's getting first aid. Bristow and Burdette are being fed. They're all kind of shaky."

"Have them report to me as soon as they're able."

"Yes, sir."

•

In D Block, Crazy Sam Shockley slipped out of Dutch Cretzer's old cell and crept down the stairs to the flats. He moved slowly and cautiously, knowing that the gun gallery above D now had guards in it. Each time the outside searchlights swung their beams through the high windows, Sam stopped and ducked. Most of the light hit the middle and top tiers, but there was enough on the flats to distinguish a man's movements unless he was very careful.

Shockley worked his way around to Cell D-1, the first inmate cell next to the shower cell. Peering inside, he saw Louis Fleish sitting on his bunk, smoking. Fleish looked up apprehensively.

"It's me," said Crazy Sam. "I want to talk to you."

"What about?" asked Fleish.

"I figure we can alibi each other," Shockley said. "Let me stay down here with you and we can say we was both in your cell through the whole break."

"I don't need an alibi, Sam," the Detroit gangster replied. "I haven't done anything."

"Yeah, but the screws might think you have," Shockley told him. "They might think you had something to do with killing Corwin. Especially if I was to mention your name when this is all over."

Fleish remained silent.

" 'Course, I wouldn't do that if we was each other's alibi."

Fleish reached down in the semidarkness and gripped one of his shoes for a weapon, in case he needed it. "Beat it, Sam," he said evenly. "Find an alibi someplace else."

"How come?" Shockley asked almost indignantly. "How come you won't help me?"

"Because I liked Cecil Corwin," Fleish said. "I thought he was a good guy. I don't think you pricks should have killed him."

"If I'd known you was a fucking screw-lover, I wouldn't even have asked you," Sam said scornfully.

"You better get out of here, Sam, if you know what's good for you. I've got a shiv in my hand. Try anything funny and I'll stick you."

Shockley muttered a few obscenities and backed out. He made his way to the stairs and back up to the middle tier. That little Jew bastard, he thought. He'd fix him good. When the break was over and everybody was either dead or caught, he'd tell them that Fleish had planned the whole thing. He'd tell them that Fleish had figured it all out and told Bernie Coy what to do. He'd get Louis Fleish sent to the fucking chair!

Smiling at that prospect, Shockley went back into Dutch Cretzer's old cell and lay down on the bunk.

•

At about 2:00 A.M., a young Marine corporal patrolling a section of the north wall looked down into the prison yard. The two hundred-odd convicts were huddled together in a great mass, some lying next to the wall, some sitting hunched over their knees, others squatting on their haunches with chins down, forearms across their stomachs. All were trying to stay warm. Most were still awake, although the ones up closest to the wall appeared to be sleeping.

The Marine watching them was only twenty, but he was old beyond those years. He had joined the Corps at seventeen. Six months later he had been in jungle combat in the Pacific. Until he was nineteen, he had spent his time in an infantry unit, island-hopping. He had helped bury his best friend on an island that had a name he could not even pronounce. He won a Purple Heart for three mortar fragments in his left thigh. For a year after the surrender he had served with the occupation forces in Tokyo. One night he had fought a Japanese pimp in an alley and strangled him to death.

The Marine was very contemptuous of the convicts in the yard. As far as he was concerned, they were a collection of scum who had sat out the war in a nice safe, dry, warm place where they were fed three hot meals a day. And all the while he had been getting shell chips in the leg and his best buddy had been getting killed. Somehow, none of it seemed very fair.

The corporal suddenly felt the urge to go to the bathroom. He turned to face the outside of the wall that looked down on a slope of rocky hill. Slinging his rifle, he unbuttoned his trousers. In the split second between the conscious thought and the physical act, he remembered some of the scathing filthy insults the convicts had yelled up at him earlier.

Turning in the darkness, the corporal urinated down on the prisoners.

•

In San Francisco, newspaper reporters from every paper were looking for Alcatraz stories from every source imaginable. One group of reporters was waiting at the Hyde Street pier when an Army launch docked to pick up some emergency food rations prepared by the Red Cross. The captain in charge of the detail was interviewed briefly and hectically. Most of the questions asked were at that moment unanswerable; most of the answers given were nonresponsive. But one question and one answer stood out glaringly from the rest.

"Captain, do you have any idea how much ammunition the convicts have?" a reporter asked.

"It is my understanding that they have enough to last them forty days," the captain replied.

No one knows why the captain made that statement. He was never identified.

Other reporters were at Marine Hospital, where the men wounded in the earlier gun-gallery battle had been taken. The California Highway Patrol had given the ambulances a motorcycle escort from the dock to the hospital. One motorcycle officer, Patrolman James Morgan, was surrounded by reporters after he returned from helping attendants carry one of the officers into the emergency room.

"Did you talk with the wounded officer?" a reporter wanted to know.

"A little. While he was waiting for the doctor, I stayed with him."

"Did he tell you how the break started?"

Patrolman Morgan nodded. "He said a convict named Coy had overpowered a guard in one of the towers. He took the guard's machine gun, then forced the guard to lead him to a room where some other guards were changing clothes to go on duty. After capturing all those guards, this Coy threw a switch that opened all of the cellblocks. He invited all of the convicts to join him in the break. Only twelve joined him. They made their way to an arsenal where guard weapons were kept and loaded up with guns and ammunition."

"Did the officer give you any other details?" the reporter asked, making notes furiously.

"No," the patrolman replied, "that was about all I got from him."

The officer that Morgan spoke with was never identified, and Morgan himself was never requestioned about the conversation.

At the U.S. Marine Corps base at Treasure Island, still another story was being given out. This one came from Marine Major Albert Arsenault, a public-relations officer who had just returned from the island.

"The way I understand it," Arsenault said, "a convict trusty named Coy somehow obtained a ladder and a T-square. He went to a point below the elevated gun gallery and somehow got up on the ladder unobserved. He hooked the T-square around the neck of the gallery guard, pulled him to the bars, knocked him out, seized his rifle, and ripped the keys from his belt. Another trusty named Thompson was there helping him."

To the outside world who read the various stories in print later that day, most of it probably sounded reasonable. One had to be acquainted with reality to see the absurdity of it all. Coy overpowering a *tower* guard; the convicts having enough ammunition for *forty days*; a ladder-and-T-square assault on the gun gallery (Coy would have loved that one; it sounded so easy, while the actual taking of the cage had been so brutal). The most ludicrous part of all was referring to Buddy Thompson as a *trusty*. Thompson, with a record of eight jailbreaks; a trusty in a prison where there *were* no trusties.

One reporter, at least, dealt only with pure fact. Ed Montgomery, after leaving the San Francisco police boat, hurried back to the *Examiner* offices to write his story. Rolling a sheet of yellow paper into his typewriter, he wrote the first sentence of what would be the least sensational but most factual story of the day.

"For a few hours last night," he wrote, "the Rock in San Francisco Bay was the hottest spot on earth."

•

By 3:00 A.M., both Captain Henry Weinhold and Lieutenant Joe Simpson were undergoing emergency surgery at Marine Hospital. In one operating room, a team of doctors removed a .45 slug from Weinhold. In another, a second team removed two similar slugs from Simpson. That neither man had been killed after being shot almost point-blank by what was then the world's most powerful handgun was incredible. Weinhold's life had probably been saved by the slug deflecting slightly on one of the cell bars; it hit him in a flopping forward motion instead of its natural spiraling velocity which would have drilled it into his chest. As for Joe Simpson, the explanation was much simpler and far more obvious. His life had been saved because Cretzer's second bullet, which hit him squarely in the chest, struck his tie clip, bent it into a U-shape, and embedded it in his chest. In doing so, the slug was deflected and prevented from going into his heart.

After the operations, the two senior guards were moved into intensive-care units. Despite their extreme good fortune in still being alive, doctors unanimously agreed that neither would survive the night.

In another part of the surgical ward, Officer Bill Miller was lying on a gurney after finishing his own turn in surgery. With him were his wife Josephine and two FBI agents. Miller, who was very weak from loss of blood, and whose stamina was rapidly diminishing, had just recited a deathbed statement for the two federal agents.

"Let me read this back to you, Bill," one of them said quietly. " 'On this date, May 3, 1946, at about 3:00 A.M., I, William A. Miller, being in a critical condition and believing I am now dying, make this my sworn statement that I was shot with a .45 Colt revolver by convict Joseph Cretzer, who I can positively identify.' Is that accurate, Bill?"

Miller nodded a barely perceptible nod. Technically, it was not accurate. The weapon had been an automatic, not a revolver. But Bill Miller was too weak to correct it. He could barely nod.

"Can you leave him alone now?" Josephine Miller asked tearfully.

"Of course," the agent replied. He gently touched Miller's hand. "Good luck, Bill."

Miller was wheeled into a hospital room and put to bed. Josephine, a deeply religious woman, laid a crucifix on his chest and took a prayer book from her purse. She began reading from it in a whisper.

•

Across the street from Portsmouth Square, on the edge of Chinatown, Hal Stites's body had finally arrived at the San Francisco morgue. Because he was dead and could not be helped in any way, Stites had been put aside on the Alcatraz dock as the wounded from the gun-cage battle were transported to the mainland. Then the dock was closed temporarily after darkness to avoid giving the convicts a lighted target; later, the launches were used to take the wounded from 402 and 403 to the Marine Hospital.

When the body finally did arrive, it was in the final stages of rigor mortis. A great deal of blood had left the body while it lay on the pier. Most of that blood had seeped down, saturating the back of the dead guard's uniform coat and drying into an almost black crust. When the body was lifted and moved about in the morgue, that grisly crust of dried blood split and cracked like rust that had eaten through a pipe. A morgue attendant got a brief glimpse at it when Stites was rolled onto his side for his uniform to be scissored away. That attendant was questioned a little while later by several reporters who had been assigned to the morgue.

"Can you tell us what kind of wounds the dead officer had?" a reporter asked.

"A single row of machine gun bullets right up the back," the attendant said. "I saw the crusted blood and the bullet holes myself."

The reporters hurried off to call in this latest piece of news.

CHAPTER TWENTY-FIVE

5:20 A.M.

In the storage pantry in the far corner of the cellhouse kitchen, Bernie Coy finally woke up. He blinked his eyes several times, then jerked up like a frightened animal and looked around desperately, as if seeking a route of escape.

"You sure did sleep, old buddy," a voice said from across the pantry. Coy snapped his head around. He saw Marv Hubbard, propped up on a sack of beans, grinning at him.

"What time is it?"

"Hell, I don't know," Hubbard said. "You're the one that stole Lageson's watch, not me."

"Huh?" Coy frowned. Then he remembered. He looked at the strange watch on his wrist. "Jesus, it's almost five-thirty. What's been going on?"

"Not a hell of a lot," Hubbard said. "There was a lot of shooting for a minute or two around midnight. I was out in the kitchen getting some coffee. Been quiet since then."

"Know where any of the others are?"

Hubbard shook his head. "You feeling better?" he asked.

Coy stood and stretched, grimacing. "I feel like a Mack truck done run over me."

"Hungry?"

"Christ, yes!"

"I'll get us some grub."

Hubbard left the pantry and cautiously searched the kitchen. It was empty. He peered into the big dining hall. The milk pitcher Buddy Thompson had left was still on one of the tables; other than that, the dining hall was empty, quiet, and spotlessly ready for the next meal. Hubbard listened for a moment, but heard not a sound from Times Square or the cellblocks beyond.

When he returned to the pantry, Hubbard had a metal pitcher of coffee from the automatic urn, a loaf of bread, preserves and butter from Bristow's private refrigerator, and, stuffed inside his shirt, half a dozen oranges. The two convicts put a sack of beans between them and spread out their food.

"Wonder where everybody is?" Coy said as he ate.

"Hard telling," answered Hubbard.

"Wonder if the screws got out last night?"

"Probably. The cell doors weren't closed." Because they had been sequestered in the pantry, they had not heard Cretzer firing into 402 and 403.

Coy wondered how Bill Miller was. All right, he guessed, except for a sore face.

"Got any idea what we can do now?" Hubbard asked.

Coy shook his head. "That son of a bitch Cretzer," he said. "I should have knowed better. All my life I've knowed that hotshots like Cretzer and Dillinger was just headline hunters. None of them gave a goddamn what they had to do, just as long as they got to see their names and pictures in the papers. Jesus! Why did I ever bring that bastard in on this?"

"Connections on shore, remember?" said Hubbard. "The car and the clothes and the hideout waiting."

Coy looked disgusted. "If I had it all to do over again, it'd be just me and you and the Kid." For a brief, suspended moment, Coy stared into space. "If I just had it all to do over again," he repeated, slowly and sadly. It was as if he were talking about his whole life.

Marv Hubbard saw the distant look in his friend's eyes and nodded understandingly. "I know what you mean, partner," he said quietly.

When they finished eating, Hubbard put the empty pitcher, the preserves and butter containers, and the orange peels over next to the door. Being a kitchen worker had made Hubbard a very tidy man; he liked to clean things up immediately. When he got back to the bean sacks, Coy handed him a neatly rolled cigarette. The two of them lighted up and smoked in silence for a while, each with his own thoughts. After a few minutes, Hubbard said, "Bernie?"

"Yeah?"

"How in the hell did two ol' hillbilly boys like us end up in this here room?"

Coy grunted wryly. "Just lucky, I guess, Marv."

•

Across the water at the Marine Hospital, a team of plastic surgeons finished a five-hour repair procedure on Officer Cecil Corwin's face. It had been a grueling, frustrating operation and the doctors were exhausted. In the post-op room, one of them pulled off his surgical mask and sank wearily into a chair. "Jesus Christ. Talk about a mess."

One of his colleagues nodded agreement. "Like trying to put a meringue pie back together after it's been dropped."

"What kind of animal would shoot a man in the face like that?" a young intern wondered.

"An Alcatraz animal," someone answered. "A rabid rodent in a human body."

"Instead of locking up people like that, why don't they just execute them and be done with it?"

"That wouldn't be civilized, Doctor," one of them said sarcastically.

The young intern went over to the chief surgeon. "Doctor, will he ever have a face that *looks* like a face again?"

"Maybe," the older man said. "But it'll take a lot of years and a lot of surgery."

As the doctors talked, Corwin was being wheeled into the intensive-care unit, where Weinhold and Simpson still clung tenaciously to life.

In Washington, D.C., it was shortly after 9:00 A.M. At the Department of Justice, Attorney General Tom Clark had just finished the second of two telephone calls. The first had been brief and Clark had immediately recognized the voice of his caller.

"What the hell is going on out there at Alcatraz, Tom?" asked Harry Truman. "On my morning walk a little while ago, the reporters were asking me more questions about that than about Jimmy Byrnes over in Paris."

"I'm holding for a call to the prisons director now, Mr. President. We should have it cleared up in a few hours. I'm sorry the reporters bothered you about it."

"Hell, it wasn't any bother," the President declared. "Kept those fellows from asking me questions about important matters. But you get it under control out there as quick as you can."

"I will, Mr. President."

The call to Bennett had been completed just as the President was hanging up. Clark talked with the prisons director for five minutes. When he finished, he buzzed for his aide.

"I have a brief statement I want distributed to the press this morning," he said. "You can write it yourself. In essence, what I want to say is that I am extremely proud of the officers on Alcatraz who advanced into the cellhouse under heavy fire and brought out their wounded comrades. What they did was an act of collective heroism worthy of the finest traditions of the federal prison service. Something like that."

In the formal statement later released, Attorney General Clark did not comment on the fact that the rescue team had entered the cellhouse unarmed, because he had not been made aware of that fact. Nor had he been told that all but two shots of the "heavy fire" under which the rescuers advanced had come from the weapons of other guards.

•

In San Francisco, the first morning newspaper for Friday, May 3, came out. Its headline read:

14 GUARDS SHOT, 1 KNOWN DEAD IN ALCATRAZ BATTLE

Considering the rampant rumors and unreliable stories being spread by misinformed sources, the headline was remarkably accurate. At that time, a total of thirteen guards had been shot, including Hal Stites, the then sole fatality.

At about the time the majority of San Franciscans were reading the story, however, the death toll was doubling.

At 7:00 A.M., Officer Bill Miller slipped deeper into shock and died. The first man to be attacked in the break attempt thus became the second to die.

Josephine Miller was still with her husband when he passed away. The crucifix was still on his chest and she was still reading from her prayer book. She continued reading even after the dead man's eyes had been closed. Finally a Navy doctor knelt beside her chair and put his hand over the book.

"Is there anyone you'd like us to call, Mrs. Miller?"

"Could you call Monsignor Cantwell for me?" the woman asked. "At St. Brigid's Church. The sisters are looking after my two children." She looked over at her husband. "We have a girl, Joan Marie, who's thirteen. And a boy, Billy, who's ten—"

She broke down then and started weeping. The doctor left a nurse with her and started to go make the call. The widow called to him at the door.

"You'd better call the warden too, I expect," she said. "He'll want to know at once."

•

Warden Johnston took the call from Marine Hospital in his office. Sitting in chairs facing him were Lieutenants George Boatman and Isaac Faulk, and the three uninjured rescued officers, Robert Bristow, Joe Burdette, and Carl Sundstrom. They watched in silent apprehension as the warden listened quietly, spoke a few words, thanked the caller, and hung up. He looked solemnly at his men.

"Bill Miller's gone," he said in a strained voice. He poured a glass of water from a pitcher on his desk and drank it. "Cecil Corwin will live. Captain Weinhold and Lieutenant Simpson are still critical."

Johnston looked down at a list of names on his desk. They were the same six names that Officer Lageson had scribbled on the wall of 403 a few moments before Dutch Cretzer started shooting. The warden stared at the list for a moment. Then his eyes shifted to a second, longer list; one with thirteen names on it. The second list read:

> Dock Tower—Besk
> Cell 403—Weinhold, Corwin, Lageson, Miller
> Cell 402—Simpson, Baker
> Gun Gallery—Cochrane, Stites, Richberger, Oldham, Maxwell
> Rescue Squad—Roberts

The name of Stites had a circle around it. Now Johnston picked up a fountain pen, uncapped it, and circled Miller's name also. He picked up his phone and when an armory guard answered, said, "Get Lieutenant Bergen for me, please."

Bergen was contacted on the gun-gallery phone. It was now left hanging down the wall so that the officers in the cage did not have to expose themselves to use it. When the switchboard had a call for them, the operator blew a whistle loudly into the transmitter.

When Bergen got on the line, Johnston drew the first list of names in front of him.

"Phil, two things. First, pass the word along that Bill Miller is dead. Second, give these six names to all personnel at that end of the cellhouse. Coy, Cretzer, Shockley, Hubbard, Buddy Thompson, and Dan Durando. I want everyone to start looking for those six men. When any of them are located, I want to know at once."

"Right, Warden," said Phil Bergen.

Johnston nodded as if Bergen could see him, and hung up.

•

In Cell 142, on the Michigan Boulevard flats near the cutoff, Danny Durando was trying for the fifth time to roll a cigarette. He had tobacco spilled on his trouser legs and bunk, and several crumpled sheets of cigarette paper thrown on the floor. Finally, on his sixth attempt, he got a halfway decent one rolled, twisted the ends as he had seen Louis Fleish do, and stuck it between his lips. Lighting up, he lay back on the bunk and took his first deep drag. He got a little dizzy almost at once.

The Kid had been in his cell most of the night. He had run away from D Block, frightened, when the cellhouse lights were turned off. The darkness of the big cellhouse had really spooked him. He had run down Seedy to the cutoff, then dashed across Broadway to Michigan Boulevard. With tremendous relief, he had found his cell door still racked open. On his way across the flats the terrible thought had occurred to him that somehow his cell door might have been closed. Then he would have been trapped in the cellblock aisles, with no place to go, no place to hide. But the tiny little cell, which Durando had joined the break to get away from, was like a blessed refuge to him in the scary blackness of the cellhouse.

The Kid had blood on him from being in Cells 402 and 403; he could smell it. It was a smell familiar from the whippings he had taken in the Oklahoma reformatory, and the fights he had been goaded into at Leavenworth. In his dark cell, he stripped off his clothes and washed himself well with cold water from the sink. When he had dried off, he put on his mealtime coveralls. They reminded him how hungry he was. He got down his tin cup and drank several cups of water.

For a couple of hours the Kid lay or sat quietly in his cell. Several times he considered sneaking back over to Seedy to see if the guards were still there; but he rejected the idea each time. He was not going to prowl around that huge, dark cellhouse by himself, and that was that.

Just after midnight he had heard muffled footsteps down at the east end of Michigan. Leaping from his bunk, he peered out. The sounds were coming closer. Every few seconds they stopped and a light flashed on briefly. The Kid's bowels churned with fear. Quickly he kicked the bundle of bloody clothes under his bunk and stepped out of the cell. Jumping up, he grabbed the lower pipe of the middle-tier rail and silently swung his shoeless feet onto the range. He rolled under the pipe and lay absolutely still.

The guards had found his cell open; they discussed it briefly; then, because no one was in the cell, they quickly moved on. When they got to the end of the aisle, Durando dropped down to the flats and went back into his cell.

It was only minutes later that he heard the gunfire. Two quick pistol shots first; then a thundering barrage of machine-gun fire. Durando lay terrified through all of it. He was certain that the guards would be returning at any moment to kill him. For a while he cried. Then he just lay on his bunk shivering. Finally, sometime between midnight and dawn, he fell asleep.

Now daylight came, and a very tense, nervous Danny Durando awoke to face what he was certain would be his day of reckoning. He faced it not bravely, not confidently, not even hopefully. Instead, he faced it in utter despair.

As he lay on his bunk nervously indulging in his newly acquired vice of cigarette smoking, a tear again streaked each cheek on the young Chicano's face. For him, once more, life had somehow gone wrong.

CHAPTER TWENTY-SIX

9:05 A.M.

Warden Johnston was at his desk, kneading a throbbing headache with the tips of his fingers, when a call came from the gun gallery. "Lieutenant Bergen, sir," Johnston's secretary said.

Johnston picked up his phone. "Yes, Phil?"

"We've spotted Shockley in D Block, sir. He's on the middle tier in the area of his own cell."

"Armed?"

"Can't tell, Warden. He's just peeked out a couple of times."

"Any sign of the others?"

"Nothing definite. Every once in a while we hear some noise from the top of C Block, where the shots were fired down at Roberts. But we can't be sure who's up there."

"Did they get some food to you and your men?" Johnston asked, abruptly changing the subject.

"Yessir. We've got rolls and coffee."

"Is Officer Burch still all right?"

"He's fine, Warden."

"At the first sign of unusual fatigue, he should be relieved. An officer cannot function at peak efficiency without proper rest and nourishment. That's one of the prime rules for keeping fit and alert in this business, Lieutenant. I established that criterion when I was warden at Folsom back in—let's see, this is 1946—"

There was an unusually long silence on the open circuit. In the gallery, Bergen glanced uncomfortably at Bert Burch and Fred Mahan. Finally, after the silence became strained, Bergen interrupted it.

"Warden?"

"Yes, what is it?" Johnston answered absently.

"Sir, we were wondering if there are any immediate plans for regaining control of the cellhouse?"

"Yes, that's being worked on, Phil. It's absolutely essential that we regain control."

"Do you have any idea when we'll be able to do it?" Bergen asked outright.

"I'll let you know when there's something definite," the warden answered. "In the meantime, you notify me at once if you or any of your men want to be relieved. Understand?"

"I understand," Bergen replied.

The warden hung up. Bergen let the gallery phone hang back against the wall again. He looked silently at Burch and Mahan. There was nothing he could say.

In Johnston's office, the warden's secretary entered. "Sir, General Stilwell and General Merrill are here. They're just coming through the reception area."

Johnston quickly rose and went out to meet his two visitors in Admin. Stilwell, bone-thin and leather-tough, had a combat pistol strapped to his waist and an ancient campaign hat on his bullet head. He had canceled his San Diego speech and come to Alcatraz instead. The old war horse smelled a battle. Frank Merrill, in deference to his commander, also wore a web belt and holster. Merrill, who had met Johnston at the Commonwealth Club in San Francisco, introduced him to Stilwell.

"General, this is an honor," said Johnston.

"Wish it was under more pleasant circumstances for you, Warden," said Stilwell.

"I want you to know I'm very grateful for the help you've given us."

"We're happy to help, sir," said Merrill.

Johnston ushered the two generals into his office and poured coffee for them. Stilwell sipped briefly at his and put a thin cigar in his mouth. Merrill lighted it for him. "Frank and I have been going stale over at the Presidio," Stilwell said. "We're glad to have something besides paperwork to occupy our thoughts. Have you pretty well got your situation here under control?"

"As a matter of fact, I haven't," Johnston said.

Stilwell frowned slightly and glanced at Merrill. "Is there any way we can be of further assistance?"

"I could use some expert tactical advice," the warden said frankly. "Let me show you what my problem is." At his desk, he unrolled a scale drawing of the building. "There are two ways into the cellhouse," he pointed out. "The sallyport entrance at this end, and the yard door at the other end. Both doors are covered. There is absolutely no way for the convicts to get out. Now then, there are six men in on the break. One of them we know to be isolated in this wing here, called D Block. Another one is up on top of C Block, somewhere in this area. We don't know where the other four are."

"Warden, if you like," said Stilwell, "I'll send in a couple of search-and-destroy platoons and wrap this thing up for you in an hour."

"I'm afraid that's not possible, General, although I certainly appreciate the offer. But the fact of the matter is, no firearms are allowed inside the cellhouse."

Stilwell frowned again. "Why is that?"

"The cellhouse was designed so that no guns would ever have to be taken into close proximity with any prisoners. There are some sixty-odd extremely dangerous criminals in there, General. If I allowed armed troops to enter the cellhouse, and the prisoners took their weapons away from them, I could end up with a major insurrection on my hands."

"Warden," said Merrill, "the men we would send in there would be career soldiers. Combat veterans. I can assure you that no one would take their weapons away from them."

"Naturally, I respect your opinion on that," replied Johnston. "But I still cannot permit it. The principle of no guns on the floor of the Alcatraz cellhouse must be upheld. The reputation of the prison depends on it."

Stilwell rubbed his chin uneasily. There was something irrational about Johnston's position that stuck in his craw. But he was all military, and he respected the boundaries of command. Alcatraz was the warden's outfit, and that was that.

"Warden," said Stilwell, "are you saying that you want your cellhouse retaken from the *outside*? Because it would be suicide to try to do it by sending unarmed men inside."

"Can it be done from the outside?" Johnston asked almost eagerly.

The two generals exchanged glances again. "Certainly," said Stilwell. "You have to realize, of course, that to do so will mean structural damage to the cellhouse itself."

"No matter," Johnston said at once. "It can be repaired."

"Consider too that an outside assault will jeopardize *all* the men in the cellhouse, whether they are involved in the break or not."

"I'd rather jeopardize every convict in the prison than expose another one of my officers," Johnston said firmly.

"Okay, it's your baby," said Vinegar Joe. "Let's get to work." He turned back to the scale drawing of the cellhouse. "We'll start with the two men that have been located. This one in D Block: what's his patrol range? That is, where can he go from where he is now?"

"Nowhere. He's confined to D Block. The rescue team that brought the hostages out locked the connecting door."

"And the man up on top of this block here: where can he go?"

"Down into this utility corridor that separates the backs of the cells."

"What's in there?"

"Heating ducts, ventilation shafts, water pipes, that sort of thing."

Stilwell turned to Merrill. "Frank, you remember that Marine warrant officer who was in charge of cleaning out those Jap caves on

Bougainville and Guam? Remember, he got the Silver Star for it?"

"Sure. Charley Buckner. He's stationed over at Treasure Island now."

"Exactly. I was thinking of the way he used to drop shape charges through overhead holes to drive the Japs out of those caves. He'd be a natural for this."

Merrill nodded. "I'll get hold of the Marine commanding officer at T.I. and have him detach Buckner to your staff. What do you want to use on D Block?"

"I'd say launchers, Frank, wouldn't you?"

"Yes, sir, I think launchers would do it."

"Warden," said Stilwell, "as soon as we get back to the mainland, we'll see that you get the men and equipment you need. General Merrill will come back over to brief Warrant Officer Buckner. In the meantime, if there's anything we can do for you, don't hesitate to call us."

"I appreciate this more than I can tell you, General," said the warden. "I've got two officers dead and eleven wounded. It's a great relief to know that I won't have to risk any more of them."

The three men shook hands and Stilwell and Merrill left.

"I can't believe it," Merrill said on their way to the dock. "He's going to turn a minor mop-up job into a battle."

Stilwell shrugged. "It's his island, Frank."

•

Later in the morning, Johnston decided to walk across the plaza to his home for a few minutes. He had not seen his wife since noon the previous day when he had gone into their bedroom to nap. He told his secretary where he would be, then walked through Admin and out the front of the building. Halfway across the plaza outside, he looked up and saw three Piper Cub airplanes circling and flying low over the island. His jaw clenched at such a flagrant invasion of Alcatraz's air space. Turning around, he returned to the building and went directly to the armory.

"Officer Fish," he said to the armory guard, "get me the commanding officer at Hamilton Field."

Johnston went into his office and sat down again. The call to Hamilton Field was put through. The commanding officer was off the base, but Johnston was able to speak with his adjutant. He asked if something could be done about the private civilian aircraft circling his island. The adjutant replied that since the planes were civilian, and since Alcatraz was not a military prison, the Air Corps had no jurisdiction to interfere. Very well, said Johnston, he would then go directly to General Stilwell, who was cooperating with him during the emergency. Was that General Joe Stilwell, the adjutant wanted to know, commanding officer of the Sixth Army? It was, Johnston assured him. In that case, perhaps the Air Corps *could* assist, after all.

Within an hour, the adjutant had an AT-6, a fast, single-engine trainer, in the air over the Rock. The Piper Cubs were radioed away. The Air Corps maintained an air patrol over the prison for the remainder of the emergency.

Warden Johnston never did get over to his house that morning.

Before noon, the San Francisco newspapers were getting out extra editions almost as fast as the public was buying them. Some of the headlines and stories were conservative and close to factual. Others were pure sensationalism. Some, like the *Chronicle,* were a combination of both. The *Chronicle*'s first headline of the day read:

ONE GUARD KILLED, NINE INJURED IN ARMED REVOLT ON ALCATRAZ

That was conservative. But one of the stories following the banner headline was *not* conservative. It was strictly sensational. That story reported that Officer Hal Stites had been machine-gunned in the back at close range.

•

Some newspapers were having difficulty getting a story on Alcatraz. The armory operator answered one call that morning and heard a distinctively British voice from halfway around the world.

"Is this the American prison where the riot is going on?" the caller inquired. The operator said it was. "This is the London *Times* calling. Connect me with the warden there, will you?"

The operator obediently rang Johnston's office. "Warden, the London *Times* is on the phone. Do you want to talk to them?"

"No calls from newspapers," the warden said. "I told you that."

"Yessir, but I thought because it was London—"

"No calls from newspapers," the warden reiterated. He hung up.

The operator got back on the line to London. It did not seem right to turn them down so brusquely when they were interested enough to call all the way from England. Because the London reporter was so polite and sounded so dignified, the operator himself talked to him for ten minutes and gave him the complete story of the break—as much as was known—up to that time.

•

At Marine Hospital, Officers Hersh Oldham and Fred Richberger, wounded in the gun-gallery battle, and Elmus Besk, wounded in the Hill Tower, were sharing a three-bed room. An FBI inspector and two special agents from the San Francisco office were interviewing them.

"Of the six convicts named by the rescued hostage officers, who do you think would most likely be the ringleader?"

"Dutch Cretzer," Oldham said at once. Besk and Richberger nodded. "He's the only one of the six who's got sense enough to organize a thing like this. Thompson always worked alone; he wouldn't know how to plan a group break like this. Coy and Hubbard are just a couple of hick hillbillies. The Indio Kid is all muscle. And Shockley is a goddamned idiot. It had to be Cretzer."

"How did they get into the armory?" the inspector wanted to know.

Richberger's eyebrows shot up. "The *armory!* Who said they got into the armory?"

"One of the papers."

"The papers are crazy," said Besk. "There's no way a con could *ever* get into the armory."

"You're sure of that?"

"Of course we're sure," said Richberger. "Oldham and I were in the armory ourselves *after* the break started."

"Where did they get the machine gun, then?"

"I'm not even sure they had a machine gun. All three of us were hit by rifle slugs. And when Oldham and I were in the gun gallery, we didn't hear any machine-gun fire."

The inspector shook his head and looked at the two agents. "You don't suppose the newspapers are *all* wrong, do you?"

"Wouldn't be the first time," the agent answered. "When will we be authorized to go over to the island for some first-hand evidence?"

"Not until it's over," the inspector replied. "Washington feels there are enough agencies involved already. The Army, Navy, Marines, Coast Guard, Air Corps, San Francisco Police, California Highway Patrol, San Quentin guards, and the Red Cross. If anything goes wrong, nobody's going to know *who* to blame."

"That won't be a problem for us," Fred Richberger said quietly.

"What do you mean?"

"Something's already gone wrong. Two of our men are dead. And *we* know who to blame."

"That's right," said Besk. "You're wasting your time collecting evidence against those six."

"Why is that?"

"Because they'll never get out of that cellhouse alive."

•

Back on the island, the prison launch pulled alongside the Alcatraz pier. A broad, husky man in Marine dungarees stepped ashore. He had a small field pack slung over one shoulder. On his dungaree cap was the gold-and-red bar of a warrant officer, the only rank in the Corps entitled to the privileges of both enlisted man and commissioned officer.

The man was Warrant Officer Charles Lafayette Buckner, a twelve-year veteran Marine who, as Vinegar Joe Stilwell had said, was a survivor of the bloody battles of Guam and Bougainville. A demolitions expert since before the war, Buckner had devised numerous new ways to use conventional explosives in warfare. A native of Memphis, Tennessee, he grew up just a few miles from where Marv Hubbard was shot down in a police ambush, and he once worked only blocks from the Beale Street bar where Machine Gun Kelly had asked Tennessee Slim Howard to join him on the Urschel kidnapping.

Buckner reported to the warden's office. General Frank Merrill was waiting there to brief him.

"This is the situation, Buck," said Merrill, pointing to the diagram. "We've got an armed man on top of this cellblock, with no way to get to him except to send men climbing up through this utility corridor. If we do that, he can pick them off one at a time until he runs out of ammunition." Merrill purposely avoided telling Buckner that the warden refused to let armed men enter the cellhouse. There was nothing to be gained by letting a story like that get around. "We need a way to get him out of there, Buck. General Stilwell thought perhaps it could be done the way you handled the caves on Bougain. What do you think?"

Buckner looked at the drawing for several moments, studying both the top and side views. Then he nodded to Merrill.

"I'll need an electric drill and about a thousand feet of string, General. That ought to get the job done."

Merrill picked up the warden's phone to get what the Marine explosives man wanted.

CHAPTER TWENTY-SEVEN

10:40 A.M.

When the electric drill arrived on the island, it was treated like a VIP. Three guards and a car were waiting for it at the dock. Two of the guards held the drill and its accessories on their laps while the third drove them up the hill to the plaza in front of the main building. It was carefully carried inside, and after Warrant Officer Buckner had a look at it, taken up to the roof of the cellhouse. There it was placed next to a chalk mark that had been made to indicate a place directly above the west section of C Block.

Buckner followed the drill to the roof a few minutes later. He placed his small pack in a corner of the big roof away from all activity, and covered it with his field jacket. Rolling up his sleeves, he pulled the power line up the roof stairs a little to give him more slack to move. Then he hefted the drill into place, put its steel-tip bit firmly against the concrete of the roof, and turned it on. The bit began eating away at the rough concrete.

Four guards armed with rifles stood like ring posts fifteen feet away. They watched curiously as the brawny, silent Marine turned the chewing bit first one way, then another, while it ate slowly but surely into the roof and began to form a rough indentation as big around as a man's boot top. Every once in a while one of the guards would look ominously over at the bundle in the corner—the field jacket with the pack under it, a pack that Buckner had handled so delicately, as if it might explode. The guards had not been told exactly what Buckner was doing, but by now all of them had guessed. As men trained to guard and possibly shoot a man once in a while, they stood in awe of this tough professional who could so calmly prepare for wholesale killing.

As Buckner worked the big, noisy drill, the sun moved around in front of him. The big Marine began to sweat.

•

Just below where Buckner began drilling, Dutch Cretzer opened his eyes and looked up at the noise. He frowned briefly; then his eyes grew frightened. Grabbing the gun at his side, he sat up and looked around the top of the cellblock. It was still empty, still silent—except for the muted noise above him.

In a crouch, Cretzer hurried across the block roof toward the west bars. When he was near enough to see the curved top of the upper gun-gallery tier, he dropped to his stomach and wiggled forward until he could look across into the cage. In the top tier he saw three guards with submachine guns. They were crouched down behind the shield. Only one of them had his head up, just enough to see over the rim of the shield to watch the ranges and the few feet of the block roof that were visible.

Cretzer wiggled back before the guard could see him. When he was back far enough, he rose and ran to the end of the roof that looked down on the cutoff. He saw no sign of life. Following the bars to the corner of the roof, he scrutinized Seedy Street. It was deserted. He saw that the D Block door had now been closed. That meant that Shockley was probably locked back inside. Cretzer wished now he had brought Sam with him. At least he would have had someone to talk to, someone to encourage him when the screws started coming after him and the battle—short though it would be—started. But it was too late now.

The drilling noise was still going on above him as he walked back to the middle of the roof. He sat down next to Miller's coat, which was rolled up as a pillow. His tobacco pouch and cigarette paper were lying nearby; he reached for them and rolled himself a smoke. On the first drag, he felt his stomach churn and growl, and he realized how hungry he was. Except for the coffee he drank when he and Coy talked in the kitchen, he had not had anything to eat or drink since the previous noon. He wished to hell he had thought to bring some food up on the roof with him.

Thinking of Coy made him remember his damaged face. Gently he touched his lips and felt a line of dried blood where Coy had struck him with the rifle muzzle. That dirty little hillbilly son of a bitch. What he wouldn't give for one clear shot at that skinny cocksucker.

Sighing, he stretched out and put his head on the rolled-up coat. As he smoked, he thought of Eddie, his ex-wife, who was living over in San Francisco. He remembered some of the good times they had

had together—times in Chicago and Denver and Los Angeles, living it up, spending money like it was going out of style. They didn't give a damn that it was money taken in bank robberies, or that J. Edgar Hoover was slowly moving the name of Joseph Paul Cretzer toward the top of the Most Wanted list. They didn't even *think* about the time that was rapidly running out on them. They just *lived.*

Then he was captured. Convicted of three bank jobs. Sent to McNeil Pen. He tried a break and almost made it. Almost. At his escape trial, he had seized a likely moment and tried again. He missed by seconds. And that goddamned old federal marshal had croaked. He beat the chair but got life. And the Rock. Then five years in D for trying to beat the Rock.

Eddie had stuck by him for a few years. Then she had gradually drifted into another life. Because he was in D, he was not allowed visitors and had no mail privileges. Legal matters were an exception, however, and one day his lawyer appeared on the island and had divorce papers sent in to him. Eddie did not want to wait any longer. She had met a truckdriver and wanted to marry him and settle down. Cretzer had signed the papers, with no hard feelings.

Now, as he finished his cigarette and crushed it out in the dust on top of C Block, he thought about Eddie and how he had once called her his "good-time kid." Somehow he just could not picture her married to a square-john truckdriver. He wondered if she ever thought of him; wondered how she would feel when she read that he had been killed in the break.

Cretzer sighed again. It was an odd feeling to be so resigned to dying. It did not seem to bother him at all. He wondered if it was because in a way he was already dead.

And had been since the day they brought him, in chains, to the Rock.

•

In downtown San Francisco, a real estate agent named Morris O'Hearn returned from lunch to find a *Chronicle* reporter waiting in his office.

"Mr. O'Hearn, I understand you used to be a guard out at Alcatraz," the reporter said. "Would you give us some comments on the break?"

"What kind of comments?" O'Hearn asked.

"Well, for instance, do you have any guesses as to how long the convicts might hold out?"

"I shouldn't think very long," the former guard said. "Maybe another day."

"Another *day.*" The reporter laughed. "You must not read the papers, Mr. O'Hearn. It's been estimated that they have enough guns and ammunition to hold out for a month!"

O'Hearn shook his head. "The papers are wrong. Look—" He drew a quick sketch on a pad of paper. "This is the cellhouse, see. There's a gun gallery at each end, east and west. There would be a guard in each cage. He'd have one pistol and one rifle. It's possible that the cons could have somehow forced the two gallery guards to throw out their weapons, maybe under threat of some of the floor guards being killed. But there's absolutely no way they could have reached a tower or got into the armory. The most they could have is two .45s and two Springfield rifles."

"I take it you don't want to be quoted on that," the reporter said knowingly.

O'Hearn shrugged. "Quote me if you like."

"But what you're saying conflicts with every report we've gotten up to now. We *know* that the cons have a machine gun; one of the dead guards was riddled with it."

"You'll probably find that he was shot several times with a rifle or pistol. There's no way a con could get his hands on a machine gun."

"Mr. O'Hearn," the reporter said in exasperation, "how long has it been since you were a guard on Alcatraz?"

"About four years."

"Don't you think things could have changed in that length of time?"

"Not on the Rock," O'Hearn said unequivocally. "Not with old Jim Johnston running the place."

"Then you want to stick by your theory?"

"Definitely."

The reporter thanked O'Hearn and left, convinced that he had just wasted his time. What he had no way of knowing was that he had just heard the first sensible analysis yet given of the escape attempt. Morris O'Hearn was mistaken in one conclusion: some things *did* change on Alcatraz. Only one gun gallery was now manned during daylight working hours. While the in-grades were down at Industries, the east cage above the sallyport entrance was not manned. Had O'Hearn known that, he doubtless would have revised by half his estimate of the number of guns the convicts had captured. Had he done so, he would have guessed it exactly.

As it was, on speculation alone, the real estate man knew more about the mechanics of the break than anyone else in San Francisco.

•

One hundred miles away, at Warden Johnston's former place of employment, Folsom Prison, another interview was being held. This one was with Warden Robert A. Heinze, the current head of California's maximum-security penitentiary. An *Examiner* reporter asked Heinze if he expected any trouble in his own prison as a result of the continuing conflict at Alcatraz.

"We always expect trouble," the warden replied. "That's what we're paid for. We have two thousand of the state's worst felons in this institution. With that many inmates, trouble can be touched off at any time."

"Is there any way you can sense trouble? Anything that tips you off when it's about to happen?"

"Sometimes," said Heinze. "Now and then you'll get a *feeling* that something's in the air. Other times you just have to guess. Right now, we're guessing. We don't know whether the trouble on Alcatraz will cause any problems here or not. But we're keeping in extra-close touch with convict activities right now, and will continue to do so until the Alcatraz matter is settled. I would imagine that Warden Duffy is doing the same thing at San Quentin."

"I take it then that you're not alarmed at all," the reporter said.

"Alarmed, no. Extra-cautious, extra-sensitive, yes."

"If trouble should come at Folsom, do you have any doubts that you can handle it?"

"None whatever."

"How many guards do you have here, Warden?"

"One hundred forty."

"Is that your full strength?"

"No," Heinze admitted. "Our full strength guard line is one hundred fifty-four. We're fourteen men short right now."

"That doesn't bother you?"

"Not in the least," the Folsom warden said, smiling.

When the reporter left, Heinze breathed a sigh of relief. He *was* bothered by the shortage of guards on his staff. Right then he had one guard for every fourteen convicts. Even when he had a full complement, there was still only one guard for every thirteen cons.

The safe ratio, as any good penologist would agree, was one for seven.

Warden Heinze fervently hoped that the Alcatraz trouble did not spread to his pen. If it did, there would be a bloodbath.

•

In the gun gallery on the Rock, Lieutenant Phil Bergen received a call from Warden Johnston. "Phil, we have a Marine rocket launcher squad standing by on the south slopes to assault D Block. Before we resort to that, I want to give Shockley one final chance to surrender. Yell down into D and see if you can get him to throw down his gun and come out. I'll wait ten minutes. If I don't hear from you, I'll instruct the Marines to commence firing. Warn your men to stay low in the gallery."

"Yes, sir." Bergen turned to Burch and Mahan. "I'm not even sure Crazy Sam *has* a gun," he said irritably. "No one has been seen with guns except Coy and Cretzer." He looked at Burch. "The Marines are getting ready to launch an attack, Bert. Don't you think this would be a good time for me to relieve you?"

Burch shook his head. "I'm okay."

"You've been in this cage for twenty-eight hours, Bert. You've been beat up, you've been cold, you've gone hungry—"

"Miller, Lageson, and I came on duty together yesterday," Burch said stubbornly. "Now Miller's dead and Lageson's been shot. I'm the only one left out of the three of us. I want my chance at those killers, Phil. You told me I could have it. You're not going back on your word, are you?"

"You know me better than that," Bergen replied, a slight edge to his voice. "I just don't want you to collapse."

"I'll be okay," Burch assured him.

Bergen sighed quietly and edged past him to the D Block door. He crawled into the D section of the gallery. Two other officers were on duty there. Bergen crawled over between them.

"The warden wants to try to get Crazy Sam to come out," he told them. "I'm going to call down to him. Stay alert in case there's a gun down there somewhere and they decide to use it to answer us."

Bergen got into a crouch, sitting back on his heel with one knee forward. He raised his eyes an inch above the top of the shield.

"Shockley!" he yelled. "Sam Shockley!"

The lieutenant waited a moment. There was no answer.

"We know you're in D Block, Sam! Throw your gun out onto the flats! Come out with your hands raised!"

Bergen paused again. Still there was no answer.

"We won't fire if you surrender quietly, Sam! Come on out! This is the only chance you'll have to give up!"

From the cells of D Block Bergen heard only silence.

•

Along the flower-covered slopes on the south side of the island, Marine Corps rocket-launcher gunners and their fire teams had set up bazookas in strategic positions facing the outside wall of D Block. There were four fire teams of four men each: a gunner, a loader, and two ammo bearers. The gunners were firing from kneeling positions, awkwardly maintained due to the angle of the hill. They had to aim their tubelike launchers uphill, which gave them difficult trajectory and reduced velocity. The loaders had to practically lie flat in order to slip the miniature bomblike shell into the back of the tubes and connect the two firing wires. And the ammo bearers had to be particularly careful where they knelt, because the back-blast from the launchers, tilted at that angle, would burn up anything on the ground behind it.

Even with all those drawbacks, the four teams were in place and ready when the officer in charge gave the command to fire. All four gunners fired simultaneously. They had zeroed in on the middle window in the row of seven that looked in on Sunset Boulevard. Three of the rockets hit the bars and glanced back out the broken window to explode harmlessly on the slope beneath the catwalk. The fourth, a low shot, exploded against the concrete wall, barely denting it.

"The shells won't get through those window bars without tearing them to pieces," the Marine officer said to his sergeant. "Have them lower elevation and aim for the wall halfway between the bottom of the window and the catwalk."

The order was passed on and the men prepared to fire again. This time, on command, all four rockets struck the wall where the officer had indicated. They made a lot of noise and sent up a great puff of white smoke, but they only chipped a quarter-inch of concrete off the thick, solid wall.

The officer had his gunners try twice more, then gave up. "Cease fire!" he yelled to the men. To his sergeant he said, "Tell whoever's in charge of this lash-up that bazooka shells won't get through. Tell them we'll need mortars."

"Beats me why they don't just send in half a dozen good flamethrower men and burn the whole goddamned bunch out," the sergeant said. "That's what we did on Iwo."

"Those happen to be *white* men in there, Sergeant," the officer said in a distinctly cool tone. "Now get the word up the hill about those mortars."

"Yes, *sir!*" The sergeant hurried off.

Briefly, the siege that thousands were eagerly watching from shore was interrupted.

CHAPTER TWENTY-EIGHT

11:05 A.M.

Coy and Hubbard were in the kitchen pantry when they heard the repercussions of the first rocket shells hitting the outside of D Block.

"What the hell was that?" Coy said, getting to his feet at once and instinctively reaching for the rifle.

"Sounded like dynamite," Marv Hubbard said.

They opened the door and peered out. No one was in sight. Cautiously they eased out of the pantry and crossed to the door leading to the dining hall. They looked across the dining hall and through the entry to Times Square. No one was in sight; they heard no sound. Quickly they crossed the open doorway to the south side of the kitchen. In the southwest corner of the room, they looked out one of two corner windows, the one facing south. From that vantage point, they were able to see the Marine launcher squads on the flower-covered slopes below.

"Looks like soldiers down there," Coy said, frowning. He and Hubbard watched curiously as the launchers were raised and a second volley was fired, this time against the concrete below the middle D Block window. Again the repercussion rattled the building.

"Jesus Christ," Marv Hubbard said incredulously, "they're shooting D with *bazookas!*"

Coy stared in disbelief at the dungaree-clad men. "It was a simple little prison break," he said, shaking his head cheerlessly. "Twenty-four hours ago, it all looked so easy. Just six cons taking a few hostages down to the dock, getting aboard the launch, and telling the pilot where to take us. Now it's turned into a goddamned war."

As Coy spoke, neither he nor Marv Hubbard paid any attention to the fact that while they were looking out the south corner window, they were standing fully exposed in front of the west corner window.

•

One of two guards in the Hill Tower focused in on the west corner window of the kitchen with a pair of high-power binoculars. At first he frowned; then his mouth dropped open slightly. He had been scanning the windows for more than six hours; this was the first sign of life he had seen. "It's Bernie Coy," he said almost to himself.

"What?" said the other guard.

"Coy!" the spotter said urgently. "The corner window there!"

The second guard looked, saw the shadowed figure, and immediately raised his rifle. "You're sure it's Coy?" he said as he drew a bead.

"Positive. He's wearing a guard's coat, but it's Coy all right."

The guard with the rifle steadied his shoulder against the tower doorframe. Slowly and carefully, he squeezed off a single round.

The glass in the west kitchen window shattered and the figure pitched back violently.

•

At his desk, Warden Johnston picked up a call from the armory switchboard.

"Warden," the guard said excitedly, "the Hill Tower officers report seeing Bernie Coy and another con in the southwest corner of the kitchen. One of the officers shot Coy."

"Kill him?" Johnston asked. He could not keep a trace of hope out of his voice.

"They're not sure, Warden. They saw him fall but they don't know if he's dead or not."

"All right," Johnston said. He rose and hurried into Admin. Looking around, he spotted a lieutenant and summoned him into his office.

"Lieutenant, I want you to take a dozen men with Springfields and spread them out along the slopes facing the south side of the kitchen. Coy and at least one other con have been seen near the southwest corner windows. A tower officer hit Coy with a rifle shot, but we don't know if he's dead or not. If he is, another con probably has the rifle now. We know there won't be any officers in that area, so order your men to shoot at anyone they see in the kitchen or dining hall. I'm going to alert Lieutenant Bergen and the men in the west gallery to watch for cons in the dining hall."

The lieutenant acknowledged the order and left. As he was going out, another officer hurried in. "Sir, the Marines report that bazooka fire won't penetrate D Block. They want to set up some mortars."

"Have them do it then," Johnston said. "Have them use whatever it takes. Bombs, if necessary."

"Yes, sir."

When he was alone in the office, the warden got on his phone and flashed for the operator.

"How's that Marine on the roof doing?"

"I'll check and see, sir," said the operator.

Johnston hung up. He never did get around to calling Bergen.

•

Warrant Officer Charles Buckner finally felt the drill bit break through the concrete roof. Breathing heavily, his entire body layered with sweat, he pulled the heavy electric tool out of the fist-size hole and laid it aside. Experienced combat veteran that he was, he cautiously stayed back far enough so that anything fired through the hole could not hit him. From holes that he had drilled or dug on Bougainville and Guam, he had been shot at by rifles, pistols, and machine guns; had Japanese sabers and bayonets shoved out in an effort to stab him; and once even had a grenade pushed back out the hole after he had dropped it in. He knew from vividly remembered experience that a hole in the roof above a desperate man could be deadly both ways.

"I'm going down to wash up and put on some dry clothes," Buckner told the four guards. He took an extra set of dungarees from his pack. "I'd stay away from that hole if I were you."

As Buckner spoke, there was a muffled report of two pistol shots under the roof and the whine of two slugs coming straight up out of the hole.

"See what I mean?" the Marine said.

•

Below Buckner and the guards, Dutch Cretzer had cautiously approached the hole in the roof. He was far enough out of sight of the gun gallery so that it was safe to stand up. The hole was about four feet over his head. Peering up through it, he saw only a ragged circle of sky. He thought for a moment that he heard a voice somewhere near the hole, but he could distinguish no words.

There's got to be somebody up there, he told himself. The goddamned hole didn't drill itself.

Raising the automatic over his head, he fired twice, point-blank into the opening. His bullets went harmlessly into the sky.

Goddamn it, he chastised himself. Never should have done that. Waste of two good shots.

Disgruntled, he moved away and sat down to wait and see how the men above him intended to use the hole in the roof.

•

Across the water at the Marine Hospital, two reporters were talking to Officer Robert Baker. He was in bed, his gunshot leg swathed in surgical dressing.

"You and Lieutenant Simpson and Officer Sundstrom were the last three of the nine officers to be taken hostage, is that right?" one of the reporters asked.

"Yes," Baker verified. "Lieutenant Simpson had taken Sundstrom and me into the cellhouse to see if we could find out what had happened to Captain Weinhold and the others. And to see why none of the floor guards were answering their phones."

"Can you tell us exactly how they captured you?"

Baker shrugged. "We just went into the cellhouse and ran down one of the aisles. Before we knew it, ten or twelve of them jumped us. They caught us off guard."

The interview continued, and was not particularly unusual except for that one reply in which Baker indicated that the three-man party led by Lieutenant Joe Simpson had been taken hostage by ten or twelve convicts. Like many other erroneous news reports taken as gospel during the forty-one-hour siege, his statement was simply reported, published, read, digested, and apparently forgotten.

No one knows why Officer Robert Baker exaggerated the number of convicts who captured him. As far as is known, he was never asked.

•

In Seattle, Washington, another interview was taking place. An Associated Press newsman was talking with Captain Richard Mahoney, the Seattle police detective who had gone in to see Dutch Cretzer in April, 1940, just after the former public enemy had been given a life sentence for the killing of federal marshal Chitty.

"Dutch told me the night he was sentenced that he'd try to crash out of Alcatraz," Mahoney recalled. "He said he would either escape, get killed trying, or kill himself if he couldn't make it."

"Did he say why?" the AP reporter asked.

"Sure. He said he grew up in San Francisco. Said that being able to see the city lights go on each evening from his cell would be too much for him."

And so another fallacy was created. Dutch Cretzer, driven mad by the glittering lights of San Francisco, unable to stand it any longer, decides to escape or die. That was the headline on the story the following day: "Escape or Die, Cretzer Vow."

When in fact, Dutch Cretzer had not been able to see San Francisco at all from his cell. He could see nothing except the north wall of the cellhouse and a rectangle of sky through one of the high windows. His cell did not even face San Francisco. Even when he had been in D Block, the closest thing he had seen to San Francisco was the Marin County side of the Golden Gate Bridge.

•

In the warden's office, Johnston was on the phone briefing prisons director Jim Bennett on the current status of their situation. Bennett was not altogether certain that the outside assault plan was the best procedure to follow. But Johnston was insisting on it.

"I have been assured by no less a personage than General Joseph Stilwell that this is the safest method of attack under the circumstances," Johnston told the director.

"From a military standpoint it might well be," Bennett allowed. "But I'm trying to consider what public reaction will be if a large number of innocent inmates are unnecessarily killed."

"Mr. Director, there are no *innocent* inmates in here," the warden said, a bit stiffly. "Now, I'll abide by whatever decision you make, of course. But I think the public is going to take into consideration that two brave and dedicated prison officers have been killed. Both of them good men, family men. Both with young children who are now fatherless. And we have three more officers who are critically wounded. My personal opinion is that it would be criminal for us to jeopardize the lives of any more such men." Just then, Warrant Officer Buckner, who had finished cleaning up, came to the door. "One moment, please, Mr. Bennett," Johnston said. He covered the speaker with his hand. "Yes, Mr. Buckner?"

"The hole in the roof is ready, sir," Buckner told him. "I can start trying for the man on top of the block any time you say."

Behind Buckner, the warden's secretary came in. "Warden, the Marine rocket launcher squads have been replaced with mortar teams now. They're ready to begin firing at D Block."

"Have everyone stand by," Johnston said. He uncovered the

phone and relayed to Bennett that all was in readiness for the assault. "It's up to you, Mr. Director," he said.

Bennett pondered a moment longer. Finally he sighed quietly. "All right, Warden. Go on with your plan. But first I want as many inmates as possible moved out of the line of fire. Take the men in the yard and move them inside to A Block. Also make sure all lockup prisoners in C Block and the Broadway side of B are moved back out of range."

"That'll take time," Johnston said reluctantly. "We'll have to unjam the yard door first—"

"Do whatever you have to do, Jim," the director said firmly. "Just get those men to safety."

"Yes, Mr. Director." Johnston hung up. He glanced at his watch. "Warrant Officer Buckner, we're going to postpone our assault until about three o'clock. Will you stand by until then, please?"

"Yes, sir," Buckner replied. "I'll be ready when you are."

As the Marine left, Johnston turned to his secretary. "Notify the officer in charge of the mortars to hold off his attack until further orders. Also get word to the officer in charge of the twelve riflemen on the south slopes to cease firing into the kitchen and dining hall for the time being. Then get Mr. Waller up here to work on the yard door."

Earl Waller was the prison locksmith. Someone was finally going to unjam the west cellhouse entry—the door that would not open.

•

In Washington, James Bennett drummed his fingertips soundlessly on the telephone he had just hung up. The situation on Alcatraz did not sound good at all. More than twenty-four hours had passed since the break began. Two guards were dead, several more possibly dying, and a score of others wounded or otherwise injured in some way.

And the six convicts still had control of the cellhouse.

Bennett looked at his watch. It was a quarter of six, Washington time. He buzzed for his secretary, who was working late.

"Call the airlines and see if you can quietly get me on a plane to San Francisco. Later tonight, if possible."

"Yes, Mr. Bennett."

When he was alone again, Jim Bennett hoped he had done the right thing giving Johnston permission to assault the cellhouse from the outside. A very humane man, Bennett detested any unnecessary loss of life.

Even convict life.

•

Within an hour, under the watchful protection of the armed men in the east and west gun galleries, Earl Waller unjammed and opened the door that had held Bernie Coy and his escape gang in the big Alcatraz cellhouse.

When the door was open, the convicts who had spent the night on the yard were moved quickly into the cellhouse, across Times Square, and over to the unused A Block. All 126 cells in A were racked open. In addition, the 87 cells of B Block which faced Michigan Boulevard were also opened. The 200-odd Industries prisoners, singly and in pairs, were hurried into the cells and quickly locked in. Alvin Karpis, Harold Brest, and the others under the yard steps were also brought into the cellhouse, after spending all night in their makeshift pillbox.

After the in-grades were locked up, squads of guards hurriedly went around releasing lockup prisoners from the Broadway side of B and all of C. Naturally wary because they were armed only with riot sticks and knew that two cons with guns were still at large somewhere, the guards rushed through the process of transferring the lockup prisoners to A Block. In their haste, they overlooked seven men in the three rows of cells.

One of these men was in Cell 216 on the Broadway side of B. Another was in Cell 297 on the Broadway side of C. A third was in Cell 378 on the Seedy side of C.

Those three men, all in cells on the flats, along with four other men in upper tier cells, would remain where they were throughout the break.

•

While the in-grades were being moved back inside, Warden Johnston's secretary returned to his office.

"Sir, I think I ought to remind you that the switchboard is still being flooded with calls from the press. They're getting pretty sore because we won't give them any information about what's going on."

Johnston considered the problem. "All right," he said after a moment, "let's give the names of our killers to the papers so that the public can see why we're attacking in force. Get your note pad. I'll give you a statement to pass on to any paper that inquires."

Johnston took the prison records of the six convicts from his desk drawer and, when his secretary was ready, began his statement.

"Tell the press that the following men are the mad dogs of Alcatraz who are the known ringleaders in the revolt we are now attempting to put down. Refer to them in just that phrase: mad dogs.

"First, Joseph Paul Cretzer. Say that he's the head of the escape gang. Refer to him as a murderer. Tell the press that in dying statements, several guards have branded him a cold-blooded killer." The warden tossed Cretzer's record across the desk. "Get the rest of the facts from this.

"Second, Marvin Franklin Hubbard. Call him a Tennessee kidnapper. Make sure you mention that he participated in the uprising at Atlanta before he was sent here." He tossed another file across.

"Next, Bernard Paul Coy. A Kentucky bank robber. There's really not too much to say about Coy. Maybe you can find something in his record; some kind of brutality committed during a robbery, something." Johnston's voice trailed off, as if disappointed that Coy was not more of a monster.

"Sam Shockley," he continued. "Kidnapper. Be sure to emphasize the kidnapping aspect where it applies. The public detests kidnappers. Mention that Shockley was involved in the 1941 break attempt with Cretzer.

"Miran Edgar Thompson. Kidnapper. Killer of a Texas policeman. Eight jail breaks.

"Dan Durando. Kidnapper. Killed a man in a robbery when he was sixteen. Several escapes." He tossed Durando's file over. "That's it. Get something prepared. Make it sound as bad as possible."

"Yes, sir," said Johnston's secretary. He glanced at the clock. "It's a little past one, Warden. Is the assault still set for three?"

"Definitely," said Johnston. "Maybe we can get this thing wrapped up before dark."

CHAPTER TWENTY-NINE

3:00 P.M.

Bernie Coy and Marvin Hubbard were no longer in the kitchen area where they had spent the night. They were now in the west end of the C Block utility corridor.

After Coy had been hit by the single rifle bullet from the Hill

Tower, Hubbard managed to drag him away from the windows and get him safely around the corner of the tray-washing room.

Hubbard had been standing on Coy's left when the guard in the Hill Tower fired. The rifle slug had ripped into Coy's upper right shoulder and sent him pitching back onto the kitchen floor in a spray of ground glass. Hubbard, an old hand at being shot and shot at, quickly and instinctively dropped down and pressed himself against the wall beneath the windows. He knew in a glance that the impact of the slug had knocked Coy well out of the line of fire of whoever was shooting. What he was not sure of was whether the shot had been a single sniper effort, or if he could now expect a hail of gunfire through all the windows.

Hubbard did not move for a full minute. He knew Coy was not dead. The wounded man was groaning softly and trying to roll onto his side. His thin body was jerking spastically now and again from the trauma of the bullet. Hubbard wanted to get over to him as quickly as possible; the bullet had hit high on the shoulder up near the neck; he wanted to see if it had nicked Coy's jugular vein. Hubbard hoped desperately that his friend was not mortally wounded. He liked Bernie Coy as much as or more than he had ever liked any man. But more important than that, Hubbard dreaded the thought of being left all alone if Coy died.

When no subsequent shots were fired, Hubbard snaked along the floor under the windows until he judged himself to be out of the line of fire. He got quickly over to Coy, examined him enough to assure himself that the wound was not a bad one, and immediately dragged the fallen man to the protection of the corner outside the tray-washing room. Pausing there, Hubbard quickly examined the wound.

"It ain't bad at all, Bernie," the Alabaman said. "Slug went clean through. You lie here and keep still. I'll get something for it."

Hubbard moved in a crouch across the kitchen. In a couple of minutes he was back.

Hubbard washed the wound with water and an antiseptic powder that the kitchen help used for minor cuts. Coy, recovered from the initial shock of being hit, had tears in his eyes and was grimacing in pain.

"First time you been shot, Bernie?" Hubbard asked as he worked.

"Yeah."

Hubbard grinned tightly. "Smarts, don't it? I been shot four or five times. This one here's probably going to hurt like hell for a spell."

"Thanks for the news," Coy said.

When the wound was clean, Hubbard bound it with strips of a freshly laundered baker's apron. "I'll see if I can find you some aspirin for the pain," he said. "Chief Bristow used to keep a box in the kitchen for his sinuses."

Hubbard started to move away again.

"Do me a favor, will you, Marv?" Coy said.

"Sure, Bernie. What is it?"

"If you see a rifle lying around out there somewhere, bring it back with you."

Hubbard's mouth fell open. "Goddamn!" he said. In his rush to drag Coy to safety, he had left their one weapon lying out on the kitchen floor where it had fallen when Coy was shot. "I'll get it right away, Bernie," he said, embarrassed.

"Appreciate it, Marv," Coy drawled.

Hubbard slipped back across the kitchen and made his way to where Coy had hit the floor. About five feet from some spots of Coy's blood lay the rifle. Hubbard retrieved it, then made his way in a crouch over to Chief Steward Bristow's desk. Kneeling behind the desk, he went through the drawers. He found a tin box of aspirin, an unopened package of Camels, and one stick of Doublemint chewing gum. Sitting down, he carefully tore the stick of gum in half. He put one piece in his mouth and the other in his pocket for Coy. Then he started back for the far corner where Coy lay.

He was about halfway back to the protected corner when the first barrage of concentrated rifle fire crashed through the kitchen windows and sent slivers of glass raining across the room. Before Hubbard even knew what was happening, his face had become a mass of blood.

Hubbard rushed back to Coy. The escape leader looked at him in horror. "Jesus Christ, you're shot!"

"Glass," Hubbard said, panting, "just glass." He looked around frantically as more rifle fire ripped through the windows. "We got to get the hell out of here, Bernie!"

"Help me up!" Coy said.

Hubbard got him to his feet and Coy took the rifle. "Look through the dining hall and see if anybody's in the gun cage." Hubbard moved cautiously out to the wide doorway leading from the kitchen area into the dining hall. Above the far doorway which led on out to Times Square, the west gun gallery had a bulletproof window on the dining-room side to allow the gun cage officer to watch the dining room during meals. As far as Hubbard could see, there was no one on the other side of the window.

"Looks clear," he reported to Coy.

"Okay, give me a hand," Coy said. "Let's try to make it over to A Block. There are some stairs there that go down to the dungeons. Maybe there's a way out from there."

With Coy's good arm around Hubbard's shoulders, the two men half-ran, half-staggered down the center aisle of the dining hall.

•

In the gun gallery, Bergen, Mahan, and Burch had been peering over the steel shield in the direction of the cellblocks. The bazooka shells had hit the side of D Block about five minutes earlier and the three officers were watching intently to see if the reverberation would drive any of the escapees out into the open.

When they decided that no one was going to show himself, they knelt back down on the floor of the lower tier and resumed watching both the cellblocks *and* the dining hall.

By that time, Coy and Hubbard had crossed the dining hall and were under them.

•

Standing under the gun-cage overhang, next to the cellhouse officer's desk where the break had begun, Coy and Hubbard heard the movement of the officers in the gallery. They looked in the curved mirror but could see no one in the cage. The officers were either crouching or sitting down.

"We'll never make it to A," Coy whispered, looking down Times Square to the north wall.

"Where else can we go?" Hubbard asked nervously.

Coy, carefully scrutinizing everything he could see, noticed that the C Block utility corridor door was not closed all the way. The door was not open, not actually moved out from its steel jamb; but Coy, who knew the Times Square corridor as well as he knew his own cell, could tell that the door was not closed flush; therefore the lock could not be engaged.

Coy touched Hubbard's arm and motioned toward the door. He pulled Hubbard closer and whispered something to him, handing him the rifle. Hubbard nodded, and with the rifle moved silently back toward the dining room.

Moving out from under the gun gallery on the dining room side just enough to aim the rifle almost straight up, Hubbard blasted the gun-cage window with three quick shots. The bullets immediately ricocheted up to the ceiling; the gallery officers spun around to cover the dining hall. As they did, Hubbard moved quietly back to where Coy waited.

The two men crossed the flats and quickly entered the C Block utility corridor.

●

Coy and Hubbard had been in the corridor for an hour, crouched just inside the door, when they heard footsteps down Seedy Street. By bending down to floor level, they could listen through the air vent that led into Cell 404, the last cell at the west end of the block. Reserved for use as an officer's toilet, 404 was next to the two hostage cells. Through the vent, Coy and Hubbard had heard Earl Waller working on the lock of the yard door. Coy had grunted quietly.

"I hope he has better luck than we did," he said dryly.

A while later, they knew that Waller had successfully unjammed the lock, because the rumble of several hundred feet told them that the in-grades were being brought in from the yard. Shortly after that they heard hurried footsteps and the sound of individual cells being racked open, and knew that the lockup cons were being moved.

Now all had been quiet for what seemed like a long time. Coy wished he knew what time it was, but he had no way of telling. Lageson's watch had stopped. Coy had forgotten to wind it.

If it had been running, he would have known it was three o'clock.

●

Precisely at 3:00 P.M., all assault forces attacked the cellhouse.

From the south slopes, the twelve riflemen resumed firing and poured a continuous rain of Springfield fire through the kitchen and now the dining hall windows. Within minutes, there was not an unbroken pane of glass in the west end of the building.

Marine mortarmen on the slopes adjacent to D Block commenced lobbing heavy shells into the side of the wall. Some of them bore through the barred windows and exploded on Sunset Boulevard. Others burst through the concrete wall and blew cement fragments all over the block. Inside, some of the D Block prisoners began screaming.

On the roof above C, Charley Buckner began performing his specialty. Through the fist-size hole in the roof, he lowered a fragmentation grenade on a string. When it was as far down as he wanted it, he pulled a second string attached to it. The second string yanked out the spoon pin. Eight seconds later, the grenade exploded into forty-eight pieces of flying shrapnel.

On top of the west half of C Block, Dutch Cretzer, like the trapped men in D, screamed.

•

Below the roof over C Block, Dutch Cretzer had watched wide-eyed as the first grenade was lowered through the hole. Rising from where he had been lying, he started to move toward it. Then he saw the pin yanked out and the spoon fly off. Cretzer was not familiar with the operation of hand grenades, but some animal instinct deep inside warned him that he was in immediate danger. He turned and ran toward the cutoff end of the block.

As Cretzer was running, the grenade exploded. Four needles of shrapnel hit him in the back. He screamed and pitched forward onto his face in the dust.

Groaning and cursing, half-choking from a puff of dust that got into his mouth and nostrils, he crawled on his hands and knees to the deep utility corridor dividing the block. He slipped quickly over the edge. Using the pipes and conduit as ladder rungs, he started climbing down into the darker recesses of the narrow corridor.

Just before his head dropped below the roof's edge, he saw another grenade being lowered through the hole.

•

Because of the noise of the bombardment, neither Coy nor Hubbard had heard Dutch Cretzer's scream, and neither of them heard him now as he climbed down the narrow corridor to the flats level. Coy and Hubbard were crouched near the door at the far west end of the corridor; Cretzer was climbing down at the far east end. There was some light in the corridor filtering over from the fifteen big skylights above Broadway and the ten smaller ones above Seedy; but it was still too dark in the narrow enclosure to see from one end to the other. So Cretzer had no idea that Coy was that near; and Coy, with Hubbard, did not know that Cretzer was already deep in the corridor.

The noise of the grenades exploding on top of C Block echoed like thunder down in the corridor. Hubbard covered both ears with his palms, and saw that Coy was trying to do the same; but Coy, because of his wound, could not get his right hand all the way up. Hubbard quickly pulled a folder of cigarette papers out of his shirt pocket, rolled several of them into a ball, and handed them to Coy to stuff in his right ear. Both men were trying to talk at once, but under the combined noise of Buckner's grenades, the firing of the twelve riflemen, and the intermittent explosions of mortar shells against D Block, it looked to each as if the other was mouthing silent words. Finally, they both gave up.

As the assault continued, the two convicts crouched as far down in the corner as possible and each pulled his coat up over his head. They huddled together in their respective darknesses.

•

In D Block, Robert Stroud came out of his cell on the top tier. Holding his mattress in front of him for a shield, he looked over the rail. Below, the flats of Sunset Boulevard were littered with mortar fragments, concrete chips, and broken glass. A heavy layer of smoke clung to the ceiling overhead. The air was acrid with the smell of cordite.

Stroud moved downrange to Cell 34. He looked in and saw an Isolation prisoner named Burton Phillips lying under his bunk. "You okay, Crow?" he asked, calling Phillips by his prison name.

"So far," Phillips answered. "You?"

"Just mad," Stroud replied. "Those sons of bitches are trying to kill us all. I'm going down and see if I can put a stop to it."

"Don't be a goddamned fool!" Phillips said. "You go down there and you're as good as dead."

Stroud snorted. "Those dirty bastards have been trying to do me in for better than thirty years. They aren't about to do it today. I'll live until I get ready to die."

Laboriously, the old convict made his way along the range to the stairs. He walked down to the middle tier and over to Shockley's cell. There was no one there. He looked next door in Dutch Cretzer's old cell. Shockley was huddled back in a corner.

"Have you got a gun, Sam?" he asked evenly.

Crazy Sam, terrified by the mortar barrage, shook his head. "N-no," he answered in a quavering voice.

"Are you sure?" Stroud challenged. His old eyes were like ball-bearings. "If you lie to me, I'll kill you. I've killed two men already."

"I ain't g-got no g-gun," Shockley stuttered. He was trembling and his teeth chattered.

Stroud went back to the stairs. He sat down, wrapping the thin mattress around him as best he could. Earlier, he had heard Lieutenant Phil Bergen calling to Shockley from the gun gallery. He yelled now to see if Bergen was still there.

"Mr. Bergen! This is Stroud! Can you hear me?"

"Get back in your cell, you old bastard!" one of the guards in the cage yelled back.

"I want to talk to Mr. Bergen!"

"Shut up if you don't want your ass shot!"

"I have something important to tell Mr. Bergen!" Stroud said. "If you don't get him for me, the warden will hear of it!"

There was some muttered conversation in the gallery; then one of the guards opened the door into the main cellhouse. A moment later, Bergen crawled into the D Block cage.

"Stroud! What do you want?" the guard lieutenant yelled.

"Can't you call off this shelling?" Stroud shouted back. "You're going to murder every man in D Block!"

"There are armed men in D Block!" Bergen said. "We want them to surrender!"

"There are no armed men in D Block!" Stroud told him. "There is no gun in D Block!"

"I'd like to believe you, Stroud! But I can't!"

"Call the warden for me!" Stroud said. "Tell him he has my word that there is no gun in D Block! I will personally walk in front of any guards he wants to send in here! If you don't stop this shelling, you'll murder us all!"

There was a long pause, the block and the cage completely silent. Finally Bergen shouted, "All right, Stroud, I'll call the warden!"

•

In the intensive-care unit of Marine Hospital, a Navy doctor had been checking on Weinhold, Simpson, and Corwin every twenty minutes. There had still been no improvement in any of them; all three hovered in the cloudy area between life and death. As the doctor finished checking the vital signs of the last one, he shook his head hopelessly.

"Let's get oxygen tents over all three of them," he said to a corpsman. "It might help, but I doubt it. Personally, I think all three of them will be dead before dinnertime."

•

On the roof of the cellhouse, Charley Buckner was on his knees studying a diagram of the cellblocks below. Two of the guards were looking at it with him.

"Is this utility corridor open all along the top?" the Marine asked. "No grille or anything covering it?"

"Not a thing," one of the guards replied.

"How wide is it?"

"Two and a half feet."

Buckner tapped the diagram with a blunt forefinger. "If that guy's got any sense at all, he'll be down inside there by now. I've had shrapnel flying all over the top of that block. The only place he can hide is in that corridor."

"Can you get to him in there?"

"I think so," said Buckner. "I'll show you a little trick I figured out on Guam."

Buckner cut two pieces of string longer than he had been using earlier. He attached one to the pin and one to the neck of the grenade. The pin string he tied to a belt loop to keep it out of his way. The neck string he used to lower the grenade through the hole, letting it out a little at a time, like a fishing line. When the line went slack, he knew that the grenade had reached the top of the cellblock. He immediately drew it back up about six feet. Then he started moving the top of the string back and forth above the hole. Because of the size of the hole, it would only move three inches each way. But those three inches were enough to start the hanging grenade swinging: first three inches, along with the top of the string; then four inches and six and ten and more as it gained momentum from the weight of the grenade. Soon it was swinging in a wide arc six feet above the C Block roof, with Buckner maintaining the movement by the same simple three-inch manipulation of the top of the string.

When he had the grenade moving the way he wanted it, Buckner began lowering it again. He waited until it was swinging toward the top of the utility corridor, then let out the string twelve inches. The grenade swung back toward Broadway, then returned. As it arced over the edge of the corridor again, Buckner dropped it another foot. Six swings back and six swings forward; then, on the seventh, when Buckner let out the line, the grenade stopped and he knew that it was hanging a few inches into the corridor.

Quickly, before anyone who happened to be in the corridor could get to it, Buckner dropped the neck string and jerked smartly at the pin string tied to his belt loop. The pin was pulled, the spoon flew away, and the grenade, armed, dropped down the corridor, hitting pipes and shafts and conduit along the way. It exploded halfway down, between the two back-to-back middle tiers.

•

Dutch Cretzer heard the grenade swing into the corridor. Its quilt-like steel jacket made a sharp plunking sound as it hit against the concrete wall five inches below the rim of the corridor. A frightened, animal sound rose from Cretzer's throat when he looked up and saw it. He knew he did not have time to get to it, to grab it and throw it over the block roof down onto Broadway or Seedy Street; so he frantically tried to get as far away from it as possible. He scrambled toward a bank of large steam ventilator shafts. He managed to get partway behind them before the grenade exploded. He screamed as two slivers of shrapnel sliced into his left thigh and his left forearm. A fourth and fifth piece, both small like fingernail clippings, stuck in his neck and left cheek.

"You dirty sons of bitches!" Cretzer screamed at his unseen tormentors.

Even as he yelled, he could look up and see another grenade swinging ominously over the top of the corridor.

•

"Did you hear a scream just then?" Coy asked, sticking his head up from the crouch he was in.

"I didn't hear nothing except that goddamn noise down at the other end," Hubbard said. "What in the hell was it?"

"Hand grenades, I reckon," Coy told him.

"Jesus Christ! You'd think we was a bunch of goddamn Japs or something."

Coy paid no attention to Hubbard's complaint. He was staring at the darkness that pervaded the middle of the long, narrow corridor. His thin face, dark with more than a day's growth of beard now, was held rigid by a frown.

"I could have sworn I heard a scream," he said, as much to himself as to Hubbard. "A scream from close by."

"It was probably somebody in one of the cells," Hubbard said. "I bet those guys are scareder than we are."

Coy listened intently in the silence that followed the next explosion. He heard nothing. "You're probably right," he finally said. "Some of the lockups must have been left in their cells."

But even after he agreed with Hubbard, Bernie Coy continued to stare at the blackness for a long time.

CHAPTER THIRTY

6:40 P.M.

As the sun went down and cast a twilight over the bay, tens of thousands of San Franciscans again lined the shore to watch the spectacle of Alcatraz under siege. Police Chief Dullea had issued a strong interdiction the previous day against hilltop parking, but for the most part it turned out to be a paper order only: too many citizens ignored it.

Every vantage point from Coit Tower to Russian Hill was again jammed with shoulder-to-shoulder spectators equipped with everything from cameras and field glasses to toy telescopes. Automobiles were parked three deep along every curb. Near the Marina and on Telegraph Hill, it was virtually impossible for even pedestrian traffic to move freely.

The siege being watched was a colorful one. As the day turned gray, the riflemen on the south slopes began using tracer bullets furnished by the military. The ammunition bore bluish streaks through the darkening day. Farther along the same slopes, the mortar shells fired by the Marines threw out brilliant yellow flashes as they struck the D Block wall. An occasional incendiary shell burst into an eerie green light as it exploded in the cellhouse kitchen or in D Block.

From the shore, it was like a spectacular fireworks display. Inside the prison, it was more the wrath of God.

In the warden's office, Johnston had just finished talking with Bergen in the gun gallery. He turned to his associate warden, Ed Miller, now back on duty with his burned face dressed.

"Bergen says Stroud claims there's no gun in D Block. He gives his word on it. Says it's murder if we continue the shelling."

Miller grunted softly. "Murder's a subject he should be well versed in." The associate warden rubbed his chin speculatively. "I don't like Stroud, never have. But I've got to admit that his word has always been good. Back at Leavenworth and out here too."

Johnston nodded. "I'm inclined to believe him. He's too smart to lie to us; he knows we can put him in a dark cell—permanently."

The warden got up and walked to the window of his office. Outside, the gray of the evening was beginning to darken. "It'll be night in a little while. I'd just as soon no heavy shells be fired after dark. Too much chance of a few of them making a hole large enough for some of the Treatment Unit inmates to crawl through." He turned back to Miller. "What would you say to a cease-fire until daylight?"

Ed Miller agreed at once. "I think that's a good idea. The men need rest and some hot food."

Johnston returned to his desk and picked up the phone. He issued an order for all firing and shelling to stop at once. Then he put through a call to Bergen in the gun gallery.

•

Bergen was back in the main section of the cage when Johnston's call came. He talked to the warden for less than a minute, then told the other men that the shelling was going to stop. It was getting dark in the cellhouse now, the light filtering into long shadows. Bergen crawled back into the D Block section of the gallery.

"Stroud!" he shouted. "Are you there?"

"I'm here," the old Birdman said.

"Listen carefully, Stroud. The warden has ordered the shelling of D Block stopped. All inmates are to remain in their cells. If any gunfire comes from this block, the shelling will resume at once. Is that understood?"

"Understood," Stroud confirmed. "I'll pass the word in case everybody didn't hear. Thank you, Mr. Bergen."

Stroud pulled himself to his feet. Two other cons were out on the middle range, listening. Stroud motioned them over.

"Did you hear the lieutenant?"

"We heard," one of them answered.

"Pass it along to everybody then. I'll have a word with Crazy Sam, then I've got to get back up to my cot. My goddamn lumbago is killing me."

The two cons parted to spread the word. Stroud left his mattress on the stairs and walked stiffly back to the cell where Sam Shockley was hiding.

"Listen to me, Sam," said Stroud. "As long as you stay in your cell and there are no shots fired from this block, they won't shell us anymore. But at the first sign of trouble in here, they're going to start bombing us again. If that happens, we'll probably all end up dead.

I say probably, because I imagine some of us would come out alive. But since you're one of them that started this fucking fiasco, I just want you to know that you won't be among the survivors. You get my meaning?"

Shockley, staring at the Birdman over the edge of the bunk he was crouched behind, did not reply.

"Answer me, you son of a bitch!" Stroud growled. He took a threatening step forward.

"All right, I understand!" Shockley screamed. "Now get away and leave me alone, you fucking old creep!"

Stroud grunted derisively at the insult and went back to the stairs. Dragging his mattress, he made his way slowly up to the top tier. When he had walked all the way down to Cell 41, the next to last from the end, he stopped at the door and looked inside. Usually neat and tidy, the cell was now a wet, sopping mess. One of the mortar shells had hit a water pipe. Stroud shook his head in disgust.

"Shit," he said wearily.

•

In the corridor, Bernie Coy and Marvin Hubbard heard the shelling stop and an ominous silence descended over them. They exchanged nervous looks.

"Do you think they're coming in?" Hubbard asked.

"I don't know," Coy replied. "It must be dark by now. I don't think they'd rush us in the dark, do you?"

"Who knows what a bunch of goddamned screws would do?" said Hubbard.

They sat there quietly for a few minutes, listening, wondering. After a while, they lighted tailormades from Bristow's pack of Camels and began to talk again.

"Looks like we're pretty well hemmed in, don't it?" Hubbard said, more a statement than a question.

"Maybe," said Coy. "But we might still stand some kind of chance."

"How do you figure?"

"Two ways. First, for as long as I been on this rock, I've heard stories about there being a drainage canal or something under the cutoffs. It's supposed to lead right out to the water somewhere. Maybe there's one, maybe there ain't; maybe it goes out to the water, maybe not. If it just went outside this goddamned cellhouse, I'd be happy. Anyway, it's a chance."

"I ain't very impressed," Hubbard drawled. "If there was a tunnel, *some*body would have tried getting out that way during the twelve years this dump has been running. What's the other way?"

"If there's no drain or sewer or anything, we can still crawl under the cutoff and come up in the east end of the utility corridor. We've still got a rifle. When they come looking for us and open the door at that end, maybe we can grab a couple of screws and find a way to make them let us out through the sallyport."

"Might as well try to walk through the wall," Hubbard said.

"You're probably right," Coy agreed. "But look at it this way: it's a hell of a lot better than just sitting in here like a couple of knots on a log."

"I think you might have a point," Hubbard admitted. He leaned back against the wall and blew smoke at the ceiling.

Coy looked thoughtfully down at the dark end of the corridor again.

•

There was no drainage canal under the cutoffs. Dutch Cretzer had already found that out.

Bleeding from a dozen minor shrapnel wounds, Cretzer had crawled around on the bottom of the utility corridor until he had found the tunnel that Coy had spoken of to Hubbard. But that was all it was: a tunnel. Pipes and conduit ran through it, under the cutoff, to connect the west end of the corridor to the east end.

Cretzer had not been looking for a drainage canal. He was looking for a way to get away from the grenades. His body ached and burned everywhere the hot slivers of metal had hit him. His neck was swollen from one of them and he could barely swallow. To him the tunnel by itself was a happy discovery.

Cretzer got down on his stomach and wiggled through the tunnel with little effort, coming up beyond the cutoff in the east end of the block. He stood there in the dark for several moments, uncertain as to what he should do next. The east corridor was silent and still; compared to the west corridor, it was like going from a foxhole to a grave.

As he stood there, Cretzer was not entirely sure that he was alone. It was possible, he thought, that a goon squad had already come into the corridor, earlier, when the Industries cons had been run back in from the yard. There was only one way to find out, he decided. He aimed the .45 from the hip and fired a single round straight down the corridor.

After the explosion of the shot echoed away, Cretzer heard only silence again. There was no one else in the corridor. As he had done in the west end, he then climbed up through the intertwined pipes and shafts and came out on the barred east roof of C Block. The cutoff was now west of him instead of east. He no longer could see Times Square and the west gun gallery; now he could crawl almost to the opposite end and see the east gun gallery and the cross aisle into which the sallyport door opened.

Cretzer was pleased at having found a way to get on the other half of the C Block roof. He was safer now; the grenades could not get to him. And the guards would not know where he was; they would think he was still on the west roof. Maybe now he could get some rest. He flicked a dry tongue over his parched lips, wishing for the fiftieth time or more that he had some water. He lighted another cigarette, hovering over his cupped hands to conceal the match. He knew the smoke was going to raise hell with his stomach, but at that point he did not care. He needed something to relax him, to help him forget his aching cuts for a minute or two. He lay down on his side, with one outstretched arm under his head. The left side of his neck was swollen and throbbing; he was sure the sliver of shrapnel was still in it. He thought briefly about the possibility of blood poisoning; then just as quickly dismissed it from his mind.

It was much more pleasant to close his eyes and think about his ex-wife Eddie and all the other people who would be reading about the bloody last stand he made on the Rock.

•

The shot that Cretzer fired to determine if he was alone in the corridor had almost hit a guard. Officer Joe Steere, one of several guards making routine spot checks to see if the aisles between the cellblocks were still clear, was just walking past the east corridor door when he heard a muffled shot. He froze as an instantaneous *thud* hit the door from the inside, and a bullet ricocheted off the concrete wall on the other side of him. Staring at the single-sheet steel door, he saw a finger-size hole about chest high.

Steere quickly reported the incident to Associate Warden Ed Miller. Several minutes later, Miller, Steere, and three other guards, armed with shotguns, came through the sallyport and quietly approached the door. Miller unlocked it and opened it a foot, making certain that he and his men stayed well back out of view.

"You men better surrender!" he yelled into the corridor.

There was no reply, no sound.

"Do you hear me?" the associate warden yelled. "Cretzer! Coy! Whoever's in there, you'd better surrender and come out!"

Still only silence came from the dark passageway.

"All right, boys," Miller said to his men, "move up to the door one at a time and unload one in there. But don't open the door any more than it is already."

The men took turns at the door, each awkwardly shoving the barrel of his riot gun around the edge of the jamb and firing one shell. The line of fire was too restricted at the angle from which they were forced to fire; all of the shells hit the north inside wall about ten feet down the corridor, tearing up a ventilator shaft and some low-voltage conduit.

After everyone had fired, Miller slammed the door and locked it. He and his men retreated to the sallyport. Their effort had been completely wasted. Coy and Hubbard, still in the west-block corridor, barely heard the blasts. Cretzer, lying flat on top of the block, ignored it.

•

As full darkness spread completely over the big cellhouse, the six men who had started the battle of Alcatraz were spread out in five different locations, and each man had his own private thoughts about the present and the future.

Danny Durando, the Indio Kid, was still in his cell, 142-B, on the flats of Michigan Boulevard. He was locked in, now that the Industries prisoners had been brought in and all the cells racked shut. He lay on his bunk, staring at the ceiling. Only rarely did he get off the bunk even to go to the toilet or get a drink of water. For hours he just lay there, very still, his dark young face sad, his insides sick from the knowledge of what he had been a part of and the ultimate price he knew he would have to pay for it.

In a locked A Block cell to which he had been removed, Buddy Thompson paced like a nervous coyote. Things were not working out exactly as he planned, but they still might turn out all right. The hostage guards were all dead—or so he thought. That meant there could be no guard testimony tying him in with the escape attempt. The guards who had moved him from C Block did not treat him any differently than they did the other lockup cons, so in all probability they did not know he was in on the break. Maybe his luck was holding.

Thompson had not been able to locate Durando to agree on a

mutual alibi, but the Kid was certain to deny his own participation in the break. So all Thompson had to do was back the Kid's story, and in doing so establish his own. If Cretzer and Coy got killed— and Thompson felt there was a very good chance of that—so much the better. Hubbard would almost certainly die with Coy. That would leave only Shockley, and he was so goddamned crazy that no one would believe anything he said. So for Buddy Thompson, everything could still fall nicely into place.

In Dutch Cretzer's old cell on the middle tier of D, Sam Shockley still cringed on the floor at the end of the bunk, even though the shelling had long since stopped. Shockley was trying not to be afraid of what was coming next. He tried to make himself concentrate on something pleasant, like the pancakes he loved so dearly and missed so much. But his mind, over which he had so little control, kept going back to Cecil Corwin's horribly grotesque face.

Bernie Coy and Marvin Hubbard were hiding in the west end of the C Block utility corridor. Resting now, they were quiet, subdued, even a little drowsy. Hubbard's thoughts were of his wife Tola and their little girl, and of what might have been. Coy's thoughts were of the escape, and of what might be done to salvage something— *anything*—from his extraordinary accomplishment of capturing the "invulnerable" west gun gallery. As Coy evaluated their position over and over again, he still wished in the back of his mind that he had killed Dutch Cretzer.

Cretzer, at that moment, was giving no thought at all to Bernie Coy. All he could think about, as he lay on the east roof of C Block, was the excruciating headache he had: a throbbing pain just behind his eyes. He had been walking around earlier, and a sudden dizzy spell had dropped over him like a shroud. His vision had blurred, then doubled. When he looked at the bars that extended from the cellblock roof up to the inside of the cellhouse ceiling, they had merged into a wavy wall of almost solid steel. When that had happened, he had dropped to his knees and crawled back to the center of the roof, where he now lay. From time to time, when he thought about going blind, Dutch Cretzer would quietly cry.

Thoughts of death pervaded the cellhouse that night as the hour moved toward midnight. Thoughts not only in the minds of the six escape plotters, but also in the minds of all the prisoners now locked in A and B; of the seven lockup cons who had been overlooked when C Block was emptied; of the D Block cons in the Treatment Unit;

of the guards who were manning the east and west gun galleries; and of other Alcatraz officers who knew that sooner or later some of them would have to go into the cellhouse after the armed convicts.

The break was then in its thirty-fourth hour. Two men were dead. Within the next seven hours, another three would die.

PART THREE

SATURDAY, MAY 4, 1946

CHAPTER THIRTY-ONE

12:35 A.M.

During the post-midnight hours, with the electricity still turned off in the cellhouse, Coy and Hubbard relaxed as well as they could in the cramped, uncomfortable utility corridor. All of Chief Bristow's Camels were gone now, and they were back to smoking roll-your-owns from the makings Hubbard still had in his shirt pocket. In the silent, still hours, the two convicts reminisced, speaking in soft, sometimes melancholy voices.

"Marv, did you ever wonder how life would have been for you if you hadn't been born so poor?" asked Coy. This was not Coy the Depression-era bank robber or Coy the convict speaking. It was Coy the dreamer; the artist; the student of psychology.

"I used to think about that when I was little," Hubbard admitted. "Used to wonder why some folks was borned rich and others wasn't. Then for a long time, after I started stealing, I didn't think about it no more. But it's funny: after I got sent here, I begun to think about it again. I begun thinking that if I'd been borned rich, I never would have ended up on this stinking rock." Hubbard took a drag on his cigarette and grunted softly. "I might be wrong about that, though. Even if I'd had lots of money, I might still have wound up in the pen. My daddy always told me I was borned bad. Maybe he was right."

Coy shook his head emphatically. "No, he wasn't, Marv. Hell, no. Not by a long shot. I don't mean no disrespect to your daddy, so don't take offense. But he was as wrong as he could be. There ain't *nobody* ever been born bad. If I didn't learn nothing else from the books I been reading these last nine years, I sure as hell learned that. Not even Dutch Cretzer was born bad, or that fool Shockley. And not you and not me. I don't think none of us ever *wanted* to be outlaws and get put in cells and herded around like cattle. You didn't want it, did you, Marv?"

"No, I didn't *want* it," the fiercely proud Alabaman answered. "But I was willing to chance it to get what I did want."

"What was that, Marv?" Coy asked with a sudden consuming interest. For the first time in his life, he felt intimately close to another human being. "What was it you wanted so bad?"

In the darkness, Marv Hubbard blinked back tears that rose with his memories. "I wanted some glasses so's I could see. I never had good eyes, since I was little. And there wasn't never no money to buy me glasses. When I was a kid, I can't never remember being able to see more than ten feet in front of me. Not until I got old enough to steal and get me some money for glasses."

Coy shook his head in wonder. "A pair of glasses to see with? Is that what done it, Marv?"

"That's what *started* it," Hubbard said. "After that, every time I needed something I didn't have money for, I'd always go back to stealing. Oh, I tried living like ever'body else; I got married to Tola and we had us a little girl. But stealing had give me the eyes to see more than ten feet in front of me, and stealing was always waiting for me to come back when I needed it." Hubbard took off his thick glasses and rubbed his eyes. For a few minutes, he was silent. When he spoke again, his voice was sad. "I ain't complaining. And I ain't got no regrets. Except maybe one. I sure do wish I'd been able to do better for my wife and little girl." He sighed wistfully and put the glasses back on. "You ain't never said if you've got any family, Bernie. Not aiming to pry, understand."

"Yeah, I got some family," Coy told him. "I got a few people somewheres. Folks might even still be alive, I don't know." He sighed as Hubbard had sighed a moment earlier: painfully, sadly. "My people are just hill folks back in Kentucky. Daddy never did care nothing about me. Mamma neither, I don't expect. They never had nothing except a sharecropper's shack and us kids. Never gave us nothing 'cause they didn't have it to give. All I ever got from my daddy was strappings; all from my mamma was rotten teeth."

The two Southerners both fell silent for several moments. Neither had ever been as frank and honest with another man before. Each was a little embarrassed by it.

Coy finally laughed quietly and poked Hubbard on the arm. "Hey, I just thought of something funny. It's a good thing we didn't know one another as kids. We'd have made a sorry pair: your eyes and my teeth."

In the pitch-black darkness, Marv Hubbard laughed with him.

•

Across the water in San Francisco, fresh headlines were being set and updated stories being written about the break.

At the *Chronicle,* Saturday's headline would read:

PRISON BATTLING RESUMES
AFTER FOUR-HOUR TRUCE;
FELONS WON'T SURRENDER

Exactly when the four-hour truce had been in effect was not made clear. In a follow-up story, other items were clear, however. A casualty list published that day again described the body of Hal Stites as "riddled by machine-gun bullets." And a hospital or morgue report from some source stated unequivocally that Bill Miller had been "tortured" by the convicts prior to being shot. How he had been tortured was not indicated.

The *Examiner* headline was much more sensational and considerably less factual. Their Saturday banner was:

9 CONVICTS STILL SHOOTING!
Alcatraz Felons Reported
Making Last Grim Stand

The main headline was set strictly to sell newspapers. There was absolutely no basis for it. And no excuse.

The *Examiner*'s story of the official toll of casualties as of midnight Friday was very close to accurate, however. They listed two dead—correct; and fourteen wounded—almost correct. There were thirteen officers who had suffered actual wounds up until that time, not including Burch and Sundstrom, who had fistfight injuries; and another officer who had a tiny nick in the tip of his nose, presumably from a ricocheting sliver of lead. Inclusion of the latter officer would have made the *Examiner* count exact, but it hardly seems fair to include what was little more than a scratch, while excluding the cuts and bruises of Burch, who fought so tenaciously to retain control of the gun gallery, or Sundstrom, who made a superb effort to avoid capture and sound the alarm earlier.

The accuracy of the *Examiner's* casualty list was not that important, however. Nor was its statement that there were "strong indications that a number of convict dead" existed, when in fact no convicts had yet been killed.

That was a fact which would be altered before San Franciscans read either of the papers that day.

•

By 4:00 A.M., Coy and Hubbard had begun to move quietly and tentatively farther into the corridor. They did not know what time it was, and both kept looking up toward the roof for the first signs of a predawn softening of the night sky. They had stayed awake all night and their throats were hoarse from talking and smoking. Their stomachs felt queasy from too little food, too little rest, too much tension, and the stale, strong tobacco they had smoked. Coy's wounded shoulder was almost immobile with stiffness and was throbbing again, even though during the night he had taken all twelve aspirin in the box Hubbard had got from Chief Bristow's desk. Oddly, through all the thirty-nine hours since the crashout started, Coy's damaged gums had given him little or no pain. He supposed there was a limit to how many places a man could hurt at one time.

Hubbard was in much better shape than Coy. He had a dozen small slices in his face and neck from flying glass, but none of them were deep or painful. His thick, healthy body was built to withstand abuse and fatigue. He was ready for any task, any challenge, as the final hours of the escape approached.

One slow, careful step at a time, they moved deeper into the corridor.

•

On the east roof of C Block, Dutch Cretzer also watched for the first light to give some relief from the long, dark night he had just endured. Cretzer was in miserable shape now. He had not eaten in forty hours, had nothing to drink for thirty-five. There were ten shrapnel wounds in his body, one of them—in his neck—now festered and swollen to the size of a walnut, and burning like fire. His face where Coy had raked him with the rifle was also very sore, and between that and his neck wound, one of his eyes had closed to a slit. On top of it all, he had run out of tobacco to roll cigarettes.

Nothing left now, he thought. Old Public Enemy Number Four

is all washed up. He patted the folded poem in his pocket. Only one way to go out now. Like they all knew he would: plugging away at every screw in sight. That's the way the people who knew him would expect him to go out. That's the only way Dutch Cretzer *could* go out.

Might as well get on with it, he decided. The longer he waited, the weaker he would become. Sam, Coy, Thompson, and the others were probably all dead by now. With all the heavy stuff he had heard shaking the cellhouse the previous day, it wouldn't have surprised him if every lock-up con in the joint was dead—

A sudden awful thought hit him then. Suppose the cons in D Block had bought it? Stroud, Fleish, the others. There would go his headlines. The Birdman and the others would get all the play. Unless, of course, he himself went out in such a blaze of glory that it would make everyone else look sick. Like for instance, taking about ten screws with him. Now *that* would be something.

Thus inspired, Cretzer snaked close to the east end of the C roof and peered over the barred edge. He saw three guards in the top tier of the east gun cage. I'll start with those three right there, he thought.

Cretzer wiggled forward and put the barrel of the .45 through the bars. He took aim on one of the guards, steadied the gun, and squeezed the trigger.

The bullet missed the guard by a foot and ricocheted harmlessly away from the cage. Immediately a blistering barrage of machine-gun fire spiked the air above Cretzer's head as he scurried back out of range.

"Goddamn it!" he said with tears in his eyes. He had *missed*!

•

In his office, Warden Johnston received a call from the east gun gallery. He talked with the officer in charge. When he finished, he looked across the desk at Associate Warden Ed Miller. "Someone just fired a pistol shot at the east gun cage from that end of the C Block roof."

Miller frowned for a moment, tightening the now-unbandaged, burned skin on the right side of his face. "I guess that means there's still a gun in the east corridor. I thought after we blasted in there last night, we might have finished whoever shot at Steere." He and the warden stared at each other for a moment. "You know," he said, "that could mean that *both* guns are in there."

"Exactly what I was thinking. All the previous fire, with the exception of the shot at Steere, has come from the west end. Of course, there still might be just one man—and one gun—in there. He could have crawled through the cutoff tunnel. But since we haven't pinpointed the second gun anywhere else, I think we ought to go on the assumption that there's a gun in each section of the block. One in the west corridor, and one on the east roof. We know it's the man with the pistol on the east roof, so it must be the con with the rifle at the west end."

"If you're right," Ed Miller said, "and we can drive both of them into the east section of that corridor, we'll have them caught in a perfect trap."

Johnston picked up his phone and called the armory. "Is Warrant Officer Buckner still here?"

"No, sir. He left the island late yesterday when the cease-fire went into effect."

"Well, locate the officers who were on the roof with him and had a chance to observe his technique. Have them go back up and resume grenading the west utility corridor."

"Yes, sir."

Johnston turned to Miller again. "That should drive the man with the rifle either back out onto Times Square or under the cutoff into the east corridor. Either way we'll have him."

"Perfect," said Miller. "What we have to do now is drive the con with the pistol down off the east C Block roof. Then we'll have him *and* the one with the rifle both in the east corridor."

Johnston nodded. He had allowed Miller to take weapons onto the cellhouse floor the previous evening to fire into the corridor. The east corridor door was only a dozen steps from the sallyport, and the officers were well covered from the gun gallery. Johnston had finally conceded to himself that the principle of no weapons on the cellhouse floor simply was not going to work in this break, any more than assaulting D Block with mortars had worked. He was going to have to force the action *inside* the prison—or he would never be able to put an end to the nightmare.

"After we're sure they're in the east corridor," he told Miller, "we can have men jerk the door all the way open and blast that corridor to pieces. There's no way we can miss. Question is, how do we drive the pistol-shooter off the east roof? We don't want to waste time drilling another hole to drop in grenades."

"Suppose we toss the grenades onto the roof from the top tier of the east cage?" Miller suggested. "I know it's tricky; most of them will hit the roof bars and bounce down onto the flats. But there's nobody down there to get hurt when they explode. And all we have to do is get two or three through the bars to drive him down into the corridor."

"It might work," said the warden. "Let's give it a try."

"Yes, sir."

"But first get your team with riot guns and rifles ready at the sallyport door," the warden said. "Let them stand by until we're sure one or both of the cons are in the corridor. Then have them hit that east door—hard and fast. No surrender pleas, no warnings; just blast the dirty bastards out."

Miller nodded soberly. "Yes, sir."

•

On the mainland, the prison launch was waiting at the dock when a gray U.S. Government sedan pulled up and Director James V. Bennett got out. He had come directly from the airport and his dark, vested suit was wrinkled from the overnight plane trip. He wore a snap-brim hat and carried a topcoat. An Alcatraz lieutenant met him at the edge of the pier and escorted him aboard the launch. Half a dozen news photographers took his picture in the process.

"Any change in the situation, Lieutenant?" the director asked as the launch moved away from the pier.

"Not yet, sir. But the warden is very close to regaining control."

Bennett said nothing. He looked back at the shore. There were thousands of people lining the waterfront. Many of them had binoculars or telescopes; others merely shaded their eyes.

"They're waiting for the end of the show, I suppose," Bennett said.

"They won't have long to wait," the guard lieutenant replied.

CHAPTER THIRTY-TWO

6:10 A.M.

Both ends of the utility corridor were very dimly lighted now by shafts of daylight coming through the skylights high above Broadway on one side, and overlooking Seedy Street on the other.

In the west corridor, Coy and Hubbard made slow but steady progress through the maze of pipes and shafts and conduit, many of which had been blown apart or twisted by the concussion of

Buckner's grenades. Water leaked steadily from a number of damaged pipes, making the sunken floor of the tunnel wet and slippery. A few live but low-current electrical wires were hanging loose overhead, but the two convicts easily avoided them. The entire length of the corridor was pungent with gunpowder.

"Jesus, it looks like a bomb was dropped in here," Marv Hubbard whispered. Hubbard was now wearing an old prison coat that Coy had kept hanging just inside the corridor door for cool mornings. It was tight across the Alabaman's barrel chest, but at least it was warm. As they moved slowly along, Hubbard looked around edgily. "It's spooky as hell in here," he said. "Whereabouts is that tunnel anyway?"

"I told you, under the cutoff," Coy said. "I hope to hell it leads us someplace. There sure don't look like no other way out—"

As Coy was speaking, they heard a sharp metallic *plunk*! Looking up at the top of the corridor, where it opened onto the roof and was much lighter, they saw a hand grenade hanging by a string some five or six inches over the side. As they watched incredulously, a second string pulled the grenade's pin, its spoon handle flew off, and the grenade began tumbling and bouncing downward.

"Oh, Christ!" Coy said. He grabbed Hubbard's sleeve. "Duck down, quick!"

They had eight seconds. In that time they both squeezed partway behind a ventilator shaft. The grenade, delayed by too many obstacles, got down only as far as the middle tier. There it exploded far enough above Coy and Hubbard to miss them entirely with any of its shrapnel.

When the blast was over, Coy pulled Hubbard on toward the cutoff wall. "Come on, let's get the hell out of here!"

Hurrying, they reached the mouth of the crawl tunnel that extended under the cutoff. Coy looked up and saw another grenade swinging back and forth over the top of the corridor. He slapped Hubbard on the back. "Get in there, quick!"

Hubbard dropped down and wiggled headfirst into the tunnel.

Coy heard the ominous *plunk* again and looked up, frightened. The swinging grenade was now hanging into the corridor. He flattened himself at the mouth of the tunnel. Marv Hubbard's feet were just disappearing into the opening. Coy pushed on them, trying to make Hubbard move faster.

Above Coy, the grenade fell.

•

Inside the sallyport entry, Garand rifles and Remington 12-gauge shotguns had been issued to four officers.

"This is the way we'll work it," Ed Miller said. "I'll go up to the top tier of the east cage and have the men up there toss a few grenades on top of C Block. They'll be pitching them up, between the roof bars, so some of them are going to bounce back and blow up on the flats. You men keep the door closed until I give you the word to open it. As soon as I think the con with the pistol has gone down into the corridor, I'll call the armory from the cage. When you get a signal from the armory, that's when you go in. I want one man on each side of the utility door, facing away from the door in case anybody comes around Broadway or Seedy to jump you. I want a third man to jerk open the door, and the other one to blast the corridor. Then change positions and let the other man fire. You've got five shells in those riot guns, eight in the rifles. Keep one in reserve for when you retreat into the sallyport. Close and lock that corridor after you finish. Any questions?"

The four men shook their heads.

•

In the west corridor, Coy frantically scrambled into the cutoff tunnel and drew his legs up as the second grenade exploded. Flying shrapnel tore into several ventilator shafts nearby, and two pieces ricocheted off the wall just above the tunnel, but none came into the low, narrow access through which Coy and Hubbard crawled.

"They must know we're in here," Coy said tightly. "Maybe when we opened the corridor door, it tripped an alarm or something. Can you see anything up ahead?"

"Yeah, the other corridor," Hubbard said. "I knew there wasn't no drainage canal under here. I got a feeling we ain't going nowhere at all, Bernie."

"We've still got a chance. The east door. It's close to the sallyport. Maybe we can grab a couple of screws. Keep moving, Marv—"

"I think we're washed up, Bernie," Hubbard said quietly.

"Just keep going, goddamn it! We've got a chance, I tell you!"

"Okay, Bernie. Okay. I'm moving."

Marv Hubbard started inching forward again.

•

In the top tier of the east gun cage, Ed Miller and two other guards got ready to toss the first grenades. Two officers with machine guns were crouched on either side of them. At a nod from Miller, the machine-gunners stood up and sprayed the top edge of the block with a sheet of fire. The instant they ceased firing, Miller and the others rose, pulled the pins from their grenades, looped their arms through the gallery bars, and tossed the grenades underhanded toward the top of C Block. One of the three grenades went through to the top of the roof without hitting the long bars extending up to the cellhouse ceiling. The other two dropped to the flats. Miller and the two guards ducked behind the shield before the grenades exploded.

They quickly tried it again. Grabbing more grenades from a gas mask bag, Miller passed them out and nodded to his machine-gunners. They swept the roof edge with more fire. Miller and the others tossed the second round of grenades. They all bounced off bars and fell to the flats. The men ducked again; the grenades exploded below.

During the next ten minutes, the men in the cage tossed grenades twelve more times. On the seventh and tenth tosses, one grenade made it through the bars each time. All the rest exploded on the flats. Miller decided to keep tossing them until one more got through.

•

On top of the block, the first grenade had blown up twenty-five feet from Dutch Cretzer. He was crouched down near the back of the east section, momentarily distracted by string-lowered grenades which were again being dropped into the west corridor. In the echo of the concentrated machine-gun fire, and with his head turned to look across the cutoff at the west block, he did not hear the grenade tossed by Miller. It landed about fifteen feet past the bars and exploded five seconds later.

A sheet of shrapnel hit Dutch Cretzer. His back and left side were stitched with it. He screamed and fell, his scream lost in the concussion noise. Rising quickly to his knees, he began firing the .45 blindly in the direction of the gun cage. As he fired, there was another burst of gunfire and then more grenades were tossed at him. They hit the bars and fell to the flats. Cretzer whimpered in fear and crawled frantically toward the top of the corridor.

In seconds he was lowering his bleeding, hurting body down through the maze of pipes and conduit again.

•

At the bottom of the corridor, Marv Hubbard was out of the tunnel. He adjusted the kitchen knife that was still stuck in his belt and bent to pull the wounded Coy through. As he got Coy halfway out, the second grenade exploded on top of the block.

"We're washed up, Bernie," Hubbard said nervously. "They're going to blow our asses off!"

Coy struggled to his feet, clutching the rifle. "Let's get to that door! See if it's unlocked!"

They stumbled forward, hitting their shins and ankles against pipes and airshaft edges. Hubbard was leading the way now; he had come out of the tunnel first and there was no room in the narrow corridor for Coy to get past him.

Halfway to the east door, they heard a low, growling noise. They stopped. Coy crouched, the rifle ready. Hubbard, squinting through his rimless glasses, peered down the narrow corridor ahead of them.

Without warning, a grimacing, blood-soaked figure leaped from behind a ventilator shaft and began firing a .45 at them.

Hubbard dropped down and managed to find a few inches of cover at the side of the corridor. Behind him, Bernie Coy was not as lucky.

Cretzer's bullets hit Coy in the neck, shoulder, and face. He spun sideways, violently, and slammed against the wall of the corridor. Then he dropped to the plank floor and rolled over.

"Jesus," he moaned. "Jesus. Jesus."

•

Above, Associate Miller's eighteenth grenade made it through the bars and exploded on the roof. Miller immediately snatched up the gallery phone, which was already hanging off the hook, a line open to the armory.

"Send them in; hurry!" he ordered the armory officer.

In the armory, a signal was waved and the deadlock guard unlocked the big steel sallyport door and pulled it inward. Then the barred door beyond it, which swung out to the right. The cellhouse entry was then fully open.

Slowly, carefully, the four heavily armed officers moved onto the flats toward the utility-corridor door.

•

In the corridor, Marv Hubbard twisted around in his crouched position and crawled back to where Coy had fallen. He looked down at his groaning friend and then over at Dutch Cretzer.

"You son of a bitch!" he screamed furiously at Cretzer. The former public enemy sneered and raised the pistol again. But before he could fire, there was the loud clang of a steel door being thrown open, and sounds of running footsteps coming from the sallyport. Cretzer whirled and faced the east corridor door. Hubbard frantically began dragging Bernie Coy deeper into the corridor.

The hurrying footsteps came closer to the east door. Defiantly, Cretzer started for the door, .45 raised and ready. But in the cluttered corridor, he stumbled; the gun fell from his hand. He heard it clatter noisily into a maze of pipes. In near panic, he dropped to his knees and began to search for it. He scrambled around in the narrow corridor like a madman.

"My gun!" he screamed. "I can't find my gun!"

When he heard the footsteps stop at the corridor door, Cretzer froze for an instant. Then he turned and ran wildly along the plank flooring toward the back of the corridor. When he got to where Hubbard was dragging Coy, he bulled his way over both of them, stepping on Coy's face and half-crawling over the bent form of Hubbard.

"Let me by!" he yelled. "Let me by!"

•

On the flats outside the utility corridor, the four guards were all in place: one on each side of the door, about six feet away, facing the two aisles; one standing to the right of the door, ready to open it; one standing to the left, a rifle at high port, ready to fire.

The guard on the left found that his hands on the trigger housing and barrel grip of the rifle were slick with sweat. He had never had to shoot at another human being before. But he was girded up for it. The memory of easygoing Hal Stites and of patient, concerned Bill Miller was still fresh in his mind. Clenching his jaw, he nodded tensely to the man at the door. In a blur of motion, the door was jerked open. The guard stepped into the open doorway and leveled the rifle.

Down the corridor, Hubbard threw himself flat on top of Bernie Coy. Just feet behind him, Cretzer stopped and looked back at the open door.

The guard fired seven times, rapidly, randomly. Six of the bullets ripped into water pipes, conduit, and ventilator shafts.

The seventh drilled Dutch Cretzer in the left temple as he started to turn and run away. He was dead before he hit the floor.

•

After the first guard had fired all but one shell from his rifle, the second stepped into the doorway and let go four shotgun blasts. Then they slammed and locked the door, and ran back to the sallyport.

Because all three convicts were flat on the plank floor of the corridor, none of the shotgun blasts hit them. Not that it would have mattered if they had. Cretzer was dead and Coy was dying, and Marv Hubbard must have known that his life was as good as finished too. Pushing himself to a sitting position, Hubbard cradled Coy's head in his arms.

"Does it hurt, Bernie?" he asked in a sympathetic voice.

Coy's answer was spoken too softly to be heard.

If it had been heard, it probably would have been a negative answer. Bernie Coy had hurt too much for too long to let those last bullet wounds bother him. If anything, they were probably a relief.

It was then 6:40 A.M., exactly forty-one hours after the crashout began. For all practical purposes, the battle of Alcatraz was over.

CHAPTER THIRTY-THREE

9:00 A.M.

Coy was dead, Cretzer was dead, and all the fight had at last gone out of Marv Hubbard. But the Alcatraz officers had no way of knowing that. And with two guards in the San Francisco morgue, they were not inclined to take chances. So for the next two hours, until nearly nine o'clock, they continued to assault the east utility corridor.

It was like a stage scene being rehearsed over and over. Four guards entered from the sallyport. Two covered the aisles of Broadway and Seedy Street. One jerked open the door. A fourth fired into the dim fifty-foot corridor with a rifle. Then the one who had opened the door took his turn firing, using a shotgun. Every length of pipe, conduit, and shaft in the corridor was shot apart.

So too, finally, was Marv Hubbard. Sometime during the lengthy barrage, he was hit above the left eye by a rifle slug. He was standing up, facing the door, and must have spun to his right, because a second bullet hit him in the left temple before he had time to fall.

The impact of the two bullets sent him reeling back into the dark reaches of the utility corridor. He sprawled face-down on the plank floor.

The thing Marv Hubbard feared most—dying alone—was finally over.

•

At 9:00 A.M. a mass force of unarmed guards moved in and secured the big cellhouse. Four officers with shotguns remained on guard at the east utility corridor door, while other guards in relief shifts covered the west corridor door from the gun gallery.

A special team of guards led by Associate Warden Ed Miller entered the cellhouse and headed directly for Cell 142-B. Two guards dragged a terrified Danny Durando from the cell and slammed him back against the door bars. Taking no chances with him, they spread his arms out wide and cuffed his quick, dangerous hands to the door. They hit him several times in the stomach and kidneys with billy clubs, then systematically tore every stitch of clothes from his body.

In A Block, Buddy Thompson was pulled from his temporary lockup cell by his hair and punched in the face four times. His nose began to bleed. "What the hell are you doing?" he pleaded. "I wasn't even a part of it!" The guards hit him again, with clubs this time.

"You lying son of a bitch!" stormed Ed Miller. "You're the one got Cretzer to shoot those officers!"

They continued to hit him until he fell to his knees. Then, like Durando, they stripped him naked.

Finally, the team unlocked the D Block door and went into the Treatment Unit after Shockley. They found him in the bunk in Cretzer's old cell on the middle tier.

"Come out, you crazy bastard," Ed Miller ordered.

"I didn't do nothing," Shockley said. He cringed back in the cell and began to cry.

The guards dragged him onto the range and ripped off his clothing. For some reason none of them could bring themselves to hit him with their fists or clubs; but they slapped him freely with their open palms. He cried loudly, like an injured child.

"Are you going to give him a trial or kill him now?" a voice called from the top tier. Everyone on the block, guards included, knew it was the Birdman.

"Shut up, you murdering old son of a bitch, or we'll come up and give you a dose of it!" Ed Miller yelled.

"Come ahead," Stroud challenged. "Then you can all go home tonight and brag to your wives and kids about killing a helpless old man. You'll all be heroes."

Miller said nothing more. The guards dragged a groveling, pleading Shockley along the range, threw him halfway down the stairs, and shoved him through the big steel door into C Block. They locked the Treatment Unit behind them.

All three men were taken, naked, over to A Block, and down a flight of stairs to where the dungeon cells were located. The dungeons had not been used for eight years. Theoretically, their use had been abolished when the present D Block was constructed. The dungeon cells were pitch black, empty, with no water or sanitation facilities. A bucket substituted for a toilet. It was emptied once a week. One full meal was served every third day. Between those meals a con in the dungeon got two cups of water and one slice of bread daily. From 6:00 A.M. until 6:00 P.M. he was chained standing up to the wall. The other twelve hours he was given a blanket and allowed to rest on the concrete floor. He was completely naked at all times.

Now, for the first time since 1938, three dungeon cells were opened and their wall shackles unlocked. Into the darkness went Thompson, Crazy Sam, and the Indio Kid.

•

Outside the east utility corridor door, two officers turned on portable battle lanterns with large, bright beams. Other officers stood ready with riot guns. The door was slowly opened and the lights directed inside.

Bernie Coy's body was nearest the door. He was still, eyes open and staring, face beginning to bloat from the multiple wounds. Rigor mortis was setting in; one of the Kentucky outlaw's arms was bent at the elbow as if still holding a rifle.

The beam was thrown farther. Dutch Cretzer was found next. Rigor mortis, advancing on him also, had captured his face in an agonized, terrified expression.

The light went farther still. Marvin Hubbard was farthest back. His body was still warm, indicating that he had been dead but a short time. The rifle bullets had done considerable damage to the left side of his face. But, incredibly, his rimless, thick-lensed glasses had not been touched.

The bodies were dragged out of the now stinking corridor that was slimy with sewage waste and seawater used for the prison toilets. They were laid side by side on blankets and dragged over to the flats on the east end of A Block. Guards who volunteered for the job, with handkerchiefs tied around their noses and mouths, systematically stripped the bodies and placed the clothing in laundry bags brought up from the basement.

After the bodies were stripped, numerous guards who had seen the three men many times while they were alive, now came in curiously to see them in death.

•

Warden Johnston and Director Bennett walked around the south side of the cellhouse, along the steel catwalk under the D Block windows, and around to the entrance to the west gun gallery. They shook hands with all the officers who were manning both sections of the lower level, and chatted for several minutes with Bert Burch, who had been relieved the previous night but had voluntarily reported back to duty early that morning; and with Fred Mahan, the only one of Bergen's original assault team, besides Bergen himself, who had not been shot down in the recapturing of the gallery.

Lieutenant Bergen then led the two prison executives up the steep metal ladder to the top level and showed them the spread bars where Bernie Coy had dropped into the gallery. The bar spreader had been found in the gallery; Johnston and Bennett both examined it carefully.

"I'll be a son of a bitch," Johnston said quietly. He could not conceal the hint of admiration that crept into his voice. Bennett, when he spoke, did not even try.

"Incredible," the director said. "Absolutely ingenious."

The two men left the gallery and went back around to the front of the building. They went in through the sallyport and entered the cellhouse for another look at the bodies. Bennett looked at all of them in turn, but Johnston seemed to concentrate his attention on Coy. How many times over the past years had he seen that thin, homely, often sad-looking man pushing his blanket broom down the highly polished flats of Broadway or Seedy or Michigan Boulevard? How insignificant had he considered this quiet, almost meek Kentuckian next to the likes of Machine Gun Kelly, Alvin Karpis, Doc Barker, and all the other public enemies the bureau had sent him. Even after the hostages had been brought out, when Johnston had learned who was in on the break but before he had time to get any specific details from Sundstrom or Baker, he had marked Cretzer, not Coy, as the leader of the crashout. And now it turned out that it was Coy all along. Coy who planned it, Coy who accomplished the impossible feat of capturing the gun gallery, Coy who almost brought off what would have been the greatest prison break in history.

Johnston shook his head in wonder. Bernie Coy, a Kentucky hillbilly. Not even doing life, only twenty-five years. The last man on the Rock that Johnston would have believed could do what had been done to Alcatraz in the past three days.

Quiet, mild Bernie Coy. The still water that ran deep.

•

Late in the morning, word began to spread that it was all over.

People on the island found out about it first. Officers, a few at a time, were let off duty to hurry down to the personnel compound to assure their families that the danger was over and that they had come through it unharmed. Then they had to go right back up to the cellhouse to relieve other officers for a few minutes.

The Marines were relieved as soon as the prison personnel had secured the cellhouse. Most of them were glad to leave the island. They were fighting men, not jail guards, and almost unanimously they regarded the inmates as phony tough guys who would not have lasted a week at Parris Island boot camp. Most of them had been bored stiff with the Alcatraz duty, and like Vinegar Joe Stilwell and Frank Merrill, considered the entire operation a drawn-out farce that could have been wrapped up six to eight hours after it started.

The people on shore began to find out that it was over when first the Air Corps patrol plane returned to base, then the San Francisco police boat and Coast Guard cutters terminated their patrols. Word spread quickly through the city, almost on a person-to-person basis. People stopped strangers on the street to tell them it was all over. It was the second time in slightly more than a year that information was passed so rapidly and indiscriminately. The other time had been thirteen months earlier, when President Franklin Roosevelt died.

Warden Clint Duffy's contingent of San Quentin guards boarded the Alcatraz launch and were taken back to the mainland. The federal prison guards from Leavenworth, McNeil Island, and Englewood stayed on to help get the prison organized again. A massive cleanup and repair job lay ahead.

•

In D Block, the Treatment Unit cons waited patiently for the guards to return. They had come in earlier to remove Shockley, then left, locking the block behind them. An hour later a different group had come in, ordered all men into their cells, and racked all the cell doors closed. The convicts assumed that the locking of the cells was a preliminary to being fed and moved to dry cells. All three levels in D were flooded now from the broken water pipes. The main valve had finally been shut off, so no more water was seeping in, but that also meant no tap water in the sinks and no toilet water after one flushing. The men had been without drinking water for twelve hours, without food for nearly forty-eight. Toilets in the cells of men who had to use them more than once, including Birdman Stroud, were creating a collective stench that was slowly becoming unbearable.

"Hey, Bob," yelled Fleish from the flats, "when do you think they'll feed us?"

"Soon," Stroud replied. "Old Saltwater Johnston's a fair man. He must know by now that nobody left in here had anything to do with the break. And he knows we've been without food for two days. He'll have us fed soon."

"Christ, I hope so," said Fleish. "I'm starving."

"When they bring the steam carts in, I'll ask them to feed the gangsters first," Stroud said wryly.

"Very funny," Fleish replied humorlessly. He sat on his bunk and stuffed a wad of toilet paper into each nostril to cut down on the putrid stench. That goddamn Coy, he thought. He sure had caused a lot of trouble for the rest of them. Wait until he saw that hillbilly prick again; he'd tell him off but good.

Fleish, like the rest of the men in D, had no way of knowing that Coy's body, along with Hubbard's and Cretzer's, was now lying over at the east end of A Block.

CHAPTER THIRTY-FOUR

1:00 P.M.

Early that afternoon, a squad of FBI agents arrived on the island. Led by an inspector, they reported to Bennett and Johnston in the warden's office just as the long-distance call came through for Bennett from J. Edgar Hoover in Washington.

"Jim, have my men arrived yet?" Hoover asked.

"Your timing is perfect, as usual, Edgar," Bennett replied. "They just got here."

"I've talked to Frank Hennessey, the U.S. Attorney out there,"

Hoover said. "He tells me there are three survivors who were major participants in the break. He has orders from Clark to prosecute to the limit. My men need to start gathering evidence before it gets cold."

"We're still in the process of getting order reestablished, Edgar," the prisons director said reluctantly. "The place is a mess. Your men are just going to add to the confusion."

"The attorney general is especially concerned with this," Hoover emphasized. "You should be too, frankly. It doesn't look too good when a smalltime bank robber can take over the nation's toughest prison and hold it captive for three days."

"That's not exactly what happened, Edgar," the prisons director said patiently.

"That's what it *looks* like. And with two guards dead, you know the public is going to have to be appeased in some way. Stiff prosecution of the survivors could do the trick."

"All right, Edgar," Bennett said finally. He knew from experience that Hoover would not take no for an answer; the bulldog little FBI head would argue all day and all night unless Bennett let his agents on the island. "We'll cooperate with your people to the fullest extent possible under the circumstances."

"Very good, Jim. I appreciate that. If we turn up anything that is —well, not favorable as far as your prison people are concerned, rest assured I'll keep it confidential until you and I can chat about it."

"I don't think you'll find anything of that nature, Edgar," said Bennett, a trifle stiffly. "But I appreciate the thought."

When he got off the phone, Bennett summoned the agents from an outer office. "Can you give me some idea of what you require, Inspector?"

"Yes, sir. First of all, we'd like to secure any weapons the convicts used, for fingerprints and other physical evidence. Then we'd like a list of all convicts who were locked in the cellhouse during the time the guards were held hostage. If there's a small office where we could conveniently interrogate them one at a time, it would help. We'd like to have the clothes of the three dead convicts, too, and inspect the cells each one of them occupied when the break started. Also we'd want to talk to the men who celled near them and the men who worked with them, and take a look at the places where they worked. And, of course, we'll want to conduct lengthy interrogations of the three survivors."

"That's quite an order," Bennett said, glancing at Johnston. "But I think we can accommodate you on most of it, can't we, Warden?"

"Yes, I believe so," said Johnston. "There may be some problem with that last part: interrogating the three survivors. You can talk to them all you want, of course, but you'll have to do it underground. They're in dark cells down on the subterranean level. And that, by God, is where they are going to stay."

The FBI inspector exchanged glances with his men, much in the same way Stilwell and Merrill had. It was as if they were silently asking themselves if this man was real. Did his penological mentality actually believe that it was more important to keep the surviving perpetrators in a dark solitary confinement cell than to bring them out in the open for the purpose of getting evidence to put them on trial for what they had done? Maybe that was the Alcatraz idea of justice, the inspector thought, but it sure as hell wasn't the FBI way. One look at Johnston, however, told him that any argument right then would be futile. The warden's will would have to be circumvented in another way.

"We'll work it however you wish, sir," the inspector said deferentially.

•

In the San Francisco federal building, a press conference was being held by U.S. Attorney Frank J. Hennessy and his assistants, William C. Licking and Daniel C. Deasy.

"Mr. Hennessy," a reporter asked, "will the three survivors of the break be charged with murder in the deaths of the two guards?"

"We think so," the U.S. attorney replied. "The FBI is gathering evidence at the prison right now. That evidence will be presented to a federal grand jury with a request for indictments for the crimes of murder, conspiracy to commit murder, and conspiracy to break jail. If those indictments are granted, then this office will vigorously prosecute on those charges."

"Will you ask for the death penalty?"

"We could prosecute for first-degree murder. Under federal law, capital cases originating within a government prison must be tried under the statutes of the state in which that prison is located. In this instance, if the defendants are found guilty of murder in the first degree, and there is no jury recommendation for mercy, the death penalty would be automatic under California law."

"Where would they be executed?"

"In the gas chamber at San Quentin."

•

Back in the warden's office, Prisons Director James Bennett was working on a statement of his own to be released to the press. He had been dictating and rewording it for half an hour and now had it as he wanted it. "Read the whole thing back to me, please," he said to Johnston's secretary.

The secretary flipped back one page and cleared his throat. " 'There was not the least indication of negligence or carelessness or inefficiency in this affair. The felons found and took advantage of a weakness which not even the most experienced and able prison man could have anticipated. When the emergency broke, it was handled intelligently, courageously, and with great devotion to duty.' "

"How does that sound, Warden?" the director asked.

"It's an excellent statement, Mr. Director," Johnston replied. "The men will appreciate it as a statement of confidence from you. And of course I am personally grateful for that same confidence."

"All right," Bennett said to the secretary, "get that to the press right away."

"Yes, sir. Warden, regarding the press, we're being hounded by them every hour for permission to come onto the island. They keep reminding us on the phone that this is a public institution, supported by tax dollars, and that the public has a right to what they call first-hand reportage on the break. One editor said he was sick and tired of getting second-hand, watered-down press releases from the bureau. He said unless we started recognizing freedom of the press, that his paper was going to call for a congressional investigation of the entire prison system."

"To hell with them all," Johnston said. "This is Alcatraz, not some minimum-security reformatory. No reporters are going to come snooping around here."

"Yes, sir." The secretary left.

"Jim, I may have to overrule you on that business about the press," Bennett said when they were alone. "This is no ordinary prison disturbance that happens today and is forgotten about tomorrow. We've got five men dead, a dozen wounded, and three convicts that will probably be tried for murder. The whole country and a lot of the world has been watching this rock for three days. If we keep the press off the island, if we continue to operate Alcatraz like it was some big secret, I have a feeling the newspapers are going to crucify us. Nothing makes a goddamn newspaperman angrier than somebody who deliberately tries to keep him from getting a big story. Especially a story he thinks he's entitled to."

"Be that as it may," Johnston said stubbornly, "I won't have a lot of reporters wandering around my prison like tourists on Fisherman's Wharf."

"I wasn't thinking about anything like that," Bennett said easily, trying to placate the older man. "What I had in mind was a formal press tour."

"A tour?"

"Yes. With you as the guide, of course. I'd stay completely in the background. You could show a selected number of reporters and photographers where Coy got into the cage, where the officers were shot, the utility corridor where your men ended it, that sort of thing. We could outline the route ahead of time. The entire thing would be controlled by you."

"A tour," Johnston said, his interest obviously growing. "With me as the guide. Yes, that might be a very good approach." He got a pad of paper and opened his fountain pen. "What were those points of interest again?"

Late in the afternoon, the bodies of Coy, Hubbard, and Cretzer were wrapped in blankets and put onto canvas stretchers. Twine was used to bind the blankets around the heads of the dead men so that their faces would not be exposed during transfer to the San Francisco morgue.

The bodies were carried, each by two officers, to the Alcatraz dock and put aboard the prison launch. Because they would not fit anywhere else, they were laid on the bow of the vessel. The six stretcher-bearers accompanied the dead convicts on the twelve-minute boat ride to Dock Four at Fort Mason. There, with the help of several military policemen, the stretchers were transferred from the launch to a waiting ambulance and driven away.

Coy, Hubbard, and Cretzer were finally off the Rock.

CHAPTER THIRTY-FIVE

7:00 P.M.

At seven o'clock that night, Warden Johnston met with twelve reporters and photographers from San Francisco and Oakland newspapers and the national wire services. He briefed them in Admin.

"Gentlemen, first of all, let me tell you that aside from our physical damage, the situation here is now almost normal. Regular routine is being restored very rapidly. This has been a bitter experience for all of us. However, as Director Bennett pointed out in his statement earlier today, we are satisfied that there was nothing irregular, nothing we can criticize in the conduct of our personnel. The United States government is still in control of this island. The whole affair has only served to demonstrate that this is still a pretty tough place to get out of."

Following his comments and a few preliminary questions, the warden conducted the group through the deadlock and into the cellhouse. He took them down Broadway. As they walked along the wide main aisle, there were several loud taunts behind them.

"Hey, Scoop, make sure he tells you the whole story!"

"Tell 'em the whole truth, Saltwater!"

"Like hell he will!"

Johnston ignored the shouts. He led the reporters to Times Square and pointed out where the now dead Bill Miller had been jumped. Then he moved over to the west end of Michigan Boulevard and pointed up to where Coy had climbed and spread the bars. He then had an accompanying guard unwrap a canvas parcel and display the ingenious bar-spreading device that had been designed by Coy and manufactured right there in the prison.

When they were finished on Times Square and the photographers had taken as many pictures as they wanted, the warden took them around to Seedy Street. "These are the two execution cells," he said, pointing to 402 and 403. There was dried blood on the floor, walls, and mattresses of both cells. From some notes he had, Johnston read off the names of the officers who had been held captive in each cell. "All nine of them were shot down in cold blood," he emphasized.

That comment, heard by the convicts now back in their C Block cells, drew a rash of hoots and jeers.

"Sure, sure! Nine screws just stood there and let one con shoot 'em down one by one!"

"Bullshit, Saltwater!"

"Tell 'em another one, Warden!"

Johnston continued to ignore all the convict voices.

Next, the warden led his visitors up Seedy and around the corner to the east utility-corridor door. A guard on duty there opened the door and two battle lanterns were turned on to light the inside.

"There," Johnston said, "that's where the bastards died. In there, in the filth, in a dirty hole, like the rats they were."

From above him and around the corners of both Broadway and Seedy came a tumultuous roar of disapproval from the celled men who could hear his voice.

"Fuck you, Johnston!" one yelled.

"And fuck all your newspaper friends!"

"They were better men than you, you old cocksucker!"

"Why don't you tell them about the fucking dungeons and the chains and the way you starve some of us!" came one particularly emotional scream.

There was such pandemonium from the flats and the two upper tiers that Johnston's voice could no longer be heard. He gestured to his visitors and they followed him back through the sallyport to Admin.

The enraged convicts continued yelling for twenty minutes after they were gone.

•

In D Block, it was beginning to get cold. Night had fallen and the damp bay air was whistling in through the mortar and grenade holes in the windows and wall. There was now neither light in the block, nor water. Some of the prisoners in flooded cells had no place to lie down because their bunks were soaked and more than an inch of water stood on their cell floors. Their only alternative was to sit on the metal seat that folded out from the wall. The break had been over for more than twelve hours but they still had not been fed.

"Hey, Birdman!" somebody yelled from below. "I thought you said they'd feed us soon!"

"Yeah," shouted another con. "Didn't you say old Saltwater was a fair man?"

"I guess I was mistaken," Stroud answered. "We all make mistakes. You'll agree to that, won't you, boys?"

No one else yelled anything else derisive at the old convict.

Later that night, when it became obvious that they were going to be left in their wet cells all night, Stroud put his face to the bars and shouted to the guards in the gun gallery. "Hey, you up there! Officer whoever-you-are! Why don't you go ask the warden if he's ever heard of uremic poisoning!"

"Shut up, you senile old bastard!" a guard answered.

"Uremic poisoning is what a man gets when he can't piss the poisons out of his system," Stroud went on undaunted. "It's caused by lack of drinking water. The condition can be accelerated by lack of food and by exposure."

"If you're so goddamned smart, how come you're in here?" another guard yelled.

"I'm in here because I killed a son of a bitch just like you," Stroud told him. "Now you listen! We've had no food for sixty hours, no water for twenty-four! I warn you, the courts and the newspapers are going to hear of this!"

"Go play with your bird, Birdman!" was the reply. There was laughter from both tiers of the D Block gun cage.

•

Stanton Delaplane, a reporter for the *Chronicle,* made more of an effort to analyze the escape attempt than the other newsmen assigned to the story. After the warden's guided tour of the cellhouse, everyone knew how the break had begun, what had transpired during the incident, who had been killed, and all the rest. But Delaplane, more than anyone else, recognized the high level of human drama involved in the story and was able to inject that feeling into his coverage. Perhaps even more important, he was the only reporter whose instincts directed him to Bernie Coy when everyone else was touting Dutch Cretzer as the ringleader. Delaplane somehow *knew* that Coy, not Cretzer, had been the catalyst responsible for the episode. And he somehow sensed that it was Coy's inconspicuousness, his unimportance compared to major criminals like Cretzer, that made the whole thing possible.

Delaplane's remarkably accurate conclusions were aptly summed up in one passage of the story he wrote that night for the Sunday editions. He said:

Every guard goes into the lion cage knowing that convict eyes appraise every move. Watching and waiting. Just when things look safe, along comes a tractable con like Coy to tear the place apart.

No words could have better described the entire affair.

PART FOUR

SUNDAY, MAY 5, 1946
TO
FRIDAY, DECEMBER 3, 1948

CHAPTER THIRTY-SIX

SUNDAY, MAY 5, 1946

Early Sunday morning, in the autopsy room of the San Francisco morgue, Dr. George Kerhulas, in surgical gown and mask, stood over the body of Bernie Coy and with rubber-gloved hands probed the brain for bullet fragments. He found several and selected the largest one.

"We'll call this one the cause of death," he said to Chester Goodwin, the morgue attendant. He dropped the fragment into a small porcelain pan. "The way he's shot up, nearly any of the bullets could have done it. But let's keep it simple. Dead's dead. Call it this one." He removed specimens of Coy's brain to be examined by a pathologist and a toxicologist.

Dr. Kerhulas turned to the next table. On it lay Dutch Cretzer. The doctor studied the dead man for a moment. "Not a bad-looking fellow," he said. "Interesting face. Intelligent-looking. Ah, well." He began probing in a hole that coursed behind the left eye and dug out a rifle slug. Again, he also removed specimens of the dead man's brain.

As Goodwin wheeled Coy into an anteroom, Deputy Coroner Harold Honore entered the autopsy room. "Morning, Doc," he said.

"Good morning, Harold," said Kerhulas.

"How goes it?"

"Two down, one to go," said Kerhulas. "They're all multiples, so I'm just picking one at random."

Honore shrugged. "Dead's dead," he said. Kerhulas stared at him.

"Amazing."

"What is?"

"I just used that exact same phrase to Chester not five minutes ago."

As if his name had been a cue, Chester Goodwin wheeled in the body of Marv Hubbard. The doctor turned to the new arrival, and Goodwin, as he had done with Coy, put a spotless white sheet over Dutch Cretzer and rolled him out. As Kerhulas worked on Hubbard, the deputy coroner said, "You know, Doc, it's too bad all the young punks in town can't be brought in here to see how guys like this finally end up. Might keep some of them from growing up bad."

"I doubt it," said Kerhulas. "A certain number of kids are just naturally going to turn out bad and there's not a damn thing anybody can do to prevent it. It's just human nature, Harold." He extracted a flattened piece of slug from Hubbard's left temple. "Okay, that's it." He quickly took two brain specimens.

"We're taking some pictures in the anteroom, Doc. Want to get in any of them?"

"No, thanks," said Kerhulas. "I never pose with corpses."

In the anteroom, the three wheeled tables were put side by side and their brakes set. The heads of the tables were cranked up, like hospital beds, raising the three corpses. Because rigor mortis had now markedly decreased, the bodies were no longer rigid. Twice Coy almost rolled off the table. Finally he was wheeled in between the other two and propped up more steadily. The crisp white sheets were tucked in snugly so that only the heads and feet of the dead men showed. Each had tags on both of his big toes with his name on them.

When they were ready, Harold Honore ushered in some city government officials and let them have their pictures taken with the three dead men. While the photographing was going on, Coy started to slip sideways again. Chester Goodwin moved to straighten him, but then the body stopped slipping. The morgue attendant left him that way, tilted slightly to his left.

Cretzer was on Coy's right. Even in death, the Kentucky bank robber leaned away from the former public enemy.

•

One of the people who read the official version of the break attempt that Sunday was Congressman George P. Miller (no relation to deceased officer Bill Miller or Associate Warden Ed Miller). Representing California's Sixth Congressional District, which embraced

Alameda and Contra Costa counties, Miller contacted the press immediately after reading the papers to say that he was of the opinion that some kind of coverup was being employed and that the true story of the escape attempt and its cause had not been disclosed.

"Upon my return to Washington," the congressman pledged, "I will ask the Department of Justice to undertake a full investigation of the matter. If results in that quarter are not satisfactory, I will call upon Congress, by resolution, to dig to the bottom of the whole affair."

As far as can be determined, the publication of that statement was the whole extent of Congressman Miller's interest in the case. He was not heard from again.

●

At the First Baptist Church of San Francisco, a Youth for Christ Rally was being held. The main speaker was the Reverend Winston T. Nunes, a chaplain at Carrera Prison, the British penal colony off the coast of Trinidad.

Chaplain Nunes, in his sermon that day, told the congregation that in his opinion, the escape attempt at Alcatraz had been caused by a lack of religious belief among the convicts. Prisoners who had not accepted Christ as their savior were not contented prisoners, he explained. What was needed on Alcatraz, he said, was a return among the inmates to the gospel of Jesus. That would solve everything.

Following the chaplain's sermon, a group of young Baptists, the Melody Girls, sang for the congregation.

●

Over at the prison, there was little thought of religion *or* young girls in D Block. More than twenty-four hours had passed since the escape attempt had been quashed, and still the D Block lockups had been given no food or water. They remained locked in their flooded cells.

Stroud by then was on the verge of collapse. His tired old body was weak from hunger and thirst, and his voice had shrunk to a whisper from yelling at the gun-gallery guards intermittently during the night. Only his blood pressure remained strong, due to the outrage and fury he felt at the unwarranted treatment being imposed on him and the other D Block cons.

While Stroud was quiet, however, many younger, stronger prisoners were not. From all three levels came constant obscenities directed toward the guards in the cage, especially from those men whose cellfronts permitted them an occasional glimpse of an officer drinking coffee or smoking a cigarette.

"I hope you choke on that, you fucking queer!"

"Hey, stupid! The screw that you relieved said he was going to fuck your wife while you were on duty!"

"You'll get yours, you cocksucker! I've got a friend in Frisco who'll poison your groceries!"

By noon Sunday, the block was growing quieter and quieter as the seventy-two hours without food and thirty-six without water began to take their toll. On the flats, in Cell D-1, Louis Fleish was beginning to worry about Stroud. "Bob!" he called up to the top tier. "How you doing?"

Stroud's voice, when he answered, was very weak, barely discernible. "I'll make it. The pricks won't get me this way."

"Hey, you in the gun cage!" Fleish yelled. "You'd better do something about Stroud! I think he's dying!"

"Let us know when he's finished," a guard answered. "We'll bury him."

"You dirty son of a bitch!" Fleish yelled back. Half a dozen other men joined him in cursing the unknown officer.

Finally, at four in the afternoon, thirty hours after the cellhouse had been secured, a contingent of guards came into the block and lined up on the flats facing the cells. "All right, you monkeys, we're taking you out of here!" the officer in charge told them. "When your cell doors are opened, strip down to your bare asses and drop your clothes on the range. Then come down here and line up at the door!"

Guards with clubs climbed to the two upper tiers to supervise the stripping. One of them saw that Stroud was having a difficult time of it. He put down his club and helped the old convict get out of his clothes. Then he found a dry blanket in one of the unoccupied cells and draped it around the Birdman's frail shoulders.

As they got ready to leave the cell, the guard stuck a cigarette between Stroud's lips and lighted it for him. After his first dizzying drag, the old man nodded his thanks. "I never thought the day would come when I'd be happy to see a hack," he said hoarsely.

"A lot of you guys are probably glad to see us," the officer said. "Some of us would have been in here a lot sooner if it had been up to us."

The guard helped Stroud down the two flights of stairs to the flats.

There the cons lined up and were taken to temporary cells in A Block.

•

Across the water at Marine Hospital, the day-shift nurses were getting ready to go off duty. One of them had just typed a new critical list to be posted at the main nursing station of the intensive-care unit.

The names of Captain Henry Weinhold, Lieutenant Joseph Simpson, and Officer Cecil Corwin were still on the list.

The three men shot with a .45 at close range by Dutch Cretzer were not improving, but they still clung tenaciously to life. By now the trio was the main topic of conversation around the hospital. The doctors were unanimously amazed. The Alcatraz guards simply *refused* to die.

All over the hospital, people whom the three officers did not know, and would never know, were secretly saying prayers for them.

CHAPTER THIRTY-SEVEN

MONDAY, MAY 6, 1946

On Monday morning following the escape attempt the seven-o'clock mass at St. Brigid's Catholic church was dedicated to Bill Miller. The mass was celebrated by Monsignor James Cantwell, who had been the Miller family's parish priest ever since Bill Miller had transferred to Alcatraz from the federal prison at Lewisburg, Pennsylvania.

The mass was more of a memorial service than anything, since Miller's body was not brought to the church. Some of his fellow guards attended, but not many; the hour was early, not much notice had been given, and many of the officers were temporarily assigned extra duties at the prison. The lack of mourners did not disturb Miller's widow, Josephine. The service in San Francisco was merely a token one; Bill's real funeral would be conducted when they got back home to Pennsylvania. Besides, as long as the children were there, that was what mattered. They sat on either side of her: Joan Marie, fourteen, on her left; Billy, ten, on her right. During the mass, they comforted her as much as she comforted them. Perhaps even more.

When the services were over, Monsignor Cantwell rode with Josephine and the children to the Halstead and Company funeral home. There the monsignor blessed the mortal remains of Bill Miller. Later, his casket was closed and taken to the depot, where it was put on a train for the east. His widow and two children rode the train with him.

Because her husband had been killed in the performance of his duty, Josephine Miller would now begin to receive $61.50 per month for the rest of her life. In addition, until they were eighteen, she would get $17.50 per month for each child.

The United States Bureau of Prisons bought men cheap.

•

In his office on Monday afternoon, Warden Johnston received a telegram that had been delivered to the pilot of the prison launch. Johnston opened it, read it, grunted softly, and handed it back to his secretary.

"Send this over to the morgue in San Francisco."

The telegram went back to the pilot of the launch, who was left with the task of finding some way to get it from the dock, which is as far as he went, to the morgue. Finally, late in the day, an officer leaving the island for the night agreed to drop off the telegram at the morgue on his way home.

Morgue attendant Chester Goodwin was on duty when the Alcatraz officer arrived. He was busy at the time—two bodies had just come in from an automobile accident in North Beach—so he merely thanked the officer and laid the envelope on the desk. As the officer was leaving, a draft came through the front door and blew the telegram onto the floor.

Another morgue attendant came on duty later that evening, relieving Chester Goodwin, who by then had forgotten all about the telegram. Fortunately, the relief attendant accidentally found it a few hours later. He opened the envelope and read the message. It was a request from a Gadsden, Alabama, undertaking parlor authorizing the remains of Marvin Franklin Hubbard to be shipped to them C.O.D. as soon as possible upon formal release of the body.

Hubbard's body was sent to the Julius S. Godeau funeral home for preparation. Later, in a travel coffin, it was put aboard an eastbound train.

Marv Hubbard was finally going home to Tola and their little girl.

CHAPTER THIRTY-EIGHT

TUESDAY, MAY 7, 1946

In Washington, D.C., another California politician decided to make a statement on the Alcatraz incident. He was Congressman J. Leroy Johnston (no relation to Warden Johnston). The congressman, representing the Stockton congressional district, proposed that legislation be drafted making the death penalty mandatory for any federal prisoner participating in a jailbreak. The congressman was questioned as to whether he really meant jailbreaks in which guard or other deaths occurred. This apparently was not what he had in mind. He meant *all* breaks, regardless of whether anyone was killed or even injured. A Washington reporter who had done his homework on Alcatraz pointed out to the congressman that if such a law had been in effect for the past decade, the United States government would have had to execute 16 men at Alcatraz alone, not to mention Atlanta, Leavenworth, McNeil Island, and Lewisburg.

Congressman Johnston was not impressed by the figures. He still proposed the death penalty for *all* participants in *all* federal prison breaks.

Such ludicrous legislation was never passed, of course. And there has always been a gnawing suspicion in the minds of some that the two Johnstons *might* have been distantly related.

●

Services for Hal Stites were somewhat more ceremonious than they had been for Bill Miller. Stites was to be buried locally, so his widow and children were not rushed to catch a train. The services were held a day later, so the Rock itself was a little more organized and officers could be excused from duty to attend. And, too, Hal Stites had been on the island for a number of years and was the hero of the Franklin-Lucas-Limerick break eight years earlier.

The funeral was held at Maneely Chapel at one o'clock in the afternoon. It was a full Masonic service. Director Bennett and Warden Johnston sat in the front pew. In the family section was Bessie Stites, the widow; a grown daughter, Thelma Elson; and three sons: James, seventeen; Robert, fourteen; and Herbert, nine.

Following the chapel services, a funeral procession drove to Golden Gate Cemetery where a short service was conducted at graveside prior to burial.

•

Like Josephine Miller, Bessie Stites would now receive from the government a death pension of $61.50 per month for herself and $17.50 per month for each child under eighteen. That, in effect, was all she would get. The Bureau of Prisons had no provision to even pay for the funerals of guards killed in the line of duty, so that cost had to be borne by the two widows. Fellow officers across the country knew that, of course, and it was easy for them to project themselves and their families into the predicaments of the Miller and Stites families. So a collection was started.

Money came in from the big pens: Atlanta, Leavenworth, and the others. It came in from the reformatories at El Reno and Alderson. From the medical center in Springfield, Missouri. From federal prison camps in Florida, Alabama, and Arizona. From correctional centers at La Tuna, Texas; Lompoc, California; Milan, Michigan; Seagoville, Texas; and others. Even from federal juvenile homes in Kentucky, Colorado, and West Virginia.

In all, nearly $7,000 was collected and divided between the two widows. If the bureau bought men cheaply, its officers did not.

•

At the Marine Hospital, there was finally a note of good news. Lieutenant Joseph Simpson was removed from the critical list. There was still no guarantee that he was going to live, but his condition had improved enough, at least temporarily, to make the doctors' prognosis a little more hopeful.

There was still no change in the condition of Captain Weinhold or Cecil Corwin. They did not improve, but they would not die.

CHAPTER THIRTY-NINE
FRIDAY, MAY 10, 1946

At the San Francisco morgue, an Oakland attorney presented a letter to the deputy coroner requesting delivery of the remains of Joseph Cretzer to a local crematorium. Attached to the letter was a notarized statement from Cretzer's ex-wife, Eddie, now the wife of a San Francisco truckdriver. The statement declared that at the time of their divorce, Cretzer had made a verbal request of her, through their lawyer, to take possession of his body if he died while still on Alcatraz. She had promised to do so. The attorney attested to Cretzer's request.

After due consideration by the coroner's officer and approval by the San Francisco city attorney, the request was complied with, and Cretzer's body was picked up by a crematorium hearse.

The mortal remains of Joseph Paul Cretzer were later cremated and his ashes placed in a small vault at Cypress Lawn Memorial Park. In attendance at the brief ceremony were his former wife and his attorney. No one else. No reporters attended and no headlines told of the former public enemy's final departure.

•

In the federal building, Assistant U.S. Attorney Daniel C. Deasy presented to a federal grand jury the evidence in the government's case against the surviving Alcatraz escape plotters. That evidence was impressive and its presentation thorough. Most of the facts had been compiled by the efficient FBI agents who had arrived on the island just hours after the escape attempt had been stopped.

The FBI had finally been allowed to interrogate Buddy Thompson, Sam Shockley, and Danny Durando someplace other than the dungeons. This had been accomplished by explaining to Warden Johnston that the agents conducting the investigation would be subject to cross-examination by the defense when they testified at the subsequent trial. They pointed out that such cross-examination could only benefit the defense if the agents had to admit that at the time of interrogation the defendants had been chained naked to the wall of a subterranean dungeon, and had only been fed one full meal in the four days they had been kept there.

Johnston, although still reluctant to release the three men from the dungeons, had nevertheless regained his normal mild composure enough to compromise. He had the trio brought up to D Block, which was unoccupied except for Whitey Franklin in Cell 14, and put into Cells 9, 10, and 11, all solid-door dark cells. Before being interviewed, each of them was fed, allowed to shower, and given fresh clothes. The FBI interviews were conducted with the agents standing in the access area of each cell, between the solid outer door and the inner barred door.

None of the interrogations was particularly helpful to the government. Buddy Thompson denied being a part of the escape plan and claimed he had never left his cell. Sam Shockley stated that he was mentally unbalanced, suffered from long periods of amnesia, and did not even remember the break. Dan Durando simply refused to talk. No matter what question was asked of him, even what his name was, the Indio Kid maintained a stonefaced silence. He did not speak a single word to the agents.

Cooperation from the three accused men was not expected or required, however. Five of the nine hostage guards were able to testify as to exactly who was in on the break, and who did what from the time it began until the horrible moment that Dutch Cretzer began shooting into Cells 402 and 403. The evidence was clear and irrefutable.

At the end of the taking of evidence, the federal grand jury returned indictments of first degree murder, conspiracy to commit murder, and conspiracy to break jail, against all three.

CHAPTER FORTY

WEDNESDAY, MAY 15, 1946

An unidentified federal agent arrived at the San Francisco county morgue shortly after the business office opened and presented a U.S. government authorization to have Bernie Coy buried.

"We were under the impression that his body was to be held for thirty days, in case someone wanted to claim it," a coroner's representative said. "It's only been eleven days."

"The government has decided to go ahead and bury him," the agent said. "There's no problem with jurisdiction, is there?"

"No problem at all," the coroner's representative said. "The body's yours anytime you want it. It's just that it's customary to wait thirty days—"

"We'd like to do it today."

"Whatever you say. We'll send the remains over to Godeau's Funeral Home. They'll bill the government for preparation and burial. But you'll have to go over there and sign some forms for them."

"Okay. And your office will file the death certificate today, right?"

"Correct."

"Okay. Where's Godeau's Funeral Home?"

"Forty-one Van Ness Avenue."

The agent thanked him and left.

Later that morning, the body of Bernie Coy was removed to the Julius S. Godeau Funeral Home. At the time the body was accepted, a Godeau funeral director and an embalmer signed the death-certificate form, to be taken back to the coroner's office. Coy was then wheeled into a refrigerated room to be held until someone arrived to sign burial forms. By the end of the day, no such person had arrived. Bernie Coy was held overnight.

In the meantime, the death certificate was filed in the Vital Statistics section of the San Francisco Department of Public Health, indicating that Bernard Paul Coy was now buried. The date of burial was not entered, but the date stamped on the certificate was May 15, 1946.

Anyone inquiring about the body of Bernie Coy after that date would have been told he was already in the ground.

CHAPTER FORTY-ONE
SATURDAY, MAY 18, 1946

After Wednesday, Thursday, and most of Friday had passed, the people at Godeau's Funeral Home began to grow concerned. Their representatives had signed the undated burial section of Bernie Coy's death certificate, and, after checking back with the coroner's office, they had learned that the certificate had been filed on Wednesday. But by late Friday, the body of Coy was still in their refrigerator room, still not even embalmed. It was the custom at most San Francisco funeral homes to sign the blank burial section of the death certificate for the coroner's office, and later phone them the facts of the burial to be filled in on the form. But burial usually took place within a day, and the certificate was never filed until it had. In the case of Coy, he had officially been buried two days earlier.

Godeau's began to worry. They contacted the coroner's office and insisted that the matter be straightened out at once. The coroner's office called the prison. They were referred to the San Francisco office of the Department of Justice, under which the Bureau of Prisons operated. After a great deal of insistence, the Department of Justice finally agreed to attend to the necessary burial forms. Apparently all they had been concerned with was getting Coy in the ground *on paper,* in case anyone inquired about him. Now they finally took care of the formalities to have him actually buried.

Because it had been too late Friday to proceed with the burial, Bernie Coy remained in the refrigerated room for a third night. Godeau's agreed to bury him on Saturday. The coroner's office, on Friday, had the Bureau of Vital Statistics put Saturday's date, May 18, in the burial section of the death certificate. The Department of Public Health then had a registered death certificate, dated May 15, attesting to the burial of a corpse on May 18.

•

Finally, on Saturday morning, the body of Bernie Coy was removed from the refrigerated room and taken to the mortuary room. There it was tubed and drained of all remaining blood. A mixture of embalming fluid was injected into his veins. When the remains had been prepared, a long sack of gray-black cotton was slipped over the body from the feet up. It was pulled up to the neck and buttoned there. The morgue tags on Coy's big toes were left attached. The body was then lifted into a plain wooden coffin and the lid nailed shut at the four corners.

Two morgue attendants put the rope-handled box into a plain black panel truck and drove it out to the potter's-field section of Woodlawn Cemetery. At the caretaker's office, they presented a duly authorized burial-permission certificate from the federal government. The caretaker logged the name of the dead man in his burial book and inserted a grave number after it. When he came to the classification column of the book, he asked, "Pauper, unknown person, or criminal?"

"Jesus Christ, pop, don't you read the newspapers?" one of the attendants asked, taking a toothpick out of his mouth. "This here is Coy. From Alcatraz!"

"Oh, yeah," said the caretaker. He entered "criminal" in the book.

The panel truck was driven far back into the cemetery where an open grave and two Negro gravediggers waited. The two morgue attendants helped them lower the wooden coffin into the hole.

"Okay, boys, he's all yours," one attendant said. He tossed his toothpick into the hole, onto the coffin.

After the morgue truck left, the two husky blacks went to work filling the grave. The two men did not talk, because one of them was a deaf mute and could not. So the other usually passed the time humming or singing softly to himself. On this particular day he sang "Rock of Ages." It was a religious song he had learned as a boy back in Kentucky during the hard times of the great Depression.

Bernie Coy, if he could have heard it, would have recognized the tune at once.

CHAPTER FORTY-TWO

MONDAY, JUNE 24, 1946

In D Block, a guard opened the outside doors of the three dark cells where Thompson, Shockley, and Durando were being held, and handed each man a hanger with a new suit, shirt, and necktie on it. He also passed a new pair of shoes through the bars for each one of them.

It was 6:00 A.M. They had been awakened at five and taken one by one down to the end of the flats to the shower cell to clean up and shave. Now they were told to get dressed. After they dressed, they would be given a tray of breakfast which they had to eat either standing up or squatting down, because there were no fold-down tables in the dark cells. All three of them were tense and nervous. This was the day they were to be taken over to San Francisco to federal court and formally arraigned for murder.

"These must be the suits they plan to bury us in," Buddy Thompson yelled to the others as he put on the gray-black trousers and vest. "Christ, we're going to look like undertakers."

"It don't look too bad to me," Danny Durando answered. "Feels pretty good after prison duds."

"What do you know about clothes, anyway?" Thompson said. "They should have given you a serape and a sombrero."

"Fuck you, gringo," said the Kid.

"Better watch your spik mouth, Pedro," Thompson warned. "I'll bust your ass when we get out of these holes."

"I hope you try, punk," the Kid said quietly.

From the third cell down came a plaintive cry. "Son of a bitch!" Crazy Sam said in frustration. "I don't remember how to tie this tie."

"Take it easy, Sam," Durando said gently. "Somebody will do it for you." The Kid's attitude toward Shockley had softened considerably during the seven weeks since the break attempt. Durando was now convinced that Sam was actually crazy, in the literal sense of the word. "He don't belong in here," the Kid had said several times to Thompson. "He belongs in a hospital or someplace where they can help him."

"He belongs in a fucking padded cell," the Texan had replied each time. Durando had dropped the subject. It was useless trying to talk to Thompson. He never had a good word to say about anything.

At seven o'clock, the prison launch arrived with a contingent of federal marshals aboard. The three prisoners were taken from their cells and marched into C Block. It was the first time they had been in the main section of the cellhouse since the morning they were brought up from the dungeons, cold, hungry, and naked. Now, as they came onto the flats of Times Square, the first thing they noticed was that a thick metal grille had been put over the entire west gun gallery, extending from the bottom of the lower tier all the way across the curved bars on top. In addition, thick, flat, steel cross-bars had been welded on to reinforce the weak curved bars that Bernie Coy had managed to spread.

"Jesus," Durando whispered. "Nobody'll ever take the gun cage again, that's for sure."

He was right. Nobody ever did.

As the trio was led up Seedy Street, both Thompson and Durando glanced self-consciously into Cells 402 and 403. Shockley, dull-eyed and expressionless, just looked straight ahead. Some of the lock-up cons in C Block saw them being led out and began whistling and cheering. Thompson alone waved to a few of them.

In the deadlock, they were met by the federal marshal. Each man was given a hat and had his wrists cuffed. Then a marshal started to chain them all together.

"Better keep these two separated," said an Alcatraz officer who had overheard Thompson and Durando threatening to fight.

Shockley was put between them and a chain was run through and looped around each set of handcuffs.

"What about my tie?" Shockley pouted. "Somebody's got to tie my tie."

"I'll do it for you, Sam," a guard said. "If you'll let me tie it as tight as I want to."

"Here, I'll do it," said one of the marshals.

They all went down to the dock, where the launch was waiting for them. During the short trip across the water, all three convicts were transfixed by the sight of San Francisco getting closer and closer. At the dock they were hurried into a waiting police wagon and the doors were quickly closed. When they arrived at the federal courthouse, again they were moved briskly along so that they would not be out in public any longer than absolutely necessary. Even so, they all had chances for brief glimpses of the outside world: the new cars, the new clothes styles, most of all the women. For Thompson and Durando, it was a treat to be out on the streets again, even briefly; but for Crazy Sam it was like an incredible dream come true. Thompson had been on Alcatraz only eight months, the Kid a little over a year. But Shockley had been there since September, 1938, nearly eight years. To him, the postwar world of 1946 was something almost futuristic. He stared open-mouthed at the women. He was thirty-six years old and had not seen a woman since he was twenty-eight.

Upstairs in the waiting room, the restraining chain was removed. When the case was called, the three handcuffed prisoners were led before a federal judge and formally charged with first-degree murder and conspiracy to commit murder, both in the death of William H. Miller. They were not charged in the death of Hal Stites.

Each defendant was handed a copy of the indictment against him. The court appointed a free attorney to defend each of them. Trial was set for November 20, nearly five months away.

Each carrying the single-page indictment, the three were led back into the waiting room and chained together again. Apparently the federal marshals had forgotten the Alcatraz guard's admonition about keeping Thompson and Durando apart; the Kid was chained in the middle this time, with Shockley on his left, Thompson on his right. Even so, there was no difficulty taking them back to the prison.

Facing death in the gas chamber, Buddy Thompson and Dan Durando figured they had enough trouble already without looking for more.

•

At the Marine Hospital, Captain Henry Weinhold and Officer Cecil Corwin were at last taken off the critical list. Lieutenant Joseph Simpson, who had been off the list for seventeen days, continued to improve. It was now considered a certainty by the doctors that all three would, to some degree, recover from their wounds.

Medically, that would prove true. Practically speaking, it would not. None of the men would ever completely get over his wounds.

Captain Henry Weinhold, later that year, would be classified as permanently disabled. He would never work as a keeper of men again.

Lieutenant Joseph Simpson, after three months and three days, would be released from the Marine Hospital but indefinitely continue on the out-patient roster with his condition listed as guarded. He would return to Alcatraz to recuperate under the watchful eye of his wife Marian. Back on the island that they both loved, back among the flowers of the compound, back to his dog Honey and his cameras, back among the island children who idolized him, Joe Simpson would gradually regain his strength, stature, and military bearing.

On May 14, 1947, a little more than a year after he had been shot, Simpson would be reinstated to active status. He would be assigned as a Custodial Instructor at Leavenworth Prison in Kansas, where he had begun his prison service fifteen years earlier. Although he would be able to perform training duties competently, Simpson was to endure chronic discomfort from the two bullets Dutch Cretzer had fired into him. With his ribs resectioned and one lung gone, even normal breathing was to take its toll on the former military officer over the years. Six years later, at the age of sixty-one, he would retire from the prison service.

For Officer Cecil Corwin, the years that were to follow would be both painful and rewarding. The single bullet that hit Corwin entered his face just below the left eye and came out on the right side of his lower jaw. Literally going all the way through his head, it broke his jaw, destroyed a dental bridge, knocked out a wisdom tooth, and finally lodged in the shoulder padding of his coat.

Although he lost most of the sight in his left eye, Corwin's face, incredibly, did not require any plastic surgery at all. It healed naturally and normally, and after a while he looked almost as good as he previously had. Three months after the shooting, he would return to Alcatraz and be assigned as office manager of Prison Industries. His chief clerk there, a man for whom he was to develop a genuine fondness, would be Machine Gun Kelly.

Unfortunately, Corwin's health would soon begin to deteriorate. Three months after his return to work, he would have to spend eight days back in the hospital for a septectomy: the removal of tissue masses building up in his wound. A month after that, he would faint in public and be rushed to the hospital again. This time he would be kept two weeks and ordered to rest at home for a week. Over the next year, he would experience frequent headaches, episodes of momentary dizziness, nervousness, and chest pains. Finally, on May 25, 1948, two years after the shooting, Corwin would undergo a thorough physical examination by Dr. Walter C. Clowers, senior surgeon at the Marine Hospital. Dr. Clowers would diagnose him as unfit for further prison bureau service and recommend his disability retirement.

Cecil and Catheryn Corwin would move to Stockton, California. Unable to accept the inactivity of retirement, Corwin would begin studying psychiatry. He would learn enough to pass the California state examination for psychiatric technician. He and Catheryn would subsequently move to Pomona, California, where Corwin would be employed by the Pacific State Hospital.

In his new field of endeavor, Cecil Corwin would again become engrossed in helping a less fortunate segment of society. As he had done on Alcatraz, he would attempt not merely to perform what his duties called for, but to find other ways in which he could impart something extra to those in his care. Above all else, Cecil Corwin would continue to be a man who would feel an acute need to contribute.

CHAPTER FORTY-THREE

TUESDAY, OCTOBER 12, 1946

Shortly after the noon meal, the D Block guard racked open Cell 41 and shouted, "Okay, Stroud, come on down. The warden has granted your request for an interview."

The old convict removed his green celluloid eyeshade and put on his seldom-worn prison cap. As he walked along the range, the other D Block prisoners began to boo and taunt him and make loud sucking noises. They all knew that the Birdman was as loyal a supporter of the convict code as any man who ever lived, but they could not resist this opportunity to chide him for asking to see Johnston.

"No more secrets in D Block," one of them yelled. "The Birdman's turning canary!"

"That's right," Stroud said loudly. "I'm going to tell the warden about the filthy things you men do to yourselves after the lights go out. It's disgusting."

"Hey, Mr. Stroud," said a big Negro con who, like many, always respectfully called Stroud "mister," "the onliest reason you think it's filthy is 'cause you's too old to enjoy it anymore!"

The D Block cons laughed, Stroud along with them. "I think maybe that's an accurate analysis," he said.

An officer met Stroud at the D Block door and escorted him down Seedy Street toward the sallyport. Curious lock-up cons in C Block stood at their cell doors and stared at this living legend who had been in prison before many of them were born. This was only the second time since his arrival that Stroud had been in the main section of the cellhouse. The first had been when he and the others were temporarily quartered in A Block while the Treatment Unit was being repaired and cleaned up.

In the deadlock, the door officer asked, "Do you have anything in your pockets?"

"Just guns and knives," Stroud said dryly.

The door officer clenched his jaw slightly but passed the old man without a search. Stroud was taken through Admin and into the warden's office.

"Well, Stroud," said Johnston, "this is a first for both of us. I don't usually see prisoners in my office, and you don't usually get to take this kind of walk."

"I appreciate the courtesy, Mr. Johnston." He stood uneasily before the warden's desk. Johnston did not offer to let him sit down.

"You said it was important, Stroud. What is it?"

"In the matter of my correspondence, you've been more than fair to me, Warden. Even though my transfer here from Leavenworth, taking me away from my birds and my laboratory, was nothing but vindictiveness on the part of Director Bennett and the others at the bureau, you have been very kind in allowing me to continue to subscribe to bird journals and to correspond with bird owners and breeders. You have even extended that privilege to include my publisher so that I can conduct personal business affairs."

"I am aware of the privileges I have given you, Stroud. Please get to the point."

"I wanted to tell you something personally rather than have the mail censor bring it to your attention. The trial of Thompson, Shockley, and Durando starts in five weeks. I intend to write my publisher and have him direct two hundred dollars of my royalties toward Shockley's defense."

Johnston frowned. "But why? The court has appointed attorneys for all of them."

"The money is to be used for an independent psychiatric examination. I want to help them prove that Sam is mentally deranged and should not be executed."

"I see." Johnston drummed his fingers on the desk. "Why just Shockley? Why not Thompson and Durando too?"

"Sam's the only one who's crazy," Stroud replied. "Anyway, things will work out right for the other two. The Kid doesn't deserve the gas chamber and I personally don't think he'll get it. Thompson does deserve it and probably will get it."

The seventy-year-old warden, who had spent thirty-five years as a penologist, stared thoughtfully at the nearly sixty-year-old inmate who had spent more than forty years as a prisoner.

"All right, Stroud," Johnston said at last. "I commend you for having the integrity to tell me about this yourself. It won't affect your special correspondence privileges."

"Thank you, Mr. Johnston. I sincerely appreciate it."

When Stroud got to the open door where the escort guard waited, the warden said, "Stroud," and the convict turned back.

"Yes, sir?"

"You're wasting the two hundred dollars. Shockley's going to the gas chamber for what he did."

Johnston nodded to the escort guard and he took Stroud away.

•

Across the water at the Presidio that day, General Joseph Stilwell died quietly at the age of sixty-three.

The official cause of death was listed as heart failure. Many of his fellow officers believed that the old war horse simply died of boredom.

The battle of Alcatraz was his last involvement in an armed skirmish of any kind. It was a poor conclusion to a magnificent career.

CHAPTER FORTY-FOUR

WEDNESDAY, NOVEMBER 20, 1946

The case of the United States versus Miran Edgar Thompson, Samuel Richard Shockley, and Daniel Durando began at 9:00 A.M. The charge was conspiracy to commit murder on the person of William H. Miller.

The selection of the jury took three days. Chosen were an architect, the president of an export firm, a civil-service clerk, an engineer, the vice president of a sugar company, a retired clothing salesman, and six San Francisco housewives.

The government's case was simple. The three defendants had been part of a concerted effort by six inmates to unlawfully escape from Alcatraz federal penitentiary. They had all known about the escape plan and agreed to participate in it prior to the time the break actually began.

During the escape attempt, nine prison officers had been captured and held hostage by the escape gang of which the three defendants were members. During the time the officers were held hostage, two of the defendants, Thompson and Shockley, openly encouraged another member of the escape gang to murder the nine hostages. As a result of that urging, the other member did in fact fire numerous pistol shots at the hostage officers in an attempt to murder them. As a direct result of said shooting, Officer William H. Miller suffered a gunshot wound and did thereafter die.

The evidence was virtually indisputable. The urging by Thompson and Shockley was witnessed by Officers Lageson, Bristow, Burdette, Baker, and Sundstrom, two of whom had been wounded in the subsequent shooting and three of whom had been missed completely. Medical testimony left no doubt that the gunshot wound suffered by Miller put him in such a reduced state of strength that he was unable to recover from the trauma, lapsed into shock, and died.

The defense tried in every way imaginable to distract the jury from the main issues of the case. They said that the second dead officer, Harold Stites, had been killed by *guard* fire rather than convict fire, which was the reason their clients had been charged with only one killing. The judge ruled that even if true, it had no bearing on the present case. The defense then delved at length into the conditions on Alcatraz: the deprivation of simple pleasures such as chewing gum and candy; the lock-up policy that kept men in isolation for years at a time; the maddening monotony of a never-changing routine; and even instances of outright cruelty and brutality on the part of some prison personnel. Again, the judge ruled that such evidence was irrelevant to an acceptable defense. An inmate could not attempt escape and in doing so commit a killing simply because he did not like the conditions of a prison to which he had been lawfully committed. The defense attempted to convince the jury that Shockley should not be held answerable for his conduct because of his mental condition. Psychiatric testimony proved him to be legally sane.

The efforts of the defense attorneys were commendable but futile. The government's case against the trio was simply too strong.

The trial lasted a month. The case was given to the jury at 9:00 A.M. on Saturday, December 21, 1946. By twelve noon, the group had decided unanimously to send Sam Shockley to the gas chamber. Fifteen minutes later they went to lunch.

The jury lunched at the Hotel Whitcomb for an hour and forty-five minutes. At two o'clock, they resumed their deliberations. After another four and a half hours, at six-thirty, they returned to the Whitcomb for dinner. By eight, they were back in the jury room. At midnight they announced that they had reached a verdict in all three cases. At forty minutes past midnight, with all parties present, the jury announced its decisions.

Sam Shockley, as they had decided early on, was found guilty and sentenced to die.

Buddy Thompson was found guilty and also sentenced to the gas chamber.

Danny Durando was found guilty, but the jury recommended mercy in his case. Because of his youth, the Indio Kid was spared the death penalty.

In brief statements to the press after their convictions, Buddy Thompson was philosophical about his fate. "It's just as well," he said. "I'd rather have it this way than have to go back to the Rock. At least in the gas chamber a man dies fast."

Sam Shockley grinned moronically at the reporters. "They'll never gas me," he said confidently. "I'm crazy."

Danny Durando, who was physically limp from the ordeal of

having so narrowly escaped death, was unable to speak with reporters.

•

The next morning, as Durando was being led out of the federal
lockup in chains to be returned to Alcatraz, he was allowed to stop
briefly at the cells of Thompson and Shockley.

"I know we ain't never been good friends, Buddy," he said to
Thompson, "but no hard feelings now, huh?" He stuck a shackled
hand through the bars to shake.

"Go fuck yourself, Mex," Thompson said flatly. He did not even
get off his bunk.

Durando shrugged and went two cells down to see Shockley.
"Hey, Sam, I got to go back to the Rock now," he said easily. "Don't
you worry none, hear? You're sure to beat the gas on appeal."

"I know it," said Shockley. "I'll beat it. They won't gas a crazy
man."

Crazy Sam and the Indio Kid shook hands for the first and only
time in their lives.

"So long, Sam."

"So long, Kid."

An hour later, Danny Durando was back in the Alcatraz deadlock, taking off all his clothes. When he was naked, Warden Johnston
came out of Admin and spoke to a guard lieutenant. "Put this man
on lock-up status in D Block," he said.

"Yes, sir. For how long, Warden?"

"For as long as I am warden of this institution," Johnston replied.

Durando was walked naked down Seedy Street, past 402 and 403,
and into D Block. He was taken to the last cell, number 42, on the
top tier, and locked in.

After the guard left, Bob Stroud spoke to him from 41 next door.
"What did you pull, Kid?"

"Life," the young Chicano answered.

"And the other two?"

"The gas chamber."

Stroud thought of Sam Shockley. "Barbaric," he said.

"What? asked the Kid.

"Nothing," said Stroud. "You play chess?"

"Me? No. I ain't smart enough to play chess."

"You will be when I get through with you, Kid," the old con said
confidently. "Tomorrow you begin chess lessons."

On his bunk in 42, where no one could hear or see him, Danny Durando buried his face in his strong hands and cried.

CHAPTER FORTY-FIVE

SATURDAY, MAY 1, 1948

Just before noon, one day short of the second anniversary of the escape attempt, the prison launch brought a new warden to the Rock. His name was Edwin B. Swope. He was sixty years old, a native of New Mexico, and he wore a string tie and a Stetson. Johnston met him at the dock and the two were driven up the hill to the warden's home for lunch.

Jim Johnston was now seventy-two years old. He had designed the Alcatraz prison, overseen its construction, opened it, and served as its sole warden during the fourteen years it had been in operation. Now he was retiring from active prison duty to accept an appointment to the United States Board of Parole.

As the two men talked that day in 1948 when the prison was formally changing hands, Johnston told Swope some of the things he had planned to do on the Rock but never got around to. "I've been meaning to do something about the interior colors of the cellhouse: get rid of the gray and see if the place can't be brightened up a little. And I've thought about landscaping some of the south slopes a bit to make the island itself a little more scenic. I think improvements of that nature would have an excellent therapeutic effect on the prisoners."

"I'll certainly keep your suggestions in mind, Warden," said Swope.

"I've been thinking too that some gradual reduction in the rigidity of our rules might be in order now that the days of wild gangsterism seem to be over. It's 1948; the country isn't producing any more Machine Gun Kellys or Alvin Karpises or Dutch Cretzers. I've been wondering if perhaps the time hasn't come to gradually increase the prisoners' privileges."

"Did you have anything specific in mind?" asked Swope.

"I've been seriously considering having radio jacks put in the cells and letting them listen to monitored radio broadcasts."

"It's certainly something to think about," Swope admitted. "Alcatraz gets all the rotten apples out of the barrel. Maybe a little different treatment from what they've been used to might save a few of them from spoiling completely."

On his inspection tour of the prison later that day, Swope kept all of Johnston's suggestions in the back of his mind. He noted how relatively uninvolved it would be to wire B and C Blocks for radio jacks. And he went one step farther with Johnston's idea of brightening up the cellhouse: he decided he would purchase a selection of colors and let every prisoner paint his own cell whatever color he desired. There was a lot that might be done in the area of rehabilitation on the Rock.

But only for the prisoners who deserved it, he decided. Only for those whose attitudes were acceptable and whose conduct was above reproach. For the others, the recalcitrants who did not care and did not try, Alcatraz was going to remain as tough as it had ever been.

Perhaps even tougher.

Shortly after Swope took over the prison, he had four new gun portholes installed in the outside wall of D Block. The new portholes would allow guards to stand on the catwalk outside the cellhouse and, if the situation called for it, fire into the Treatment Unit without exposing themselves to danger.

One of the next things he did was to revoke all of Robert Stroud's special correspondence privileges, and to order that Danny Durando's lock-up status in D Block be continued indefinitely.

CHAPTER FORTY-SIX

THURSDAY, DECEMBER 2, 1948

Shortly before 10:00 A.M., Warden Clinton Duffy of San Quentin took a walk into Death Row to see if the two federal prisoners were having any problems getting organized for their move downstairs. It was approximately twenty-four hours before their scheduled executions, and they were due to be moved to the holding cells a few steps from the gas chamber to spend their last day and night of life.

Buddy Thompson and Sam Shockley had been paying guests at San Quentin for a few weeks short of two years. The U.S. Bureau of

Prisons paid the State of California $3.25 per day per man for their cell and board on Death Row. Tomorrow morning, barring any eleventh-hour reprieves, the federal government would pay $300 to have the men put to death in the state's gas chamber.

The first cell at which Duffy stopped was the one occupied by Sam Shockley. Crazy Sam was a pathetic sight now. Dull-eyed and spiritless, he had spent the last several months in utter despair. He had been eating only about one-third of each meal served to him; sometimes not even that. His weight was down to 120 pounds; he reminded Duffy of some of the concentration-camp photos that had been publicized following the war.

When Duffy looked through the bars now, he saw the condemned man sitting on the edge of his bunk, staring morosely at the floor. A box just inside the door contained his few pitiful belongings: toothbrush and powder, a writing tablet and pencil, a broken comb, some letters from his sister, two well-read *Batman* comic books, and a copy of the death warrant ordering his execution.

"How are you today, Sam?" the warden said, more of a greeting than a question.

Crazy Sam shrugged his frail shoulders. "Okay, I guess." His face was empty of expression, desolate.

Duffy's jaw clenched slightly. He hated capital punishment with a passion. "Have you picked out your menu yet for that big feed tonight?" he asked with forced enthusiasm.

"No," Sam replied. "I ain't felt too much like eating lately."

"I'm sure you could get your appetite back, Sam, if you picked out something special to eat. Why don't you think about it?"

Sam nodded lethargically. Duffy walked down the Row to Buddy Thompson's cell.

"Hello, Tex."

"Hiya, Warden," Thompson replied cheerfully. He presented a startling contrast to Sam Shockley. Bright, alert, hopeful, he was the picture of optimism. Still handsome and innocent-looking, his hair was just slightly tinged with a few hints of grey. It was twelve days before his thirty-first birthday. He was convinced that he would not be executed. "Know what this is?" he asked, holding up a sheet of paper on which he had been writing. "It's a telegram I'm composing. Know who to? The President of the United States, that's who. I go right to the top, Warden."

"As soon as it's ready, send it down to me. I'll see that it goes right out." Duffy looked at Thompson's personal belongings: five boxes full—books, copies of appeals, pinup photos, model planes he had built, toilet articles, extra felt slippers, jigsaw puzzles, several packets of letters, and a variety of other items he had collected during the past two years.

Thompson saw Duffy looking at the boxes. "Listen, Warden, don't let nobody unpack my stuff, okay? I've got everything in order the way I want it. I'll unpack it myself when I get back up here."

"All right," said Duffy. They chatted for several minutes, then Duffy had to go. "I'll drop in on you later after you're settled downstairs," he said.

When the warden was gone, and after Thompson had finished composing the telegram and sent it down, the Death Watch squad came for him and Shockley. These were the guards who would lead them into the gas chamber. They instructed the two men to strip, then had them step naked into the wide Death Row corridor. Each had his wrists cuffed together and the cuffs strapped to a leather restraining belt that was put around his waist and buckled in the back. Then they were walked toward the Death House elevator to be taken down to the holding cells.

On the way, Buddy Thompson stopped to say good-bye to a newcomer who had arrived on the Row five months earlier. A cocky young man of twenty-seven, he had a severe widow's peak and a hook nose that served collectively to give him a sneering, arrogant countenance. Thompson had found him to be much like himself: a loner with a natural dislike and distrust of most people. He was the only man on the Row who had never killed anyone. His two death sentences were for kidnapping during a robbery, with subsequent sexual offenses against the victims.

"What the hell are you doing with your pecker hanging out, Tex?" the newcomer asked.

"Just airing it out, kid, letting it see daylight for a change." Thompson winked. "I'll be back up in a few hours. Play you some casino during rec tomorrow."

"You're on, Tex."

Buddy Thompson walked on away, following Sam Shockley into the elevator.

Back in his cell, the newcomer, Caryl Chessman, watched him go.

•

CHAPTER FORTY-SEVEN

FRIDAY, DECEMBER 3, 1948

Twenty-four hours later, Duffy again visited Buddy Thompson, this time in one of the two holding cells next to the gas-chamber entrance.

"Any answer from the President yet?" Thompson asked eagerly when the warden walked up.

"Sorry, Tex, nothing." And there *won't* be an answer either, Duffy thought. Harry Truman was the wrong man to ask for a pardon for killing a prison guard.

"Jesus, what am I going to do now?" Thompson said nervously to no one in particular.

The Death Watch brought Thompson a pair of dark trousers and a white shirt, both new. They were the only two articles of clothing he would wear into the death cell. While he was changing, Duffy stepped over to the adjoining cell to see Shockley.

"Hello, Sam. Can I do anything for you?"

"I'm crazy, you know," the condemned man said.

"I know, Sam," Duffy replied quietly.

When both men had changed into their execution clothes, a doctor taped a stethoscope head over each of their chests. A rubber tube from it dangled out the front of the shirt after it was buttoned up.

At ten, a carpet runner was quickly rolled out from the cells to the chamber entrance. The Death Watch guards led Shockley out first. He was almost limp and had to be supported. Thompson came next, taking short, hesitant steps with his bare feet.

"Any chance of holding off for a few minutes?" Thompson asked Duffy at the door. The warden shook his head and motioned the Death Watch to get on with it.

Shockley was already seated in one of the two chairs when Thompson was led over the lip of the door into the chamber. Crazy Sam's head flopped back and forth and his eyes were rolled back to their whites as if he were already dead and this was merely a ceremony to formalize it. Thompson, trembling, was put into the chair next to him. Just before he sat down with his back to the three observation windows, he recognized one of the official government witnesses:

Officer Robert Baker, who had been in Cell 402 with Simpson and Sundstrom.

The well-worn leather straps were quickly secured on both men and the stethoscope tubes attached to two longer tubes leading out of the chamber for the doctor to monitor their last heartbeats. In seconds the Death Watch left the chamber. The big steel door was closed with a *whooosh* and was pneumatically sealed from the outside.

Buddy Thompson looked at Sam Shockley and said, "I never thought this would really happen."

There was a subdued splash, barely audible, as a cheesecloth bag of cyanide eggs was lowered into a lead well of sulphuric acid under each chair. In seconds, the chamber of death was filled with the odor of sickeningly sweet, almond-scented fumes. Shockley, in a stupor, head down, breathed the fumes normally and died easily, his body only twitching a few times. Thompson jerked and coughed and choked and his eyes watered and saliva drooled from both corners of his mouth. He died with difficulty.

At 10:12 A.M., both men were pronounced dead. The witnesses signed the log and filed out. An hour later, after a powerful exhaust fan had blown the deadly gas out and distilled water had flushed out the acid well, the chamber was opened and the two bodies were sprayed with liquid ammonia to neutralize any death fumes caught in their clothes. Then they were removed and released to local undertakers.

Sam Shockley was picked up by Keaton's Mortuary in San Rafael. His body was embalmed and shipped that same day to his sister in Idabel, Oklahoma.

Buddy Thompson's body went to Harry M. William's Mortuary, also in San Rafael. It was supposed to be claimed by a brother and sent to Texas. The mortuary held Thompson's remains for six days. When no one claimed it, the body was buried on the grounds of the Marin County Farm. It was not embalmed prior to burial.

PART FIVE
THIRTY YEARS LATER

CHAPTER FORTY-EIGHT

SUNDAY, MAY 2, 1976

On the thirtieth anniversary of the day the 1946 break began, a slightly overweight, balding man of forty-nine boarded a Harbor Carriers boat from Pier 43 at Fisherman's Wharf. He walked down the gangplank with some two dozen Sunday-afternoon sightseers, presented his two-dollar ticket to the man at the dock's edge, and took a seat on the big, open, upper deck.

The boat docked at the Alcatraz pier ten minutes later and the passengers debarked. They were assembled on the big prison dock by a pretty, dark-haired young woman wearing the olive-drab and khaki uniform of a National Park Service guide. As soon as the visitors were in a group, the guide gave a short introductory speech and then led them up the winding road for their tour of the cellhouse.

For three years now, the prison had been open to the public as part of the National Park Service. Prior to that, it had been virtually abandoned for a decade. The prison had been closed on May 15, 1963, by order of Attorney General Robert F. Kennedy. The reasons were two. First, the cellhouse structure was deteriorating from constant exposure to the dampness, salt water, and erosion. To continue to keep federal prisoners there would have required renovations costing an astronomical sum. Second, the prison itself, and the principles of strict isolation for which it stood, had become archaic by the standards of modern penology.

On this Sunday afternoon, as the tour group reached the front of the cellhouse and was taken into what had once been the deadlock, the guide stopped them briefly to deliver another part of her tour speech. The balding, overweight man at the back of the group adjusted a pair of rimless glasses and looked curiously into the big, now-empty room that had once been Admin. For a brief instant, he stared at the door leading into Admin, almost as if he expected old Saltwater Johnston himself to come walking out.

•

(Warden James Johnston died in 1958 at the age of eighty-two. He outlived many much younger men who had been in his keeping on Alcatraz and had sworn to celebrate on the day he died.

Johnston's immediate superior, Director James Bennett, remained as head of the Bureau of Prisons until 1964 when, at the age of seventy, he retired. He had run the nation's federal prison system for twenty-seven years, having been appointed by Franklin Roosevelt, and reappointed by Presidents Truman, Eisenhower, and Kennedy.

Attorney General Tom C. Clark, Bennett's superior at the time of the 1946 escape attempt, was appointed to the U.S. Supreme Court in 1949 and served as a member of that august body for eighteen years.

In addition to Clark, Bennett served under ten other attorney generals.

Bennett, now eighty-two, and Clark, seventy-seven, are still alive.)

•

As the tour moved into the cellhouse, the guide took the group over to Seedy Street and led them into D Block. There she talked about the six dark cells on the flats and let some of the more daring members of the group go into a dark cell and have the door closed behind them. But only for a few seconds.

The guide talked about the Birdman too, and pointed out Cell 41, where he had lived.

•

(As Robert Stroud grew older, his health failed by degrees. He suffered chronic kidney and gall-bladder disorders, as well as a myriad of other ailments that attack a body kept at severely subnormal activity for so many years. Through all his pain, he continued to work diligently on his massive history of the federal penal system. It was to be done in two volumes; he had completed the first part, which ran to 100,000 words.

In 1949, due to his deteriorating physical condition, the Birdman was taken out of D Block and removed to a private cell-room in the prison hospital. There he was again kept isolated except for contact with prisoner patients who rested in a ward down the corridor from his cell-room. Stroud lived like that, alone and ailing in the hospital room, for ten years.

In 1959, at the age of sixty-nine, the old convict was finally taken off the Rock and transferred to the federal prison hospital at Spring-field, Missouri. There he lived for four more years, dying in 1963 at the age of seventy-three.

The U.S. Bureau of Prisons confiscated his written history of federal prisons as he had known them for fifty-four incredible years. They have never let the work be made public.)

•

When the tour group left D Block, they walked onto the flats of Times Square, passing within several yards of the two cells where Dutch Cretzer had shot down the hostages. It was the second time on the tour that the group had been close to those two cells. Neither time were they pointed out or mentioned by the guide. The numbering sequence of the cells had been changed since the escape attempt of 1946. What were once Cells 402 and 403 are now C-102 and C-104.

As the guide led her tour toward the now-empty dining hall, the heavyset man with the glasses paused to look at the hostage cells. He thought of the nine men who had been held in those cells.

•

(Bill Miller dead, the morning after the break began. Captain Weinhold now dead. Carl Sundstrom dead. Chief Steward Bob Bristow and Cellhouse Officer Ernest Lageson had both resigned from the prison service more than twenty-five years earlier. Lageson had died an untimely death from cancer shortly after that. Joe Burdette and Bob Baker were still alive.

Lieutenant Joe Simpson's health had gradually begun to deteriorate following his retirement. To make matters worse, his devoted Marian had passed away, and that had taken something important out of his spirit. Shortly after New Year's in 1960, he quietly checked into a veteran's hospital for treatment. But it was too late: his overtaxed heart had run its gallant course. On January 31, 1960, Joe Simpson died.

At his request, Simpson was buried in the cemetery at Ft. Leaven-worth. As his flag-draped coffin was being borne through the fort, all traffic stopped to pay homage to a returning soldier. At the graveside, his daughter was presented with the forty-nine-star flag from her father's coffin. She still flies that flag from her home every national holiday.

For Cecil Corwin, life gradually improved. For a number of years, he had suffered a series of coronary thromboses that attacked him like sudden blows. Usually occurring at night, the bloodclot onslaught would awaken him with a terrifying jolt. He would sit up in bed, trembling and gasping until it passed. The seizures got so bad at one point that he was forced to give up the psychiatric work he was doing and retire to inactivity a second time. Mercifully, however, as the years passed, the attacks grew more infrequent and less severe.

On July 18, 1967, Corwin suffered a final heart attack and died in Long Beach, California. He had been on his way to the bus station to go to Sacramento to represent the Long Beach Chapter at a convention of the Veterans of World War I.

Cecil Corwin was seventy-four when he died. His widow, Catheryn, still has the bullet that went all the way through his head twenty-one years before his death.)

•

In the big dining hall, the guide was showing her tour group a typical Alcatraz menu lettered on a large board above where the serving tables once stood. As she talked, the balding man caught up with the group and looked thoughtfully back into the kitchen area.

•

(Alcatraz's last Public Enemy Number One had continued working in the Rock's bakery for sixteen more years. Alvin Karpis eventually became a superb baker of bread and pastry. Living in constant hope of ultimate release, Karpis remained on the Rock until 1962, when he was transferred to McNeil Island. He was then fifty-four years old and had served more than twenty-five years on Alcatraz, longer than any other man.

Karpis remained at McNeil Island for seven years. During his stay there, he resumed what had once been a consuming hobby of his: playing the guitar. In January of 1964, he was approached by a young forger of government checks who asked the old con to teach him to play. Karpis agreed. He found the young man a clever and adept student who played well almost from the first lesson. They often played duets together during their recreation time. Then, in 1967, the young forger, Charles Manson, was paroled.

Alvin Karpis was finally released from prison in January of 1969. His total career in crime had lasted only five years, and for that he had served thirty-three years in prison. Upon release, he was deported to Canada, where he had been born. He is sixty-nine now and lives in Montreal.)

While the tour guide talked to the group about the food on Alcatraz, the man with the glasses wandered over to the south windows and looked down at the abandoned Industries building. It was dilapidated now, rust-covered and corroding, used only as a nesting place by the big seagulls of the bay.

•

(It was down in Industries that George "Machine Gun" Kelly could have started a chain of events that would have wrought havoc throughout the island, simply by agreeing to participate in a break from there while the escape attempt was going on in the cellhouse. But Kelly was far too bright to endorse anything that insane. Throughout his tenure on Alcatraz, he remained convinced that the Rock was escape-proof. No one has ever proved him wrong.

In May of 1951, after nearly seventeen years in the island prison, Kelly was finally transferred to Leavenworth. Three years later, on his fifty-fourth birthday, he suffered a heart attack in his cell and died later that night in the prison hospital.

Kelly's body was claimed by R. G. "Boss" Shannon, father of Kathryn Kelly, who was still in prison. The former Public Enemy Number One was laid to rest in Willow Springs, Texas, under his true name of George Barnes.)

•

When the group left the dining hall and was guided down Michigan Boulevard, the balding man lagged behind and stayed for a moment on the flats of Times Square. He adjusted his glasses again and bent his head back to look up at the top of the west gun gallery, where the bars curved back to meet the wall. They still were not set in concrete; but with the flat cross-bars holding them together and the heavy-gauge grilles over the outside of the whole structure, it did not much matter. The taking of the gun cage by a convict from the cellhouse floor had been a once-in-a-lifetime feat.

•

(During the Rock's twenty-nine years as a federal penitentiary, a total of 1,033 inmates were incarcerated there. In addition, more than 400 men served as guards on the island. Add to those numbers the medical and miscellaneous prison-bureau personnel, and you have a total of roughly 1,500 men who at one time or another moved in and out of the big cellhouse.

Yet of all those men, only one recognized the structural defect of the west gun-gallery bars.

Of the 1,033 inmates, only one was clever enough to devise a way into that gallery and courageous enough to use that method of entry to accomplish the extraordinary feat of capturing it.

Of the 39 convicts who attempted to escape over the years, only one had figured out a way to secure weapons with which to try it.

Bernie Coy came within minutes and feet of accomplishing what would have been the most incredible prison break of all time.

But in the end, Alcatraz held him. And he went to his final peace, if there was such a thing for him, in an unmarked grave that no one has visited for thirty years.)

•

When the balding man finally walked down Michigan Boulevard, he found the tour group looking into a cell that the park service had furnished as a convict's cell might have been in the old days: bunk made up with a coarse blanket, metal chair and table pulled out from the wall, convict coat hanging from a peg. The guide was talking about the size of the cell and the daily routine of the prisoners. As she spoke, the balding man moved unobtrusively behind the group and walked up to a cell near the cutoff. The number on it now was B-126, but thirty years earlier, when he had lived in it, it had been Cell 142.

Looking at the tiny, barren cell now, Dan Durando sighed a deep, hollow sigh.

•

(The Indio Kid had stayed in lockup in D Block for seven years. Warden Swope finally let him out in 1953. By that time, although he was still under thirty, his once superb body and flashing hands had become convict-slow. He smoked heavily by then and no longer even thought about exercising. Most of his time in D had been spent reading or bent over a chessboard studying intricate, complex moves for hours on end. His muscles slacked; his middle thickened.

Upon his release from D Block, Durando was given Bernie Coy's old job of cellhouse orderly. Later he worked as a library clerk. In all, he served eighteen years on the Rock.

When Alcatraz was closed down, the Kid, who was then nearing forty, was transferred to Leavenworth. There he undertook a plan of formal study and eventually earned a high-school diploma. He served another seven years in Leavenworth; then he was paroled to the state of Oklahoma: he still had that life sentence waiting for him. But Oklahoma kept him inside for only another three years, then it too paroled him.

On Christmas Eve, 1973, after nearly twenty-nine years in prison, Dan Durando was granted parole and released.)

•

The tour finally ended, and the group was led back down the hill to the dock. The boat for the return trip was not there yet, so the visitors had to wait. Most of them looked back up at the summit of the island, at the big cellhouse.

Durando did not. He stood on the dock with his back to the prison and looked across the bay. As he stared out at the water, he decided that he would never visit the island again.

There were too many ghosts on Alcatraz.

AFTERWORD

Six Against the Rock contains a number of reconstructed incidents which have never before been made public. Perhaps they were concealed, perhaps merely overlooked. Perhaps, examined out of context, they seemed unimportant. As an example, the fact that Cellhouse Officer Ernest Lageson and Officer Bill Miller changed lunches on the day the break began may of itself seem insignificant; yet their doing so interrupted Bernie Coy's timetable for several minutes—and caused Miller to slip the 107 key into his pocket instead of returning it to the gun gallery. Had Lageson been on duty at his usual time, he would probably have summoned Bert Burch back to the lower level of the cage and sent the key up to him. Lageson was like that; he went by the book. Miller was a little more flexible—and it was Miller's flexibility that kept Coy and the other five convicts from getting out of the cellhouse. More than any other single individual, Bill Miller prevented the break from succeeding. At the cost of his life.

A point with which some will disagree was whether Coy used a one-inch crescent wrench or a pair of pliers to spread the gun-cage bars. Warden Johnston showed a pair of pliers to the press along with the bar-spreader Coy had designed, indicating it was the tool used to rotate the spreader. Where the pliers came from and where the wrench disappeared to is something we cannot answer. It makes no difference, of course, whether it was a wrench or pliers. The author went along with the wrench theory because the majority of the book's informants thought it was a wrench. And because Bernie Coy, if he had a choice, would certainly have opted for the tool easiest to use.

The differences, the disagreements, and the ultimate fight between Coy and Dutch Cretzer will probably be disputed. In any version of the break ever written, Coy, Cretzer, and Hubbard stuck together valiantly until the bitter end, and went down shooting together. That is simply not so. There was friction among them from the moment the break began to go wrong—which was almost as soon as it started. Only a few prisoners—kitchen workers who had gone to their cells on the flats of Broadway, and some lockup cons on the upper tiers—witnessed the final eruption between them, when Coy hit Cretzer with the rifle butt. The reason this incident has never been brought to light appears to be simply that no previous researcher went to the trouble of locating former inmates to obtain their side of the break story.

Another incident either overlooked or purposely concealed is the unidentified convict who secured towels from other cells to help the wounded guards in Cells 402 and 403. Some speculate that the man was Louis Fleish, who earlier in the break had tried to keep Cecil Corwin from being hurt. Others say it was the person represented in this book by the character of Dan Durando. If so, that person has never admitted it.

The seven lock-up prisoners who were overlooked when C Block and the Broadway side of B were emptied on Friday afternoon remained in their cells to witness the remainder of the break from the best vantage point possible. They had no water (except for two of them who had the foresight to fill their basins), no food, and no protection from badly dropped grenades which could have exploded in front of their cells at any time. But with hand mirrors they could see a lot of what was going on in the cellhouse, and through the six-by-ten-inch grille-covered air vents at the bottom rear of their cells, they could hear much of what was said in the utility corridor behind their cells.

As far as the deaths of Coy, Cretzer, and Hubbard are concerned, the reconstruction in this book is based on several sources of information. The first is that part of the conversation that was overheard just at dawn on Saturday morning. The second is medical opinions that Dutch Cretzer's behavior would have been highly irrational by then: Cretzer, as the autopsy later showed, was suffering from encephalitis. That was undoubtedly the reason for the double vision that had convinced him he was going blind. And for the headaches and dizziness. And, finally, for his last, insane acts in the death corridor.

Add to the above that the death certificates for Cretzer and Marv Hubbard specify "Justifiable Homicide" because they were killed by guard fire; while Bernie Coy's death certificate lists only "Homicide," with the "Justifiable" noticeably absent. No one is certain just when the federal agencies involved in the subsequent investigation learned that Coy had not died as the other two had; but it must have been sometime prior to May 14, because it was the following morning that the hasty arrangements were made for filing his death certificate. Coy's body should have been held through June 3, and buried on June 4 if not claimed. As it turned out, he was buried sixteen days earlier than that—and his certificate of burial filed three days before *that.* Someone clearly was in a hurry to make Bernie Coy's corpse unavailable for claiming *or* examination. The story had already been written across the nation how the Alcatraz guards had gone in and killed the mad-dog escapees. Apparently the Department of Justice wanted that version of it to stand.

•

In researching *Six Against the Rock,* the following ad was run in the PERSONAL column of metropolitan newspapers across the country:

> ALCATRAZ. Writer wishes to contact former inmates of Alcatraz federal prison. Write Clark Howard, Box 5306, Las Vegas, NV 89102.

The response to the ads was considerable. In an introductory reply, the respondents were advised of the nature of the project and cautioned against cooperating in it if they were still under federal jurisdiction of any kind. A few never wrote again, but with most of them it was the beginning of an extremely interesting period of correspondence. Some of the men used their real names and addresses; others used aliases, no name at all, post-office boxes, or General Delivery. Some wrote letters longhand, some typed them, others used cassette tapes, and some, after asking for a phone number, telephoned. Most, naturally, requested and were assured of anonymity. Almost without exception, after the first suspicions were alleviated, they were candid and, I feel, truthful, even about their own crimes and, in some cases, their own involvement in previous Alcatraz escape attempts. Many of the answers they gave to my questions, and much of the information they volunteered, was verified by other sources.

Most of the former inmates of Alcatraz with whom I corresponded and, in some cases, personally visited, are men who now range in age from sixty to eighty-five years. Without exception, they now lead honest, productive lives, and in many cases have raised respectable families of children and grandchildren. The press still quite often refers to these men as "gangsters." That is a misnomer. Al Capone was a gangster; Machine Gun Kelly and the others of whom I wrote in this book were Depression-era outlaws. The two categories are worlds apart.

In thanking the ex-Alcatraz cons who helped me so much in preparing this book, I want to say that I found them all, without exception, to be complete gentlemen. This is especially true of Willie Radkay and Dale Stamphill, the former a close friend of George Kelly, the latter a break partner of Doc Barker. Between the two of them, I learned enough about the Rock to feel almost as if it were *my* alma mater as well as theirs. Willie is a family man with grandchildren today, and Dale is president of the Kansas Council on Crime and Delinquency. Both men are now responsible citizens—in spite of the Rock.

•

I want to express a special note of thanks to Father Joseph M. Clark, S. J., who was the Catholic chaplain on the Rock for 17 years. Father Clark not only put me in touch—and vouched for me—with several key sources of information, but also shared with me nearly two decades of memories and numerous boxes of Alcatraz notes and other material he had collected over the years.

Father Clark is an extraordinary person, both as a man and as a priest, and becoming his friend was a very rewarding part of writing this book.

Another friend I was happy to make during my research was Bruce Barnes, the youngest son of George Kelly. Bruce, a successful California business owner, provided me with considerable factual information about his father—information that further laid waste to the mad-dog myth applied to Kelly by Hoover and his bureau (the FBI, in reality, knew so little about George Kelly that even today their files do not reflect his correct birthday). I hope that some day Bruce will tell the *true* story of the man the press called "Machine Gun" Kelly.

•

On the guard side of the story, the U. S. Civil Service Commission in Washington was most helpful in forwarding letters to surviving guards and the next-of-kin of those who were deceased. Mr. Wilmer R. Haack was particularly helpful and cooperative, as was John G. McCarthy, Associate Director for Operations, who arranged to have the mail forwarded.

Through the Civil Service Commission, three excellent sources of information were established. The first was the family of the late Cecil Corwin: his widow, Catheryn Corwin; his stepson, Brigadier General Harold A. Strack, USAF (Retired); and General Strack's wife and daughter, whose memories were also plundered. From them I received not only an abundance of recollections, clarifications, and verifications, but also a personal narrative of the break written by Officer Corwin shortly after he had recuperated from his wound. Cecil Corwin's entire family devoted considerable time to helping research this book, and their assistance and cooperation are gratefully acknowledged.

Another very valuable source of personal information was the daughter of Lieutenant Joseph Simpson, who was most helpful in providing not only many recollections of her late father, but also numerous photographs, clippings, medical files, and other documentation. Lieutenant Simpson's memory of the break, and his later comments on it to his daughter, were rare rewards for a grateful researcher.

The third source was the widow of Dr. Louis Roucek, the prison psychiatrist on the Rock at the time of the break. Dr. Roucek had Bernie Coy in private therapy for a time and was intimate with the escape leader's complex personality. Of all the prisoners Dr. Roucek attended, he collected and saved the writings of only one: Bernard Paul Coy. Mrs. Roucek generously shared with me the more than 100 pages of those writings, as well as some of her personal recollections. Her help is most appreciated.

Letters were also forwarded to two surviving guards: Joe Burdette and Robert Baker. No reply was ever received from Burdette. Baker responded with a short letter asking how much I was offering for his story. I wrote back and asked him to set a price for a half-day tape-recorded interview. I never heard from him again.

The Alcatraz Alumni Association, an organization comprised of former guards and their families, was contacted by letter requesting assistance. They never replied. After a period of time, the secretary of the group was contacted by phone. She was most cooperative. Among the things she agreed to do was put my request for assistance in their newsletter; put me on their mailing list; and obtain permission for me to attend their annual weekend convention so that I could personally meet some of the men who served on the Rock during the break. I was naturally quite pleased with such a splendid spirit of cooperation. Unfortunately, I never heard from the secretary or the alumni association again.

A special note of thanks must go to Jerry L. Schober, Superintendent, Golden Gate National Recreation Area, and Carnell Poole, Supervisor of Alcatraz, for allowing me unlimited access to the island to take photographs and measurements, and in general to follow as closely as possible, step-by-step, the break as it happened.

From the U.S. Bureau of Prisons, I naïvely expected the cooperation that, as a taxpayer, I had received from the Civil Service Commission and the Department of the Interior. I was badly disappointed. In my first letter to Norman A. Carlson, director of the bureau, I outlined my project and asked for information on the five deceased convicts and the nine hostage guards. I received no reply. Sixty days later, I sent a follow-up letter. A month later I received a letter signed "for Norman Carlson" with an illegible signature advising that signed releases from the convicts were necessary to look at their records. Regarding the officers, the letter provided only sketchy information, part of which I later learned was erroneous (they advised that Joe Burdette was deceased, when in fact he was very much alive and receiving a civil service annuity). I wrote a subsequent letter inquiring whether Whitey Franklin and Jimmy Lucas, who had been involved in an earlier escape attempt, were still in federal custody or had died while in custody. No reply. A follow-up letter was sent requesting an answer. A reply was eventually received from the bureau's Philadelphia office (my letters had been directed to the Washington office). The reply simply stated that Lucas and Franklin were not presently incarcerated within the federal system. I wrote back, again asking specifically if they had died while in custody. A reply was received advising that there was no record at all of either individual, and referring me to the bureau's Burlingame, California, office. A letter was directed to that office. In reply, they wrote back that my inquiry was being forwarded to their Washington office (where it originally had been sent by me). I never received an answer.

In a subsequent letter to Mr. Carlson of the Prison Bureau, I requested, under the Freedom of Information Act, a copy of the Report of the Alcatraz Prison Escape Attempt and Riot, prepared by Assistant Director William T. Hammack, and submitted to then Director James V. Bennett under date of May 24, 1946. I received no answer to that request. About that same time, I wrote Clarence M. Kelley, Director of the FBI, and requested, again under the Freedom of Information Act, a copy of FBI Report I.C. #7012090 (Official Report of the Alcatraz Island Escape Attempt of May 2–4, 1946). From the FBI I received a six-page condensed report, dated December 12, 1952 (six years after the break), which appeared to be written for elementary school consumption. No other information was ever furnished.

After six months of time-consuming attempts to secure cooperation from these bureaus of the Department of Justice, I was finally forced to proceed without the benefit of their help—or their files on the break, which I am certain would have been very interesting.

•

One last note which may be of some interest to the reader. Throughout the research on *Six Against the Rock,* I often wrote to various state agencies for background information on the men involved. Eventually I found that the same states kept turning up over and over again. Out of curiosity, I decided to geographically chart the families involved. I found that all the men and most of their parents were native to six states. Beginning in the west, Buddy Thompson was born in Oklahoma, Sam Shockley grew up there, and the person represented by the character of Dan Durando was born and raised there. Moving over to Arkansas, Shockley was born there, as was Thompson's mother. Up to Missouri: Cretzer's mother was born there. Over to Kentucky, which was the birthplace of Bernie Coy, his father Samuel Coy, and Shockley's father, Richard Shockley. Down to Tennessee, where both Shockley's mother and Coy's mother were born. Then down to Alabama, where Marvin Hubbard and both his parents were born and raised.

The odd thing about it is that these six states are contiguous. You can travel through all six of them without having to enter or cross any other state lines.

I found that almost as curious as the Bureau of Prisons' and the FBI's concealment of their official reports on the break.

A FINAL NOTE

What caused the break? What was the one element that acted as a catalyst for the desperate, bloody forty-one hours that followed? Perhaps this portion of a letter will tell us.

> One year and five days ago, I arrived here. At times I can hardly remember much of what went before; and then again everything seems as vivid as though it were yesterday. 1963 is a ways off yet. I can't imagine that far ahead. It never worries me, either. I feel that whatever the world is man enough to do to a fellow is okay. I believe in every man being what circumstances make of him.
>
> —Bernie Coy, in a
> letter written from
> Alcatraz on August 4,
> 1938.

Maybe the catalyst was hopelessness.

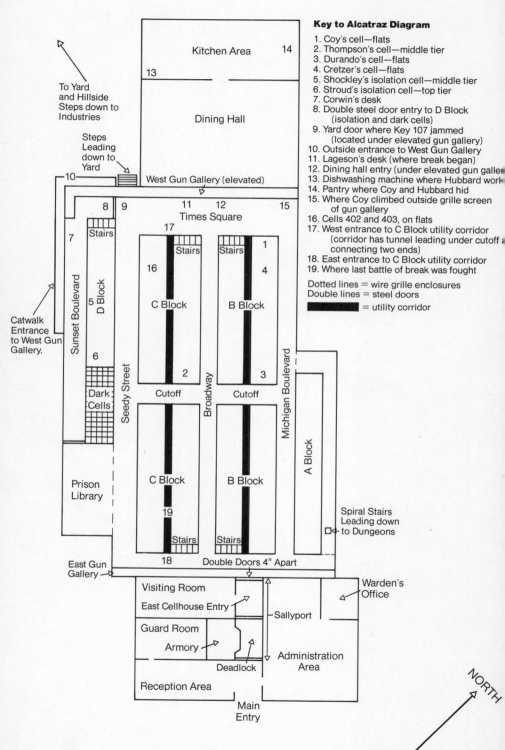

ALCATRAZ

Key to Alcatraz Diagram

1. Coy's cell—flats
2. Thompson's cell—middle tier
3. Durando's cell—flats
4. Cretzer's cell—flats
5. Shockley's isolation cell—middle tier
6. Stroud's isolation cell—top tier
7. Corwin's desk
8. Double steel door entry to D Block (isolation and dark cells)
9. Yard door where Key 107 jammed (located under elevated gun gallery)
10. Outside entrance to West Gun Gallery
11. Lageson's desk (where break began)
12. Dining hall entry (under elevated gun gallery)
13. Dishwashing machine where Hubbard work
14. Pantry where Coy and Hubbard hid
15. Where Coy climbed outside grille screen of gun gallery
16. Cells 402 and 403, on flats
17. West entrance to C Block utility corridor (corridor has tunnel leading under cutoff connecting two ends)
18. East entrance to C Block utility corridor
19. Where last battle of break was fought

Dotted lines = wire grille enclosures
Double lines = steel doors
■■■■■ = utility corridor